PROKOFIEV'S BALLETS FOR DIAGHILEV

Sergey Sergeyevich Prokofiev (1891–1953)

Prokofiev's Ballets for Diaghilev

STEPHEN D. PRESS
Illinois Wesleyan University, USA

ASHGATE

Published by
Ashgate Publishing Limited
Wey Court East
Union Street
Farnham, Surrey
GU9 7PT
England

Ashgate Publishing Company
Suite 420
101 Cherry Street
Burlington, VT 05401-4405
USA

Ashgate website: http://www.ashgate.com

British Library Cataloguing in Publication Data
Press, Stephen D.
    Prokofiev's ballets for Diaghilev
    1. Prokofiev, S. S. (Sergei Sergeevich), 1891–1953 – Criticism and interpretation 2. Prokofiev, S. S. (Sergei Sergeevich), 1891–1953 – Friends and associates 3. Diaghilev, Serge 4. Ballet
    I. Title
    780.9'2

Library of Congress Cataloguing-in-Publication Data
Press, Stephen D.
    Prokofiev's ballets for Diaghilev / Stephen D. Press
        p. cm.
    Includes bibliographical references (p.) and index.
    ISBN 978-0-7546-0402-0 (alk. paper)
        1. Prokofiev, Sergey, 1891–1953. Ballets. Selections. 2. Diaghilev, Serge, 1872–1929. I. Title.

ML410.P865 P74 2002
781.5'56'092—dc21

2002074723

ISBN 978 0 7546 0402 0

Reprinted 2009

Mixed Sources
Product group from well-managed forests and other controlled sources
www.fsc.org Cert no. SA-COC-1565
© 1996 Forest Stewardship Council
FSC

Typeset by Bournemouth Colour Press, Parkstone, Poole.

Printed and bound in Great Britain by MPG Books, Bodmin, Cornwall.

To Angela

Contents

List of illustrations

Figures
(Between pages 142 and 143)

Frontispiece   Sergey Sergeyevich Prokofiev (1891–1953). Photo by Hulton Archive / Getty Images.

1   Sergey Pavlovich Diaghilev (1872–1929). Photo by Sasha / Getty Images.

2   Contemporary British caricature of some violent acts in *Chout*. From *London Evening News* (1921).

3   Prokofiev in New York, 1918–19 season. Reproduced from the collections of the Library of Congress.

4   Larionov's sketchbook for *Chout*, opened to sketches and descriptions for the "Danse du rire". From Réné Fülöp-Miller and Joseph Gregor (1929), *The Russian Theatre*, Philadelphia: J.B. Lippincott Co.

5   Pencil sketch of Larionov by Juan Gris for the Paris 1921 Ballets Russes program book. From M. De Brunoff (ed.), *Ballets Russes de Serge de Diaghilew. Programme. Gaité Lyrique—May 1921*, Paris.

6   Larionov's later, cubist-inspired design for *Chout* scene 1: the hero sits atop the stove hatching his plan. From Anthony Parton (1993), *Mikhail Larionov and the Russian avant-garde*, Princeton: Princeton University Press, p.185. Reproduced by permission of Princeton University Press.

7   Larionov's cubist/*lubok* design for *Chout* scene 5, the merchant's bedroom, in the Paris 1921 Ballets Russes program book. From M. De Brunoff (ed.), *Ballets Russes de Serge de Diaghilew. Programme. Gaité Lyrique—May 1921*, Paris.

8   Larionov's curtain for *Chout*. From Anthony Parton (1993), *Mikhail Larionov and the Russian avant-garde*, Princeton: Princeton University Press, p.185. Reproduced by permission of Princeton University Press.

9   The hero buffoon (Slavinsky) and his wife (Sokolova). From Réné Fülöp-Miller and Joseph Gregor (1929), *The Russian Theatre*, Philadelphia: J.B. Lippincott Co.

10   Modish costumes from *Le Pas d'acier*. From left to right: Tchernicheva, Lifar, Danilova, Massine. From Réné Fülöp-Miller and Joseph Gregor (1929), *The Russian Theatre*, Philadelphia: J.B. Lippincott Co.

11   Excerpt from the Paris 1927 20th season Ballets Russes program book. From Willy Fischer (ed.), *Saison de Serge de Diaghilew. 10 Galas des Ballets Russes. Programme. Théâtre Sarah-Bernhardt—1927*. Paris: L'Edition Arstique.

12   Baba-Yaga and the crocodile. From Dmitry Aleksandrovich Rovinsky (1900), *Russkiya narodnïya kartinki*, St Petersburg: Izd. R. Golike.

13   Tchernicheva and Lifar with hammers in the factory finale. Photo by Sasha / Getty Images.

14   Closing scene of *L'Enfant prodigue*: Lifar crawls to his father. Photo by Sasha / Getty Images.

15   Nikolay Rimsky-Korsakov (1844–1908), Anatoly Lyadov (1855–1914) and Alexander Glazunov (1865–1936). Glazunov welcomed the thirteen-year-old Prokofiev to the St Petersburg Conservatory. There he studied orchestration with Rimsky-Korsakov and composition with Lyadov. Photo by Hulton Archives / Getty Images.

16   Doubrovska as the Seductress in *L'Enfant prodigue*. Photo by Sasha / Getty Images.

17   Prokofiev's "General Aid" for *L'Enfant prodigue*'s original number 4, the male servant's dance. In the boxes from left to right: "Introduction; main part/animated; procession/animated; secondary/fem.; development/evil [or angry]; reprise/animated; coda/animated" [at the bottom] "(given to Diaghilev)." The Prokofiev Archive, London.

18   The portrait of Diaghilev that hung above Prokofiev's desk in his Moscow apartment. Photo: akg-images, London.

Charts

List of music examples

Preface and acknowledgments

Although the topic at hand concerns ballets written for western audiences by a composer who was domiciled in Western Europe much of the time, a great proportion of the relevant documents and informative correspondence is in Russian. Very few translations of these sources have been made, which might account for the paucity of original work in the West. Thus, the Russian language is unavoidable when investigating the life and works of Sergey Sergeyevich Prokofiev. The researcher's lot is not an easy one given the peculiarities of the composer's style of informal writing and his sometimes difficult-to-decipher handwriting, nor is it any easier when deciding how to present one's work to the general reader. A simple, consistent system of transliteration from Russian Cyrillic script is desirable but nearly impossible to realize in anything approaching normal, that is, nonacademic syntax. A brief explanation is in order regarding the system chosen for this book.

I have elected to follow Gerald Abraham's method created for the *New Grove Dictionary of Music and Musicians* (1980, see vol. 1, pp. xvi–xvii). However, bowing to convention and to facilitate reading by nonspecialists, I employ widely accepted spellings for names such as Fokine (instead of Fokin), Massine (instead of Myasin), Diaghilev (instead of Dyagilev), Glière (instead of Glier), Nijinsky (instead of Nizhinsky) and so on. When these names appear as part of Russian titles or in quoted passags, however, they will be transliterated systematically. In cases where the artist is perhaps less well known I have retained the *New Grove* system, that is, Lyadov, Myaskovsky, Cherepnin, and so forth. My use of Chaikovsky instead of "Tchaikovsky" or even "Tschaikowsky" is prompted by the former's closer phonetic equivalent: the silent "T" or "Ts" appropriated from the French and German transliteration is useless, indeed, ridiculous for English use (Tchernobyl? Tchekhov?). Consistent use of an English transliteration for English readers is long overdue. In order to achieve a more uniform appearance I have opted to transliterate 'uǔ' and 'ыǔ' as simply 'y', and to ignore the Russian soft sign except in quotations or formal titles. Hence the text employs, for example, Musorgsky (instead of Musorgskiy), and Prokofiev (instead of Prokof'yev). Thus my spelling of the central figure's name is yet another concession to convention. When the composer signed his name in Latin letters he regularly spelled it Serge Prokofieff (Diaghilev similarly, Serge de Diaghileff). Patronymics are provided in the index. As guides, Richard Taruskin's *Stravinsky and the Russian Traditions* and *Defining Russia Musically* have been very helpful in this endeavor.

Most titles of musical compositions are given in their original language or languages (Prokofiev's scores for Diaghilev displayed both Russian and French titles). French equivalents are used if the first performing venue was France (hence *Petrouchka* and *L'Oiseau de feu*). English will be used secondarily to facilitate recognition, for example, *Gadkiy utenok* (The Ugly Duckling), or alone in cases of widely recognized classics, for example, *Sleeping Beauty*. I am responsible for all the translations herein unless otherwise credited.

Russia changed from the Julian to the Gregorian calendar on 1 February 1918. Up until 1900 Russian dates were 12 days behind those in the West, but due to the Julian leap year of 1900, they became 13 days behind beginning 29 February 1900 until the changeover. Dates in the text are based on the Gregorian calendar, except for events occurring in Russia, which will be dated according to the Julian calendar if appropriate and will include an appending "OS" for Old Style at the beginning of the passage. In cases where dates are mentioned in the body of excerpted material, I have retained the originals, and when applicable, added "OS" along with the equivalent date in the "new style" (NS) in parenthesis. St Petersburg was renamed Petrograd on 31 August 1914 (OS), then Leningrad shortly after Lenin's death in January 1924.

This book is a significantly revised and greatly expanded version of my thesis submitted in 1998 as partial fulfillment of a Doctor of Philosophy degree from the University of North Carolina at Chapel Hill. Many of the revisions were mandated by the publication of the composer's 1600 page diary covering the years 1907–1933 by the Serge Prokofiev Estate in September 2002 (three volumes: *Dnevnik 1907–1918*, *Dnevnik 1919–1933*, *Litsa*). I am grateful to Ashgate for extending my deadline so that I could that advantage of it. Chapter 3 is largely based on my article "Diaghilev and the two versions of Prokofiev's *Chout*" from the February 2001 issue of *Music and Letters* (pp. 51–77), which in turn is based on a presentation I made at the 1997 annual meeting of the American Musicological Society in Phoenix, AZ. I am grateful to Oxford University Press for allowing it to appear in these pages.

There are many people whom I would like to acknowledge for their generous assistance and encouragement. My deepest thanks go to Mikhail Saponov of the Moscow "Chaikovsky" Conservatory, Natalia Savkina of the Moscow State University, and M. Elizabeth Bartlet of Duke University for their time and effort in pursuit of materials in Moscow and Paris, respectively. My sincere thanks go to Noëlle Mann, Archivist of the Prokofiev Foundation at Goldsmiths College, London, for her helpfulness and warm hospitality during my visits, as well as for her ready assistance through correspondence and for her role as a conduit to the composer's family.

I am especially grateful to Malcolm Hamrick Brown for his hearty encouragement at the outset for this project, and to Arthur B. Corra for his ongoing fatherly cheering. For their generous assistance at various times I would like to thank Harlow Robinson (Northeastern University), Margarita Mazo (The

Ohio State University), John Bowlt (The University of Southern California), Serge Prokofiev, Jr. (Paris), Lee Grady (State Historical Society of Wisconsin), J. Rigsbee Turner (Pierpont Morgan Library), Rob Bennett (Illinois Wesleyan University), and Jon W. Finson, Evan Bonds, John Nádas and Thomas Warburton (University of North Carolina at Chapel Hill).

Above all I am indebted to my wife Angela, not only for her assistance and valued opinions, but her patience, understanding and support.

Introduction

Sergey Sergeyevich Prokofiev is well known to audiences as the composer of the popular *Peter and the Wolf*, *Alexander Nevsky* and *Lt. Kizhe Suite* as well as the ballets *Romeo and Juliet* and *Cinderella*. But the success of these and other compositions of his later career in the Soviet Union has overwhelmed his early work for Sergey Pavlovich Diaghilev's Ballets Russes: *Chout* (1921), *Le Pas d'acier* (1927) and *L'Enfant prodigue* (1929). These ballets usually garner no more than brief mention in the plentiful surveys of the Ballets Russes or in Prokofiev biographies. True, only *L'Enfant prodigue* remains in the active repertory; *Chout* and *Le Pas d'acier* had just passing success. But in light of their importance to Prokofiev's oeuvre, these works deserve more attention than they have received. Despite his devotion to opera, Prokofiev's first theatrical success came in ballet. More than his operas and symphonies, and at least as much as his concerti and solo piano pieces, Prokofiev's ballets for Diaghilev were the works for which he was best known in Western Europe before his return to the Soviet Union in the 1930s. Furthermore, these three ballets and the *Scythian Suite* (extracted from his rejected first balletic attempt, *Ala i Lolli*) not only demonstrate the range of his style during this period, but most clearly reveal his shift from aggressive modernism towards simpler lyricism. As exemplars of a fully formed balletic style, these works measure up to *Romeo and Juliet*, often considered Prokofiev's greatest achievement in the genre.

Extramusical factors have determined the ballets' life spans. Each ballet is dramatically unique; each resulted from a different hierarchy of collaboration. The stories span a wide range of topics: a long-winded, farcical adaptation of Russian folk tales (*Chout*), a series of vignettes suggesting post-revolutionary Soviet life (*Le Pas d'acier*), and a timeless parable taken from the Bible, colored by images from Pushkin (*L'Enfant prodigue*). Each production was lavish and striking in typical Ballets Russes fashion. Mikhail Larionov designed garish, neoprimitive/cubist sets and costumes for *Chout* which nearly overpowered the other elements of the ballet. Georgy Yakulov's constructivist designs for *Le Pas d'acier* provided an arresting visual setting for a topical ballet that became a document of its time. Georges Rouault's somber sets for *L'Enfant prodigue* evoked images of stained-glass windows and set the tone of the ballet. *L'Enfant prodigue* remains popular today, in part, because it is a virtuoso show piece for solo *danseur* and because of the high esteem in which dance aficionados hold its choreographer, George Balanchine. The two earlier ballets had choreography

1

that was, by turns, too untutored or too faddish. While it is essential to understand the collaborative product when appraising these ballets, Prokofiev's music deserves to be judged on its own merits as well.

The value and significance of Prokofiev's western works in general and his seeming chastened return to Soviet Russia remain lively topics for discussion. The Russian Prokofiev scholar, Mikhail Tarakanov sees the Soviet period ballet *Romeo and Juliet* as a focal point in the composer's career, calling it "a consummate example of neoclassical style ... in which all the separate lines of his work unite, and, colored by the lyricism of the theme, form a perfect example of the romantic ideal."[1] Richard Taruskin calls Prokofiev "a halfhearted modernist who achieved his best work after returning to Soviet Russia where he could be himself without pressure from the likes of Diaghilev to keep up with Parisian taste."[2] Others claim that the western and Soviet phases of Prokofiev's career differ according to style: the one modern, the other traditional.

While each of these positions has an element of truth to it, each misjudges largely due to an underestimation of Prokofiev's ballets for Diaghilev. Focusing on *Romeo and Juliet* slights the composer's self-proclaimed shift of emphasis to "a new simplicity" 10 years earlier in *Le Pas d'acier*. The "keeping up with the Jones's" assessment ignores the fact that Prokofiev sought fame in Paris by accentuating his own, well-established stylistic practices (for example, a layering technique which often resulted in strident dissonances). Moreover, the suggestion that the western works are of a lesser musical value is undermined by the composer's own assertion to the contrary, "without it [the period spent abroad] what followed would have been on a lower level."[3] Separating Prokofiev's ballets into "modern" and "traditional" is also misleading: when the music is divorced from its context, as it ultimately must be in order to make unbiased musical comparisons, there is fundamentally very little difference in musical style between the western ballets and those of the Soviet period. Modern and traditional traits coexist in virtually all of Prokofiev's music. Despite his decision to emphasize a simpler, more euphonious style beginning in the mid-1920s, Prokofiev was a composer of amazing stylistic consistency. His mature ballet style—the manner of characterization, formal preferences, and harmonic vocabulary—was established in the revised version of *Chout*. Prokofiev's ballets for Diaghilev do stand apart from the Soviet ones by their shorter duration and less rigorous approach to traditional forms and conventions. They also differ in tone: the malevolent fantasy in *Chout* and the heady futurism of *Le Pas d'acier* have no counterpart in the Soviet period. Yet there are examples of "humanistic warmth" in *Chout* (the music for the merchant) and *Le Pas d'acier* (that for the sailor and female worker). But the western ballets' greater use of emphatic dissonance, rhythmic intensity and restive juxtaposition of thematic material does not undermine the consistency of Prokofiev's ballet style. Each of these modern elements is to be found in his work from *Chout* through to his last ballet, *Tale of the Stone Flower* (see, for example, no. 37 "Severyan Follows the

Mistress," and no. 46, "Epilog"). The difference is only a question of degree. Prokofiev established his wide stylistic palette early on, and in his ballets he fully exploited it in service of heightened theatricality.

Prokofiev owed much of his success as a ballet composer to Diaghilev's encouragement, and the composer's gratitude for this help is well documented. Theirs was a far more convivial relationship than the composer would have with choreographers and theatre officials in the Soviet Union. There, at times, he would be treated like some insignificant nineteenth-century ballet hack. In the West Prokofiev was restricted only by the given story or scenic conception. While he readily absorbed Diaghilev's suggestions and revisions, he adamantly refused to alter one note of *L'Enfant prodigue* for Balanchine. The situation is reversed in the Soviet period. The litany of nitpicking and interference with his ballet scores by choreographers and producers (often behind his back) makes for distressing reading.[4]

The scope of this book is tempered by the limited availability of research materials. A considerable number of drafts, sketches and manuscripts are extant from the 1920s onward, but only a mere handful exists for the earlier works under consideration. Prokofiev's departure from his homeland in 1918 and the Russian Revolution are the primary causes. For example, if the scenario drafts for *Ala i Lolli* and *Chout* and the musical manuscripts for the former were saved, they would have been among the documents that the composer left behind when he departed for his tour of America; a great many of these were subsequently destroyed during the revolution, probably used as heating fuel.[5] Microfilms of the extant sketches are now centrally located,[6] but they have yet to be thoroughly analyzed and catalogued. We do know, however, that they did furnish material for the ballets, and that some of the sketches predate the finished product by several years. This ready supply fostered quick starts on a number of occasions: for example, with *Ala i Lolli*, *L'Enfant prodigue* and Prokofiev's last ballet written for the West, *Na Dnepre* (Sur le Borysthène). A number of documents and manuscripts from the ballets were part of Diaghilev's possessions and were carried off by Kochno and Lifar after the impresario's death.[7] Some of these, like the incomplete holograph of *Chout* that was used in rehearsals, have emerged at Sotheby's auctions only to revert to inaccessibility. There is no reason to believe that Prokofiev deliberately destroyed any sketches, yet only one has thus far surfaced for *Chout*—an uncharacteristic gift to a colleague. The publishing exemplars and the 1915 holograph of *Chout* are available for examination (copies of the former at the Prokofiev Archive, the latter at the Pierpont Morgan Library); the whereabouts of all other musical manuscripts for *Chout* and *Le Pas d'acier* is presently unknown.[8] One must reluctantly draw the conclusion that much of this material is irretrievably lost.

Enough material exists, however, to fashion an understanding of Prokofiev's ballets for Diaghilev. Fortunately, the music has been published in trustworthy editions in both full score and piano reductions, the latter created by the composer himself. Prokofiev had a keen eye for detail and methodically reviewed his proofs. He sometimes solicited his colleagues' help in this task. The lack of motion picture film documentation presents a major challenge to understanding the relationship between dance and music. There are a fair number of photographs from the ballet productions, but most are poses. Although plentiful, newspaper and magazine criticism yields little of substance, especially with respect to the music. Journals such as *La Revue musicale* are usually more helpful in this regard than reviews in the major dailies. Much can be gleaned from Prokofiev's own correspondence with his colleagues such as Nikolay Myaskovsky, Boris Asafyev (also known as Igor Glebov) and Vladimir Derzhanovsky, his Diary (covering 1907–33), and from his autobiography penned many years later.[9] Indeed, researchers in this field quickly become very grateful for the composer's candid, straightforward reporting (if not for his quirks of writing style). His recently published Diary covering the years 1907–33 is especially helpful: it not only corrects much received knowledge, but it fills in countless details in the composer's life and his compositional process. It allows the reader to get to know the man as never before and to share in his day to day thoughts and activities. What emerges is a new, deeper understanding of this too-frequently misunderstood artist. There are several instances where the Diary contradicts the autobiographies which were written at many years' remove. A case in point: Prokofiev played four-hand Stravinsky with the composer in Rome before Diaghilev, Massine and some of the futurists in April 1915. In his autobiography he says they played *Petrouchka*, but in the Diary entry recorded that very evening Prokofiev says *Le Sacre du printemps*, and goes on to describe the experience. In such cases it stands to reason that the diary is the more reliable source.

In light of these restrictions this study focuses on three interrelated issues: Diaghilev's important role in establishing and guiding Prokofiev's balletic career, the highly personal nature of the composer's balletic style, and its underlying unity from *Chout* onward. With his legendary prescience, Diaghilev launched Prokofiev on his tremendously successful ballet career despite two false starts. He later directed Prokofiev to acquire a recognizably Russian style, provided an important lesson in the special needs of the ballet, and encouraged his turn towards a new, simpler style, all the while holding him to the highest standards. Aside from being successful in their own right, Prokofiev's ballets for Diaghilev demonstrate a fully mature musical style that is consistent with that of the later, better-known examples.

A word or two about Diaghilev's musicality is in order since many continue to underestimate him. Diaghilev (1872–1929), who claimed to be a distant relative of Peter the Great, was raised in Perm, then a fairly cultural town of some 33 000 inhabitants. His prosperous family had been cultural leaders for generations. As befitting members of the nobility (albeit of a low rank) the

Diaghilev household was alive with music: Sergey's father was an amateur singer, his uncle played the cello and conducted an amateur orchestra, and his stepmother's younger sister was a professionally trained singer who was highly esteemed by Chaikovsky (young Sergey first met the composer at his home in Klin).[10] A room was specially built in the Diaghilev house for concerts, opera productions and pantomimes.[11] During his high school years Diaghilev aspired to become an artist, nevertheless he played the piano, sang (he became an ardent singer, a baritone), and even composed small pieces such as romances for piano and voice. During his university years in St Petersburg (1890–96) he became increasingly absorbed with music: whereas he was at best dutiful in his studies at law, he reveled in the excitement at the opera and concert hall. He took singing lessons from his step-aunt, played piano four-hands with his friend Walter Nouvel, studied the theory of music here and there, and composed—even undertaking a setting of *Boris Godunov*. During these years Diaghilev made several trips abroad, absorbing as much Wagner as he could, and seeking out famous composers such as Brahms, Verdi, and Chabrier, not for guidance, rather, just for the experience of being in their presence. His interest in music grew to such an extent that in 1894 he approached the august Nikolay Rimsky-Korsakov, professor of composition and orchestration at the St Petersburg Conservatory, with the goal of becoming a composer. Rimsky's brusque rebuff and the wounded Diaghilev's parting "We will see which of us will be more important in history!" have become legend.

All of this musical activity served Diaghilev well when he was at the helm of the Ballets Russes. He had developed a keen ear: the conductor Pierre Monteux recalls that Diaghilev once called out to him during a rushed rehearsal in London, "That second trumpet is playing a C natural and it's a B flat!"[12] He could audition new scores by sight-reading them at the piano, though he usually had a friend such as the musically gifted Misia Sert play through them as he listened. One hearing was generally all he needed to size-up a piece and gauge its suitability for the ballet. He could accompany singers at the piano if need be, even the likes of Chaliapin. When the contracted tenor canceled at the last moment for a performance of *Pulcinella*, Diaghilev coached one of his character dancers, Michel Pavloff (who sang by ear) to take his place. He selected all the company conductors and was the "keeper of the tempi" and woe betide the conductor that crossed him.[13] It was he who selected all but two of the 21 pieces Stravinsky used in *Pulcinella*, and all of the Rossini that Respighi then orchestrated for *La Boutique fantasque* (1919). He was clearly respected by the musicians who worked for him. Years later Stravinsky recalled that "he loved music passionately," adding, "and understood it very well."[14] During orchestral rehearsals his suggestions were readily accepted, even when Stravinsky was conducting his own music. Ballets Russes conductor Eugene Goossens believed that since Diaghilev knew all of the music for his ballets "forwards and backwards," he could conduct the ballet orchestra himself in a pinch;[15] on at least one occasion he did, briefly, during a rehearsal of Auric's *Pastorale*.[16] He was interested in a wide range of new music, from futurist sounds to Hindemith to the latest music from Soviet Russia, yet through it all Diaghilev remained fondest of deeply emotional romantic works such as Wagner's opera *Tristan and Isolde* and Chaikovsky's Pathétique Symphony.

His most remarkable musical talent was his intuitive discernment and ability to stimulate his composers to new heights. A comparison of Prokofiev's originals with their replacements from both ends of their collaboration provides some of the proof. Prokofiev was not an isolated case, however; Nicholas Nabokov (composer of the ballet *Ode*) claimed that Diaghilev could immediately see what was good and what was bad in a new work.[17] George Auric (composer of *Les Fâcheux*, *Les Matelots* and *La Pastorale*) said "If you placed twenty scores before him, he would pick out the best and give his reasons too."[18] Igor Markevitch, the impresario's last discovery, called him the "most extraordinary *agent provocateur* in history."[19]

Diaghilev was certainly not infallible. Most of his musical misjudgments had the company's bottom line or personal prejudice at their source. He disliked choral ballets, even the visual spectacle of the chorus itself ("Hide them! Hide them!" composer Vittorio Rieti recalled him once saying).[20] To Diaghilev a chorus was just an unwanted expense; he either endeavored to cut their parts (*Daphnis et Chloë*)[21] or quickly dropped ballets that used them (*Barabau*). His high-handed musical cuts in, for example, *Apollon musagète* (Terpsichore's variation) and *Chout* (the end of scene five) demonstrate that he valued theatricality higher than musical integrity. He also had an aversion to American composers and to jazz as well, in complete opposition to the prevailing taste of 1920s Paris. Diaghilev enjoyed recognizing and molding new talent, but sometimes, despite his best efforts, expectations were not fulfilled. Scores such as Constant Lambert's *Romeo and Juliet* and Henri Sauguet's *La Chatte* are serviceable but hardly distinguished. Late in his career, personal interests such as book collecting and the indoctrination of the young composer Igor Markevitch kept him away from the company when his presence was sorely needed. Increasing deference to his secretary Boris Kochno and periods of disinterest and ill-health suggest that had he not died in 1929 he may not have continued much longer at the head of the Ballets Russes.

Given the success of the *Scythian Suite*, Diaghilev's rejection of *Ala i Lolli* might seem to be a serious misjudgment. But as we shall see, this ballet had no chance whatsoever in the Ballets Russes of 1915. Still Diaghilev was wise enough to offer Prokofiev another chance, and then another when the original version of *Chout* proved not to his liking. In 1920 he directed the revision of what was to become Prokofiev's first great ballet. Despite the false starts and his disappointment with the composer's magnum opuses of the period—*L'Amour des trois oranges* (*Lyubov' k tryom apel'sinam*; The Love for Three Oranges) and *Ognennïy angel* (Fiery Angel)—Diaghilev maintained his faith in Prokofiev. For that, we remain grateful.

Once Prokofiev entered the limelight of Western Europe he had to contend with the occasional charge of composing in Stravinsky's shadow.[22] In certain quarters today Prokofiev's early ballets are still dismissed as pale reflections of that composer's great trilogy, *L'Oiseau de feu*, *Petrouchka*, and *Le Sacre du printemps*. Although they do share some precompositional strictures, the music clearly reveals the respective composers' unique styles. Notwithstanding his flair for caricature in the manner of Musorgsky and his studies under both Lyadov and Rimsky-Korsakov, the independent-minded Prokofiev fulfilled Diaghilev's requests and became an heir to the Russian tradition on his own terms. From Igor Stravinsky he received far more in the way of inspiration than outright influence. Unlike Stravinsky he used Russian folk song anthologies only as a point of departure and subjugated *neokuchkist* practices to sound theatricality. By *neokuchkist* I mean a revitalization of the practice whereby folk songs are conspicuously used in art music; the *kuchkists* (that is, *moguchaya kuchka* or mighty little heap) being the Balakirev-led group of composers that included the well-known "Five" (Balakirev, Cui, Musorgsky, Rimsky-Korsakov and Borodin) as well as other associates of the "New Russian School," for example, Chaikovsky and Dargomïzhsky *c*.1869. *Chout* shares hardly any of *Le Sacre du printemps*' musical style, forged from the very essence of folk songs and texts. Although Prokofiev and Stravinsky shared a common heritage — both *L'Oiseau de feu* and *Chout* do reveal an assimilation of traditional techniques — the independence of the respective composers' personal styles yielded quite different results.

Despite his adoption of '*neokuchkist*' Russianness in *Chout* and topical references in *Le Pas d'acier*, Prokofiev's means of expression remained basically the same, that is, fundamentally lyrical. Though often decidedly unvocal and enlivened by relentless ostinati, this music does not make a break with the past, rather it is characterful music built on the lyrical phrase. This music is completely unlike the spatiotemporal manipulation of harmonic and melodic cells found in Stravinsky's ballets beginning with *Petrouchka*. If one were to strip away Prokofiev's clangorous layers of surface activity there remains an almost textbook clarity and reserve. Of course, conservative audiences in Russia and the West heard only the former and voiced their disapproval. While it is not modernistic, his ballet style does stand apart from that of its forebears such as Glazunov and Chaikovsky. And it has an amazing stylistic consistency which will become evident during the course of this survey.

Prokofiev's relationship with Diaghilev spans the entire war and postwar era of the Ballets Russes (1914–29). Clearly envious of Stravinsky's acclaim and material success, Prokofiev ventured West to meet the sagacious impresario upon graduation from the St Petersburg Conservatory in 1914. Ever on the lookout for new talent, Diaghilev for some time had had his eye on this young firebrand whose music outraged provincial Russian ears. They met in London that summer and Prokofiev received his orders to write his first ballet. By then Diaghilev had been experimenting with modernism in décor (Goncharova replacing Bakst) and had fallen under the spell of the Italian futurists who were presenting their novel sounds in a series of concerts at the London Coliseum. Domiciled in Italy at the start of the Great War, Diaghilev wholly embraced modernism, with choreographer Massine replacing Fokine.[23] When Stravinsky balked at composing a Mass or religious piece for the proposed ballet *Liturgie*, Diaghilev considered accompanying it with a futurist "orchestra," or just silence.

Prokofiev's first ballet for Diaghilev, *Ala i Lolli*, stood no chance of success in such a hotbed. With the novelty and audacity of *Le Sacre du printemps* in his mind, the composer had subverted his first ballet into an orchestral tour de force of musical primitivism. Stylistically, however, the two works are poles apart, a fact not lost on Diaghilev who dismissed *Ala i Lolli* as something old-fashioned and generic besides. The impresario exhorted Prokofiev to try again with something "truly Russian." He even called upon Stravinsky, then consummate Russian nationalist, to help with the reorientation process. For a weekend in April 1915 Prokofiev apparently became his aspiring disciple.

Awaiting Stravinsky's completion of *Les Noces*, Diaghilev wanted something as intensely Russian from Prokofiev—playing his exotic card always led to a favorable reception in Paris and London. So Massine, Prokofiev and Diaghilev concocted a ballet entitled *Skazka pro shuta* (*Chout* in French transliteration) based on Russian folk tales from the Afanasyev collection, one well-suited, the impresario believed, to the composer's natural talent for the grotesque. After being delayed by the war and undergoing a major, Diaghilev-directed revision, *Chout* was finally premiered in Paris in May of 1921. It was Prokofiev's first professional theatrical work to be presented anywhere.

Prokofiev's understanding of ballet, and hence his success in it, was greatly indebted to Diaghilev. Prokofiev had composed *Chout* in 1915 back in Russia without any supervision or choreographer's input. While the score demonstrates the composer's gift for characterization, its dramatic sections were overly detailed and it provided too little opportunity for dancing. Diaghilev met with Prokofiev in 1920 in order to salvage the dramatically ill-paced score. His recommendations are preserved by Prokofiev's penciled-in instructions on the manuscript. As many have pointed out, Diaghilev had uncanny musical and theatrical wisdom. Prokofiev acknowledged as much saying he was a "subtle and discerning critic ... [who] argued his point with great conviction."[24] That he indoctrinated Prokofiev to the needs of ballet (as Fokine had done for Stravinsky in *L'Oiseau de feu*) and helped separate the wheat from the chaff in *Chout* certainly deserves recognition.

During the postwar period the Ballets Russes more often chased trends than set them: the company's precarious financial condition necessitated an aesthetically mobile stance. This changing artistic outlook greatly affected the nature of Prokofiev's commissions. After having been cast apart during the heyday of French influence in the early mid-1920s, Prokofiev reentered the Ballets Russes circle in 1925 shortly after the lackluster premiere of his Second Symphony. Diaghilev came through with a timely commission for a ballet on contemporary life in Soviet Russia which would be called *Le Pas d'acier*. As soon as designer Yakulov joined the project it became both futurist and constructivist as well. Futurist-inspired pieces such as Honegger's *Pacific 231* (1923) and his ballet *Skating Rink* (1921) were then in vogue. Jazz and ragtime had begun to influence ballet as well. Though eager for the commission, Prokofiev felt the need to refocus on lyricism. Despite the seeming incongruity with the proposed topic, Diaghilev encouraged him to write in his own style. Thus alongside some of the most trendy music he ever wrote, Prokofiev penned his first romantic pas de deux. In the end his new simplicity was nearly imperceptible—the ballet's stunning finale with its highly representational noises of a factory at full production overshadowed the more lyrical sections. *Le Pas d'acier* brought Prokofiev considerable success and a closer relationship with Diaghilev. It and its more timeless (and obviously prefiguring) successor kept his name on the playbill for the company's final three seasons.

As the decade progressed the heady, carefree, postwar climate in Paris gradually gave way to a more melancholy (though not yet financially morose) mood that welcomed the sober *L'Enfant prodigue* in 1929. When Rolf De Maré's Ballets Suédois folded in 1925 Diaghilev's primary competition became dancer-led troupes that presented less experimental fare. The conservatism of the Ballets Russes' financial backers also influenced the company's esthetic in the waning years of the decade. Amidst monetary devaluation and new fascism there arose in many a concern for social order and a need for orthodoxy. The overriding musical tenor had taken a similar course since the middle of the decade as the more daring aspects of Parisian modernism succumbed to increasingly ubiquitous "neoclassicism." Wistful eighteenth-century retrospectivism had occasionally surfaced in the ballet throughout the decade, but concurrent with the dissolution of the "Roaring Twenties" a touch of melancholia appeared in the ballet music of many Paris-based composers—from Stravinsky (*Apollon musagète*) to Prokofiev (*L'Enfant prodigue*) and even Poulenc (*Aubade*)— occasioned by even more archaic plots. This context provides both the impetus and a fitting aura for Diaghilev's swan song.

While composing *L'Enfant prodigue* Prokofiev had confidently claimed in a letter to a colleague in Russia that it "will undoubtedly be one of my most successful works." Although each of his ballets for Diaghilev was born from a different kind of collaboration, this time a viable scenario came before the music, and the décor (by Georges Rouault) and choreography (by Balanchine) followed its completion, in turn. For the first time in Prokofiev's work with the Ballets Russes there were no undermining aspects to the collaboration (although the composer considered much of the choreography repugnant). The result, not surprisingly, has stood the test of time. Once again the ever-discriminating

Diaghilev encouraged the composer to make important improvements in the score. The production of Prokofiev's first ballet after Diaghilev's death, *Sur le Borysthène*, would suffer from the lack of such guidance.

Though only *L'Enfant prodigue* belongs with *L'Oiseau de feu*, *Petrouchka*, *Le Tricorne*, and *Les Noces* at the pinnacle of the company's collaborative artistry, each of Prokofiev's ballets for Diaghilev was significant. Each was prefigured in the Soviet theatre, each attracted the close attention of the impresario and each culminated a chapter in the company's esthetic: *lubok*-inspired Russian modernism, topicality and the brief return of high drama, respectively. Together these ballets are testimony to the mutual respect between the composer and the impresario.

Prokofiev did some of his best work for Diaghilev. He obviously respected his judgment and valued his approval. Beyond their fine craftsmanship and engaging theatricality, the ballets Prokofiev composed for him are consistent in compositional style and manner of characterization. This consistency further links them to his later ballets. Prokofiev's ballet style is not indebted to any person or school—it lived and died with the composer himself. Nevertheless, the ballets he composed for Diaghilev reflect and extend the traditions of the colorful and characterful Russian theatre.

Notes

1. Mikhail Tarakanov, "Prokofiev: Legende und Wahrheit," trans. by Margaret Weiss, in the program book for the 1991 Cologne Sergey Prokofiev Symposium, p. 23.
2. Richard Taruskin, "The Anti-literary Man: Diaghilev and Music," in *Art of Enchantment: Diaghilev's Ballets Russes, 1909–1929*, ed. by Nancy Van Norman Baer (San Francisco, CA, 1988), p. 121.
3. These are Prokofiev's words challenging Soviet biographer Israel Nestyev's statement in his first biographical sketch that the period spent abroad was of lesser significance. Nestyev, "New Discoveries About the Great Master," in *Sergey Prokofiev: Materials, Articles, Interviews*, ed. by Vladimir Blok (Moscow, 1978), p. 90.
4. See, for example, the interview with conductor Gennady Rozhdestvensky, "Besedï s masterami," in *Sovetskaia muzyka*, no. 5 (May 1971), 32–6; or Harlow Robinson's account of the collaboration between Prokofiev and the Bolshoy theater staff on *Tale of the Stone Flower*, Robinson, *Sergei Prokofiev* (New York, 1987), pp. 484 and 492.
5. Prokofiev saved what he wanted from the ballet in his *Scythian Suite*. He took the Suite along with his Symphony No. 1 (the "Classical"), First Piano Concerto and some piano pieces when he left for America in 1918. The remnants of *Ala i Lolli*, if retained, were probably not highly valued. They were not among the items his widowed mother carried when she left Russia in 1920, nor among those he had stored at his publisher's office and reclaimed when he returned to Russia in 1927. And it is highly doubtful that they were among the composer's manuscripts that Koussevitzky carried with him when he left Soviet Russia for good in May 1920.
6. They are available at the Serge Prokofiev Archive, Goldsmiths College, London, England.

7. Lifar sold his holdings bit by bit over the course of many years. The remnants of Kochno's collection was purchased by the French government upon his death and is now held at the Paris Opéra library. See John Drummond, *Speaking of Diaghilev* (London, 1997), pp. 29 and 74.

8. This problem also exists for other theatrical works of the period, such as the operas *L'Amour des trois oranges* and *Igrok* (The Gambler).

9. Actually, there are two autobiographies. The more lengthy one is a detailed memoir of childhood through age 17 (July 1909), assembled by the composer beginning in 1937–39 and resumed in 1945 with the help of his second wife, Mira. The truncated English version (318 pp.) is entitled *Prokofiev by Prokofiev, a Composer's Memoir*, trans. by Guy Daniels. Also in English translation is his "Autobiography," penned in 1941, which breaks off in 1937. It is part of *S.S. Prokof'yev, materiali, dokumenti, vospominaniya*, ed. S.I. Shlifshteyn (Moscow, 1961) and also *Sergei Prokofiev, Soviet Diary 1927 and Other Writings*, trans. by Oleg Prokofiev and David Mather, ed. by Oleg Prokofiev and Christopher Palmer (Boston, MA, 1991). I will refer to the more detailed earlier one as "first autobiography," the other as simply "autobiography."

10. Israel Nestyev, "Diaghilev's Musical Education," trans. by Robert Johnson in *The Ballets Russes and Its World*, ed. by Lynn Garafola and Nancy Van Norman Baer (New Haven, CT, 1999), p. 25.

11. Evgenia Egorova, "The Diaghilev Family in Perm," trans. by Irene Huntoon in *The Ballets Russes and Its World*, ed. by Lynn Garafola and Nancy Van Norman Baer (New Haven, CT, 1999), p. 16.

12. Doris Monteux, *It's All in the Music* (New York, 1965), p. 88.

13. Désiré Inghelbrecht did once, leading an early 1927 rehearsal of Debussy's *L'Après-midi d'un faune* at a "breathless" pace. Diaghilev corrected him and then they argued, the conductor claiming he well knew the tempo for French music. But the impresario trumped him saying that the tempo for the ballet had been set by Debussy himself. True or not, Inghelbrecht was replaced just as soon as Desormière became available.

14. Igor Stravinsky, "The Diaghilev I Knew," *Atlantic Monthly* (November 1953).

15. Eugene Goossens, *Overture and Beginners* (London, 1951), p. 247

16. Conductor Roger Desormière objected that the orchestra could not play the "circus-like" D-major theme any faster, whereupon the impresario began to conduct in the tempo he desired. Apparently Diaghilev requested the *prestissimo* because of his dislike for the music. See *Sergey Prokof'yev, Dnevnik 1919–1933* (Paris, 2002), vol. 2, p. 707.

17. Quoted in Drummond, p. 302.

18. Quoted in Arnold Haskell, *Balletomania: The Story of an Obsession* (London, 1934), p. 121.

19. Quoted in Drummond, p. 282.

20. Hilary Ostlere, "Rieti and Balanchine," *Ballet Review* (Spring 1982), p.14.

21. Diaghilev claimed that the wordless chorus was an "experiment" that proved to be "detrimental" to the ballet. To his budget, perhaps it was.

22. For example, Prokofiev was accused of being a Stravinsky "follower" by the caustic and sometimes brutal Warsaw critic Piotr Rytel in a 15 January 1925 concert review for *Gazeta Warszawska*. Prokofiev was in town for a performance of his Third Piano Concerto with Fitelberg on 15 January and a "Klavierabend" four days later. In an interview with Ye. Shevchenko for the Russian language Warsaw newspaper *Za svobodu!* he was compelled to protest against that judgment (19 January 1925, p. 3).

23. Nijinsky's modernistic choreography—*L'Après-midi d'un faune, Jeux, Le Sacre*—lasted only through the summer of 1913. After his marriage and subsequent dismissal

in the fall of 1913, Fokine was reengaged as company choreographer for the 1914 season.

24. Sergey Prokofiev, "Autobiography," p. 268.

CHAPTER 1

Prokofiev and Diaghilev: the collaboration

Sergey Sergeyevich Prokofiev (1891–1953) was introduced to Sergey Pavlovich Diaghilev (1872–1929) in July 1914 during the Ballets Russes' London season. Despite Diaghilev's later reference to him as "my second son" (his "first" being Igor Stravinsky) their relationship until the impresario's death in 1929 was variable, inconstant and frequently complicated by the presence of Stravinsky (1882–1971). The same Diaghilev who would write highly critical letters and call Prokofiev an "utter imbecile" behind his back would prove his loyalty and trust with ballet commissions even in the wake of unsuccessful compositions. For his part Prokofiev was not so blatantly duplicitous, although he did complain to his friends about the delays in bringing his works to the stage, negotiated with "competitors," and tried to arrange illicit performances of his Ballets Russes commissions. There were periods when the relationship was strained (after Diaghilev sided with Stravinsky in criticizing *L'Amour des trois oranges*, and when the impresario promoted Poulenc and Milhaud) and when it was tempered by geographic remove (for example, during and immediately after World War I). At the outset Prokofiev could play at best a distant second to Stravinsky in Diaghilev's esteem. But by 1929 the prospect of *L'Enfant prodigue* and Stravinsky's and Diaghilev's recurring estrangements had turned the tables. Then in the final weeks a dark cloud appeared. These inconsistencies in their relationship notwithstanding, Diaghilev produced three of Prokofiev's ballets— *Chout* (1921), *Le Pas d'acier* (1927) and *L'Enfant prodigue* (1929). These ballets not only garnered a fair measure of success for Diaghilev's company and provided gratifying critical recognition for the young composer, but they laid the groundwork for the genre in which Prokofiev would achieve great renown.

Prokofiev first saw the Ballets Russes in mid-June 1913 at Paris's new, elegant Théâtre des Champs-Élysées while on a summer trip to France, England and Switzerland with his widowed mother. They arrived at Paris's Gare du Nord in the late afternoon of Sunday 15 June.[1] After settling into their hotel on the rue du Helder, Prokofiev ventured out onto the Boulevard des Italiens in search of friends from home: Nikolay Cherepnin, his favorite professor at the Conservatory, Mikhail Shteyman (Steiman), a former classmate in Cherepnin's conducting class and now an assistant conductor for the company, and the Andreyevs, professional singers he knew from St Petersburg. Anna Andreyevna, a mezzo, was a Professor at the St Petersburg Conservatory and Nikolay Andreyev, a tenor, sang at the Mariinsky Theatre. This season he was assuming the roles of the Scribe and Prince Shuisky in Diaghilev's productions of *Khovanshchina* and *Boris Godunov*, respectively. Prokofiev liked the "noisy boulevard" and quickly realized that the "celebrated liveliness and joy" of the French people was really true. Not having any luck in his quest, he stopped by the Élysées Palace Hôtel where Diaghilev was staying to ask for his assistance. Prokofiev had never been introduced to the impresario, nevertheless he sent him his card with a note asking if he knew his friends' whereabouts. Diaghilev was not in but his valet appeared with the name of the Andreyevs' hotel and the news that Cherepnin had just departed Paris for Russia.[2] This last information was disappointing: Prokofiev had hoped that Cherepnin would help him interest local musicians in several of his manuscript scores which he had brought along.[3] After visiting three different hotels named Terminus without finding the Andreyevs he abandoned his search and dined at the Café de la Paix. He finally located the couple the following noon. They warmly welcomed Prokofiev and convinced him that he and his mother should take adjoining rooms at their new quarters, a *pension* on the rue du Marbeau, "with excellent air," just a stone's throw from the Bois de Boulogne.

Not surprisingly, this bustling metropolis of nearly three million made a tremendous impression on the 22-year-old. He was charmed by the Parisian tempo of life and general level of culture. He found certain aspects to be vexing, however; for example, his encounter with a street vendor who tried to sell him dirty postcards along with the street map he wanted,[4] and the necessity of wearing a top hat to formal occasions, such as Ballets Russes intermissions. Along with visits that week to the Louvre (on a guided tour that was "very interesting, then boring, then torture") and the Eiffel Tower (which he found fascinating), Prokofiev saw *Khovanshchina* starring Chaliapin on 16 June and attended the ballet on 17 June and 19 June, viewing Stravinsky's *Petrouchka*, Fokine's ballet *Schéhérazade* set to Rimsky-Korsakov's score, the "Polovtsian Dances" from Borodin's *Prince Igor* and Ravel's *Daphnis et Chloë* among other works. He had missed by two days the final performance in the premier run of *Le Sacre du printemps*, but the opening night riot, Stravinsky's audacious music and Nijinsky's shocking choreography were still the talk of the town.

Prokofiev was too early by two weeks to see *Le Sacre* in London, where he was "dragged" for five days beginning 22 June by the Andreyevs, lodging in their *pension* on Clifton Gardens. He enjoyed strolling along Oxford and Regent Streets, but complained about "fast buses" and traffic on the wrong side of the street; he summed up, "Paris is prettier." At Hyde Park Prokofiev happened onto a procession with King George and French President Poincaré in "splendid old carriages." He greatly enjoyed visiting Westminster Abbey, where he stood before the monuments to Handel and Shakespeare "for a long time." He finally met Shteyman at a rehearsal of *Boris Godunov* and chatted briefly with the opera's conductor Emil Cooper. Prokofiev wrote home to Cherepnin that he attended the "glittering" opening night performance of *Boris Godunov* featuring Chaliapin at Drury Lane Theatre. The performance was sold out so he had to sit in the wings with Shteyman but he was still able to mingle with the elegantly attired guests during intermission. This was Chaliapin's London debut and from his vantage point Prokofiev could see how nervous he was, "pacing like a beast in a cage." He considered the basso "an artist before whom I bow." The performance made a tremendous impression on the young composer; he reported in his Diary, "Boris is a wonderful opera. Musorgsky really understands the stage and that is how one should write. I really want to write an opera. I will have a good, genuine [nastoyashchaya] opera!" His whirlwind visit to London concluded with a trip to Windsor in the company of Shteyman, but only half was accessible due to the state visit. In his letter to Cherepnin, he admitted that he "suffered not knowing the language." But in his Diary he wrote "I decided to study English. It is absolutely necessary for future trips."

Although he would not enter into Diaghilev's circle for another year, Prokofiev was well aware of the fame the Ballets Russes had brought to Stravinsky, an acquaintance from St Petersburg since the spring of 1910. Despite his keen interest in Stravinsky's music, Prokofiev was hardly swept away by it as his unreserved criticism shows (see Chapter 2). Even though the notorious Pavlosk premier of his Second Piano Concerto was still weeks away, Prokofiev was already quite proud of his own reputation as an *enfant terrible* of the avant-garde in St Petersburg, and at this stage he failed to appreciate his colleague's neonational style which had been fashioned at Diaghilev's behest. Likewise, Prokofiev would, by his own admission, fail to immediately grasp the significance of *Le Sacre du printemps* when he first heard it at a concert performance in St Petersburg led by Serge Koussevitzky in February of 1914. Nevertheless, his trip West in 1913 made a tremendous impression and broadened his horizons. Shortly after his graduation from the Conservatory the following spring, Prokofiev departed for London hoping for a commission from the crafty impresario who seemed to hold the keys to success in the music capitals of Western Europe.

Traveling alone but armed with letters of recommendation from Cherepnin, Prokofiev arrived in London on 22 June 1914 and headed once again to Clifton Gardens. He spent his first days meeting his friends the Andreyevs, acclimatizing himself and settling into a studio provided for him by Otto Kling in his music shop at 54 Great Marlborough Street, the London branch of the German music publishing company Breitkopf and Härtel. There from 10 in the morning until he broke for lunch at 1 p.m. he began rewriting his *Sinfonietta*, a work he had begun in 1909 and would not finish tinkering with until 1929. Prokofiev asked Andreyev to find out Walter Nouvel's address as he was a member of Diaghilev's circle and a useful conduit to the great impresario. Unaware of the reason for the request, Andreyev asked Diaghilev for the information the next day during a performance of *Prince Igor*. The impresario responded by requesting that Prokofiev be brought to meet him in the wings the next day, adding that he wanted to discuss a business matter. The next day Prokofiev duly arrived, but the meeting did not take place until the following day after a performance of Stravinsky's *Le Rossignol*: 29 June, one week after he arrived. Prokofiev recalled that the impresario with his monocle, frock-coat, white gloves and top hat was a sight worth seeing (Fig. 1). He recorded in his Diary that Diaghilev extended his hand in a white glove saying that he was very pleased to meet him and that "for a long time he wanted to ask me to attend his shows ... and in the near future he had to have a serious talk with me and hear my music, about which we would make an appointment through Nouvel. We parted on that. I soon met Nouvel who told me that Diaghilev wanted to order a ballet from me." Prokofiev had achieved his goal. The fateful assassination in Sarajevo on 28 June seems not to have fazed him in the least, nor, for that matter, Diaghilev, who still anticipated the company's tour through Germany beginning in October.

Already in the middle of its season at Drury Lane Theatre, the Ballets Russes appeared as spectacular as ever, though it was actually in a state of flux. During the previous year the company had endured Nijinsky's sudden departure, the strained but necessary return of Fokine, and financial uncertainty bordering on outright collapse. The current season, another joint venture with the conductor Thomas Beecham, was taking place due to the largesse of his father, Sir Joseph of "Beecham Pills" fame. But even more significant was Diaghilev's gradual shift in artistic vision away from long standing *Mir iskusstva* (World of Art) ideals[5] towards an interest in modernism and the futurist movement.[6] The arrival of the young dancer Léonid Massine (1896–1979), who had recently debuted in the title role of *La Légende de Joseph*, and the painter Natalya Goncharova, who had painted the fresh, neoprimitive décor for the surprisingly successful *ballet-chanté* staging of Rimsky-Korsakov's opera *Le Coq d'or*, fueled the transformation.

Prokofiev journeyed north to Birmingham for a few days as the guest of the composer, conductor and university professor Granville Bantock, whom he had met through Kling. Upon his return to London he received a letter from Nouvel saying that Diaghilev had invited him to a luncheon on Friday, 3 July. Prokofiev arrived at the restaurant with Nouvel (who, quite perceptively, teased him about his extraordinary careerism) and after some time Diaghilev arrived accompanied by Massine. Stravinsky missed this and all subsequent meetings since he had left for Russia to gather materials for what would become the ballet *Les Noces* soon after the rather tepid London premier of his "conte lyrique" *Le Rossignol*. The discussion opened on the subject of the ballet, Diaghilev expounding on the latest trends, namely that the choreographer and the scenarist now follow a completed musical score. Prokofiev was uninterested and tried to steer the conversation towards opera, specifically his plans to set Dostoevsky's "The Gambler." It was

Diaghilev's turn to be uninterested and the conversation returned to ballet. Diaghilev firmly believed that opera was passé and ballet was flourishing, but probably did not add that he staged operas only when it was financially prudent to do so. After lunch the group headed to Kling's shop where Prokofiev played his Second Sonata, his opera *Maddalena* (1911, revised 1913) and his Second Piano Concerto. According to the composer, *Maddalena* was liked least of all whereas the last two movements of the Sonata and and the entire Second Concerto "sent Diaghilev into ecstasy." The impresario exclaimed, "Now we should eat from the beginning," as if to say (in Prokofiev's interpretation) "that now he understood how and about what he should talk with me." Prokofiev was given a pass to all Ballets Russes performances and after several days was invited to the salon at the Hôtel Cecil for further conversations.

At their next meeting Diaghilev toyed with the idea of staging the Second Concerto as a ballet pantomime with Prokofiev as soloist. The second theme of the finale (reh. 99ff), which resembles a Russian peasant *chastushka* and clearly has a *kuchkist* air about it,[7] suggested to Diaghilev a Pan-like creature such as Lel in Ostrovsky's *Snegurochka* (Snow Maiden), but one who was "gently grotesque and mocking." Prokofiev was reluctant to use his Concerto as a ballet accompaniment, but surely he realized that performing it with the famous Ballets Russes would, as he wrote to his mother, "launch me on a dazzling career as a pianist." The idea was eventually dropped due to the difficulty in adapting a story.

Prokofiev suggested writing a new ballet but Diaghilev wondered if there was enough time, although adding that he definitely wanted to present a ballet with the composer's music in the next season. Diaghilev then had an idea for a plotless ballet set to a suite of the composer's piano pieces which would be orchestrated. This, he believed, could serve as a stopgap in case the *ballet d'action* would have to be postponed until 1916. They decided to discuss this further with Nijinsky, who would be coming to London any day. Diaghilev and the famous dancer/choreographer, now married and recently a father, had made an uneasy rapprochement earlier that spring. Apparently the impresario's negative feelings about his avant-garde choreography for *Jeux* and *Le Sacre du printemps* in 1913 had passed—that July at season's end he had told the dancer's sister that it was not the type that could "sustain the success [read financial viability] of the Ballets Russes."

Nijinsky did not come, however, and at their next meeting Diaghilev was accompanied by the Spanish painter José-María Sert. Prokofiev again played the Second Piano Concerto, and Diaghilev again praised it highly. After the first movement cadenza Sert blurted out, "Mais c'est une bête féroce," unaware that the composer understood French. The impresario recognized the composer's tendency to write in a Russian national style, but added that this was lost amidst a prevailing international style. By this time Diaghilev knew exactly what western audiences expected from Russian composers—music that recalled the *kuchkists*, not the sort of fare that was presently being composed back in Russia.

At the following meeting on 14 July, Diaghilev introduced Prokofiev to his chief conductor, Pierre Monteux. Beecham was to have joined them but had been urgently called away. This was unfortunate, because, as Prokofiev acknowledged in a letter home, "to meet and get along with the wealthy and influential Beecham was essential." After lunch at the Savoy Prokofiev played for them his First Piano Concerto, which was appreciated more for its sweep than for the music itself, some solo pieces from his op.12 and the first *Sarcasm*. He received a most favorable response. Monteux invited Prokofiev to perform with him the following winter at his Concerts Monteux at the Casino de Paris (in April Monteux had led a highly successful concert performance of *Le Sacre* at these concerts). Since negotiations about Prokofiev's first ballet were still in progress it was decided that Monteux would present the composer's Second Concerto unless it was to accompany a ballet, in which case he and the composer would perform the First Concerto. Since the time of Prokofiev's departure was nearing, Diaghilev ended the meeting by saying, "Don't leave without talking to me."

Before departing for home on 20 July Prokofiev went to see the impresario in the wings of the Drury Lane Theatre. Because he was distracted by some performance crisis, Diaghilev's thoughts were scattered and his parting words rather vague: upon arrival in St Petersburg Prokofiev was to appeal to Nouvel or Karatïgin (critic, composer and promoter of Prokofiev's music) to introduce him to a "real Russian writer, for example, Gorodetsky," who would make a ballet plot on some Russian fairy-tale or prehistoric theme. In August Diaghilev would be in Russia and would contact him then for further explanation and the signing of a contract. With that they parted. Prokofiev was satisfied, and considered the trip a good career move. He recorded in his Diary, "To succeed on the European road, which is still wide, like the Diaghilev road, this is very successful … . For a long time I had felt that I should work with Diaghilev." The lack of a contract did not seem to bother him; Prokofiev was convinced that the impresario's reaction to his music was so strong that if Diaghilev's company remained in existence then his ballet would surely come to fruition. However, the planned August meeting never took place, and this proved to be a bad omen.

Prokofiev's reputation had preceded him, yet it was still an act of faith for Diaghilev to request a ballet on the basis of these piano auditions alone. Diaghilev had an uncanny gift for spotting talent: after hearing *Scherzo fantastique* at a Ziloti concert in St Petersburg in early 1909, he had commissioned the young Stravinsky to orchestrate two pieces by Chopin for the upcoming production of *Les Sylphides* and later to compose *L'Oiseau de feu* for the 1910 season.[8] Diaghilev always enjoyed molding fresh talent. Both Stravinsky and Prokofiev were unproven in composing for the theater when they received their first Ballets Russes commissions. But at least Stravinsky had the advantage of collaborating with established artists close to Diaghilev's circle (Fokine as choreographer and Alexander Golovine in charge of décor) and of writing music to a well-known Russian fairy-tale. It was most unusual for

Diaghilev to assign such a vague balletic concept to novices like Prokofiev and Gorodetsky and leave them to their own devices. Though he must have been preoccupied with financial shortcomings, futurism, and—as the news grew more bleak—the company's future in the event of a war, Diaghilev seems to have held little enthusiasm for this project from the start. Prokofiev's youthful arrogance and abrasive personality may have been a factor.

Prokofiev had nevertheless entered into Diaghilev's circle even though he would not receive a proper contract until 1915. He had been given complete access to the theater, "in order to get to know the business," as he wrote to a former classmate back home. One of Diaghilev's four seats in the seventh row was always available to him. "At night, I put on tails and a cloak and go to the Ballets Russes ... . Backstage I meet heavily made-up celebrities and half-naked ballerinas." In his Diary and letters home Prokofiev related his activities, mentioned his new acquaintances in the Ballets Russes circle and provided typically frank impressions of the ballets he saw. While in London in the summer of 1914 Prokofiev saw Ballets Russes productions of *L'Oiseau de feu* (again), *Daphnis et Chloë* (again), *Narcisse* (with music by Cherepnin), the calculated extravaganza *La Légende de Joseph* (Massine's debut, with music by Richard Strauss), the experimental, danced staging of Rimsky-Korsakov's opera *Le Coq d'or* and Stravinsky's opera *Le Rossignol* (like the company's production of *Le Coq d'or* with a double cast of singers and dancers) among other works. Prokofiev was notoriously hard to please. Regarding the music his opinions ranged from tepid praise to downright dismissal. In his letters home he called *Midas* (with music by Rimsky-Korsakov's son-in-law Steinberg) "boring," and *La Légende de Joseph*, "horrible," "hastily written," and "ludicrously insignificant." About the ballets in general, only *Schéhérazade* garnered his unqualified acclaim. He called the staging of *Petrouchka* and *L'Oiseau de feu* "very amusing and inventive," but did not care all that much for the music. In July 1913 he had written to Cherepnin that "he rejoiced" in *Petrouchka's* wit, but was "exasperated by the music, or more truly, by the low level of Stravinsky's standards." After his 1914 encounter he called this score "odna truka" (garbage) in a letter to his friend and colleague Myaskovsky. Prokofiev penned more detailed criticisms about *Cockerel* and *Midas*. He did not comment on the "Polovtsian Dances" from *Prince Igor*, but its staging, like that of *Schéhérazade*, was, by all accounts, stunning—capable of firing the imagination of a novice ballet composer. Though Prokofiev would be forced to compose his first ballet for Diaghilev's company back in Russia, this trip at least provided a partial indoctrination into its aesthetics and performing style.

In addition to the important career moves, Prokofiev had time for more frivolous activities: playing bridge with the Andreyevs, attending a boxing match where he watched with delight as the fighters "beat each other into unconsciousness and spit their teeth out in a bucket of water,"[9] and engaging in some youthful nighttime voyeurism in Hyde Park:

Hundreds of couples settle down on the soft grass in the park, kiss and lounge around embracing each other, and pay absolutely no attention to the passersby. You can stand near them, learn pleasant positions, and recall your own youth [!]. Since there was so much fun at 9:00 p.m., I decided that at 11:00, when darkness falls upon the earth, it would be even more interesting ... . Alas, the evening turned out to be wet and cold, so I didn't get a chance to see what I was hoping to spy on ...[10]

Prokofiev returned to St Petersburg through Berlin and Moscow on 24 July (NS), just eight days before Germany declared war on Russia. His mother wanted to depart soon for their vacation at Kislovodsk in the Caucasus but Prokofiev needed to settle the issue of the ballet's libretto first. After spending a week tracking him down, Prokofiev finally met Sergey Gorodetsky on 17 July (OS henceforth). Probably echoing Diaghilev's advice Prokofiev explained that the ballet should be "1. from Russian life, 2. dramatic or humorous but not simply so-so, that is, it should be boiling water or ice, not warm water, 3. concise with quickly developing action, 4. no moments without action, 5. it should consist of five to six short scenes, in sum a half hour long." Prokofiev then played some of his music and Gorodetsky replied that he understood the composer, knew what was needed, and would start work straight-away on the ballet scenario. In parting Prokofiev stated that he wanted the ballet to begin with the most important part, "so that those who came late would not be able to understand what was going on," adding that the ballet could end with a wild dance in which everything would come together. Gorodetsky concurred. Both he and Prokofiev were quite satisfied with the beginning of their collaboration.

Encouraged by the seemingly limitless resources of the Ballets Russes and brimming with confidence, Prokofiev wrote to Myaskovsky, already mobilized and sent to the front, that he planned to write a "highly complicated" ballet score. Returning home to Petrograd (the new name for St Petersburg) in late September, Prokofiev was unable to begin composing the ballet because he still awaited Gorodetsky's scenario and actually had to track down the author. Biding his time he returned to his *Sinfonietta* revisions and composed *Gadkiy utenok* (The Ugly Duckling) after Hans Christian Andersen. On 8 October a madcap series of events began, alternating frenzied activity with periods of outright slothfulness, complete with missed meetings, oversleeping, deception, name-calling, and complaints about the lethargy and lack of interest by his collaborators—a bit of the pot calling the kettle black. It all began when Nouvel relayed a telegram from Diaghilev asking if the ballet was written yet; it was, after all, over three months since Prokofiev had received his instructions. The panic-stricken composer told Nouvel that there hadn't been a chance, that he hadn't gotten anything from Gorodetsky and as a result he hadn't even begun the ballet! Prokofiev quickly telephoned Gorodetsky and arranged a meeting for the following evening. There he discovered that since their last meeting Gorodetsky had written something about idols of the eleventh century, but had yet to finish it. Prokofiev thought it "highly insignificant." After an hour of lively discussion the composer and the librettist devised a ballet in five scenes (see Chapter 2). They telephoned Nouvel and asked him to telegram Diaghilev, "Prokofiev travaille avec Gorodetsky." After the next meeting on 11 October Prokofiev asked that a second telegram be sent inquiring whether or not Romanov was going to stage the ballet, since a choreographer's input was now necessary for the clarification of details. Diaghilev obviously wanted an inside man to be part of the collaboration since neither Prokofiev nor Gorodetsky knew that much about ballet dramaturgy. Originally a follower of Fokine, Boris Romanov had choreographed the Ballets Russes productions of *La Tragédie de Salomé* (music by Florent Schmitt) in 1913, as well as Stravinsky's opera *Le Rossignol* in 1914 for which the singers were placed in the pit and dancers conveyed the action on stage. By autumn 1914 he was creating experimental ballets in theaters around Petrograd. Ironically, one from this period, *What Happened to the Ballerina, the Chinese, and the Jumpers* (1915), was a forerunner to the ballet *Trapèze* (1924–25), the only true collaboration Romanov and Prokofiev would ever have.

In the following days Prokofiev and Gorodetsky were alternately at odds or mutually inspired with regard to refinements in the plot. At one point Gorodetsky strongly objected to his younger colleague's critical tone, threatening their continued collaboration. On 14 October Prokofiev received a telegram from Diaghilev requesting that he come to Rome with the ballet score and asking if he would like to perform his Second Concerto. He agreed, but this presented a significant dilemma: in the composer's own words, "the ballet [score] wasn't started and the Concerto wasn't learned." Yet the temptation was too much, "to go to a sunny place, to wear a light suit, to walk on the beach … would be fabulous … . I furiously worked on the ballet." On the next day he recorded in his Diary, "I decided to work on it for five to six weeks and write in record speed," and the day after added, "the ballet is going great, I began immediately the first, second and third scenes. I worked better than yesterday … [and] mobilized all excerpts and sketches composed in spring and summer written on scraps [of paper which are] scattered everywhere." But by 20 October he recorded that the ballet was going poorly and the pace necessarily slowed. Late in the evening of 27 October the officially designated choreographer Romanov came to see Prokofiev and the latter explained the origin and the content of the ballet. Romanov listened with apparent interest then asked for a couple of days to think over the setting and plot before returning to hear the music and to discuss the dance. This, however, was not to be. Again and again meetings between Gorodetsky, Prokofiev and Romanov were scheduled and then postponed or canceled. At best, just one meeting with all three in attendance might have occurred in early December.

Prokofiev continued to work on the ballet but irregularly: some days he worked "seriously," on the other hand he spent a whole week away from it in early November. On 17 November he confessed, "Truly the ballet would go faster if I would work on it regularly in the mornings." At times he felt stymied waiting for important details in Gorodetsky's scenario such as the sunset in the first scene during which Chuzhbog abducts Ala. Diaghilev inquired after the ballet again on 25 November, and Prokofiev told Nouvel to report: "the music is ready for four of the five scenes, and I need to know who the designer will be." That was hardly the truth, by then he had completed only the fourth part, "almost" completed the third, and the first and second were only "half done." On 27 November Nouvel and Alfred Nurok (like Nouvel a cofounder of the "Evenings of Contemporary Music" in St Petersburg and a member of Diaghilev's circle) arrived to hear the ballet. The evening went well but Prokofiev was afraid that they did not understand any of it. He was right, they hadn't. Nouvel wrote to Diaghilev that "Prokofiev was turning out some weird stuff on a weird subject." Shortly thereafter Prokofiev began orchestrating the ballet. He struggled with the concluding sunrise, but rightly recognized that this would be one of the best sections of the score. Without finishing he moved on to another section before abandoning work on the ballet altogether by 14 December. In early January 1915 he resumed work on the first scene, but still did not have Gorodetsky's final plan for the sunset. Prokofiev divided his time between the ballet and practicing his Second Piano Concerto for upcoming concerts in Petrograd and Rome. On 24 January he performed the piece to his satisfaction at a Russian Music Society concert under Nikolay Malko. Later that evening he found out that he would be leaving for Rome on 1 February with all the expenses to be paid by Diaghilev. By the time he was summoned Prokofiev had finished no more than three-fourths of the ballet, but nevertheless had begun orchestrating it, "enjoying all kinds of combinations." In those days, few composers could resist overscoring their ballets for Diaghilev.

Deeming the trip necessary for the ballet, Prokofiev left Petrograd in mid-February. Enduring a head cold, crowded conditions and a cholera scare, among other inconveniences, he traveled from Kiev to Bari circuitously through Romania, Bulgaria, and Greece, studying Italian all the way. He finally arrived in Rome on 3 March 1915 (NS henceforth).

In mid-1914 Diaghilev had come under the spell of the Italian futurist movement; in June he had attended Luigi Russolo's "Grand Futurist Concert of Noises," which was doing "turns" at the London Coliseum.[11] His interest was probably heightened by the tumultuous reception at the premiere (Diaghilev always enjoyed a good scandal, especially those of his own making). *The Times* reported that between the opening number, "The Awakening of the City," and the next, "A Meeting of Motor-cars and Aeroplanes," pathetic cries of "No More!" were heard from all quarters of the auditorium. Diaghilev considered several futurist projects, but only Giacomo Balla's light show to Stravinsky's *Feu d'artifice* (Fireworks) (presented in Rome on 12 April 1917) was to reach the stage. Still, the futurist influence was a great force in turning Diaghilev's company towards modernism. In combination with neoprimitivism (for example, Goncharova's sets and costumes for *Le Coq d'or*, and her companion Mikhail

Larionov's for the ballets *Le Soleil de nuit* and *Kikimora*) and cubism (for example, *Parade*) it gave the company a fresh new look.[12] The last component of Diaghilev's new esthetic was the rediscovery of the preromantic heritage, seen in such pastiche works as *Les femmes de bonne humeur* (1917, set to excerpts from Domenico Scarlatti sonatas orchestrated by Vincenzo Tommasini). Dance historian Lynn Garafola summarizes this metamorphosis:

> To naturalism, dramatic narrative, and psychologically motivated characterization, [Diaghilev] said goodbye. He cast out the exoticism of Bakst ... and the passéism of Benois, and threw over the symbolist thematic of *Mir iskusstva*. Henceforth, he would hang his stage with backdrops that acknowledged the revolution of cubism. Through ... Massine, he would incorporate into the ballet the dynamism and angularity advocated by the futurists, along with the impersonal performance style, discontinuous narrative, and studied incongruity that became trademarks of Ballets Russes modernism.[13]

Garafola's ensuing assertion that design overtook music as the center of gravity in Diaghilev's company is misleading, however: as descendants of the Saava Mamontov school through the artists Korovin and Golovin, Diaghilev's circle had always been design oriented.[14] And while design did occasionally control the entire production in the postwar hierarchy as in, for example, *Le Pas d'acier*, it did not do so in every case (consider Stravinsky's ballets and *L'Enfant prodigue*).

Diaghilev warmly welcomed the 24-year-old Prokofiev to Italy and introduced him to his inner circle of confidants and collaborators. Over a five-week period Diaghilev (accompanied by Massine) showed him the important sites in and around Rome, Naples, Capri, Palermo and Milan in his typical grand manner of introducing young men to treasures of art. Three days after arriving in Rome Prokofiev wrote home, "they are advertising me like the devil, and have been wearing me out with breakfasts, rehearsals, reviewers, marquis ... praising me to the sky so that I feel like some sort of Beethoven ... The [concert] posters are handsome and about 1.5 sazhen tall [roughly three meters]."[15] This heady experience was in preparation for his performance the following day of his Second Piano Concerto at the Rome Augusteum under the direction of Bernardino Molinari. Diaghilev's promotion scheme must have been successful because the concert was well-attended according to the composer's report home to his mother. In his Diary Prokofiev noted that the audience was about two thousand strong, but the hall was so large that it was far from full. The day after Prokofiev arrived, Diaghilev had telegrammed Stravinsky in Switzerland asking him to arrange for a further performance of the Concerto in Geneva on 20 March. But the primary reason for Prokofiev's trip was to let Diaghilev examine the young composer's first attempt at ballet music, and before the Sunday concert the impresario had already discovered that a tutorial visit to Stravinsky was necessary.

On his third day in Rome Prokofiev had written to his mother that the plot of *Ala i Lolli* needed revisions but claimed that Diaghilev was not yet familiar with the music. That run-through took place between rehearsals for the upcoming concert. After Prokofiev played what he had completed of the ballet Diaghilev proceeded to take him to task, "What is this? You, a Russian composer ... and you write international music? It won't do!" "International music," undoubtedly uttered with a sneer, was Diaghilev's term for the generic sounding, denationalized music then popular in the academic circles in Petrograd; such music was almost certain box office poison in Paris. The impresario clearly understood the great appeal the more overtly national or exotic music of Glinka, Rimsky-Korsakov, Balakirev, Borodin and Musorgsky had in the West. Indeed, the "Polovtsian Dances: and *Schéhérazade* remained the company's most popular repertory items along with Stravinsky's *L'Oiseau de feu* and *Petrouchka*. The last two stood apart from the latest St Petersburg fare, having been fashioned to serve, in Benois' words, "Diaghilev's foreign export campaign." Anything sounding *kuchkist*, or even *neokuchkist* was destined for certain success with Ballets Russes audiences.

Prokofiev's Diary account of the remainder of this encounter speaks clearly of Diaghilev's persuasiveness, as well as the composer's ready submission and desire to please:

> In Diaghilev's opinion international music cannot be. Of course one should not understand the term 'national' to mean [just] folk themes and in general one should not look at this narrowly, but the Russian soul should be there and I am not a stranger to this, there are examples of this, many in the Second Concerto. Diaghilev [continued]: 'After Stravinsky in Russia there remained only one composer—you ... Can a country which produced so many national composers like Borodin, Musorgsky, Dargomïzhsky, completely run dry? In Petrograd they are unable to value anything Russian. It is a swamp out from which it is imperative to drag you, otherwise it will swallow you up. But let's leave the ballet thusly, let's adjust a particularly Russian staging to your non-Russian music, also particularly Russian decorations and costumes—No! Paris is smart, Paris dismantles everything, and behind Paris the whole world goes. I don't want your ballet to be limited to three or four performances ...'
> [Prokofiev continues] I usually do not so easily step away from my position, however, Diaghilev was so convincing that I immediately agreed to throw half the music out of my ballet. [to which] Diaghilev added, 'and completely change the plot!'

In sum, the music was generic and the story passé. It apparently never occurred to Prokofiev or Gorodetsky just how old-fashioned their libretto was, even with its hero, villain, damsel in distress and benevolent protector. And its dramatic rationale—the scene one abduction of Ala—replayed the opening of Glinka's opera *Ruslan and Lyudmila*, or, without the mix of genres, the end of part one of *Daphnis et Chloë*. In the wake of *Le Sacre du printemps* this sort of fare would not do. Perhaps by this time Prokofiev had acquired his conviction that he could set anything to music and that, ultimately, it was only the music that mattered.

Diaghilev felt otherwise. This encounter was just the first of many during their fifteen-year relationship in which the composer acquiesced to the impresario's views. For all his *enfant terrible* posturing, Prokofiev remained servile to those whose judgment he respected. When defending his operas he would be far more forward, but in balletic issues he readily deferred to Diaghilev.

On the day after the concert Diaghilev posted this letter to Stravinsky:

> He brought me about one-third of the music of his new ballet. The subject is a St Petersburg fabrication; it would have been good for the Mariinsky Theatre ten years ago, but it is not for us. The music, as he says, does not look for Russianism, it is just music. Precisely, just music, and very bad. Now we have to keep him with us for two or three months. I am counting on your help. He is talented, but what do you expect when the most cultivated person he sees is Tcherepnin who impresses him with his *avant-gardisme* (!) [Diaghilev had terminated Cherepnin's services as first conductor of the Ballets Russes during the summer of 1911.] He is easily influenced and it seems to me he is a much nicer person than we suspected he would be after his arrogant appearance in the past. I will bring him to you. He must change entirely, otherwise we will lose him forever.[16]

Not only had Prokofiev failed to please Diaghilev with *Ala i Lolli*, but his debut in Rome received a mixed reception. After the Concerto's first movement the audience was divided, some applauded and some hissed, after the Scherzo they unanimously applauded, after the third movement they applauded less and at the end Prokofiev was rather warmly summoned. He felt that he had played better in Petrograd and that Molinari's accompanied was worse than in the rehearsal, but he considered it a "very good success" nevertheless. The press was far less generous. Critics accused the composer of writing a concerto that was neither modern nor traditional. Nestyev summarizes:

> Almost the entire press ... after paying due respects to the young Russian's virtuosity, severely criticized the Second Piano Concerto ('nightmarish,' 'tricks,' 'meaningless piano exercises'). 'We had expected to find a new Stravinsky, tart and interesting, but on the contrary we found an artist still lacking individuality and wandering between old and new,' wrote one of the modernist critics.[17]

When the composer first played the Concerto in public at Pavlovsk in August 1913, its perceived modernity provoked a scandal: the progressives shouted praises while the majority hissed. But to the audience in Rome this music was unexceptional. By comparison, the Romans greeted a concert performance of *Pétrouchka* earlier that season with great ovations. If nothing else, these reviews may have bolstered Diaghilev's assessment that Prokofiev needed a "major overhaul" in order to achieve success in the West.

On 8 March Diaghilev, accompanied by Massine and Prokofiev, headed south to Naples to see the sights and to talk with the futurists about a proposed ballet depicting the Neapolitan national holiday. From Naples Prokofiev wrote home that his ballet needed "important changes to which I have agreed." The day before he had written to Derzhanovsky regarding Diaghilev's plans for a new Monte Carlo season beginning March 1916 (Derzhanovsky was editor and publisher of the weekly Moscow journal *Muzïka*). After listing Stravinsky's *Svadebka* (*Les Noces*, or *The Wedding*) and *Fireworks*, there came the Neapolitan folk-festival piece (like *Fireworks*, another collaboration with Marinetti and the futurists), and a "Suite from Scarlatti." At the end of the list Prokofiev added "*maybe* my ballet" [my emphasis]. At this early date, from the composer's point of view, this would have meant a revised *Ala i Lolli*, not the yet to be conceived *Chout*. On 14 March he wrote letters to both his mother and to Myaskovsky stating that the ballet needed to be "recast" and that from Italy he would visit Stravinsky's home in Switzerland where "there are ample sources on Russian antiquity." A final letter in this series was sent by Prokofiev, now back in Rome, to his mother on 20 March, "I think that I will go to Switzerland for not more than a week, and [there Stravinsky] is to direct my steps according to his example." He added that Diaghilev wanted his ballet to be "'le dernier cri,' and besides 'Russian'; and for familiarization with these trends I need to speak with other [Diaghilev] colleagues in Switzerland."

During this trip Prokofiev and Diaghilev had many discussions about the weaknesses in *Ala i Lolli* and more lengthy ones about ballet in general. The impresario surely did most of the talking. Over the course of 12 days he pointed out that Gorodetsky's plot was dated, unoriginal and stilted, and that it was necessary to turn to a Russian fairy tale and do it "freshly and grotesquely." Such a fairy tale they would undoubtedly find at Stravinsky's. It seems likely that he was seeking a suitable performing companion for *Les Noces*. Diaghilev asserted his belief that Prokofiev's natural inclination was "grotesque, grotesque and grotesque," not "pompous narration about Wagnerian heroes." And he finally convinced the composer "to place a cross over *Ala i Lolli* and wait for Stravinsky, Switzerland and [Russian fairy] tales."

The trio returned to Rome on 19 March for a couple of days so that Diaghilev could attend to some business matters surrounding an upcoming American tour. Two days turned into nearly two weeks. Plans changed and Diaghilev was unable to journey to Switzerland, so beginning on 22 March he began sending Stravinsky a series of telegrams asking him to come to Milan "with all your music." Stravinsky was then working on what would become *Les Noces* whose completion Diaghilev anxiously awaited (during the composer's previous visit to Rome in February he had played newly completed portions of it for Diaghilev which prompted the impresario to remark, "I am in love with it"). While Diaghilev occupied himself with business affairs Prokofiev was becoming bored and wanted to return home; he greatly missed his ladylove, Nina Meshchersky (1889–1981), and had a passing idea to fetch her and return to work on the new ballet. However, after about a week Diaghilev, Massine and Prokofiev began leafing through the five volumes of Afanasyev's collected folk tales and eventually discovered a tale about a buffoon, one which Stravinsky had once pointed out as good material for a ballet plot. But the tale with all its twists and turns was not well-suited for the stage. "On one remarkable day," as Prokofiev recorded in his Diary,

> Massine tried to arrange one of the adventures into three scenes, then I added another to it and changed the chronology—both adventures united wonderfully and the plot was ready in about five minutes, amazingly having settled into six scenes. The last three to four days [in Rome] we devoted to detailing and reworking these scenes and Diaghilev participated ardently and usefully. Massine amused us very much having thought up a dance of washing the floor for the beginning [of the first scene]. I was very taken with the plot and Diaghilev was wildly happy that this was just right for me and for Nijinsky in the main role; Nijinsky would also stage it.

Diaghilev's financial matters were finally settled and the trio relocated to Milan on Friday, 2 April for the rendezvous with Stravinsky. Prokofiev looked forward to this meeting even though the two composers had met years earlier in St Petersburg. He had been hearing an earful of praise for Stravinsky's music from Diaghilev and besides, he himself now viewed it differently: "his compositions to which I had reacted almost hostilely two years ago now pleased me more and more." In his autobiography, Stravinsky recalled that he spent a "fortnight" in Milan, "in response to a new appeal from Diaghilev ... . I also saw Prokofiev ... during this stay I had an opportunity to enter into a closer relationship with this remarkable musician."[8] He was actually there for only the weekend.

Much that transpired between Stravinsky as appointed mentor and Prokofiev as apparently aspiring disciple during this three-day visit is unknown. It is likely that the composers shared their compositional plans and perhaps Stravinsky played something from his current work-in-progress, *Les Noces*; by this time he had completed the first two scenes. He had also begun the gestation of what would become *Bayka pro lisu* (Renard). Stravinsky was then, as he later claimed, "inspired by folklore," crafting texted works based on Russian folk anthologies. When told about *Chout*, he hailed the newly conceived ballet, welcomed Prokofiev into the circle and invited him to come to Switzerland. He also offered his younger colleague a mass of practical tips about publishers and, as Prokofiev recalled, "in general was nice to the extreme." After hearing Prokofiev perform his Toccata, Second Concerto and Second Piano Sonata, Stravinsky exclaimed— in true Diaghilev-speak—that he was a "real Russian composer" adding that there were no other Russian composers in Russia. For his part, Prokofiev was much taken by Stravinsky's new *Pribautki* (four songs for voice and instruments) which the composer "amusingly performed." He wrote to Myaskovsky on 4 April, "I have ... become very friendly with Stravinsky, both of us having the same sympathies. His new *Pribautki*, orchestrated, are outstanding." The *Pribautki* must have made a considerable impression on Prokofiev for it was not characteristic of him to wax rhapsodic over other composers' works. In December 1919 he again praised this composition in a letter to the composer after a concert performance in New York:

> I tell you the following with pleasure. Yesterday your *Pribautki* was performed for the first time in America ... . The success was very great, and all four songs were repeated ... . I sat with Fokine and we shouted 'bravo' as loudly as we could. ... Personally, I like most of all 'Uncle Armand,' in which the oboe and clarinet are like the gurgle of an emptying bottle: you express drunkenness through your clarinet with the skill of a *real* drunkard; the whole of 'Natashka,' but above all the last five bars with the delightful gurgling of the winds; 'The Colonel,' entirely but especially the oboe twitters and the climax on the words 'pala propala,' etc.; many things in the last song, but especially the coda: the clarinet's G and A-natural and the English horn's A-flat are most excellent and most insolent.[19]

During this visit they also met the key futurists including Marinetti, Balla and the musician Francesco Pratella. One evening they heard a demonstration of futurist music and instruments at Marinetti's studio. According to futurist poet Francesco Cangiullo an excited Stravinsky tried to match the pitches produced by one of their *intonarumori* (noise machines) at the piano. Massine began dancing to the music and Diaghilev was apparently in ecstasy. At this gathering Prokofiev joined Stravinsky to play a piano four hands version of *Le Sacre du printemps*.[20] Prokofiev felt "positively afraid" having only heard the piece once in a concert performance given by Serge Koussevitzky and "did not understand it very clearly," although he knew well that it was "unbelievably difficult." Prokofiev recalled: "Stravinsky, always small and anemic, during the playing boiled, became bloodshot, sweated, sang hoarsely and so comfortably gave the rhythm that we played *Rite of Spring* with a stunning effect [Oh, to have a recording of that!]. I completely and unexpectedly saw that the *Rite* was a marvelous piece in its surprising beauty, clarity and craftsmanship; I sincerely hailed the composer and in response he praised my reading." It seems that much of their remaining time together occurred in an alcoholic haze: Stravinsky "wanted to drink Asti on end and got tipsy," reported Prokofiev. On Monday Stravinsky returned to Switzerland and that evening Diaghilev, Massine and Prokofiev went back to Rome.

Stravinsky was then involved with the abstraction and absorption of "authentic" Russian folk music style into his own language, and for this was interested in ethnological collections of folk songs. In his studio he had a copy of pioneer ethnomusicologist Yevgeniya Linyova's *Velikorusskiye pesni v narodnoy garmonizatsii* (Great Russian Songs in Folk Harmonization; St Petersburg, 2 vols., 1904–9), a collection of folk songs transcribed from phonograph records recorded on location. But he had used "genteel" collections, for example Rimsky-Korsakov's *Sto russkikh narodnïkh pesen* (One Hundred Russian Folk Songs, 1877), as sources for earlier works such as *L'Oiseau de feu* and *Petrouchka*. We do not know the suggestions Stravinsky might have made in regards to borrowing folk material at this meeting in Milan in April 1915; however, in a letter written in mid-June from Petrograd Prokofiev adds what seems to be an indirect thanks to Stravinsky: "I'm writing the [newly commissioned] ballet with great enthusiasm; it is written easily, gaily, and with pep. Leafing through Russian songs opened to me lots of interesting possibilities." Prokofiev's new ballet, *Skazka pro shuta, semerïkh shutov pereshutivshago*, or *The Tale of the Buffoon Who Outwits Seven Other Buffoons* (the French title *Chout* being a phonetic equivalent of the Russian word for buffoon *shut*) would follow in the *kuchkist* tradition. Thoroughly shaped by Diaghilev's will and Stravinsky's guidance, Prokofiev wrote to Myaskovsky the day after he returned home from Italy: "They're turning me into the most Russian composer there is."

Chout is a satirical story from the Perm region about a mischievous peasant who dupes not only a rich merchant, but a priest and his wife as well.[21] Diaghilev and Prokofiev omitted the religious connection and accentuated the boorish, but colorful character of the hero's seven foolish neighbor buffoons. The result is a humorous and fantastical caricature of rural Russian peasantry. Its violence, not dissimilar from that of the Petrouchka or Punch and Judy tradition, was probably considered an asset in attempts to astonish western audiences. But when *Chout* finally reached the stage in the wake of the calamitous Great War and Russian Revolution, its frivolous brutality was considered by many to be in bad taste. Aware of this the composer claimed, "folk tales are often wicked, you cannot blame me for that" (See Fig. 2).

The hero buffoon and his wife conspire to sell their seven doltish neighbors a magic whip that "resurrects the dead." When the seven arrive for a visit the hero threatens his wife over her slovenly housekeeping. He "kills" her, but brings her back to life with the magic whip. After a brief discussion, the seven persuade the hero to sell them the magic whip and they hurry home. The hero and his wife joyfully dance in celebration of their cunning.

Scene two opens with the seven wives of the seven buffoons awaiting the return of their husbands. After they dance, their husbands beat them to death (they stab them in the first draft). Of course the "magic" whip is powerless to restore them to life. The scene closes with the seven carrying their wives away in a funeral procession. As scene three opens the hero and his wife are fleeing their now enraged neighbors. The hero disguises himself as "Molodukha" (*molodukha* literally means peasant woman), supposedly his own sister. The seven brutally seize her and force her to become their cook.

In scene four the seven daughters of the seven buffoons await the arrival of a rich merchant and his matchmakers. The seven buffoons enter and bully the cook. The daughters dance until they spy the arriving merchant. The seven buffoons pompously greet the merchant, and the daughters perform a *khorovod*. To everyone's horror, the rich merchant offers his hand to the cook. As he grandly leads her away, the seven buffoons become enraged again, this time beating the matchmakers as the seven daughters sob.

The fifth scene is set in the merchant's bedroom. While the amorous merchant caresses his bride, she plans an escape. Feigning illness, she is lowered by means of a drape out the window. As the merchant dreams of his beloved, the wily hero (Molodukha/cook) ties a goat to the drape in his place. When the merchant pulls up the drape he is frightened by what has become of his bride and calls for help. With the assistance of his servants and matchmakers the poor goat is shaken, twisted and turned in a ritualistic dance. At the end the goat dies.

The finale begins with the grieving merchant burying his bride/goat. Suddenly the seven buffoons jump out from behind a hedge and mock him mercilessly. Next the hero enters leading seven soldiers. He demands the return of his sister. When the seven instead produce the dead goat, he demands their arrest and financial compensation. The merchant gives the hero 300 rubles and withdraws with the dead goat. The ballet ends with a dance of celebration in which the hero and his wife brandish their extorted rubles and the seven soldiers partner the seven daughters.

Prokofiev had a major disagreement with Diaghilev over how much he should be paid for composing *Chout*: the composer demanded 3,000 rubles, a sum that was three times greater than the impresario paid for *L'Oiseau de feu*, and twice as much as he paid for *Narcisse et Echo* by Cherepnin. Diaghilev was horrified by this demand and yelled, "What ... have you lost your mind?" He began to do figures in his head, converting rubles to francs, and realized that this was more than he had paid Ravel and Debussy together for both their ballets (*Daphnis et Chloë* and *Jeux*, respectively). Prokofiev stood his ground, thinking of his needs (rather disingenuously), "it will be my yearly salary, for the ballet would take a year" and of his immediate future with Nina. Diaghilev stated that writing a ballet for the prestigious Ballets Russes would bring the young composer great fame and a Parisian debut. Prokofiev countered with an analogy, likening this to a philanthropic concert at the home of a great princess, where the artist is invited to be satisfied with playing before royalty and is paid nothing. Diaghilev took great offense and said that he didn't need any philanthropists, and left slamming the door behind him. The next day the conversation was renewed, with Prokofiev saying that he was not striving for fame in Paris since he was already loved by Petrograd. Diaghilev's anger returned but he wryly quipped that if they loved you in Kharkov, that was no great deal, and he didn't see much difference between Petrograd and Kharkov (a decidedly provincial town in the Ukraine with a population of some 250,000). This time the conversation ended when Prokofiev declared that these dealings reminded him of the publishers Jurgenson and Bessel. At the mention of the latter Diaghilev became even angrier than before and bowing at the waist said very formally, "I thank you, this conversation is concluded, I thank you," and left. At 10 p.m. the evening before his departure Prokofiev again approached the impresario, not wanting to part in disagreement over money. A contract for 3,000 rubles was finally signed at 3 a.m. with the stipulation that Prokofiev pay his own way for the return trip to finish the ballet. Diaghilev was pleased that the matter was settled and gave Prokofiev a goodbye kiss.

The impresario specified the terms of the contract for *Chout* in a handwritten letter (in Russian) to Prokofiev dated 8 April 1915. It reads in part:

> I am writing to inform you that I have commissioned from you a ballet *Chout* in six combined acts and 40 minutes in length, libretto of which was written by us together. The ballet should be presented to me by two specific dates: the piano score by 15 August 1915 and the score (orchestrated) by 1 April 1916. I will take the copying of the orchestra parts as my responsibility. The aforesaid musical composition passes into my exclusive possession for five years from the date of its first performance. I make my duty to perform the aforesaid ballet in the first season which will be arranged by me in Paris in 1916 (unless the war prevents it). However, I have the right to perform the ballet in any other city than Paris if the season in Paris should not be arranged in the mentioned year. I will pay three thousand rubles for this ballet in two installments—two thousand roubles on presentation of the piano score and one thousand roubles—on presentation of the [orchestrated] score ..."

Contract in hand Prokofiev returned home the same round about way he came and arrived on Russian soil on 3 April (OS). He stopped off in Moscow to meet with Goncharova and Larionov, and asked the latter, at Diaghilev's behest, to create the décor for *Chout*.[22] He also met with Jurgenson to negotiate the publication of the new ballet. Prokofiev quickly noted that his stock had risen while he had been away, "it seems I have become somewhat famous," he wrote in his Diary. "This happened because ... of my performance at the IRMO [Russian Music Society] on the 24th of January and the glowing newspaper accounts about it, ... and to a significant degree [because of] my trip to Italy to see Diaghilev and the news that Diaghilev had ordered a ballet from me." He continued:

> Malko [a conductor] was inviting me to play this summer in Sestrovetsk, Fitelberg [a conductor] wanted to organize an entire concert of my works in Pavlovsk, Glière [wanted] the fall in Kiev, Brïs'kin [a conductor] a tour of Russia—in a word, I did not know what to do with these invitations. Alexander Ziloti was sorry that the new ballet would not be staged in the Mariinsky Theatre and already invited me to perform it as a concert in his series next year.

By May Prokofiev was busy sketching out themes and short ideas for *Chout* in his notebook without concerning himself with where they would go. To his surprise these ideas poured out from him "like a cornucopia." In the course of two weeks he ended up with more than fifty brief sketches for the ballet and was proud of their Russian national flavor. "Now when I composed I was always thinking that I was a Russian composer and that my buffoons are Russian; this opened up for me a totally new untouched area for composition." He sent Diaghilev a telegram that he was ready to return to work on the ballet under his supervision and requested a 500 ruble advance to make the trip. But Italy declared war on Austria and the southern passage became impassable. On 7 May (NS) the *Lusitania* was sunk bringing a heightened awareness of the risks of international travel. Diaghilev sent the money and suggested the northern route, but Prokofiev replied, not discounting the news of mines in the North Sea, "serious matters keep me here in Petrograd for a while." His military status was the root of the problem although as the only son of a widow he would be exempted from military service.

By this time Diaghilev and his circle had relocated to a rented villa (Villa Bellerive) in the town of Ouchy on Lake Geneva near Lausanne, Switzerland. Stravinsky then lived in Morges—just a two-hour bicycle ride away. At Ouchy Diaghilev began to rebuild his company, disbanded on account of the war, in preparation for what was hoped to be lucrative tours of America. By July Larionov and Goncharova had arrived from Russia and installed a studio at the villa. Larionov undertook several modernist projects including the first design sketches for *Chout*, while Goncharova did the same for *Les Noces*. Larionov also assisted the young Massine with his first choreographic exercises including the Russian peasant-dance inspired *Le Soleil de nuit* (to music from *Snegurochka* by Rimsky-Korsakov).

Prokofiev was at work in Petrograd on the first scene of *Chout* by June and recorded, "My ballet is going wonderfully, quickly, easily and [it is] very Russian. There is lots of material. I am even afraid that it might become motley." In his autobiography Prokofiev expanded on this:

> Little by little I settled down to composing the thematic material for *Chout*, trying to make it as truly Russian as possible. In my childhood in Sontsovka [Ukraine] I had often heard the village girls singing in chorus on Saturday evenings or on Sundays. I do not know whether Sontsovka was especially poor in folk-songs, or whether it was the crude, raucous manner of the local singers that irritated me— they always yelled at the top of their voices—but their performances had not impressed me with the beauty of Russian folk-music and I did not remember a single tune. It is possible, of course, that subconsciously I was affected by the village songs, for the Russian national idiom came quite easily to me. It was as if I had stumbled upon an unsuspected store of wealth, or planted seeds in virgin soil that were now bearing rich fruit.[23]

Diaghilev kept after him to make the promised trip West but Prokofiev gradually convinced himself that the war would not be over by spring so there would be no Paris season for the Ballets Russes. With all his friends swept up by the wartime turmoil (Myaskovsky was at the front), and his relationship with Nina on the rocks, Prokofiev buried himself in his work. He continued composing at a rapid pace and by mid-June had completed two scenes. When four scenes were completed he considered himself ahead of schedule, certain that all six would be ready by the first of August. In the meantime he had taken another look at *Ala i Lolli* and saw that there was much good in it, so he decided to make a symphonic suite from it. *Chout* was set aside.

Diaghilev telegrammed to remind him 10 days before he was supposed to be in Lausanne to finish and polish the ballet. The day before the deadline, 2 July (OS), Prokofiev telegrammed back, "Four scenes are composed. Should I continue or is it not worth it?" He was concerned about breaking his contract, and envisioned Diaghilev receiving this news by "stamping his feet and cursing me." He would have done more than that had he known that Prokofiev had set *Chout* aside in favor of working on the rejected *Ala i Lolli!* Diaghilev did not reply, so Prokofiev sent a rather ill-conceived letter with the company's regisseur, Sergey Grigoriev, explaining his position that there was no need to hurry because the war would prevent the spring season in Paris. He received no response.

Prokofiev completed the short score by the end of the summer and sent it to Diaghilev with Grigoriev, who had been back in Russia recruiting dancers for the Ballets Russes' upcoming tour of the United States of America. By the end of September Prokofiev was officially notified that the premier was to be put off until the end of the war. Earlier that month he had heard a report that Diaghilev planned to rehearse the new ballet along with Stravinsky's yet to be orchestrated *Les noces* with the whole troop in October. Since the company was busy preparing for year end performances and a subsequent overseas tour, this was probably never seriously considered, more likely this news was intended as balm for the young composer, or perhaps it may have been incentive to finish the score quickly and give it to Grigoriev.

Diaghilev apparently did not even look at Prokofiev's ballet score until some time later, and after hearing a pianist play it for him exclaimed, "God knows what it is! I don't understand anything!" His reaction was relayed to the composer by company dancer Adolph Bolm in the autumn of 1918, prompting Prokofiev to write Diaghilev, "From Bolm's rather obscure and wordy remarks I gathered that you and everyone else have failed to make heads or tails of my *Buffoon*."[24] Indeed, the ballet had been shelved and the relationship between Diaghilev and Prokofiev, nurtured over five weeks in Italy in the spring of 1915, was essentially suspended. This did not prevent the ever-opportunistic Diaghilev from boasting in a January 1916 *New York Post* interview that the "twenty-year-old [*sic*] Prokofiev" was "our future." One month later a surprised Prokofiev received 1500 rubles for the ballet, followed in late March by yet another 1500, possibly a bookkeeping error on Diaghilev's part (by then he was only due 1000 more, and that only after the ballet was orchestrated). Prokofiev never completely forgot about this Midas who had the power to establish his career in Western Europe. The point of the aforementioned letter to Diaghilev had been to inquire about the fate of his ballet score "so traitorously buried in the secret recesses of your briefcase." Diaghilev responded with a telegram inviting Prokofiev to come to London, presumably with the intention of presenting it there. But the telegram was not received. *Chout* would not be premiered until May 1921, and only after the score was considerably revised.

This delay would bring Diaghilev's rejection of *Ala i Lolli* back to haunt him: Koussevitzky's Paris premier of the Suite from that ballet upstaged Diaghilev's presentation of *Chout*. Though not at all what Diaghilev was looking for, the Suite has proven to be one of Prokofiev's most popular pieces. When he returned to his sketches for *Ala i Lolli* during the summer of 1915 Prokofiev "found that if a few uninteresting passages were deleted the rest of the music was well worth saving. A slight revision here and there resulted in a four-movement *Skifskaya Syuita* (Scythian Suite) with the material laid out in approximately the same order as the ballet."[25] Perhaps trying to outdo the primitivism of *Le Sacre du printemps*, at least by decibel level, he scored his Suite for an enormous orchestra, often driven ostentatiously at maximum power. Just as his Piano Concerto No. 2 did in 1913, the *Scythian Suite* provoked a scandalous reception at its premier when the composer conducted it at a Ziloti concert in Petrograd on 16 January 1916 (OS). Glazunov, Director of the Conservatory, made a great show of walking out during its climactic, protracted crescendo representing the sunrise.[26] Prokofiev boasted that "Ziloti paraded the hall in fine good humor, [echoing the Futurists' mantra] 'A slap in the face! A slap in the face!'" He also noted that the journal *Muzïka* "somewhat gleefully remarked 'A scandal in high society.'"[27] Ironically, the music Diaghilev had rejected received the sort of publicity he always cherished. The fiercely polarized reception by critics and public alike obviously pleased the young Prokofiev, who at this stage was prone to egotism and grandstanding. With Skryabin's premature death at age 43 in April 1915, Prokofiev must have felt he had graduated from the rank of *enfant terrible* to become Russia's leading avant-garde composer. With Europe at war and the Ballets Russes inaccessible, Prokofiev was content to bask in his increased fame at home. When the urge to expand his audience arose he would look this time towards America.

Up until his departure from strife-ridden Russia in May 1918, Prokofiev continued to provide music that was fresh, direct and vigorous—definitely divergent from contemporary trends of veiled and understated impressionism or the highly impassioned late-romanticism of Skryabin. But Prokofiev was not becoming a one-dimensional composer: brusque pieces such as the *Scythian Suite, Igrok* (The Gambler, 1915–17, his opera in declamatory style after Dostoevsky), his primitive-texted, "Chaldean incantation," *Semero ikh* (They Are Seven, or Sept, ils sont Sept; 1917–18), and his grotesque character pieces for piano such as *Sarcasms* (1912–14) were balanced by more lyrical works such as *The Ugly Duckling* (1914), the Violin Concerto No. 1 (1916–17), the five Akhmatova songs (1916) and the Symphony No. 1 (the "Classical," 1916–17). Indeed, the lyrical, the humorous (or grotesque), and the harmonically abrasive aspects of the composer's style coexisted throughout his career, although overt lyricism would abate somewhat during his quest for leadership of the Parisian avant-garde. Between his work on the "Classical" Symphony and *They Are Seven*, Prokofiev even considered writing a small "Russian" Symphony "in the purest Russian style," and dedicating it to Diaghilev "for his fierce advocacy that I, a Russian, write strictly in a Russian way."

Intending to return within a few months, Prokofiev departed from his widowed mother, friends and revolution-torn homeland and set out for a concert tour of the Americas armed with letters of recommendation, a 6000 ruble advance from Koussevitzky on the publication of his latest music, a copy of theater director Vsevolod Meyerhold's journal *Love for Three Oranges* (which included Meyerhold's Russian adaptation of Gozzi's play of the same title), and his scores for the *Scythian Suite*, the "Classical" Symphony, the First Piano Concerto and several piano pieces. He traveled across Siberia on the last train that made it all the way through to Vladivostok. Prokofiev remained in Japan for two months since he had missed the last ship that would have reached South America in time for the concert season. He revised his itinerary and sailed for the United States of America via Honolulu and San Francisco, departing Japan on 2 August, and arriving in New York City on 6 September 1918 with only a few remaining dollars left in his pocket—money which had been lent to him along the way (as the value of the ruble plummeted his advance melted away[28]). His first domicile was a modest one on the upper West side: 107 West 109th Street.[29] But as an exotic attraction from Bolshevik Russia, and through new and renewed friendships, not to mention sheer determination, Prokofiev soon made his way. He would remain in the USA until April 1920.

During the summer of 1917 he had met the American farm machinery tycoon Cyrus McCormick, Jr. (CEO of International Harvester) at the Winter Palace in Petrograd. The latter was interested in new Russian music and as part of his effort to collect and bring back representative examples to the USA he paid to have a copy of the *Scythian Suite* made for him. (Prokofiev deposited two parcels of music, one containing this score, at the American Embassy in Petrograd that August for delivery to him in Chicago, but they were never sent.) In parting McCormick told the composer to let him know if he ever came to the USA as he had good connections in the musical world. Prokofiev first sought McCormick's help after he missed the last ship to South America. On 11 June 1918 he wrote from Tokyo (in French):

> During last summer, at the Winter Palace, you did me the honor to ask for my compositions. It is my turn to address myself to you with a request—and I ask pardon for abusing your great kindness. Being in Japan I wish very much to visit America. As Russian subjects cannot have their passports viséd unless a well-known and influential American testifies that he knows them, I beg you to be good enough to communicate with Washington in order that they may telegraph to the American consulate in Yokohama permission to visé my passport. Your kindness, which I have already observed in Petrograd, will give me the opportunity to become acquainted with your beautiful country.[30]

McCormick forwarded this request with a covering letter to the Russian Embassy in Washington on 12 July. On 31 July he received word that the State Department had cabled the Ambassador in Tokyo with the necessary instructions, and Prokofiev set sail 3 days later.[31] Having such an influential, politically connected corporate executive as a sponsor surely helped ease his way through the immigration formalities once his ship, the S.S. *Grotius* docked in San Francisco on 21 August 1918. But he was, after all, arriving from the land of the Bolshevik revolution and there was great fear of spies entering the country.

Prokofiev had filled out the requisite entry forms, but he was one of twenty passengers singled out by Bureau of Immigration officials for face-to-face interrogation. He was first questioned on board ship shortly after it docked. Seeing his musical manuscripts the agents asked him to play something on the piano to prove that he really was a musician. The melody—from a Sonata for Unaccompanied Violin composed during the journey—did not please them, but the Funeral March from Chopin's Second Piano Sonata (a request) did. The whole ordeal dragged on for days due to gross inefficiency: one had to wait one's turn to be questioned, the questioning of some went on for hours, and the officials only interviewed for four or five hours each day. The first night Prokofiev was detained onboard his ship, and thereafter in a military hospital at the Angel Island Immigration Station. There his party was forced to arise at 6 a.m. even though the officials would not arrive on the island until 11 to resume their questioning. When his turn to be questioned finally came, the officials' greatest concern, it seems, was that Prokofiev only carried $100 ($50 was all that was required). But he was allowed to enter the United States of America at noon on Saturday 24 August. He and his companions throughout this ordeal, an Italian couple named Ernest and Gabrielle Vernetta, were met at the Plaza Hotel by a recent acquaintance, a financially well-off Russian engineer named Nikolay Kucheryavy who had been a passenger on the same ship.[32] After seeing the local sights,[33] attending his first Catholic Mass with the Vernettas, and dining well (all the time waiting for the immigration officials to return his papers, letters and manuscripts), Prokofiev and his new companions left San Francisco on the morning of 29 August via train for the East, the long way 'round, via Vancouver, British Columbia, for a more scenic journey.

He tried to telephone McCormick on his way through Chicago on 5 September but McCormick's secretary said he was too busy to speak. The two met in New York City on 9 September, three days after Prokofiev arrived there. Prokofiev thanked him for the visa, and McCormick replied that he was very keen to have the composer come to America. Over lunch the next day McCormick suggested some contacts and made many recommendations. He did indeed have good connections: in part, he introduced the young composer to the powers at the Chicago Symphony Orchestra and the Chicago Opera, and circulated copies of his music to musicians such as Ossip Gabrilovich, a former piano student of Anton Rubinstein and, from 1918, conductor of the Detroit Symphony Orchestra.[34]

Prokofiev centered most of his activities during this eighteen month stay in New York City and Chicago, but achieved only modest success as a performer (Fig. 3). Despite some sensationalist advertising and reviews ("one of Russia's young barbarians," "Wild, Willful, New, Strange, and Russian," "His fingers are steel, his wrists steel, his biceps and triceps steel, his scapula steel. He is a tonal steel trust ..." and so on)[35] his musical style proved to be too advanced for America of the 1910s. Furthermore, he had some stiff competition practically from the start, for in November 1918 his fellow countryman Rakhmaninov arrived in America to stay. In his Diary Prokofiev lamented that his rival's concerts were packed and he was raking in tens of thousands of dollars, but added "I am happy for him and for Russian music." Prokofiev would never come close to this level of popularity, nevertheless he thought he would succeed in the new world on account of his more forward-looking music.

His American debut should have come at a wartime fundraiser for Russian relief at Carnegie Hall, billed in a *New York Times* advertisement as "Liberty Loan Russian Concert." He was scheduled to perform alongside three vocal soloists, the violinist Sascha Jacobinoff, Adolf Bolm with dancers from the Metropolitan Opera Company, and the Russian Symphony Orchestra conducted by Modest Altschuler. Prokofiev had been suffering from a bad head cold and had a fever of 104 degrees Fahrenheit the day before, but he felt obligated to help the cause and so he dragged himself to the hall nevertheless. He considered himself lucky that the concert ran long and he did not have to play. His first American performance came ten days later at the Brooklyn Museum on 29 October, which was also the first time his music was used as ballet accompaniment (publicly at least). The concert was held in conjunction with an exhibit of works by Russian artist Boris Anisfeld (the future designer for the Chicago Opera's *Oranges*), presented before an invited audience of about 200. Former Ballets Russes *danseur* Adolph Bolm danced as the composer performed two of his *Visions Fugitives*, op. 22; Prokofiev recalled that Bolm's first dance was "very amusing." Prior to the dance numbers Prokofiev had played his Toccata, op. 11, the "Prelude" from his Ten Pieces, op. 12, the "Gavotte" from Symphony No. 1, and the Scherzo from Piano Sonata No. 2. He described the audience's reception as "ardent." Less than a month later he presented his first public solo recital in downtown New York City at Aeolian Hall. Being not that well known, Prokofiev wisely reasoned that it was better to have a small but full Aeolian Hall (capacity 1300) than a half-empty Carnegie Hall. For the same reason he programmed music by Skryabin and Rakhmaninov alongside his own music (op. 2 and the Second Piano Sonata). He made his Chicago debut at a matinee performance with the Chicago Symphony Orchestra on 6 December, playing the First Piano Concerto under Assistant Conductor Eric de Lamarter and, after the intermission, conducting his *Scythian Suite*.[36] The audience—90 percent ladies wearing gloves—gave him a warm, but necessarily muted ovation when he first appeared on stage and they later commanded a total of seven curtain calls from him for both pieces. After the concert Chicago Opera Association general director Cleofonte Campanini came back stage and invited the composer for talks the next morning, from which the commission for the opera *L'Amour des trois Oranges* ultimately emerged.[37] The second concert the next night was an even greater success and a proud McCormick together with the Russian and Japanese Consuls dragged the exhausted Prokofiev to a late night ball. He then had to rush back to New York for a pair of concerts with the Russian Symphony Orchestra at Carnegie Hall, performing his First Piano Concerto under Altschuler on 10 December (which followed a very well-received performance of his "Scherzo for Four Bassoons" Op. 12bis) and playing his Third Piano Sonata and some short piano pieces, as well as conducting his "Classical" Symphony the following evening.

For a while Prokofiev entertained the idea of composing his newly commissioned opera in that sunny land of orange groves, Florida. In addition to *L'Amour des trois Oranges* he completed other works during his American stay, including the nostalgic, folk-inspired *Skazki staroy babushki* (Tales of an Old Grandmother) for piano (premiered 7 January 1919) and also a bit of jobbery for some former fellow Conservatory students, the *Uvertyura na evreyskie temï* (Overture on Hebrew Themes) for piano sextet (premiered 2 February 1920 alongside Brahms's Clarinet Quintet). The Overture was the composer's first use of direct musical quotation in a mature work. On 1 October 1919 he finished *Oranges* on schedule for the Chicago Opera, despite having been bedridden the entire previous April suffering from scarlet fever, diphtheria and a throat abscess. He composed it to a Russian libretto, but curiously it was translated into French, not Italian, for the American performances.[38] The composer, in his own words, wrote deliberately in a somewhat simplified idiom to suit the local taste (that is, more tuneful, less declamatory than *Gambler*).

It appeared as though *Oranges*, not *Chout* would mark Prokofiev's theatrical debut in the West. The premier, to be conducted by Campanini, was planned for early in the 1919–20 season. Prokofiev traveled to Chicago for a pair of recitals in late October and visited the general director to discuss the opera's casting. Campanini was bedridden and looked "very bad," in the composer's opinion. Back in New York City, early in November, Prokofiev played through the opera for the company conductor assigned to coach the singers, Alexander Smallens. Then on 23 November the 59-year-old Campanini, stricken with pneumonia and suffering from complications, was taken to a Chicago hospital where he would die less than four weeks later.[39] On 27 November Prokofiev began to hear rumors that the production of his opera was going to be delayed due to the late arrival of the French singers. He also heard that some of the season's scheduled operas were going to be postponed for a year. A telegram sent by the choreographer Bolm from Chicago on 6 December bore the news that *Oranges* had definitely been dropped from the season's roster. Prokofiev's attorney encouraged him to press the Chicago Opera for damages since they had broken the contract, but counseled him to do so "quietly". The implication was that if this went to court he might not win since it would be difficult to prove the exact extent of the loss. With his checking account down to $80 and, in his words, "my whole season gone to the devil," Prokofiev resolved to demand $15,000 in compensation. He arrived in Chicago for a recital on 28 December and over the next two weeks failed repeatedly in his negotiations with the far more savvy Chicago Opera Association executives, the business comptroller Herbert M. Johnson (whom Prokofiev sometimes referred to as Johns) and one of the directors, Max Pam. Prokofiev even failed to sway McCormick's brother Harold, who was the chief financial officer of the company. They all considered his demand exorbitant. He returned to New York without one penny from the Chicago Opera but took consolation in his continuing courtship of Lina (Carolina) Codina, the woman he would marry in 1923.[40] Biding his time awaiting the now delayed first performance of his opera, Prokofiev began yet another, *Ognenniy angel* (The Fiery Angel), based upon Russian Symbolist Valery Bryusov's *roman à clef*. This work was destined to become a frustrating labor of love that would consume much of his time off and on for the next decade.[41] As he began sketching the libretto he had a backlog of two completed operas (*The Gambler* being the other) and one ballet still awaiting their premieres.

In March 1919 Prokofiev had received a letter from Larionov inviting him to Paris and informing him that the designs for *Chout*'s décor had been completed long ago. Mention of his ballet made the composer "terribly happy," because he had "become accustomed to look on *Chout* as some kind of myth" and had even "almost forgotten its music." In November 1919 he received an overture from Covent Garden about a production of *Oranges*. By February he was absorbed in the task of trying to find out whether his mother had managed to join the exodus of Russians escaping the Bolshevik tide southward. He arranged for a visa and some money to be waiting for her at the British consulate in Constantinople. Eager to help her get settled in Western Europe, and with his US career essentially at a standstill, the time was right to launch his career on the continent. For this he needed to renew his association with Diaghilev and approach the conductor Albert Coates, who had asked about *Oranges* for Covent Garden. Linette (Lina) too planned to venture eastward to study singing in Paris and thus be with Prokofiev over the summer. The last word from the Chicago Opera before he departed was unpleasant: told that the company had already lost $100 000 on his opera he was asked to proceed forthwith with legal action if he planned any so that they "would not have any new losses." Later that evening Prokofiev played through the score for Gino Marinuzzi, the new musical director. Neither Marinuzzi's remark, "it is more difficult than I imagined,"[42] nor the tone of the letter seemed to alert the composer to the dangers that lay ahead. On 27 April 1920 Prokofiev sailed from New York bound for France, his first return to Western Europe since his visit to Diaghilev in the spring of 1915. But postwar Europe was a different place with its flood of refugees, redistribution of prewar wealth and new audiences in new locales desiring the latest in entertainment.

Diaghilev's company, pared to the absolute minimum after the 1916 US tours and 1917 South American tour, had barely survived the lean months at the end of the war. The Parisian premier of *Parade* in May 1917 had occurred during an isolated and abbreviated three-week season. The company finally regained steady engagements in the spring of 1919 when they returned to London after a four-year absence, though the venue was now the lowly music hall. Nevertheless, the new middle-class London audience was treated to premiers of Manuel de Falla's *Le Tricorne* and the ballet *La Boutique fantasque* (Rossini excerpts selected by Diaghilev and orchestrated by Ottorino Respighi). After a long absence the company returned to Paris for a season at the Opéra beginning in December 1919. Stravinsky's ballet *Le Chant du rossignol* received its premiere in February 1920, while *Pulcinella* (Stravinskyized Pergolesi, or so he thought)[43] was first presented during the subsequent season in May.

New audiences and changing tastes would not only influence the style of Prokofiev's music in the years ahead, but cause Diaghilev's company to struggle for a share of the limelight in fashion-conscious, postwar Paris. An interest in jazz and other popular culture imports from America had exploded in this city so weary from war and so anxious to embrace anything new. In March 1918 Jean Cocteau's inflammatory pamphlet *The Cock and the Harlequin* appeared lauding Satie and his followers for their cultivation of a new anti-Germanic and anti-impressionistic French art based on brevity, earthiness and use of popular sources.[44] Although their association was casual and fleeting, the composers Auric, Durey, Honegger, Milhaud, Poulenc and Tailleferre, were proclaimed "Les Six"—the representatives of modern French musical art—by the critic Henri Collet in early 1920. That same year Diaghilev had serious new competition in the form of Rolf de Maré's highly experimental Ballets Suédois and Cocteau's "Spectacle-Concerts" (for example, staging Milhaud's *Le boeuf sur le toit*). Then in 1923 the Comte de Beaumont launched a dance series, *Les Soirées de Paris*. The Ballets Russes' leading status was further compromised by Russian touring theatrical companies and art exhibitions that presented the latest Soviet innovations. Dance historian Lynn Garafola observes: "After 1917 ... *le tout Paris* social et artistique so courted by Diaghilev, found other enterprises ... on which to lavish time, money, and interest. Never again would Diaghilev recover his prewar standing in the French capital."[45] Though Paris became more of a stopping-off place for Diaghilev's company between domiciles in Monte Carlo and London, it nevertheless remained potentially the most receptive locale for Prokofiev's European career. It was, after all, Western Europe's putative arbiter of culture.

When the composer arrived at Paris's Hôtel Scribe on 7 May 1920, Diaghilev, with Massine at his side, called out "Prokofiev's arrived!" and greeted the composer with kisses. The impresario stated that he was ready to stage *Chout* but this required the composer's presence; the need for major revisions in the score was not yet broached. Prokofiev dined that evening with Stravinsky and the next day sat in Diaghilev's box at the Opéra for the Ballets Russes' opening night of the season. The second performance on 11 May included Stravinsky's recent ballet *Le Chant du rossignol*, which did not overwhelm Prokofiev. He noted in his Diary, "the *Rite* which I played in Milan made more of an impression on me." Stravinsky's newest ballet, *Pulcinella*, which premiered on 15 May, had a stronger effect. After looking over the Overture before the premier Prokofiev remarked in his Diary, "the ballet is in the olden style and this is an amazing coincidence—three years before I wrote a 'Classical' Symphony and now Stravinsky, who knew nothing of this, has written a classical ballet." Following along in the score at the ballet's second performance Prokofiev found the music polished in the extreme.

Having no reason to remain in Paris, Prokofiev relocated to London on 26 May. He called on Albert Coates who again talked about a possible performance of *Oranges* at Covent Garden. On 17 June he and Coates met with Thomas Beecham, the theatre's artistic director, who discussed a production for the next summer season (May–June) with Goncharova creating the décor. Diaghilev kept abreast of these plans since it might impact his planned presentation of Prokofiev to Western Europe. He had arrived on 8 June and promised to deliver the score of *Chout* to Prokofiev on the company's opening night, two days hence, so that he could rehearse it and then play it for him. In his Diary Prokofiev recorded, "It will be very pleasant to meet Mr. Chout, I almost don't remember him." The short score[46] had been bound and then buried in a trunk with some paintings and it took more than two days before Prokofiev received it. Finally, during an intermission at a Covent Garden Ballets Russes performance, Diaghilev handed it over, "Here is your treasure." Prokofiev slipped away from Lady Cunard's loge to reacquaint himself with this music which he had not seen for almost five years. He found that much had turned out good but a lot seemed awkward and required rewriting. In general he was very satisfied with his "meeting" and returned to the loge smiling.

Prokofiev rehearsed the work on 15 June and played it for Diaghilev, Massine and Ballets Russes conductor Ernest Ansermet, probably on the next day. The latter praised it loudly but Diaghilev and Massine were more reserved; nevertheless, they acclaimed its many truly Russian passages. On the following day the entire Diaghilev circle came to hear Prokofiev play *Chout*. Stravinsky did not attend as he had returned to Morges. After Prokofiev's run-through Diaghilev made a cautious speech—cautious, Prokofiev believed, because he wanted to avoid an argument with the composer. In his Diary Prokofiev summarized Diaghilev's thesis:

> In the present state the ballet was following the action too precisely and with too many details. This was a common view at one time, for example when *Petrouchka*

was created, but now the view had changed. It was established that it is more impressive when the music is presented in long symphonic sections which correspond to whole scenes without being excessively detailed ... [and thus allowing the choreography to] become more independent and of a piece. If there is too much detail, as in my piece ... [the] choreography becomes a slave to the music and it results in just a simple pantomime. Therefore, if I would agree to change my ballet and get rid of the illustrative parts, and instead of them develop themes as I would do in a symphonic composition, then the ballet would benefit and the choreography would be freer, not tied to each musical phrase.

Prokofiev saw that this made sense and once again acquiesced. He genuinely looked forward to changing the score into a more unified symphonic work. He recorded in his Diary: "And [at] the next three visits which took place every day and sometimes [sic] twice a day, Diaghilev and I considered the details and we decided what needed to be developed and what needed to be cut." In his later autobiography Prokofiev recalled about Diaghilev:

He was a subtle and disarming critic and argued his point with great conviction. I, too, had learned enough in the past five years to be able to distinguish the good from the bad in *Chout*. So we had no difficulty in agreeing on the changes. Secondly, there were five entr'actes to be written, since Diaghilev wanted all six scenes to be presented without intermission. Thirdly, the whole thing had to be orchestrated.[47]

After the revisions were settled the subject of money arose: Prokofiev claimed that despite having been paid in full according to the contract (in fact, overpaid), the project would take his entire summer—there was no time to do it in the fall or winter—and he needed money to live on. Otherwise he would have to take up the offer he had received to go to Brazil "just to put myself somewhere." Prokofiev asked for 3000 francs a month for four months, Diaghilev countered with 3000 francs for three months and the deal was struck. Diaghilev paid a lot of money for *Chout*, but, as he told Prokofiev, he had great hopes for it since the French were now becoming angry, saying that apart from Stravinsky he cannot discover anyone. Prokofiev expressed some reservation about Ansermet and said he would like to conduct his ballet himself. Diaghilev smiled and said, "You will become the conductor of the Ballets Russes." Prokofiev demurred, but they parted in good spirits. *Chout* was to premier in Paris the following May alongside Stravinsky's *Les Noces*, and be given in London on 7 June. As it turned out, *Chout* was presented with *Les Noces*, but not until 1923 when the latter received *its* belated premier.

Prokofiev received a telegram on 20 June stating that his mother had arrived at Marseilles, and he quickly left London. Their reunion was, as he recalled, "extremely happy." Among the manuscripts his mother carried from Russia were the piano reduction of his Second Piano Concerto and detailed sketches of *They Are Seven*. Lina then arrived in Paris from New York City. He wrote in his Diary,

"So in these three or four days all the questions have been settled: Mama, Linette and Diaghilev." He rented a "spacious, very comfy even elegant" villa at Mantes-sur-Seine some 40 miles northwest of Paris and moved in with his mother on 6 July. Straight away he began revising *Chout*,

> rather quickly and with pleasure I reworked the first four scenes, inserting two new dances in a major key [sic] (Diaghilev complained that the whole ballet was in the minor) ... then I made the first entr'acte and on 21 June [sic, July] worked on the orchestration, which went along pleasantly though not very quickly; three to five pages a day. I played the piano for one to two hours a day in preparation for my program for America.

Prokofiev enjoyed this quiet haven near the Bois de Boulogne. Visitors that summer included Goncharova, Larionov, and, of course, Linette. In addition to his work on the ballet Prokofiev also arranged a toccata by Buxtehude and some waltzes by Schubert for use in his American tours. In 1923 he would recast this suite of Schubert waltzes for two pianos, in which guise it served as dance music for Boris Romanov's traveling ballet troupe (Romanov would present this "Homeage à Schubert" along with a piano arrangement of the "March" from *Oranges* to Paris at the Théâtre des Champs Élysées about the same time the Ballets Russes was premiering *Le Pas d'acier*.[48]). But most of Prokofiev's efforts went towards the revisions and orchestration of *Chout*. When the time came to set the work aside in October he had composed the remaining entr'actes and revised the last two scenes, composing the final dance anew. He had orchestrated up to the beginning of the fifth scene, the remainder he would complete when he returned to Europe in early spring 1921.[49] At the beginning of October 1920 he moved back to Paris because his mother was to have an eye operation. There he played *Chout* for Stravinsky and asked him to comment on its orchestration (through thick and thin Prokofiev always respected Stravinsky's talent in this area). According to the composer's account in his Diary Stravinsky only suggested correcting some tied notes in the winds in order to obtain more expressiveness. Nestyev suggests that more transpired, putting these words in Stravinsky's mouth: "At this spot it might be better to give it to the tuba. Here give the double basses a sharp arco instead of *pizzicato*."[50] Diaghilev appeared en route from Venice to London and praised the revised score. Prokofiev recorded that Stravinsky's and Diaghilev's comments made him very excited and proud. On the negative side the impresario said that he would not be in Paris or London in the spring, having made a commitment to go to South America. So, as Prokofiev boarded the S.S. *Savoie* on 16 October bound for New York City, the premier of *Chout* was left up in the air. But at least he could look forward to the upcoming Chicago premier of *L'Amour des trois oranges*, which would be the highlight of this visit to the USA. But bad things continued to happen: the crossing was rough and Prokofiev lost a trunk containing drawings by Larionov including an imaginary caricature of the first performance of *Chout*. He soon occupied himself by making a two-hand piano reduction of his ballet for Diaghilev, something he later described as "pretty rotten."[51]

Prokofiev had a shock waiting for him in Chicago regarding *Oranges*. After arriving in town on 31 October he wrote to Johnson requesting a meeting to settle their disagreement "peacefully." The letter he received in return on 2 November did not contain anything about an appointment, rather it bore the news that two weeks ago a telegram had been sent to him in France stating that *Oranges* had been canceled permanently. "My eyes went dark as I was reading," he recorded in his Diary. Despite the help of all the friends and sympathizers he could muster the decision was irreversible. "This is very bad," he noted, "now nothing joyful was in prospect and in my pocket is $3." Once again he was forced to turn to his financial helpmate Kucheryavy. He managed to secure a handful of concert engagements; almost all of them were in California where he spent the entire month of December and most of January. He stayed primarily in Los Angeles after performing one week of concerts in the San Francisco area. Now in a rather more relaxed mood he worked on his "Five Songs Without Words," Op. 35 for his friend, the soprano Nina Koshetz (the work was later revised for violin and piano). On 15 January he heard rumors that the famous Scottish-American soprano Mary Garden (the first Mélisande in 1902) had been appointed the new General Director of the Chicago Opera, and two days later he headed east. He successfully negotiated with her in New York City in late January and *Oranges* was scheduled for the 1921–22 season with Koshetz approved for the role of Fata Morgana and he himself slated to conduct. Just prior to Garden's takeover Marinuzzi had resigned as artistic director; shortly after it Johnson was "encouraged" to retire.[52]

With this good news Prokofiev departed the USA in early February, proceeding first to London and then to Paris. When he had renewed acquaintances with Ballets Russes personnel the previous spring (1920), he may have sensed the mounting tension between Diaghilev and Massine, no longer the promising novice he last saw in Italy in 1915, but then the company's star choreographer, and from 1920, Maître de Ballet. Prokofiev would have been unaware, however, that the rift growing between impresario and choreographer, spurred on by disagreements over the choreography for *Le Astuzie femminilli*[53] and Massine's growing need for independence, would have a profound effect on the next season's success and on the fate of *Chout*. According to Grigoriev, Diaghilev's relations with Massine had deteriorated rapidly by the end of 1920. "Knowing Diaghilev as I did, I felt sure we were headed for a crisis that might affect the whole future direction of the Ballet."[54] However the rupture actually occurred (there are differing accounts), Massine had left the company by January 1921. As a result Diaghilev lost his contract for the South American tour, since Massine was to be its star attraction.

When Prokofiev encountered Diaghilev in February 1921 he was still upset over the defection of Massine. Since he had no choreographer Diaghilev decided to put on a season of old favorites at the Paris Théâtre de l'Opéra, and invited

Fokine and Bolm to participate. But since Fokine became more competitive than cooperative that plan fell through and Diaghilev switched to de Maré's Théâtre des Champs-Élysées with *Chout* back on the bill. For Paris Diaghilev had to have something new, and at this point *Chout* was all he had. The Ballets Russes' regisseur recalled:

> In parting with Massine Diaghilev placed himself in an awkward position. For he was obliged to discover some other choreographer, since new ballets were always expected during the Paris season. He therefore surveyed the talent in the company, and fixed for this role of choreographer on a dancer named Slavinsky [Tadeusz Slaviński]—who, though young and gifted, was entirely devoid of any knowledge of choreography ... [I] felt sure that Slavinsky would be unable to cope with [Prokofiev's music for *Chout*], if not for lack of talent, at least for lack of experience. But Diaghilev countered this objection by saying that just as he had once put Larionov in charge of the youthful Massine, so now there was no reason why he should not put him in charge of Slavinsky.[55]

The difference, of course, is that Massine demonstrated great choreographic potential and seriousness of purpose, whereas Slavinsky—Diaghilev's third choice for this assignment according to dancer Lydia Sokolova—apparently had neither.

In her memoirs Sokolova (née Hilda Munnings; the co-principal female dancer in *Chout*)[56] paints a less than flattering portrait of her partner Slavinsky, a young Polish dancer who joined the Ballets Russes sometime before January 1918, and who excelled in character roles.

> Slavinsky ... danced easily and effortlessly, and if it had not been for his character he might have made a great success. He was unreliable, boastful and without a strict regard for the truth ... and since we thought of him as irresponsible and with no particular intelligence, it came as a surprise to us that Diaghilev should have thought him capable of producing a ballet. Before doing so, Diaghilev had sounded [out] a young dancer called Tcherkas, as well as Leon [Woizikovsky], to discover whether they had ambitions as choreographers ... [Both declined, the latter added that] he knew nothing about music. Nor, for that matter, did Slavinsky, and he took the whole thing as a huge joke ... Slavinsky had no more idea of inventing a ballet than flying over the moon, and what ballet there was must certainly have been the work of Larionov.[57]

It should be pointed out that Sokolova also did not care for Prokofiev's music or Larionov's staging and costumes.

The only other new work for the 1921 season was to be *Cuadro flamenco*, a work conceived by Diaghilev while visiting Seville in late March. It was a suite of Andalusian dances performed by a troupe of Spanish gypsy dancers and musicians (one singer, two guitarists) in a setting designed by Picasso. In the past Diaghilev had padded weak ballet seasons with operas, but by now his connections with Russian operatic resources were severed due to the revolution.

Furthermore, he had lost the support of Beecham as the result of a quarrel at the end of the 1920 London season, the latter paying only a quarter of what was due for their joint venture. Any chance of producing *Oranges* was now gone. The Paris season was made deliberately short (one week) with the main emphasis laid on Prokofiev's music for *Chout* and the novelty of the imported Spanish dancers. The venue would be less prestigious and smaller than usual for the Ballets Russes in Paris: the Théâtre de la Gaîté-Lyrique, located in a working class neighborhood on rue Denis-Papin off the Boulevard de Sebastopol in the third *arrondissement*. By the time the season was finalized all the good theaters had already been booked. Despite the shortened season and fewer seats than usual, Diaghilev feared not being able to fill the house.[58]

On 15 March 1921 Larionov signed a contract joining the company for three months as artistic director. Henceforth, the production of *Chout* became even closer to the experimental, commedia dell'arte-inspired fare that one-time Meyerhold pupil Sergey Radlov was staging in Petrograd. Dance historian Elizabeth Souritz calls this trend the "circusisation" of the theater.[59] Larionov had been associated with Bakst, Benois, the Moscow Art Theatre, and teachers such as Konstantin Korovin at the Moscow Art School in the early 1910s but may never have had any actual theatrical production experience until working for Diaghilev beginning in 1915.[60] His experimental nature served him well as a theoretical innovator of the dance, less so as a practical choreographer. Yet he was not ignorant of ballet steps or combinations according to Massine.[61] Boris Kochno (Diaghilev's recently appointed secretary) recalled, "Slavinsky was to be the interpreter of Larionov's theatrical ideas ... he was to translate these ideas into a dance idiom and act as intermediary between Larionov and the dancers."[62]

On 24 March Larionov wrote to Diaghilev: "I've studied *Chout* and learned it by heart. I've bought a big new notebook and am busy working out entrances and dance figures [see Fig. 4]. The whole of *Chout* is in my head and ready to be staged ..." Larionov continued:

> I'm changing the scenario because, on the whole, it is too sketchy and not very precise. Furthermore, Prokofiev constantly indicates the movements of a given character but then brings a second on stage and forgets the first. The result is that characters keep piling up on stage—but doing what one can't exactly tell. Yet the scenario never calls for them to go offstage. They couldn't, for that matter, because ten or fifteen measures later they encounter each other again.

Such *naïveté* was too much for Kochno; with barely concealed exasperation he declared that the "choreographer" seems to have forgotten that characters in a ballet are supposed to dance![63] Larionov's complaint about the "sketchy" nature of the scenario is probably due to his lack of experience with a lengthy narrative ballet. It is ironic in light of the revisions Diaghilev required from Prokofiev in 1920, virtually eliminating the original score's fussy attention to detail in order to give the choreographer more freedom. Despite his claim the story of *Chout* remained essentially the same.

Prokofiev still needed to finish the orchestration and, much to his displeasure, had to take charge of making all the parts (Diaghilev violated the contract on this). He, Linette—posing as his wife when necessary—and his mother settled in St Brevin-les Rochelets, south of St Brevin-les Pins on the Brittany coast on 21 March and he set to work on the ballet. In one week the fifth scene was completed but there were endless difficulties finding copyists to make the parts. He also finished the ballet's piano reduction, begun on board ship to the USA the previous autumn, and sent it to Madrid where rehearsals were to take place between performances. Prokofiev finished orchestrating the sixth scene, not without some difficulty in the final dance, around 20 April, and "breathed lightly." However, the copyists and their mistake ridden parts continued to give him grief. Around this time he received a telegram from Koussevitzky asking for his presence at the rehearsals for the upcoming Paris premier of the *Scythian Suite*, scheduled for the evening of 29 April, part of the conductor's second Festival of Russian Music concert at Salle Gaveau. This would be less than three weeks before the premier of *Chout*. Diaghilev soon caught wind of this concert which would upstage his long-planned presentation of the composer to Paris. In a rage he began sending a flood of "two page long telegrams" to the composer, "explaining what a horrible harm this was, and if Koussevitzky performs the Suite before *Chout* then I will perish and Diaghilev will die and the whole world will just fall apart." Prokofiev was anxious to hear how his Suite sounded from the audience's perspective, but he did not want to counter Diaghilev. Fortunately, on 21 April the impresario's tactics changed and he now asked if Prokofiev would like to proceed immediately to Monte Carlo, all expenses paid, to assist in the rehearsals for *Chout*. En route on 22 April Prokofiev stopped off in Paris in order to go over the Suite with Koussevitzky. Aware that his programing had placed the composer in the middle of an unpleasant situation the conductor nevertheless asserted that he had no intention of changing his plans, the *Scythian Suite* was to be the main piece of his concert. Koussevitzky advised him to, "just blame it all on me when talking to Diaghilev." By 6 p.m. Prokofiev was on his way to Monte Carlo.

Prokofiev had not been consulted about the desperate measures taken in the wake of Massine's departure. But there is no evidence that he was in any way dissatisfied with *Chout*'s choreography or designs. Indeed, he probably found a kindred spirit in the mischievous and witty Larionov (see Fig. 5: a pencil sketch by Juan Gris from the 1921 Paris season program book). In his Diary he called him a "talented and cunning little fellow with a brain, and his decorations are wonderful." In Larionov's hands *Chout* became a hybrid, a mixture of classical ballet, stylized folk dancing and Radlovian clowning, acrobatics and pantomime. He began composing the choreography while the company was on tour in Madrid, and continued when they settled in at Monte Carlo in mid-April.

Grigoriev recalls observing the rehearsals with interest as Larionov and Slavinsky

> assembled the component parts, as if for a mosaic, bit by bit. Slavinsky's contribution seemed to consist in doing what he was told to do by Larionov ... . When Diaghilev saw [the finished work], his enthusiasm was, to say the least, moderate; and afterwards, as we sat on the terrace, he asked me what I thought of it. I said I thought the production thin: it had the air of being by a student of dancing. 'Yes,' he agreed. 'The best part is the music. The next best is the *décor*, and the worst is the choreography. However, at least it's ready; so we're all right for the moment. But it takes us nowhere. We must find a choreographer.'[64]

That Diaghilev was not more concerned is explained by his valuation of the various components. As related by Ballets Russes composer Vladimir Dukelsky (aka Vernon Duke), the impresario "believed that the musical score was the *axis* of every ballet, sets and costumes came next in order of importance, then choreography and lastly a good or at least adequate performance by the dancers.[65] Prokofiev attended his first rehearsal on 25 April, two days after his arrival. Three scenes had already been staged, but the composer thought they looked horrible—as if never rehearsed. Larionov was still using his thick notebook full of poses and group arrangements. Prokofiev thought that Slavinsky was a good dancer, but that he had "an empty head." The composer's first concern, however, was with the person communicating his music to the dancers, the rehearsal pianist Zemskaya. "She didn't have any idea about the music or the tempo or accent ... . Fortunately they had invited me. I had to clean everything up and start over again. First of all I had to train Zemskaya with whom I had separate rehearsals, making her cry several times." During the rehearsals Prokofiev was in agreement with Larionov, "he did everything I told him to do, and I believed in his creativity and good taste. There was only one thing left, to struggle and [try to] compensate for the lack of ballet technique ... Diaghilev often visited the rehearsals which was a pleasure because he always gave great advice." After three days Prokofiev prepared to leave in order to attend Koussevitzky's rehearsals. Diaghilev found out the reason for his departure and became outraged, made a scene and then sent an abusive telegram to the conductor. As a result Prokofiev stayed on in Monte Carlo for two more days, missing all of Koussevitzky's rehearsals but arriving in Paris in time for the concert.

Prokofiev recorded that he actively participated in the staging of *Chout* during his stay in Monte Carlo; for example, insisting that Massine's dance of washing the floors which had been invented in Rome in 1915 be added to the opening of scene one. After five days in Monte Carlo (less the time for a trip to Nice to have his portrait drawn by Matisse for the program book) everything was set except for the last scene. On 27 April Prokofiev departed with Diaghilev and Kochno, on the train, de luxe class, to Paris.

On 29 April Prokofiev was finally able to hear his *Scythian Suite* away from the conductor's podium, but he found that his loge was too close to the stage and the hall too small for such a large orchestra. He thought that the opening started out a little rough, and the second part of the first movement was taken too slowly, but it nevertheless ended enthusiastically. The second movement received more applause than the first, and Koussevitzky pointed out the composer in his box. In the third movement Prokofiev took note of some passages that "did not sound" and needed fixing, likewise in the fourth. But the problems in the latter, he thought, were compensated by the sunrise "which really sounds amazing, especially the place where Glazunov stood up and walked out." Afterward there were huge ovations. Presented alongside Rakhmaninov's *L'Île de la mort*, Chaikovsky's First Piano Concerto and Rimsky-Korsakov's *Capriccio espagnol*, Prokofiev's music received great critical acclaim. His anger notwithstanding, Diaghilev must have realized (from afar) that this event could only whet the public's appetite for the 17 May premier of the composer's first theatrical work, the ballet *Chout*.

The company commenced final rehearsals at the Théâtre de la Gaîté-Lyrique on 7 May, and Prokofiev began rehearsing the orchestra shortly thereafter (he would conduct the entire premier run of his ballet in Paris). Unfortunately, the orchestra rehearsals could not take place in the theater, rather they were held in a small entrance hall which made the music sound quite different than it would from the pit. The entire company had to work around performances of Planquette's opéra-comique *Des Cloches de Corneville* which ran up to the first day of the Ballets Russes season. Prokofiev found the orchestra to be only "mediocre." He tired rather quickly while conducting, being out of practice, and after an hour or so he would pass the baton to Ansermet who would then rehearse a different ballet. During this hectic period of endless rehearsals he and Linette took separate rooms across the street from the theater at the Hôtel Vauban. According to Grigoriev the choreography was set by the time the company left Monte Carlo for Paris, although Prokofiev noted in his Diary that it wasn't— "many things had to be staged in a hurry or were not staged at all," adding that it would be better if the premier could be delayed ten days. The weather was unusually hot and Prokofiev was pushed to the point of exhaustion. He had four rehearsals each day, both orchestral and with the dancers, and he started to suffer memory losses, "I was forgetting what I wanted to say." After dinner he had to run back to the theater because, as he put it, "*Chout* was much more important than the arrival of friends."

On the morning of the premier there were two rehearsals, first for the orchestra alone, then a dress rehearsal. Prokofiev invited a number of his friends. In addition, several critics, Monteux and the American conductors Walter Damrosch (New York Symphony), Alfred Hertz (San Francisco Symphony) and Smallens (Chicago Opera) attended. Prokofiev was almost completely absorbed with the orchestra but did take note of the "weird and very uncomfortable looking costumes," and overheard the dancers' loud complaints about them. He did not believe that the dress rehearsal went all that well, but Diaghilev, either from experience or else to put a good face on the situation, countered that it was better than most. Afterwards the dancers were called upon to rehearse some more so that by performance time they were nearly exhausted.

Diaghilev had demonstrated his finely honed skill of promotion for this major event. In his interviews with the press, he encouraged comparisons between "his sons," Prokofiev and Stravinsky, sometimes provocatively. *Chout* would be presented on opening night after a revival of *L'Oiseau de feu* and the composers' portraits faced one another in the program book (Prokofiev's by Matisse, Stravinsky's by Picasso). A few days prior to the 9 June London premier of *Chout*, Diaghilev told the *Observer*: "Mr. Sergey Prokofiev has started off in a new direction. The only resemblance between Prokofiev and Stravinsky is that both are Russian, and both are living in the same century." He was carefully setting the stage for *Chout* and at the same time promoting a new production of *Le Sacre du printemps* with choreography by Massine (first seen in Paris the previous December). A concert performance of the latter ballet was to be led by Eugene Goossens at Queen's Hall the day before the London premier of *Chout*, an event that was hoped to arouse interest in the upcoming staged production. But Diaghilev had to be careful given *Chout*'s compromised production and the landmark status already accorded *Le Sacre*. He continued his interview with the *Observer* trying to put the best possible face on his newest ballet:

> The scenery and costumes have been designed by M. Larionov, and the choreography is by a young dancer, Slavinsky, after indications by Larionov. In fact, a new principle has been introduced here, that of giving to the decorative artist the direction of the plastic movement, and having a dancer simply to give it choreographic form. Both the setting and the music of this ballet are of the highest modernity and entirely in keeping with Russian Characteristic, without the musical themes being derived from folklore.[66]

As often happens in publicity, the truth gets stretched a bit, as we shall discover when we revisit some of these claims below.

Larionov biographer Anthony Parton calls *Chout*'s décor "a brilliant mélange of [Russian] neoprimitivism and cubo-futurism"[67] (see Figs. 6, 7). The first sketches, which date from the autumn of 1915, look somewhat different because Larionov absorbed other currents in theatrical design in the interim, notably Picasso's designs for *Parade*. Larionov had been in Rome with Cocteau and Picasso when these were made, and he was likely influenced by their use of cubism along with the restrictive nature of the proposed "costumes" for the French and American managers.[68]

The curtain gave the audience some idea of what was to follow (see Fig. 8). It juxtaposed drawn fragments of gothic spires, the onion domes of St Basil's, a rose window, a gargoyle, *lubok*-style animals (*lubki* being the colorful and naive Russian peasant prints), a stone saint from Notre-Dame, and opposite it, a stone statue of an old Russian woman ("baba"), each with descriptive text off to the side. This cubist mosaic is generally organized map-like by nationality, French objects and text on the left, Russian on the right; yet at the bottom inscriptions summarizing the ballet story in French and Russian Cyrillic reverse this order. The religious aspect of Afanasyev's story had been eliminated by Diaghilev and Prokofiev when they drafted the scenario of *Chout*, so the presence of religious emblems here must be due to their ready familiarity (or possibly just due to the designer's whimsy).

Scene one depicts the interior of the hero buffoons' home in *lubok* style with added "cubo-futurist spatial ambiguity"[69] (see Fig. 6). Objects not in actual use were painted onto the backdrop in a cubist manner using bold colors, making this truly look like a "crazy house of buffoons."[70] The angles and the prints used in the backdrop for the merchant's bedroom (scene five) readily display Larionov's combination of cubism and Russian peasant style (see Fig. 7). Together with his strikingly colorful, oddly shaped and futurist-inspired costumes, with their own abstract cubist designs, Larionov's décor gave off a blinding confusion between color and pattern.[71] Cyril Beaumont recalled that "the color contrasts were so vivid and dazzling that it was almost painful to look at the stage."[72]

The brilliantly colored costumes for the seven neighbor buffoons featured vertical stripes on the right leg, horizontal stripes on the left, spots and dogtooth patterns on the sleeves, vertical and diagonal lines and stylized ornamentation on the smocks. Many costumes utilized cane stiffeners or wiring so that they would maintain their proper, exaggerated shapes: the hero's baggy pants (Fig. 9), the seven buffoons' diamond-patterned, festooned panniers, the skirted bottom of the soldiers' breastplates, the wife's headdress and leaf-appended dress (Fig. 9), and the tapered sleeves of the seven daughters' dresses. Stylized hats were worn by most, face paint by some, and partial masks by the seven buffoons and seven soldiers. Clearly the most bizarre and futurist-inspired costumes were those for the soldiers, with their discus-crowned hats and free-flying epaulets, each adorned with the number "3". Although stylized Russian peasant wear, cubism and futurism may have been the bases for Larionov's designs, the boisterous garb of circus clowns could not have been far behind. Apparently the costumes proved so uncomfortable and cumbersome that the dancers had to be threatened with fines in order to wear them as designed.

Unfortunately the choreography for *Chout* is not extant and Larionov's sketchbook is unaccounted for;[73] analysis must be drawn from iconographic sources, interviews and reviews. Yet it is certain that the dancing in *Chout* was folk-influenced and mostly *terre à terre* (none of the women wore pointe shoes and most of the men wore soft-soled boots). Except for the sections in the score that were so labeled, the dancing was probably limited to brief interludes or simultaneities amidst the mimed tale. Some critics observed that *Chout* was more a pantomime than a ballet. Lydia Sokolova, who danced the role of the hero's wife, felt there was no real dancing to get her teeth into.[74] Traditional virtuosic movements such as *entrechats* or *grand jeté*'s would have been out of place here and, furthermore, would have been somewhat impeded by the restrictive costumes and the undersized stages where the ballet was presented. What little *danse d'école* vocabulary there was in *Chout* apparently came in a humorous context, for example, the seven buffoons' unceasing pirouettes as each offers his hand in turn to greet the hero in scene one. The grotesqueness of the plot undoubtedly inspired a great deal of exaggerated gesticulation, poses and running and jumping about. Not surprisingly, Larionov exploited gymnastic movements such as somersaults during the entry of the seven buffoons in scene one. When they decided to buy the magic whip they passed the purse of money through their seven pairs of legs. The ballet's surviving iconographic sources capture moments of both pantomime and of dance, the latter in both classical and modern styles. Some images reveal a combination of the two, for example, deliberately contorted *epaulement* and *port de bras* used in a classical geometric formation. The mixture undoubtedly heightened the buffoonery and cubism of the production. These sources also indicate that the seven buffoons wore the most traditional dance footwear, suggesting that theirs may have been the most demanding steps and movements in the ballet.

The audience for the 17 May Parisian premier was exceptionally wealthy and glamorous looking; the best tickets sold for 100 francs. The streets around the Théâtre de la Gaîté-Lyrique were filled with luxurious automobiles, something quite unusual for this working-class neighborhood. Residents came out of their homes to gawk at the ostentatious parade. The evening opened with *L'Oiseau de feu*, intentionally, since this was Stravinsky's first ballet. Ansermet conducted. The premier of Prokofiev's ballet came next. The composer was nervous only about the buttons he had to operate to signal the stage crew: one lifted the house curtain, another Larionov's curtain, the last brought the curtain down. The button for Larionov's curtain had to be pressed twice, first as a warning, then to follow through. He considered all this an unpleasant and difficult addition to his conducting duty. The long-awaited moment had finally arrived and he entered the pit to warm applause from the audience. He pressed the first button and the house curtain rose. When the audience saw Larionov's weird, colorful and cartoonish curtain they started to laugh and then applaud. When silence returned Prokofiev pressed the warning button and began conducting. Six bars into the score he pressed the button again and Larionov's curtain slowly rose. What followed was the only hitch at the premier: the curtain began to catch on something and go sideways. But this problem was quickly resolved, and as the composer recalled, "everything went smoothly after that ... [and] for the first performance the orchestra members pulled themselves together and played almost quite well. At the end—big success." Prokofiev headed to the stage to join the cast. By the time he arrived they had already bowed several times. At his appearance the applause significantly strengthened and the dancers shook his hand and applauded as well. With the composer on stage there were five additional curtain calls. Afterwards in the wings there was a mass of congratulations, but this came amidst preparations for the next number that evening, the premier of *Cuadro flamenco*. (The long evening finished with the "Polovtsian Dances" from *Prince Igor*.) Larionov, Goncharova, Linette, Prokofiev's friend Boris Demchinsky and the composer decided to celebrate *Chout*'s successful realization by getting thoroughly blotto at a chic bistro nearby in Montmarte. Prokofiev recalled, "our spirits were light, the heaviness abated and everything went wonderfully."

Chout was given only four times during the abbreviated Paris season (performances followed on 18, 20 and 22 May). Prokofiev thought that the orchestra played worse and worse each night and at the end of the last performance he confronted the players' manager charging that someone sabotaged the merchant's theme by playing along in thirds (the charge was denied). The orchestra members had carte blanche to send deputies at any time, and so, for example, Prokofiev had to contend with different concertmasters, each with their own inadequate rendition of the finale's solo. Despite these shortcomings Ravel told Prokofiev that *Chout* was "a work of genius," and Stravinsky said it was "the only modern work which he listened to with pleasure." Prokofiev noted that although Les Six was delighted by *Chout*, it was "a big blow" to them because it was something they should have done but could not do. Three weeks later Milhaud's strikingly scored Brazilian souvenir *L'Homme et son désir* was premiered by the Ballets Suédois, and two weeks after that, the group's collaborative *La Mariés de la tour Eiffel*, but neither of these works was considered by most critics to be as significant a musical event.

Despite all the time and money spent on *Chout*, not to mention Diaghilev's intensive publicity campaign, it was *Cuadro flamenco* that became the hit of the season, with some 30 performances in Paris and London. Prokofiev recalled in his autobiography that the production of *Chout* was received very well by both the public and the press. That is generally true regarding the Parisian reception of the music. Most of the criticism there as well as in London faulted Larionov's contributions or the story itself. One French critic dismissed Larionov's choreography as "burlesque," without realizing that that was probably quite close to his intent. Much of the attention was focused on the colorful sets and costumes. A Parisian Russian daily reported that the set in itself was very entertaining but its tumult of color was hardly consistent with Prokofiev's "westernized" and "restrained" [!] music.[75] While at least one critic (Laloy in *Comœdia*) mentioned the unity between the music, décor and the dance, Kochno remembers that many in the audience voiced contrary sentiments—that there was "no harmony between Prokofiev's limpid, cool music and Larionov's aggressive use of folk motives.[76] That observers inside and outside of the company could call this boisterous score "restrained" or "cool" implies that the shock value and eccentricity on stage far overpowered what was emanating from the pit.

Fokine had attended the opening night, drawn by the revival of his *L'Oiseau de feu*. He believed that the far greater applause for his ballet was a "demonstration of disapproval against" the "radically modernistic" *Chout*.[77] By comparison Larionov's staging undoubtedly looked somewhat amateurish, making it an easy target for the conservative faction which had grown tired of experimental works. A member of Diaghilev's own circle concluded: "the reception of *Chout* showed that extreme modernism, unless created by a master hand, was a certain failure."[78] This helps to explain the divergence of opinions regarding *Chout*'s reception: modernists generally liked it and called it a success, traditionalists hated it and labeled it a failure.

Nevertheless, Prokofiev must have been very pleased with the reception accorded his ballet score in Paris; Diaghilev's company had indeed helped to launch his European career in a major way. *Le Figaro* reported that the premier of *Chout* was a "véritable révélation," and that the audience gave "le jeune, puissant et original talent de M. Prokofiev ... superbes ovations."[79] Émile Vuillermoz cited the ballet's "allégresse, jeunesse et fraîcheur" in *La Revue musicale* and observed that Prokofiev was taking a new path, independent from Stravinsky, using his own ideals and voices: "With means as simple as those of his compatriots he obtains the effect of a delicious novelty. It is a new force, very lively and very supple. It leads not towards complication but towards simplification, towards clarity and towards generous melody."[80] The newspapers' accolades elevated Prokofiev's stature almost overnight: "Yesterday barely known to a few musicians in France, here, all at once, fame's wing has touched him. Tomorrow this young man ... will be as well-known as Stravinsky," declared *Bonsoir*, while Roland Manuel of *L'Éclair* added: "*Chout* is, at least musically, the most important work that the Russians have shown us since the War apart from the admirable [ballet] *Nightingale* of M. Stravinsky."[81]

The Ballets Russes finished their Paris season on 23 May with an all-Stravinsky evening including Massine's recent choreography for *Le Sacre*. That night Prokofiev saw that ballet for the first time and it made a tremendous impression on him. After the premier of *Chout* he had heard comparisons being made with *L'Oiseau de feu*, and some comments to the effect that Stravinsky was now defeated and was very angry. But seeing *Le Sacre* brought the full force of Stravinsky's achievement home to him.

The company quickly packed and headed for London. Originally Prokofiev had hoped Diaghilev would take him to London to conduct *Chout*, but now he felt completely exhausted and simply wanted to head back to Rochelets. Diaghilev did not mention London, rather his discussions focused on a cut he wanted Prokofiev to make, merging the fifth and sixth scenes of the ballet. The matter went unresolved for the moment and Prokofiev left Paris. In St Brevin he had a chance to work a bit on the theme and variations for his Third Piano Concerto and to catch up on some rest. Soon he received a telegram from Diaghilev asking him to conduct the London premier of *Chout* on 8 June, all expenses would be paid. Prokofiev had gradually settled into the leisurely pace of his summertime dacha life and felt too lazy to move. But move he did, returning briefly to Paris with Linette, then departing for London alone that same evening for an overnight trip. Larionov had not been invited to join the company in London and nervously probed Prokofiev for information about his current standing.

After his arrival in London at 8 a.m. it was down to business: Diaghilev took Prokofiev to the morning rehearsal in order to make the excision he had mentioned in Paris. The cut was to come in scene five after the merchant discovered the goat instead of Molodukha at the end of his drape, and eliminate everything up to the entry of the hero buffoon and seven soldiers in the last scene (from reh. 260 to 283).[82] A brief blackout would allow for the change of scenery from the merchant's bedroom to that of the finale. Prokofiev behaved like the perfect ballet-specialist composer—he immediately acquiesced. He recorded in his Diary: "I didn't protest against this although I felt bad that the whole of the final section of the fifth scene was cut [the tormenting of the goat]. Vice versa I didn't regret the bad beginning of the sixth scene. The fifth part I liked very much but you couldn't hear it very well because of talk among the audience [proto-animal rights activists, perhaps]. Thus the excision took place and was rehearsed." This only shaved about five minutes off the just under one hour long ballet but it eliminated a bit of musical redundancy with the removal of the final entr'acte. And the commotion at the end of the fifth scene and burial of the goat with the subsequent mocking by the seven buffoons at the start of scene six were rightly deemed expendable by Diaghilev. After this act of generosity by the composer in regard to his music, he was treated to lunch by Diaghilev at the Savoy before beginning his first rehearsal with the orchestra.

Ansermet had already been rehearsing them. Prokofiev found this orchestra to be far superior to the one in Paris, for one thing, he recalled, "they had a serious and attentive attitude." In addition to his ballet Prokofiev rehearsed the "Classical" Symphony because Diaghilev presented musical performances during the intervals between ballets in London. Stravinsky appeared at Prokofiev's next orchestra rehearsal and praised the Symphony, saying it was done very skillfully and full of fresh modulations. The day before when asked for his opinion by its composer, Ansermet had criticized the Symphony, but now after hearing his mentor's remarks he felt quite embarrassed and treated Prokofiev to lunch by way of apology.[83]

The Ballets Russes season had opened in London on 26 May with a program of old favorites. This would be a much longer season than in Paris with twice as many ballets presented. *Chout* was given a total of ten times in London beginning with a *répétition général* on 8 June, and ending with a matinee on 30 June. The Ballets Russes' venue was Prince's Theatre on Shaftsbury Avenue, better known for its presentations of Gilbert and Sullivan operettas and musicals than ballet. The company was cramped here: Grigoriev called Prince's "a theatre I always disliked on account of its shallow stage and general lack of space,"[84] adding, "the accommodation for performers was so restricted that some of the company had to dress and make up in other premises, specially rented."[85] The musicians did not fare well either, although Prokofiev's instrumentation was not colossal (woodwinds in threes, a regular size brass section with four horns and tuba, two harps, percussion requiring three players and strings), some of the players had to be accommodated in the stage boxes.[86] In 1927 *Le Pas d'acier*, with its bulky constructivist set would also receive its London premier in this rather confined space.

Prokofiev greatly embarrassed Diaghilev during the *répétition général*. Once again he was confused by the system of buttons that signaled backstage, and in the middle of the first scene the orchestra started playing some wrong notes. Unaccustomed to the formality of this sort of presentation with its audience of invited guests and critics, he stopped the orchestra to fix the mistakes. As he resumed conducting the impresario rushed up to him and whispered in his ear, "You've just shit all over London. Don't you dare stop again … pretend it's a real performance." At the premier on 9 June Prokofiev confessed to being slightly apprehensive just before the cut, but everything went well and the end there was a huge success. He thought the orchestra had played far better than in Paris. Diaghilev presented him with a huge laurel wreath with red and white bands. Afterwards Diaghilev, his companion, Prokofiev and Kochno drank champagne at the Savoy. Prokofiev was rather bored until the impresario began to reminisce and then perorate on the Russian Tsars.

For the second London performance on 11 June Prokofiev asked that Ansermet conduct so he could just listen to the score and watch the production. But during the interval before the ballet he conducted his First Symphony, which was "accepted well but without sensation." He then sat in a loge with Stravinsky and felt that the entire audience was staring at him.

> To listen to *Chout* from the loge was ten times more pleasant than from the conductor's stand. Everything sounds much more precise and beautiful … I could hear for the first time the trumpets and trombones loudly enough … and besides that I could really look at the stage for the first time. While conducting I only occasionally would made quick glances. It was an interesting view. There were many beautiful discoveries but many other things were not well done and there was some lack of agreement with the music. It's worth improving at least for next season.

It is doubtful that he, or anyone for that matter, ever followed through with that last intriguing statement (however, some costumes were modified). At the end the audience acknowledged the composer warmly and then it was time to bid farewell to Diaghilev. The impresario said that in August or September he would vacation in Venice and he hoped Prokofiev could come and "in the free air discuss a new ballet."

Just before leaving London Prokofiev heard for the first time Stravinsky's *tombeau* for Debussy, *Symphonies of Wind Instruments*, performed under Koussevitzky's baton. On the night of 12 June he arrived back in Paris and was met by Larionov. At the hotel Larionov was very interested to see the reviews and especially the photographs since he could not read English. As Prokofiev carefully translated the clippings he saw out of the corner of his eye that Larionov was stealing some of them and placing them in his pocket. When challenged by Prokofiev he claimed he only had his notebook in his pocket. Larionov was known to be a bit eccentric.[87] The next day Prokofiev returned to his rented villa on the Brittany coast for the remainder of the summer, and there he completed his Third Piano Concerto.[88]

The London press was overwhelmingly hostile towards *Chout*. Percy Scholes in the *Observer* found the story "outrageously dull" and the comic intent "hopelessly and stupidly flat," while Ernest Newman in the *Sunday Times* called the treatment of the "silly" story "dull and amateurish."[89] As in Paris the choreography came in for harsh criticism, Cyril Beaumont calling it "disconnected," and Newman, "feeble in invention."[90] Scholes thought that the preponderance of "pranks" on stage "precluded the possibility of any dancing whatsoever until the last five minutes." *The Times* reported that

> something might have been made of [the ballet] if it had come into the hands of the artist who devised the Children's Tales [*Le Contes Russes*] and *Pulcinella* [Massine]. Unfortunately, it had not such luck, and in spite of the brilliant Cubist scenery and dresses with which M. Larionov has provided it and the equally brilliant and equally Cubist music of M. Prokofiev, it has the effect of a loosely-improvised charade … . All the dancers jump about and pose and mime and gesticulate without achieving anything but momentary effects.[91]

The British musical press, generally a more conservative lot, was far more critical of the score than their French counterparts. Prokofiev recalled in his autobiography that the public received the ballet very well but press comment was most unfavorable. He lamented to a former Conservatory classmate that 113 of the 114 reviews were abusive.[92] Yet in a letter to a friend in Chicago Prokofiev gave a more optimistic report: "The British press was not so kind regarding my ballet, yet could not do much to harm the production, and it was given over a dozen times [*sic*], always with a sold-out house."[93] Even so, Prokofiev would never return to London for a performance of his ballets, premieres included.

There was a wide range of critical opinion concerning the music as the *Observer* summarized: "from the *Westminster*'s 'silly and childish, empty and boring trivial nonsense' to the *Pall Mall*'s 'freshness corresponding to that revealed on stage,' and 'simple in a new way.'"[94] Some reviewers recognized the score's color and effect but then tempered their praise by calling attention to its redundancies (a valid complaint which was a result of the Diaghilev-ordered entr'actes) and inability to sustain interest: "The use of a good deal of quite pleasant melodic material is to be recognized, but some of it seems to be overused ... . The whole thing seems rather commonplace, and it all drags."[95] The same reviewer (Scholes) noticed that "the fitting of the music to the action seems in most cases naive rather than clever." That ogre of the modernists, Ernest Newman, found Prokofiev's music "only a juvenile bore."[96] In the same vein "H. G." concluded his *Observer* review by stating, "'Chout' has not yet learned to walk. It can scream very piercingly while waiting for its bottle."[97]

Although Diaghilev always savored a scandalous premier, he felt compelled to respond to this onslaught of critical reviews. In a letter to the *Daily Telegraph* he lambasted the London critics for their "total lack of comprehension," singling out Newman for his "monstrous utterances" and "provincial ideas" and calling him "the viellard terribel of criticism."[98] Diaghilev claimed that *Chout* would "travel the same road" as other musical masterpieces of the Ballets Russes that were at first ill received (using *Petrouchka* as his example). From our perspective, however, the London reviews were not as bad as Prokofiev's recollection painted them. Few were totally damning, and, as the *Daily Telegraph* reported, there was much to applaud:

> We are quite prepared to believe that Serge Prokofieff's music—closely knit as it is to the action of the piece—would sound quite well apart from the ballet ... the composer is a master of climax ... a master of dynamics. The final dance is a whirlwind of cacophony, and when the curtain fell the outburst of cheering was spontaneous—mingled, it should be noted, with some booing.[99]

In this tug of war between traditionalists and modernists, it is clear that most critics failed to see the influence of the circus in Larionov's caricatures and buffoonery, and that Prokofiev's colorful, boisterous music offered the perfect accompaniment. The French composer Vincent d'Indy recognized this characteristic in the composer's music after hearing *L'Amour des trois oranges*, *Chout*'s operatic sibling. Although this arch-conservative hardly meant it as a compliment, his lapidary assessment rings true: "Prokofieff: musique de cirque!"[100] In a more friendly tone, one perceptive London reviewer called *Chout*

> perfectly childish; it is barbaric in its incentive to laughter. You are back among the truants, moved to irresistible mirth by the sight of Punch banging the life out of Judy ... [the ballet is] an hour of boisterous fun ... . You leave with the exhilarated sense of a debauch in the nursery, and the idea that you may have assisted at the revelation of a musical genius.[101]

Although *Chout* had only 14 performances its first season, it brought Prokofiev the fame and recognition he had long sought in Western Europe. Diaghilev quickly decided to present *Chout* again the following year. The conductors Ansermet and Coates pressed the composer for an orchestral suite from the ballet. The success also boosted his stature in comparison with

Stravinsky even though the number of performances given the latter's ballets vastly outnumbered those of Prokofiev's in both venues. *Chout* also helped Diaghilev's company stay abreast of the competition on the modernist-exotic front, namely the Ballets Suédois and their premier of Milhaud's and Paul Claudel's symbolic danced poem inspired by Brazil's tropical rain forest, *L'Homme et son désir*, at the Théâtre des Champs-Élysées that same June (Diaghilev had auditioned and rejected this score in July 1920). Prokofiev had clearly fulfilled Diaghilev's request to write something "truly Russian," and *dansante*, besides. These qualities were duly noted by some of the more perceptive music critics: "des thèmes russes la musique de *Bouffon* procède certainement de Rimsky-Korsakoff, mais en elle quelque chose aussi fait songer à Mozart ou plutôt à Scarlatti: sa limpidité, sa divine assurance, sa danse légère, son aimable logique, sa précision, sa grâce souriante, souvent ironique."[102] And Jean Bernier declared in *Comœdia*, "On this Russian subject Prokofiev wrote a Russian score," adding, "Russian music continues, this formidable river of Musorgsky and Borodin will not dry up after Stravinsky."[103] Thanks to Diaghilev's guidance, Prokofiev had finally created a successful ballet score— one that answered the needs of both the drama and the dance in bold exotic colors.

For the London season beginning in November 1921 Diaghilev presented a revised version of *Sleeping Beauty* at the Alhambra Theatre, retitled *The Sleeping Princess*. He hoped for a long run which, after paying off the production's enormous advances, would generate a much needed financial cushion. Instead, following the lead of a hostile press, the attendance fell off prematurely necessitating an early closing on 4 February. Sets and costumes were impounded, and the threat of further legal action prevented the company's return to London until late 1924. This was the most expensive failure the company ever suffered and it caused very lean times in the months that followed. Rumors circulated of the company's imminent demise. Diaghilev took the failure of his beloved Russian *danse d'école* as a personal rebuff. With his resources at low ebb he revived *Chout* for the 1922 Paris season with the title role danced *en travestie* by the company's new choreographer, Bronislava Nijinska (both Slavinsky and Sokolova had defected to Massine's rival company). *Chout* was presented six times, but only after the scheduled run at the Paris Théâtre de l'Opéra had been extended by an additional series at the nearby Théâtre Mogador. Prokofiev did not attend any of these performances (Ansermet conducted). In a letter dated 26 June 1922 written from his home in Bavaria Prokofiev thanked Diaghilev for his telegram relaying *Chout*'s success and invited him and Kochno to stop by for a visit on their way to Italy at the end of the season. The regular season at the Opéra had featured two premiers by Stravinsky, his "burlesque in song and dance," *Renard* and the one-act opera buffa, *Mavra*. The long-awaited premier of *Les Noces* finally came about the following season. *Chout* shared the bill with it twice that June (again at the Gaîté-Lyrique, Ansermet conducting). Thus

Diaghilev's idea of having these two ballets presented together, formulated back in the spring of 1915, was at long last fulfilled.

After the premier of *Chout* Prokofiev saw Diaghilev less and less over the next few years. In March 1922, Prokofiev settled in the tiny town of Ettal on the remote slopes of the Bavarian Alps, and, concert tours aside, remained there until he moved back to Paris at the end of 1923. Their separation became an outright rift by the summer of 1924 due in equal parts to Diaghilev's solicitation of French backers and talent, opposite opinions about the future of opera and the music of Poulenc, and Prokofiev's perceived "disloyalty," that is, his defection to the likes of Ida Rubinstein, Boris Romanov, Koussevitzky and others. Stravinsky played a key role in their relationship as usual. But after the premier of *Les Noces* in 1923, he too would drift away from Diaghilev's immediate circle, becoming increasingly devoted to concertizing.

Diaghilev still had ideas up his sleeve, but because of the financial debacle in London in early 1922 he did not have the resources to bring them to fruition. On two different occasions in the autumn of 1922 he approached Prokofiev about possible commissions, first for an opera on Mikhail Lermontov's "*Tambovskaia Kaznacheisha*" (The Tambov Treasurer's Wife, 1837–38: a young soldier is captivated by a woman with a wealthy husband) and later for a short ballet without a plot, "a 'danced symphony' of about twelve minutes." Then a blowup occurred. Diaghilev asked Prokofiev to play for him *Gambler* and *L'Amour des trois oranges*, the latter of which had finally received its premier on 30 December 1921 in Chicago (but performed there only once more on 2 January 1922, and once in New York on 14 February). One has to wonder at his motive, however, since he used the occasion to attack Prokofiev, once again, for devoting so much time to opera, and for his use of declamatory style (as opposed to traditional numbers, arias and ensembles as Stravinsky had employed in his recent opera *Mavra*). Stravinsky jumped in and asserted that Prokofiev was on the wrong path. According to the latter "there was a loud squabble with horrible shouting." At some point during this brouhaha Prokofiev yelled at Stravinsky, "And how are you able to indicate to me the [proper] path in time when I am nine years younger than you and therefore nine years ahead of you! My path is real and your path is the path of the past generation." One would like to think that there was a liquid catalyst at work here, but none was mentioned. Years later the composer recalled:

> when I played him [Diaghilev] the music [for *Oranges*], Stravinsky … sharply criticized it and refused to listen to more than the first act. In some respects he was right: the first act is the least successful. But on that occasion I hotly defended my opera and the result was a quarrel. For my part I did not approve of Stravinsky's predilection for Bachian techniques—his 'pseudo-Bachism'—or rather I did not approve of adopting someone else's idiom and calling it one's own … After this encounter our relations became strained and for several years Stravinsky's attitude towards me was critical, though not altogether unfavorable.[104]

To what extent Stravinsky's disapproval of *Oranges* affected Diaghilev remains conjecture, but the former remained in his good graces whereas Prokofiev did not. *Chout* was dropped from the repertory after 1923.[105] Even though Diaghilev had entered Prokofiev's name beside the title *Le Roi* (or *Tsar*) *Dodon* among 25 operas in his "grand project" outline in his notebook,[106] and notwithstanding the occasional social encounter, the relationship between the composer and the impresario withered until spring 1925. As so often is the case when relationships founder, money was the underlying cause.

During Diaghilev's estrangement from his second "son," the Ballets Russes set up shop in Monte Carlo and proceeded to become thoroughly Gallicized. Diaghilev had been rescued in the autumn of 1922 by an arrangement with the Théâtre de Monte Carlo engineered by Princess Polignac (née Winnaretta Singer) and the Société des Bains de Mer, whereby the company was given a permanent home at Monte Carlo and a partial year's subsidy. In return Diaghilev promised a French Festival for the season beginning January 1924. With this new support from wealthy French backers and renewed influence from Cocteau, Diaghilev's company pursued the latest French fashions. Offering ballets dealing with the leisure life of the wealthy set at the beach or in the salon, and using the music of Les Six, British dancers given exotic sounding names, chic costumes by Coco Chanel, and cinematic dance sequences (often with acrobatics), the Ballets Russes had very little Russian left in it. The esthetic shift had been ongoing for some time. Since June 1921 when Cocteau's *Les Mariés de la Tour Eiffel* with music by Les Six (sans Durey) made a favorable impression on him, Diaghilev had featured the music of this new generation of French composers during the intervals between ballets in his London seasons. Under the spell of Cocteau, Diaghilev commissioned *Les Biches* from Poulenc, *Le Train bleu* from Milhaud and *Les Fâcheux* from Auric. "Mere cocktails," ballet purists harrumphed in vain.

Prokofiev harrumphed as well and as a result he earned Stravinsky's and thus Diaghilev's enmity for almost one year. His unconcealed censure of Poulenc's ballet severed their relationship; Diaghilev's awareness that he made a misjudgment about the company's recent Cocteau-inspired "musiquette" (as this fare was derisively called in some quarters), led to its revival. Prokofiev recorded in his correspondence and in his Diary time and again his partial approval of the music of Honegger (for example, *Le Roi David, Pacific 231*) and to a much lesser extent, Auric (for example, *Les Matelots*)—he rarely gave any music his full endorsement—but he despised two works created for Diaghilev's 1924 season: *Les Biches* by Poulenc and *Le Train bleu* by Milhaud. On 26 May he went from Koussevitzky's deafening rehearsal of his own *They Are Seven* which was being prepared for its western premier to the opening night of Diaghilev's new season and the Paris premier of Poulenc's ballet. He was greatly disappointed; he thought Poulenc's music naive, calling it "organ-grinder dancing" music without form, lacking any sense of logical progression. Ever disdainful of borrowed material, Prokofiev was surely bothered by the score's eclecticism. The Adagietto's blatant reference to his "Danse des bouffonnes" from scene two of *Chout* would not have been well received. It also did not help that the next work on the program was the out-and-out masterpiece, *Les Noces*. This was the first time Prokofiev had seen Stravinsky's newest ballet; afterwards he went to the composer to congratulate him and heap abuse on Poulenc's music. He was dumbfounded when Stravinsky defended the latter.[107] "I don't believe your praise," Prokofiev said with surprise, to which the offended Stravinsky replied, "You have no basis to consider me insincere. But we look from different points of view." Clearly Stravinsky was still among Diaghilev's faithful; henceforth the gap widened between the two composers.

On 4 June Prokofiev was again at the Ballets Russes and saw Auric's *Les Fâcheux*, which he thought was not particularly good, but "not so scandalous as *Biches*." That evening Diaghilev ignored Prokofiev. On 8 June he heard a report from his friend, the émigré musicologist Pierre Souvtchinsky, that Stravinsky had said over dinner, "It's too bad about Prokofiev that he still considers himself to be a modernist." This no doubt was in response to his hearing *They Are Seven*. Prokofiev again was at *Biches* on 11 June. In a letter to Myaskovsky written on 1 June he had dismissed it as "nonsense." His second evaluation was not much better, "the motives enter your ears and play by themselves, but this is not thematic inventiveness: he simply took forgotten tangos which were fashionable at one time and then discarded because of their triviality." After the performance he spoke for a considerable time with the artist José-María Sert who was married to Diaghilev patroness Misia Sert. He shared his view of *Biches*, to which Sert replied "Ravel is of the same opinion." He added, "In art there is nothing forwards or backwards, only talented and untalented." Later when he was alone Prokofiev mused, "And the moral is unexpected: I feel comfortable in the company of backward people."

On 13 June he once again inadvertently offended the thin-skinned Stravinsky. Prokofiev thought that he might have been behind Diaghilev's ill-considered revival of French operettas with recitatives added by Les Six. For this evening's program Milhaud had performed the honors on Chabrier's *Une Education manquée*. Prokofiev found it all empty and boring. The audience was not satisfied either: there was booing, whistling and catcalls. Stravinsky was infuriated and turned around in his loge to boo in response towards the gallery. Afterwards Souvtchinsky said to Stravinsky: "I understand that there could exist well known principles which would force one to stage such a thing, but it seems to me the choice was unsuccessful: why chose such tedium?" Stravinsky immediately became enraged and said while departing "You are all savages." Soon more "savages" appeared as the curtain rose for the next ballet of the evening, *Le Sacre du printemps*. Thereafter Prokofiev went to the composer clapping his hands and saying, "Bravo, well done, old man [starik]" in the same friendly, sincere manner the French use "mon vieux." But Stravinsky flew into a rage, saying "You could be included in that category!" then abruptly turned and left.

Prokofiev was further alienated from the "new" Ballets Russes on 20 June when he saw *Le Train blue*. In his Diary he called it "the premeditated attempt to write vulgarity and orchestrate it in a vulgar style," adding "this is all in the chain of those 'new' trends, the essence of which I don't understand." That same June the young composer Vladimir Dukelsky (later known as Vernon Duke; destined to become Diaghilev's "third son" and future composer of the ballet *Zéphyr et Flore*) was warned by the impresario to stay away from Prokofiev, whom he called "an utter imbecile." Such was Diaghilev's anger when one of his discoveries dared to show some independence. Prokofiev was not sidelined during this period; on the contrary, he was busy negotiating with Ida Rubinstein, and composing a Quintet-cum-ballet for Boris Romanov. Koussevitzky was about to give him an advance towards the gestating Second Symphony and soon Inna Chernetskaya, a dancer and producer from Moscow, would approach him for a new ballet. Still Prokofiev recorded his despair in his Diary on 22 July:

> What confuses me? After all Poulenc, Milhaud, Auric—these are all attempts with unsuitable means. On the other hand, that which Stravinsky does, does not confuse me at all. What confuses me? I think it is the union of Stravinsky with Poulenc and Auric. This is completely unintelligible to me. And also, Diaghilev seized by this youthfulness and suddenly not wanting to know me ... . What they do I don't like, therefore I became an adversary. At the heart of the matter: these people are the ones in the forefront—why don't I understand them?

He did not have to wonder for long. By the following March Diaghilev began making overtures. He was curious about the ballet for Romanov and expressed interest in having Prokofiev write a new ballet. Dukelsky, who had all along befriended Prokofiev despite Diaghilev's warning to stay away, was likely the agent in bringing them back together. On 19 June 1925 Prokofiev mulled over this turn of events in his Diary:

> Why are they coming back [to me]? I'm still the same. They run forward and back while I am on firm ground. Stravinsky's attitude turned against me last winter ... [this] coincided with promotion of the French group, Auric, Milhaud, Poulenc. Stravinsky supported Poulenc and was cursing me. When Poulenc and Milhaud failed, because Diaghilev is good enough a musician to know Poulenc was not what he was looking for ... Dukelsky became his savior but he is young. Meanwhile Stravinsky left the theatre and Diaghilev for abstract music ... [thus] the main disparager of Prokofiev disappeared, that's why Diaghilev came [back] to me.

It was Diaghilev's desperation to keep his company solvent that caused him to flitter about, following rather than leading as he had done before the War. About the only trend Diaghilev did not pursue was the Parisian fascination with jazz. The more adventurous Ballets Suédois did capitalize on this: in October

1923 they presented the first "jazz ballets" shown in Paris, Cole Porter's *Within the Quota* (orchestrated by Charles Koechlin) and Milhaud's fusion of jazz, blues and modern harmony, *La Création du monde*. According to Kochno, Diaghilev "had a horror of jazz ... [and he] was outraged by the jazz invasion of Europe and by its influence on young composers."[108] He did not care for imported American popular culture in general, nor was he interested in the new generation of American composers, many of whom were then living in Paris. But once as a condition for a possible Ballets Russes tour of America, Diaghilev considered a ballet written by an American composer, John Alden Carpenter, a friend of Prokofiev's from his days in Chicago. It featured contemporary Americans at work (construction workers on girders, hammers pounding, a factory whistle), and at play (Coney Island, flappers, banjos, a 12-voice Black chorus, and bits of "Yankee Doodle"). Entitled *Skyscrapers*, this ballet eventually received its premier at the New York Metropolitan Theater in February 1926. Although Diaghilev rejected Carpenter's ballet score, it is quite possible that it had a seminal influence on the next ballet Diaghilev commissioned from Prokofiev.

After the premier of *Chout* Koussevitzky had taken Diaghilev's place as the composer's chief promoter in Paris by presenting the premiers of the First Violin Concerto (composed in 1917) in October 1923[109] and of the reorchestrated and revised Second Piano Concerto (from 1913) the following May.[110] The press reproached Prokofiev in their rather tepid reviews for living off old compositions. Being enamored of the *Scythian Suite* and *Chout*, Parisians missed the composer's "true" voice in the Violin Concerto, and found the Piano Concerto to be monotonous, dense and generally inferior to the Third. It did not help that these works shared the concert stage with fresher sounding novelties, Stravinsky's *Octet* and Honegger's *Pacific 231*, respectively. The reception of Prokofiev's recently completed Fifth Piano Sonata was also somewhat reserved when it was premiered before a small crowd in Paris on 9 March 1924, despite its liberal use of dissonance and its natty, syncopated rhythms in the finale. But another early work, the brash and noisy "incantation," *They Are Seven*, conducted by Koussevitzky on 29 May 1924 (twice on the same concert), provided Prokofiev's greatest Parisian success since the debuts of *Scythian Suite* and *Chout* three years earlier. Clearly, this was the sort of music they expected from Prokofiev.

By January 1924 the composer was involved in a greatly protracted discussion with dancer/actress Ida Rubinstein about a theater work based on the story of Judith. During this stage of her career Rubinstein was, according to Garafola, leading a "schizoid existence", working both in the lyric theater and as a straight actress. Though her dramatic style was not progressive, her musical tastes were.[111] These talks went on sporadically for nearly two years. In April 1925 Rubinstein also expressed interest in staging the *Scythian Suite* as a ballet. However, neither project went beyond the discussion stage, although Prokofiev recorded that he had made some sketches that were suitable for the biblical drama. Rubinstein's behavior towards him ranged from gracious to rude (that is, standing him up, making him wait, and so on), prompting Prokofiev at one point to exclaim in disgust, "what a pig!" Once he began working on his next ballet for Diaghilev he uttered, "to hell with that business," and all contact with Rubinstein ended.[112] By then she had approached Honegger, and by 16 July had commissioned from him what would be the first of their six collaborations, *L'Impératrice aux rochers*.[113]

There were others who encouraged Prokofiev's "disloyalty." In March 1924 Larionov requested a 15-minute score for a puppet ballet to use in Monte Carlo and Paris, but he did not provide sufficient notice—Prokofiev was too busy practicing his Second Piano Concerto for its Parisian premier to be able to accept the commission. In November the critic and writer Pierre Blois was trying to clinch Prokofiev a commission from the Ballets Suédois. This also came to nought, but it was no great loss since that company disbanded the following March. In July 1924 Prokofiev tried to solicit Boris Asafyev's help in enticing the Mariinsky Theater to present *Chout* using the music of the Suite because the impresario kept the ballet score and held production rights until May 1926.[114] Such a production was finally mounted in January 1928 in Kiev. The Suite itself was premiered in Brussels under Frans Rühlmann on 15 November 1924, at a concert which also featured the Third Concerto performed by the composer. After a critically acclaimed run of *Oranges* in Cologne from March to May of 1925 Prokofiev managed to wrest his ballet score and parts for *Chout* away from Diaghilev for a month in order to have copies made in anticipation of a performance there the following November.[115] Berlin also began discussing the possibility of presenting *Chout*. The first performance away from the Ballets Russes had occurred in March 1924, at New York City's Neighborhood Playhouse.[116] On 3 January 1924 a representative had written to Prokofiev's publisher: "As our theater seats only 400 people, we are planning to have a very small orchestral ensemble which we are having made from a piano score by a very skillful musician." Although the performance was a violation of copyright, Prokofiev was more amused than annoyed by this diminutive production (with its orchestra of six musicians)[117] and was surprised to receive 5000 francs ($272) in royalties, thinking he would be lucky to see only 1000 francs for this "Chout-taki," as he called it.

During this period Prokofiev still sought success in Paris and, despite some hostile comments about the fame of Les Six,[118] was not above being a modernist composer in French terms, that is, a willingness to astonish at all costs, usually by means of dissonance and decibels. We do not know Prokofiev's thoughts about every example in the latest trend of futurist-inspired machine music, such as the notorious "Airplane Sonata" by George Antheil,[119] but we do have a record of his fascination with the quickly acclaimed *Pacific 231* by Honegger. It is certain that Prokofiev tried to out-do them all in his Second Symphony, resolving to write, in his words, a "large symphony to be made of iron and steel."

Prokofiev's good friend, champion and publisher Koussevitzky was well aware of the composer's tenuous acceptance in the West and urged him to write "a hit."[120]

Prokofiev devoted the summer and early autumn of 1924 to the Symphony's composition. But to earn some much needed cash he accepted a commission for a chamber ballet from the Russian Romantic Theater, a traveling ballet company led by former Ballets Russes choreographer and would-be *Ala i Lolli* collaborator, Boris Romanov. With a simple, yet bizarre plot taken from circus life, the ballet, eventually called *Trapèze*, was created for a small ensemble of dancers and musicians.[121] Prokofiev regarded this commission as a pretext for writing an abstract instrumental chamber piece, something he had wanted to do for some time, perhaps since hearing Stravinsky's *L'Histoire du soldat*. It would not be the first time dance played second fiddle to instrumental concerns when Prokofiev was composing a ballet (recall *Ala i Lolli*). However, the surviving six-movement Quintet, op. 39 for oboe, clarinet, violin, viola and double bass does not belie its theatrical origins (for example, the third movement with its 5/4 gait and comic dialogue, and the highly dramatic coda to the fifth movement). Prokofiev fulfilled Romanov's request for two more movements for the ballet in the summer of 1925, an overture and a piece entitled "Matelote" [*sic*]. These did not become part of the Quintet but, fully orchestrated and revised, they serve as movements one and three of *Divertissement*, op. 43. The first of these also became an interpolation in *Le Pas d'acier* upon Diaghilev's request for more music for the change of scene in April of 1926. Romanov toured with *Trapèze* beginning in Germany in the fall of 1925, but his company folded after a poor run in Turin during March 1926. In June of that year Romanov tried to entice Prokofiev to rescore the ballet for a normal sized orchestra and add yet another number, but the composer declined.[122] *Trapèze* then entered a 77 yearlong hibernation.[123] Prokofiev played *Chout* for the choreographer at this time in preparation for a possible new production by him at La Scala in Milan. However, Romanov presented *Petrouchka* there instead; he would not choreograph *Chout* until the spring of 1931 when he replaced Nijinska as balletmaster at l'Opéra Russe à Paris.[124]

Prokofiev's new two-movement Symphony was completed after considerable effort by May 1925 and given its premier in Paris under Koussevitzky's direction on 6 June 1925. This was nine days ahead of the opening of the Ballets Russes' brief season which featured suave new ballets by Auric (*Les Matelots*) and Diaghilev's third Russian "son," Vladimir Dukelsky (*Zéphyr et Flora*). Surrounded on the program by a Mozart overture and concerto, Prokofiev's thorny, abstruse Symphony confounded its first audience and the composer even admitted that "it was too densely woven in texture, too heavily laden with contrapuntal lines changing to figuration to be successful."[125] The critical failure of the Symphony caused Prokofiev serious self-doubts about his abilities and his chosen venue:

This was perhaps the first time it occurred to me that I might perhaps be destined to be a second-rate composer. Paris as undisputed dictator of fashion has a tendency to pose as the arbiter in other fields as well. In music the refinement of French tastes has its reverse side—the public are apt to be too easily bored. Having taken up with one composer they quickly tire of him and in a year or two are searching for a new sensation. I was evidently no longer a sensation.[126]

He recorded that there were many perplexed looks after it was over and that Stravinsky merely said it was not what he expected and left. He should not have been too surprised, in a letter to Asafyev written two weeks before the premier he himself had described it as "chromatic and ponderous." *La Revue musicale*'s critic thought the first movement would make a "beautiful symphonic poem," but damned much of the second, saying that in lieu of invention the composer was reduced to "scholarly combinations worthy of Glazunov ... impulse being replaced by [just] musical grammar." In his effort to astound *le tout Paris artistique* with his compositional prowess Prokofiev had reached the apogee of his modernist tendency. Though he believed in the worth of his Symphony ("somewhere in the depths of my soul there is the hope that a few years from now it will suddenly turn out that the Symphony is actually a respectable and even well-made thing.")[127] it had brought him to an abyss.

Prokofiev's Second Symphony did not fall completely upon deaf ears, however. On 15 June Diaghilev came to the composer during the final rehearsal before the Ballets Russes' opening night, sat down beside him and uttered the words "pig's music" in reference to Auric's latest ballet.[128] He then said, "Well Serge, we have to write another ballet." The despondent Prokofiev responded, "Yes, we should, but ...," explaining he could not write in the style the impresario approved of, that is, the banal, nearly vulgar ballet music of Auric and Milhaud. Diaghilev wisely counseled Prokofiev that he must write in his own style. This timely encouragement to listen, above all, to his own voice helped impel Prokofiev's greatest stylistic redirection. Although he was not yet ready to completely abandon his quest for the vanguard of the Parisian musical avant-garde, Prokofiev did return to heightened clarity and expressive lyricism in fulfilling Diaghilev's commission. This ballet would foreshadow the musical style that would prevail for the rest of his career.

The negotiations for what eventually became *Le Pas d'acier* went on for well over one month; part of the time Diaghilev was away tending the Ballets Russes season at the London Coliseum (the Paris season lasted only from 15 to 20 June). Out of the blue on 17 June Prokofiev received a letter from the balletmaster of the Berlin State Opera, Max Terpis, also asking for a new ballet. He preferred to work with Diaghilev but decided to use this offer as a bargaining chip in their negotiations. The information was discretely relayed to Diaghilev by Dukelsky, and Prokofiev was duly reprimanded by the impresario during the Ballets Russes intermission on 19 June, "don't you dare write for Germany!" But the threat had served its purpose, Diaghilev was impelled to settle the question of a new Prokofiev ballet. On 23 June a fee of 15,000 francs was decided upon (this was a compromise, the composer thought he ought to receive 20 000 francs) but the contract was not signed until 27 July. Diaghilev had an idea for the plot but did not share it right away. At the first serious meeting on 21 June, Prokofiev had suggested a ballet with characters who are musical notes and rests (something composer Bohuslav Martinů was already in the processing of writing).[129] Diaghilev countered that the body is beautiful and he wanted no symbolic figures or anything constructivist (an interesting comment in light of what he finally received).

On the following day Diaghilev unveiled his plan, "I want you to write a modern Russian ballet." "A Bolshevik ballet?" Prokofiev interrupted with surprise. Details had to wait three weeks until the impresario returned from London. Diaghilev had been following the latest in Soviet art through his contacts with the director Vsevolod Meyerhold, the writer Ilya Ehrenburg and the artist/theatre designer Georgy Yakulov, among others. He had been very intrigued by the innovative productions of Alexander Tairov's Kamerny Theater during their Spring 1923 western tour and by the great success of the various exhibitions in Paris by Soviet artists, including Yakulov's at the Exposition Internationale des Arts Décoratifs. He surely must have heard about the avant-garde choreographer Fyodor Lopukhov's *Krasnïy vikhr'* (The Red Whirlwind)— the first attempt at a Soviet ballet—presented on 29 October 1924 in Leningrad. Using music based on the tone poem *1918, Bol'sheviki* by Prokofiev's Conservatory friend Vladimir Deshevov, *The Red Whirlwind* depicted in its two acts and prologue the polarizing buildup to the Revolution and the subsequent upheavals, struggles and profiteering, through speech, song, acrobatics and dance. There are a number of parallels between it and *Le Pas d'acier*.[130] Disillusioned by the recent turn of events in Monte Carlo (the "Affair Ravel"),[131] the impresario had been drawing closer to his roots, even to the extent of considering a trip to Russia. And while certainly no Communist sympathizer, he decided to exploit the topicality of Soviet art with an all-Soviet ballet. Once again Diaghilev's Ballets Russes would capitalize on the West's fascination with the exotic.

After Diaghilev departed for London his secretary Kochno pressed his plan for a Bolshevik ballet on Prokofiev, one which used popular Russian songs. The composer strongly disliked Kochno, for one reason because of the overly prominent billing he received for the ballet scenarios he had authored over the past few years, "ballet by KOCHNO, then down below, with music by ..." He did not want to work with him and demonstrated his lack of interest in Kochno's plan. Still he listened to him sing 10 *chastushki* which had been popular at the beginning of the Revolution. In his Diary he recorded his impressions: the village songs were "cute," but the city songs were "bullshit, too sentimental." It is doubtful that Kochno sang the factory song that Prokofiev would use to open his ballet, otherwise this self-aggrandizer surely would have demanded remuneration or at least acknowledgment. While Diaghilev was away Prokofiev tried to finalize his dealings with Ida Rubinstein over the proposed *Judith* and *Scythian Suite* ballets, especially when his good friend Souvtchinsky, who was knowledgeable about present-day Russia, stated emphatically that it would be impossible to make a Bolshevik ballet "through the glasses of western Europe."[132] Neutrality was out of the question, it would end up being pro-Red or pro-White.

Diaghilev returned to Paris on 18 July and dined with Prokofiev, Kochno and Lifar at the Hôtel Vouillement. Prokofiev asked if he was still serious about the proposed subject for the new ballet and relayed Souvtchinsky's reservations. Diaghilev answered in the affirmative, "I even spoke with our ambassador ['our'?] in London about it," and brushed the concerns aside saying "I'm not interested in politics." The names Ehrenburg and Yakulov were raised and each was brought before the group, Ehrenburg later that same day, and Yakulov on the following day. Ehrenburg did little but wax on about life in present day Russia whereas Yakulov brought a portfolio with drawings and drafts, as if he had been waiting for a moment like this to occur. Yakulov clearly was trying to impress Diaghilev but he was vague about the details of his proposed ballet and evasive when asked if he felt they could manage without Ehrenburg. The next meeting Prokofiev attended with Yakulov and the others came on 21 July (Prokofiev had moved out of Paris to his summer home at the Ville Soyer in Bourron-Marlotte, just south of Fontainebleau). Yakulov suggested a ballet in three scenes characterizing the three stages of Bolshevism: the first in Red Square with drums, commissars, crowds, sailors in bracelets (the latter was obviously a fixation of his, they remained in the final draft), the second about the NEP (New Economic Plan)—a comical performance by sly people and the third, a factory or agricultural exhibition showing the buildup of Bolshevik Russia. Diaghilev objected to the second part so Yakulov agreed to cut it out but insisted on retaining some of its elements in the surrounding parts. Prokofiev did not see how he was supposed to depict the NEP musically; Yakulov replied, "Scherzo!"

For the meeting on 24 July Yakulov brought designs for costumes and the décor, the latter all metal colored with platforms at different heights. Prokofiev was surprised by Diaghilev's unreserved praise because he usually advocated easily portable scenery. Yakulov's shortcoming continued to be his vagueness over details of the plot. Diaghilev became concerned about this and again thought of Ehrenburg, saying he was the "latest word," despite his unpleasant personality. It was agreed that he would be brought in only as a consultant, he would not write the libretto. After the meeting Prokofiev walked to the train station with Yakulov and en route, received an earful of details for a plot: cigarette girls, ladies wearing lampshades, thieves, sailors, commissars, characters escaping from level to level with ropes, workers with hammers and a speaker with a book attached to his hand by a rubber band. Prokofiev suddenly saw in front of him a Bolshevik ballet. He told Yakulov that all he needed to do was to put all of these ideas into a connected whole.

By the time Prokofiev returned to Paris on 27 July Diaghilev had met Ehrenburg. The latter did not want to be just a consultant and let slip that if he were to write the libretto he would start the ballet at a train station because that was the place where everyone congregated and where exchanges were made at the beginning of the Revolution. Diaghilev was won over and began to work out an agreement with him. However, he soon stormed out angrily, not so much because of Ehrenburg's demand for 5000 francs, but because of his confession that he really wasn't all that interested in the commission. Prokofiev sang Yakulov's praises at this meeting saying that all he lacked was organizational skills, "and I have those." He asked Diaghilev for one day to allow them to make the libretto, "if you approve it, fine, and if not, Ehrenburg will not disappear in two days." Prokofiev was surprised how quickly Diaghilev agreed to this, but added in his Diary, "Ehrenburg really annoyed him."

At 2 p.m. on 29 July Yakulov arrived in Marlotte. The two discussed the plot as they walked along the banks of the Loing River and continued as they stopped for coffee at a garden-side table outside the Hôtel La Poule d'eau. Prokofiev, who had not returned to his homeland since his 1918 departure but was increasingly interested in doing so, was undoubtedly excited about Yakulov's visual conception for the ballet. Years later he recalled

> Sitting in a tiny café on the banks of a river half an hour outside of Paris, Yakulov and I roughly sketched several draft librettos. We assumed that the important thing at this stage was not to provide mere entertainment but to show the new life that had come to the Soviet Union, and primarily the construction effort. It was to be a ballet of construction, with hammers big and small being wielded, transmission belts and flywheels revolving, light signals flashing, all leading to a general creative upsurge with dance groups operating the machines and at the same time depicting the work of the machines choreographically. The idea was Yakulov's who had spent some years in the Soviet Union and described it all most vividly. It was easy to see that the libretto had been written not by a playwright but a painter guided by his visual impressions ... . My job consisted in organizing the rather haphazard material Yakulov had given me arranging it in the form of musical numbers in a harmonious succession leading to a culmination.[133]

Prokofiev's Diary recalls this meeting more precisely. "Yakulov was giving me material and I was trying to build something out of it. I insisted on the train station—the only useful idea from Ehrenburg—and soon I was inspired and the first act promptly took shape." Taking Yakulov's ideas for the second act, Prokofiev envisioned "a factory at full speed, a small private episode, then suddenly the director says that the factory is closing due to lack of money." This is not unlike the text of the well-known song, *Kirpichniki* [lit. "Little Bricks," but known in the West as "The Brick Factory"]. Had Kochno sung this to him? Prokofiev continued, "The workers are indignant and chase him away.

The factory stops. There is a children's procession—Yakulov says this is typical for modern Moscow—a sailor and female worker in the procession encourage exercise instead of sadness, so with gymnastic exercises the ballets ends. No politics." Yakulov certainly did not want any of the latter; after all, he had to return to Russia! He came up with a working title for the ballet that day, "Ursin'ol," from URSS. Prokofiev immediately took to it because it sounded to him like a caricature of "Rossignol," that is, Stravinsky's recently restaged ballet *Le Chant du rossignol* (by Balanchine). The title of the new ballet would eventually be *Le Pas d'acier*, although this was not settled until about six weeks before the premier. Another early working title was "1920"–the date of the ballet's setting–perhaps in response to the vogue for dates as titles (for example, Hindemith's piano suite *1922*, and finale to *Kammermusik no. 1*, entitled "1921"). Lifar contends that this was rejected because it made the ballet sound dated, yet 1920 was retained as a subtitle (see Fig. 18). In fact, it caused at least one critic to believe that that was when the music was composed.[134]

The next morning at 10 a.m. Prokofiev met Diaghilev at his hotel and told him the content of the plot (Yakulov overslept and missed all but the last five minutes of the meeting). The impresario accepted it with two stipulations: Prokofiev was to further develop the private intrigue and finish with the factory at full speed with hammers swinging instead of gymnastics. Diaghilev handed Prokofiev the first 5000 francs according to their contract and Prokofiev agreed to mail the revised scenario to him in Venice after he met once again with Yakulov. The lengthy, detailed scenario was sent to Diaghilev in two parts (see Chapter 4), the first dated 2 August. Prokofiev recalled that it was "more or less" approved by Diaghilev. The ballet was to be in two acts, the first dealing with the breakdown of the old order and the enthusiasm of the revolutionaries and the second depicting the uplifting influence and comradeship of organized labor. This would be the first time the Ballets Russes addressed Soviet-style futurism and constructivism.

Once again Diaghilev had confirmed his faith in Prokofiev's talent by commissioning this "Russian" ballet in the wake of poorly received or misunderstood works. But after the lackluster Parisian reception given his dense, highly chromatic Second Symphony and even to his more Classically oriented but angular and dissonance spiked Fifth Piano Sonata, the composer resolved on his own to make "some serious changes" in his compositional style: a return to clear diatonicism and melodic writing, using a Russian musical idiom that could convey the spirit of the present times.[135] This ballet then, not *Romeo and Juliet* nor *L'Enfant prodigue*, marks the major redirection in Prokofiev's career, the beginning of a new emphasis from his established stylistic palette. But his newly revitalized lyricism would still stand alongside passages that reflected the latest in Parisian musical styles. Before he began to compose he wrote to Myaskovsky that the ballet would be simpler than *Chout* with a less complex plot [!] and with more "symphonic music" (the scenario ended up being just as prolix as its predecessor's).

Diaghilev's keen interest in this project is demonstrated by his attempt to engage some of the greatest Soviet artists: Meyerhold to direct the production and Kasyan Goleyzovsky, leader of the experimental Moscow Chamber Ballet, to choreograph it. Both Yakulov and Prokofiev wanted Diaghilev to engage Larionov as stage manager, but according to Kochno, Yakulov was to secure the collaboration of Meyerhold or Tairov upon his return to Russia in the autumn. Prokofiev recorded in his Diary that Diaghilev could not decide between Yakulov and Moscow theatre designer Isaak Rabinovich. As it turned out the only Soviet artist involved in the project was Yakulov. The choreography would be devised by Massine who had no knowledge of Soviet life, having left Russia three years before the Revolution.[136] It was Diaghilev's policy to hand the choreographer the completed score, but in this case he did not demand that the scenario to which the music had been composed, be followed. Massine's vision for the first half of *Le Pas d'acier* was to be something quite his own.

Prokofiev began composing the score in early August after completing the parts for Romanov's ballet. His work proceeded rapidly. Yakulov came to Marlotte several times, and each time they sat at the same café on the banks of the river while they refined the libretto. An early idea of Prokofiev's was to use the *chastushka* "Yablochko," (Hey Little Apple) and develop it symphonically. Had Kochno sung this to Prokofiev? Or perhaps Yakulov had mentioned that it was being used in the Second Moscow Art Theatre production of *The Flea* by Yevgeny Zamyatin, which was based on Nikolay Leskov's well-known story of 1881. Glière would use this song to great acclaim as the "Russian Sailor's Dance" in Act One of his hugely successful ballet *Krasnïy mak* (Red Poppy) composed in 1926 and premiered at Moscow's Bolshoy Theater one week after *Le Pas d'acier* was premiered in Paris. Ultimately, Prokofiev did not take up "Yablochko" but he did borrow from a "well-known" Russian factory song to set the tone at the beginning of the ballet. As he worked Prokofiev was reading Leonid Leonov's recent novel about contemporary life in Russia, *Barsuki* (The Badgers). He claimed that this story about the vastly different lives of two brothers during the years 1909–22 was very useful to him.[137]

Prokofiev played the completed short score for Diaghilev on 7 October and the impresario made a number of "very useful suggestions," the composer recalled, "as usual." In his Diary entry for that day there is a rather cryptic comment: "played the ballet twice, nine parts good (out of twelve), lengthy entr'acte." Two days later he adds: "my strange mistake about the length of the entr'acte." Apparently there was insufficient music for the change of scenes. Diaghilev would later ask for the aforementioned music from *Trapèze* to remedy that situation. Prokofiev played the score twice more for Diaghilev and his circle, presumably after revisions had been made, first on 16 October and then on 24

October with Balanchine present. Diaghilev asked rhetorically if the latter might participate in the staging. A year and a half later Balanchine would be occupied with choreographing the new ballet *La Chatte* and so Massine would receive the assignment. When he heard of this decision in late March 1927 Prokofiev was very pleased because, as he recorded in his Diary, he considered the former to be "too erotic and therefore flaccid." It is difficult to tell whether he was referring to his choreographic style or his lifestyle.

By mid-November Prokofiev was actively orchestrating the ballet. Concerned that he might not be able to complete the task on time he kept on with it while on tour in the USA: in his hotel room, over coffee in cafés and while traveling on trains. In January from St Paul, Minnesota, he sent Diaghilev a very rough (ves'ma priblizitel'nïy) piano reduction of the last numbers, suitable only for rehearsals.

The ballet was planned for the 1926 spring season; however, once again, the premier of a Prokofiev ballet was postponed, this time for just one year. The composer had been in the USA since the end of December 1925, and when he returned to Europe by mid-March 1926, he discovered that the company had not yet begun rehearsing "Ursin'ol." Diaghilev was trying to attract Meyerhold through Yakulov in order to produce the ballet, but Meyerhold was too busy so Yakulov suggested Tairov. But, according to Prokofiev, Diaghilev was not interested in the latter because he believed that "Paris did not like him." On 23 March Prokofiev recorded in his Diary: "Diaghilev was not adverse to postponing the production until the following year, since this would be his 20th anniversary, as he said, 'of glorious activity,' and he would like to have an exclusively Russian season: Stravinsky, Prokofiev, Dukelsky. But the main thing was, right now he had absolutely no money. 'Find me 800 francs and tomorrow I will begin to rehearse your ballet.'" Even though he had yet to complete the orchestration Prokofiev complained in a letter to Myaskovsky that Diaghilev had deceived him, suggesting that he knew there was more afoot than a shortfall of 800 francs. British money from conservative sponsors now supported the Ballets Russes, and it is likely that Diaghilev considered the presentation of ballets with music by British composers such as Constant Lambert (*Romeo and Juliet*) and Lord Berners (his *Triumph of Neptune* was to be premiered the following December) to be far safer than presenting a ballet exploiting Bolshevist exoticism. A healthy sum came from newspaper magnate Lord Rothermere in March 1926. When *Le Pas d'acier* was finally in rehearsal in the spring of 1927 Diaghilev received this telegram: "Rothermere wants to know which ballets to be given. No eccentric ones."[138] Rothermere's concern was real—there had been a crippling general strike in England in early May 1926. He was a man of his word: after *Le Pas d'acier* was presented in London in 1927, he refused to offer any further financial support. The one-season delay meant that Prokofiev was able to encounter the real Soviet Russia prior to seeing his balletic depiction of it, for in January 1927 he departed for a ten week trip to his homeland. The delay also meant that *La Chatte*, premiered in Monte Carlo on 30 April 1927, would be the company's first presentation of a constructivist décor.[139]

Prokofiev set off for further concert tours in Germany and Italy and returned to Paris in time for the second performance run of his Second Symphony beginning on 6 May at the Concerts Straram[140] and the opening of Diaghilev's 1926 season at the Théâtre Sarah-Bernhardt—the latter, alas, without his new ballet. "And how we busied ourselves with it last year!" he observed wryly. He was present at the opening night riot instigated by about 50 high-minded surrealists who objected to the surrealists Max Ernst and Joan Miró being remunerated for their work on Lambert's and Nijinska's ballet *Romeo and Juliet*. Prokofiev enjoyed the fracas far more than the production which was set in a dance studio.[141] In addition to this new ballet, the Ballets Russes season also featured *Barabau* a choral ballet with music by Vittorio Rieti, and *La Pastorale* with music by Auric, both choreographed by Balanchine. About the former Prokofiev was surprisingly kind with his initial reaction, "the music was sweet, simple, pleasant, happy, a little like Rossini."[142]

By the end of June Prokofiev had finally finished orchestrating "Ursin'ol." He had also revised its final number apparently upon his own instigation. His work was not yet complete, however, because a "real" piano reduction still needed to be made to replace the temporary one he had completed in America. After Diaghilev departed Paris for his usual Venetian summer sojourn Kochno visited Prokofiev with the news that "Ursin'ol" was definitely on the bill for next spring. Then in November the composer heard second hand that the impresario was going to demand a new plot for it because "the Bolsheviks are no longer in fashion." Prokofiev recorded his displeasure thusly, "Maybe a Chinese revolution is now fashionable and dear Sergey Pavlovich is planning on adapting it to my music?" When he first saw Auric's latest ballet *La Pastorale* the previous May Prokofiev had written, "God dammit, every season a new ballet is ordered from Auric." This diatribe probably had less to do with jealousy than with his frustration over the misfortunate production delays and road blocks that befell each of his ballets. The following spring the plot for *Le Pas d'acier*'s opening scene would be changed but not the Soviet theme nor the ballet's décor, which the impresario highly esteemed.

Yakulov's stage design for "Ursin'ol", with its use of a system of kinetic "machines," is not far removed from one he had designed for the mirthful, circus-like *Girofle-Girofla* produced by Tairov's Chamber Theater in Moscow in 1922 and presented in Paris in 1923.[143] Other contemporary constructivist settings included the one used by Goleyzovsky's Moscow Chamber Ballet for *The Faun* (to Debussy's score) in autumn 1922, and Liubov Popova's constructivist set for Meyerhold's *Magnanimous Cuckold* which was staged in Moscow in April 1922. A description of that stage brings up similarities with the one for *Le Pas d'acier*; it was completely denuded of curtain, backdrops, portals and footlights—a wooden installation of the strangest shape, a construction. It was assembled to look like a peculiar windmill and was a combination of platforms, ladders, gangways, revolving doors and revolving wheels … . The wings of the windmill and the two wheels revolved slowly or quickly depending on the intensity of the action and the tempo of the spectacle. The clever young actors and actresses [were] without make-up and in blue workers' overalls.[144]

Yakulov's set for *Le Pas d'acier* featured a high rostrum in the center of the stage with steps leading up to it at either side. As described by the company's regisseur, a number of wheels, levers and pistons were placed on the front and sides of the rostrum. The back cloth was gray, the wooden set unpainted, and the factory workers were dressed (as far as they were) in white and black. The dancers recalled that the actual set was much simpler than planned, yet the stage was so cluttered with the various objects that it allowed only limited lateral movement. As in the Moscow constructivist productions the action was to be performed on the platform and the ladders leading up to it as well as below and in front. During the finale of the second act, the dancers moved with increasing energy in harmony with Prokofiev's propulsive, gradually building music. Wheels were set revolving and levers and pistons moved backwards and forwards, the furnace roared and the lights went on and off in ever changing colors. The curtain fell during a tremendous crescendo from the orchestra. While still décor in the traditional sense, Yakulov's design was constructivist, that is, utilitarian and an essential part of the action.

In the first tableau signal lights on poles placed on either side of the stage suggested a generalized railroad station setting. A train is visible in the center of Yakulov's maquette (reproduced, for example, on p. 154 of Richard Shead's book *Ballets Russes*, New York, 1998), and there is a design sketch showing an abbreviated train and platform with dancers in motion, yet dance historian Lesley-Anne Sayers believes that there was no train depicted in the final set.[145] Although there are no production photographs showing one, a caricature of the train appears in the background of a cartoon in the 20 July 1927 issue of *Punch*, a composite "memory" of the Ballets Russes productions that season. Grigoriev's recollection of the gray backdrop suggests that the train, if it was used, did not remain through the entire first scene. The *Daily Telegraph* critic noted "a factory chimney that rose at the back and a rather crazy street-lamp heightened the impression that the mechanism of industrialization was indicated." During the musical section entitled "Change of décor", a massive drop with industrial-sized machines was lowered from the flies and flywheels replaced the signal lights.

Dance historian Elizabeth Souritz points out that the ballet's eccentric costumes were also a sign of the times: "The sailor had only one boot [his pants had mismatched legs] and wore a cloak that swerved behind his back, the Countesses wore lamp shades on their heads, and the clothing of the mass scenes' participants was characterized by emphatic asymmetry (the sleeves and the pant legs of different lengths and of different colors; one leg was often left bare)."[146] Many of the costumes reflect contemporary fashion as much as contemporary costume design as in Tchernicheva and Lifar's Apache clothes (see Fig. 10). Apparently, as in other Diaghilev productions of the time, chicness was an important consideration, even if it detracted from the ballet's basic concept.

What the dancers did on stage is far less certain. According to the score the first act or tableau contained seven vignettes contrasting elements of the old and new life in Soviet Russia, played out without any connecting narrative and with only occasional correspondences in the music (according to the score the seven musical numbers in the first tableau are "Entrée des personnages," "Train des paysans-ravitailleurs," "Les Commissaires," "Les Petits camelots," "L'Orateur," "Matelot à bracelets et ouvrière," and "Changement de décors"). The various activities at the train station, the street vendors (and flea market), the political orators, and the love interest between a sailor and a factory girl are all distinguished by titled sections in the music. However, episodes that are mentioned in reviews, such as the the former Countesses in ragged dresses trying to trade their clothing for flour with a speculator, are not. Nor are the modernized, symbolic fairy tales, whose inclusion did little but thoroughly confuse western audiences. These fairy tales were not part of Yakulov's and Prokofiev's original scenario, the one Prokofiev composed to, rather their inclusion came from Massine.

Below an introduction, "The two tableaux of this ballet present a series of scenes summarizing the two aspects of life in Russia; the legends of the village and the mechanism of the factory," the program lists the scenes of the first tableau as follows (also see Fig. 11): 1. Battle of Baba Yaga and the Crocodile, 2. The Street Hawker and the Countesses, 3. The Sailor and three Devils, 4. The Tomcat, Female Cat and the Mouse, 5. The Legend of the Drunkards, 6. The Female Worker and the Sailor, 7. Ensemble. Sayers has fleshed out these scenes from the various reviews, adding that in no. 2 there were four countesses trying to exchange clothes with 10 male spectators, in no. 3 the devils (dressed as firemen) pestered the sailor (Massine) until 7 workers came to his rescue, no. 4 was a comic love duet accompanied by a corps of "sarcastic mice," and no. 5 had a drunk carried away by his friends. The second tableau was much simpler, according to the program: 8. Flirtation, 9. Passage of the workers, and 10–12. Factory. After the opening pre-work flirtation between two lovers (Tchernicheva and Lifar), the action was straightforward, intensifying all the way to the close. Yet the program's titles again differ from those in Prokofiev's score ("Le Matelot devient un ouvrier," "L'Usine," "Les Marteaux," and "Finale"), but at least the correspondence is not as enigmatic as before. Prokofiev's music for "Le Matelot devient un ouvrier" could serve coquetry well given its whimsical character. However, the overriding discrepancies between the original scenario, the one in the program and the titles in the published score lead one to believe that two different scenarios exist. This is indeed the case, but the details remain sketchy.

By February 1927 Diaghilev began preparing for the ballet's presentation that spring. He telegrammed Prokofiev, then visiting Russia, to try to locate Yakulov. Rehearsals began in Monte Carlo the first week of April. Prokofiev was brought in to help acquaint Massine, who had returned to the company as guest choreographer and dancer, with the music and planned staging. Yakulov, busy with theatrical productions in Tiflis, would not arrive on the scene until 21 May. At their first meeting on 9 April Prokofiev discovered that Massine had repudiated most of the original scenario. Considering how confused his first tableau became, it is unfortunate that Prokofiev did not put up more of a fight. Instead, he believed that "it was important only to direct Massine and suppress him so that his plan would not conflict with the music." Massine had a copy of Dmitry Rovinsky's *Russkiya narodnïya kartinki* (1900), a book full of old engravings, from which he extracted folk themes such as "Baba-Yaga and the Crocodile"[147] (see Fig. 12) and the other "legends" for the ballet. After lunch Prokofiev played through the score for Diaghilev, Massine and the accompanist, Kopeikin. Massine explained his plans and the impresario and composer critiqued them. Diaghilev was present much of the time but, aside from engaging in discussions such as this one, to Prokofiev's chagrin, he remained rather aloof from the actual formation of the ballet. Perhaps this was a reflection of his confidence in Massine's talent. However, seven years after their breakup the two still had a strained relationship—they refused to dine together, for example. In his private conversations with Prokofiev, Diaghilev seemed far more interested in hearing about the composer's Russian tour and discussing the possibility of making the trip himself.

Massine suggested the title *Le Pas d'acier* on 10 April, after which Prokofiev came up with the somewhat more animated Russian version *Stal'noy skok* (*pas:* step or stride vs. *skok*: gallop or trot). Although he thought it dangerously close to "pas d'argent" Prokofiev readily accepted Massine's title. However, Diaghilev did not; it made him think of "Puce d'acier" as in Leskov's well-known story, "The Tale of Cross-eyed Lefty from Tula and the Steel Flea." The impresario suggested calling the ballet "Dragonfly and the Ant," but perhaps with tongue in cheek. This was also the time when Diaghilev forfeited his three-year production rights in exchange for a "new number" from Prokofiev to give more time for the change of scenes. This "new number" was the overture from *Trapèze* (a work scored for a mixed quintet). As a result of this bargaining Prokofiev was able to begin negotiations for a performance of his new ballet in Russia effective 1 January 1928. On 11 April Prokofiev departed Monte Carlo for Paris where his first task was to orchestrate the new number for the ballet. He wrote to Asafyev on 15 April expressing his hope that the Mariinsky or the Moscow Bolshoy Theater would now present an entire evening of his ballets: the *Scythian Suite* and *Chout* in new productions, and *Le Pas d'acier* borrowing Diaghilev's production. He had already broached the subject with the director of the state academic theaters of Moscow and Leningrad, Ivan Ekskusovich, when he was in Russia earlier that year.

On the back of the Société des Auteurs and Compositeurs Dramatiques "Bulletin de Déclaration" form for the ballet dated 27 December 1927 Prokofiev wrote a "Rémarque" with several strikeouts, stating that the ballet existed in two versions:

> les auteurs du livret de la premiere version sont M. M. Iac [Yakulov] et Prok [Prokofiev] ~~(et c'est ainsi que le clavier du ballet est publié)~~ cette version fut déclarée par MM Iac et Prok. en Juin 1927.
>   Les auteurs du livret de la seconde version sont M.M. Iac, Mass [Massine] et Prok. Le present bulletin n'est fait que pour déclarer cette seconde version ...

On the front of the form under "auteur" is written "pour livret: G. Iacoulov, L. Massine, S. Prokofieff," and below this, "pour choréographie: Massine." Given Yakulov's late arrival, it was Massine who was chiefly responsible for the revision of the first act, with perhaps some inspiration from Prokofiev's report about his recent visit. This is supported by the composer's correspondence: in two letters to Massine concerning the distribution of royalties the composer states that Yakulov was not satisfied with the changes. In a letter from Paris dated 2 July 1927 Prokofiev wrote to inform Massine in London that after his departure from Paris his "scheme" (or draft) [*proekti*] "was subjected to energetic criticism by Yakulov." Then in a letter dated 1 November 1927 Prokofiev again informed Massine that Yakulov was not satisfied with his changes. Oberzaucher-Schüller suggests that Diaghilev asked Massine to rework the first part of the ballet "soon after the Paris premier" in order that the "contrast between the life in the country and in the factory would be sharper."[148] Given the Paris performance dates—three days in a row (7–9 June) with the last performance on 11 June—and the performances of other ballets each day, a fix during the premier Paris run is highly unlikely. However, it is possible that changes were introduced before the London premier (the first performance there was on 6 July). What this change may have entailed is unknown. The bottom line is, there is still much to learn about the production of this ballet.

Diaghilev had turned to Massine because he was unable to engage a Soviet choreographer. He made no attempt to hide the fact that Massine knew next to nothing about life in Soviet Russia having left there in 1914. He told the *Observer* that "his presentation of Russia today is his own imagination."[149] This smacks of finger pointing: the Parisian audiences could not follow the action of the first act, and Londoners were sure to be as confused. In his autobiography Massine tossed the hot potato to Prokofiev, claiming that "with his intimate knowledge of the Russian people" the composer had helped him create the contrasting scenes, the first set in the countryside, the second demonstrating the "force and vitality of Communist youth."[150] Prokofiev's impressions of Soviet Russia during his winter 1927 visit were not all that favorable, however. In fact, the composer feared that some of his frank observations might get him into trouble if his Diary were to be confiscated or scrutinized by customs officials upon his departure. Diaghilev also claimed in this same interview that the ballet was really a depiction of Russia in 1920, "today, of course, it is out of date." Such excuse-making is uncharacteristic; it recalls his similar efforts on behalf of *Chout* in 1921 with the same newspaper. In the end Massine did as best he could given the circumstances; at least one Russian felt that he truly captured the new dynamic spirit of Soviet Russia.[151] This was Massine's first experience with "machine dances," but his natural inclination towards restless, fidgety choreography would seem to have given him an edge. In addition to his work on Prokofiev's ballet for the upcoming season he was also assigned to devise new choreography (replacing Nijinska's) for Auric's *Les Fâcheux* and to revive his role as the Miller in Falla's *Tricorne* as well. In early May the company departed for performances in Marseille and Barcelona prior to the Paris season. Composition of the *Le Pas d'acier* choreography continued throughout this period as time permitted. The Paris season opened on 27 May, and *Le Pas d'acier* was premiered, ready or not, 11 days later.

At the end of 1922 a Moscow group led by amateur choreographer Nikolay Foregger presented machine dances—using rhythmic acrobatic movements to imitate the different parts of working machines: transmissions, levers, wheels and pistons.[152] Though Massine had not seen any of these Soviet experiments, he surely must have seen their Italian predecessors as any number of futurist experiments in mechanized movement were demonstrated to the inquisitive impresario during the war years. One example may have been Giacomo Balla's *Macchina Tipografica* in which dancers moving like pistons or a drive shaft "drive" another dancer mimicking a wheel.[153] In the same vein, Massine fulfilled Yakulov's concept by having dancers operating machines as well as imitating them. By all accounts Massine succeeded in this aspect of the choreography; a typical review pointed out the "new postures and steps, strange contortions and movements that give the impression of powerful, complicated machinery, pistons working, wheels turning, and intense labor."[154] Massine's choreography for the first act is less well known, but apparently it consisted of a contemporary dance vocabulary including gymnastics, for example, somersaults for the vendors. He surely overstepped futuristic tenets if not official Soviet ethics in his melodramatic interpretation of the sailor-turned-worker. He recalled, "In my own role as the Young Worker I used strenuous character movements to suggest the Slav temperament and the conflict in the mind of a young man torn between his personal life and his national loyalty."[155] Whereas Yakulov's inclusion of a comic element in the original scenario was in keeping with Soviet precedents, this bigger-than-life Russian emoting, not to mention the use of chic costumes mentioned above, reduced the ballet's conceptual unity. Ultimately, it was not Massine who undermined *Le Pas d'acier*'s success; rather its faults—a weak, incomprehensible narrative and the lack of a sympathetic, that is, Soviet, choreographer—are attributable to none other than the grand overseer himself.

Once again, a Prokofiev ballet for Diaghilev would receive a compromised production.

While at a rehearsal for an orchestral concert in Magdeburg on 7 May Prokofiev discovered that a ballet set to his *Scythian Suite*, choreographed by Max Terpis, was to premier at the Berlin Staatsoper that very evening, conducted by George Szell. He boarded an express train which took him there in two hours and attended the premier incognito—he was not expected. He recorded in his Diary, "Terpis chose two scenes from Dante with demonic forces, suffering souls and an angel, their savior." The music must have well-served the scenario's contrast of "Powers of Light" with those of "Darkness." Prokofiev recorded that "It was not good and not bad, but still less bad than I expected. To unite Dante and the Scythians is in rather doubtful taste." Nevertheless, Prokofiev was probably gratified to witness this first choreographic response to his erstwhile ballet, especially since he had decided to decline Terpis's request for a new score back in June 1925.

On 25 May the Ballets Russes arrived from Barcelona and preparations for the Paris season were soon in full gear. At first the dancers were cautious when they saw Yakulov's enormous set with its many platforms, but they soon took it all in stride, along with the factory-machine movements they were required to master. The season opened two days later with the Parisian premier of *La Chatte*. *L'Oiseau de feu* was once again on the bill, but now with Goncharova's new décor, premiered the previous November in London. On the next evening Paris heard Prokofiev's Overture for 17 Performers for the first time at a Koussevitzky concert. The success was great and the conductor pressed Prokofiev to rescore the piece for a normal sized orchestra. On 30 May Prokofiev played though the ballet score for the conductor Desormière. He had declined Diaghilev's invitation to conduct the premier claiming he was out of practice, not having conducted in years. His recommendation for the job had been the Mariinsky Theater's chief conductor Vladimir Dranishnikov (who had conducted *Oranges* there in 1926), but Desormière got the nod because the former was busy conducting a production of *Wozzeck*, and Ansermet was not available. The evening of 30 May saw the premier of Stravinsky's *Oedipus Rex*, the composer's twentieth anniversary season gift to Diaghilev. "Un cadeaux très macabre," the underwhelmed Diaghilev is reported to have remarked. Prokofiev found it "boring," and not that well sung. He reported that the success was "restrained," and called the post-concert gathering for the inner circle at the Cafe de la Paix, "not especially lively."

As opening night drew closer, rehearsals for the new ballet became rather tense: by 3 June the conductor, choreographer and Diaghilev were yelling at each other, and Massine was showing signs of nervousness because it had not yet come together. Prokofiev was not in complete agreement with the staging; he believed that Massine had deviated from the original plot in vain: "In places it was expressive and strong, in other places it was unpleasant and there was a lack of respect for the music." For his part Diaghilev was extremely pleased with Yakulov's decorations and never ceased praising him. The day before the premier the impresario worked on preparations for the ballet until 3 a.m. (Yakulov stayed at it until 7 a.m.) and came back for more at 8:30 a.m.. The last orchestra rehearsal was held at 1:30 p.m., and the dress rehearsal at 3 p.m. Observing all this hubbub Prokofiev remarked how happy he was that he was not conducting.

Le Pas d'acier premiered the evening of 7 June 1927, at the Théâtre Sarah-Bernhardt. The program that night was truly cosmopolitan: it opened with Auric's and Massine's Les Fâcheux, and concluded with Lord Berners' and Balanchine's The Triumph of Neptune, with Le Pas d'acier in between. In London the ballet debuted on 4 July alongside La Chatte, Les Matelots and dances from Prince Igor in the cramped confines of Prince's Theatre. The orchestra required for Le Pas d'acier is the same as the one for Chout less the two harps, yet the cramped pit required that some brass players be seated in the audience. Eugene Goossens conducted until falling ill mid-run; Malcolm Sargent came to the rescue until Desormière could be summoned. In London Prokofiev's ballet was heard in conjunction with a Stravinsky festival which featured Petrouchka, Pulcinella, L'Oiseau de feu and Le Sacre du printemps. As in 1921 Diaghilev compared his two "sons" in the press and in one interview called Stravinsky "much more tied to the gods," and Prokofiev, "friendly with the devil."[156] Neither was in town at the time, Prokofiev was off on his summer holiday and Stravinsky was still in Paris.

In both Paris and London Le Pas d'acier was by and large a success, audiences applauded with enthusiasm. Violent political demonstrations did not erupt on opening night in Paris as Diaghilev feared, but there was plenty of noise, "deafening cheers and piercing catcalls."[157] Just as Diaghilev anticipated, Bolshevik exoticism filled the company's coffers. The Communist Director of Culture, Anatoly Lunacharsky, was there and boasted that "Yakulov, the most Soviet of all the participants involved ... was called out by the audience eight times." On opening night in London Diaghilev armed himself with a revolver and sat in the pit next to the first flute ready to fire into the air if there was a disturbance. He was probably chagrined that there was none. In addition to the predictable responses from pro-Whites and pro-Reds, the reviews focused on the lack of clarity and purpose in the opening tableau while praising the ballet's powerful finale. Prokofiev was extremely surprised by the success of his ballet in London. He had pleaded with Diaghilev not to take it there, for one, because he felt his music "was not liked in London," and two, because he feared a protest against the plot. He recorded in his Diary on 9 July, "Good news: Stal'noy skok took place in London ... with great 'noisy' success. The curtain was raised twelve times. All the newspapers verify success, although many of them also curse, calling it a 'noisy stupidity.'" Those exact words have yet to be found ("stupendous crescendo," yes), but there was a great deal of coverage.

One London critic called the stage action of the first tableau "chaotic" due to the maze of "incidental distractions."[158] Another was "puzzled" by it, while a third "gave up trying to find a meaning."[159] Some commentators mirthfully exaggerated their bewilderment in trying to sort the action out. This tongue-in-cheek account is typical:

> The first part professed to 'summarize the stories and legends of the countryside,' … What the stories and legends may have been no one could guess from either the clothes or the action, and the programme explained nothing. Among the first things we saw were a number of young men in long green coats and helmets, who hopped up and down the different platforms, alternately pursuing and being pursued by an equal number of young men in khaki. Cossacks, possible, and the Red Army; but what Cossacks ever tottered and shook as these did? And if the others were the Red Army why were they always being laid flat? Perhaps these last were the White Army, and the others not Cossacks at all, but merely legends … Danilova [a dancer], in a tartan skirt was thrown about by Massine, while a dozen proletarian ladies romped solemnly with the soldiers in the background. Possibly it was meant to demonstrate the abounding vitality of young Communists at play, but there was as little mirth in their frolic as there is said to be among the crowds in Soviet Moscow.[160]

Another critic described "a crowd of Bolshevik peasants, soldiers, policemen, seamen and working men moving unceasingly on the stage, on the wooden staircase and on the wooden platform which are all part of the scenery. They move in all directions, run up the staircase and down, pursue one another, run away, come back and so on … ." He summarized it all thusly, "The only synthesis that we can draw from the first act is that life in present-day Russia is an uninterrupted and aimless movement."[161]

The *danse d'école* lobby voiced their usual concern about the company's exploitation of vaudeville antics and circus tricks. The critic in the conservative Russian émigré newspaper, *Vozrozhdenie*, reported in seeming disbelief:

> In one of the first scenes of the second act of the ballet Diaghilev allowed … an amazing sortie: dancers coupled in pairs, grabbing the legs of their partners with their hands and depicting a living and mobile hoop, rolling out from behind the scenes on their backs by the strength of their own coordinated efforts. This device is unknown to me in the ballet tradition … but is absolutely essential for every type of clown. Such a living machine in the circus rolls out the solo, with Diaghilev the whole troop is unexpectedly and instantly cleared from the stage with this gimmick.[162]

La Revue musicale went straight to the point and called the choreography "detestable," going on to say:

> One feels quite strongly that the choreographer did not know how to fill the tableau at a railroad station, there are placed no matter what: a sorceress battling a crocodile … a vendor selling food to a countess in rags, workers raping a young girl, need I say more? As for the rest, without a livret, it is impossible to divine the significance of these diverse scenes of pantomime and dance.[163]

The critic concluded by hoping Massine would take the trouble to revise the choreography to the first part for the next season. There is no indication that he did, nor is there any clear evidence that Paris and London saw different first acts in 1927 despite some disparity between each venue's reviews.

The visceral excitement generated by the finale, however, was akin to that from the "Polovtsian Dances" from *Prince Igor* and *Schéhérazade* which had bowled over early Ballets Russes' audiences. One British reviewer recorded that the audience was "stunned by the mere accumulation of heavy sounds" with the "revolving lights, green, red, and white, flashing down on the triple tier of shining half-naked bodies, as the young workmen answered with the swing of their hammers the thunderous rhythms of the orchestra"[164] (see Fig. 13). He went on to lament, "If only the first half of the ballet had been as clear and purposeful as the last, what a wonderful invention the whole would have been!" Nevertheless, most reviews conceded the ballet's entertainment value and made note of the rapturous applause at the end; the *Daily Express* reported: "Many will dislike it, it will be overpraised, but no one will be bored by it, and, judging by the tempestuous reception it received last night, it will become a regular feature of the Russian Ballet programme."[165] There were a few, however, who saw this glorification of constructivism and futurism with foreboding:

> There is a stupendous *crescendo*, in the midst of which the curtain drops, leaving you with an uncomfortable feeling that these poor wretches must continue their various tasks to the crack of doom, because if they stopped some terrible catastrophe would happen. What the film 'Metropolis'' entirely failed to convey ... is shown here relentlessly, inexorably, in (of all art forms) a ballet.[166]

This critic concluded nevertheless, "Except for 'Les Noces' it is the strongest thing Diaghilev has produced since his prewar period. Strange to say, the effect is so dynamic that one is scarcely conscious of the music as such, but apprehends it only as a factor in a very exciting production."

This may account for the relatively little reported about the music. Yet this is somewhat surprising, especially in Paris, in that Prokofiev had clearly ended his dry spell with regards to success (London critical commentary was generally more focused on the dancers than the music, décor or choreography). A few did detect a change for the better, for example one French critic who had attacked the Second Symphony now praised the new ballet.[167] But most ink was spilled on nonmusical issues. In some cases opinions were withheld due to a lack of understanding about the ballet, for example, *The Times* critic's "since we could not make out what it [the first tableau's narrative] was driving at we are unable to judge [the music]."[168] In others the composer's music was evaluated through comparison, for example, the *Daily Telegraph*'s "Prokofiev had succeeded far better than Massine."[169] Most reviewers remarked about the relentless rhythm and power in the finale, although some (including Stravinsky) thought it all a bit excessive. Prokofiev recalled that Stravinsky was disgusted by the hammering on the stage floor, which mimicked the pounding rhythm in the orchestra.[170] *The Times* acknowledged that "Prokofiev gets from his orchestra an extremely vivid impression of the hum and roar of machines."[171] The *Daily Telegraph* noted that Prokofiev already had a "hard and steely style," but added that *Le Pas d'acier* was not "cacophonous."[172] There was some mild censure such as the *Observer*'s concluding shot "in Prokofiev there is none of the subtlety of Stravinsky."[173] This apparent divide and conquer tactic not only ignored the fact that the latter was never called upon to write a musical representation of a factory, but it also underestimates Prokofiev's carefully judged "factory music" as well (see Chapter 4).

Diaghilev forewarned the London audience in a newspaper interview that Prokofiev's music had become "very much simpler ... . He does not invent false notes merely for the purpose of inventing them. He is full of melodies, and one part of 'Le Pas d'acier' might have been composed by Mozart, if Mozart had lived at the present day [the latter being a favorite ploy of his]."[174] The unaffected, simple "train music" (no. 2), and the tender love theme for the sailor and the working girl (no. 6) do indeed demonstrate Prokofiev's renewed emphasis on diatonicism and lyricism. But with the throbbing music of the finale and the loud, grinding dissonances from the "Change of scenes" (no. 7) reverberating in their ears, it is not surprising that the critics failed to mention any examples of the composer's "new simplicity" in *Le Pas d'acier*. *La Revue musicale* did detect a "serious change in style," but not the composer's self-proclaimed redirection. Instead the critic called attention to Prokofiev's turn away from the "charming and gushing" melodies of *Chout* back to the impetuous rhythmic drive of the *Scythian Suite*.[175] The contemporary French and workaday Russian musical idioms, and, of course, the futurist machine music obviously effected the overriding impression.

Revived for a single performance in a brief gala series at the Paris Opéra that December, in Paris and London in 1928 and in Paris again in 1929, *Le Pas d'acier* fared slightly better than *Chout* performance-wise: some 26 times to *Chout*'s 20.[176] The ballet remained very popular: it opened the company's 1928 Paris season and reportedly received a 12-minute ovation from the audience. Even though it had been requested by theater managers and concert promoters Diaghilev had decided not to take *Le Pas d'acier* on the company's fall 1927 tour through Germany, Czechoslovakia, Austria and Hungary due to the difficulty of transporting the set. When he heard this Prokofiev lamented, "I am unlucky: I eternally have unwieldy stagings." Koussevitzky presented six excerpts from the ballet in a concert performance with the Boston Symphony on 21 October 1927.[177] Prokofiev fashioned a four-movement Suite in 1927 which was premiered in Moscow on 27 May 1928 at a concert sponsored by the Association of Contemporary Music. Paris heard the Suite for the first time under Desormière on 26 November 1931. The Massine choreography lived and died with the

Ballets Russes; the Stokowski-led American premier of the ballet in April 1931 at the New York Metropolitan Opera House used new choreography and designs.[178] Plans for a Moscow production to be staged by Meyerhold fell apart due to political reasons (see Chapter 4). Prokofiev had not yet written a classic ballet score, but his technique was polished and waiting for, if not a worthier story, at least a less topical one.[179]

The June 1928 Paris season of the Ballets Russes featured the first European performance of Stravinsky's *Apollon musagète*, a work commissioned by the Elizabeth Sprague Coolidge Foundation and premiered on 28 April 1928 at the Library of Congress in Washington, DC, with choreography by Adolph Bolm. Stravinsky had reserved the European performing rights for Diaghilev, who called on Balanchine to be his choreographer. On 12 June Prokofiev dined with the Koussevitzkys then accompanied them to the Théâtre Sarah-Bernhardt for the ballet's debut. Prokofiev thought the music was "absolutely pitiful ... [using] stolen material ..." and was "horribly boring."[180] In his Diary he claimed that his "rival's" ballet "annoyed him": "Stravinsky is becoming sterile. He does not exit from the stage, but only the curtain rises and lowers." For his part Stravinsky formed an equally negative opinion of Prokofiev's *The Fiery Angel*, excerpts of which were finally premiered at a Koussevitzky concert two days later. That night the audience recalled Prokofiev three times and he himself considered the performance a huge success (his friend Nina Koshetz sang the role of Renata). Yet he philosophized in his Diary about the two premiers. *Apollon* and *Fiery Angel* had summoned sharp, predictable party-line responses from the musical world, he realized, but "*Apollon* is the latest word of Stravinsky [and] *Fiery Angel* is an old thing (by design) ... from which I have moved away." Prokofiev would not have long to wait, however, before he had an opportunity to use his "new simplicity" in the creation of his own timeless, serious-toned ballet. By August, Stravinsky had committed *the* unpardonable sin in Diaghilev's eyes, he had accepted a ballet commission from the competition, Ida Rubinstein. *Le Baiser de la fée* (based on the music of Chaikovsky), premiered at the Paris Opéra on 27 November 1928, and resulted in Diaghilev's extreme and enduring animosity towards his first son. Prokofiev became the impresario's favorite: he received a commission for *L'Enfant prodigue* in October and in early January the idea of a Prokofiev "triple bill" was broached for the upcoming season with a revival of *Chout* sporting a new scenario and choreography adjusted to the music of the Suite; Larionov would design new costumes and décor. Not one Stravinsky ballet was to be presented.

According to Kochno, Diaghilev had asked Prokofiev for another ballet immediately after the 1927 production of *Le Pas d'acier*, though he did not have a specific theme to suggest. "He wanted the new work to be simple and easy to follow, unlike Prokofiev's earlier ballets, and not require a cumbersome set. He was looking for a timeless theme, some poetic episode that would be universally familiar."[181] Prokofiev never recorded such an offer, however. As Kochno's story goes, "Prokofiev grew impatient waiting for the scenario... He was on the point of giving up the commission when I had the idea of a theatrical version of the parable of the prodigal son"[182] from the gospel of St Luke (15:11–32). According to one account, some scenic inspiration, including the prodigal's return, came from Pushkin's story, "The Stationmaster," which contains descriptions of biblical story engravings that decorate the walls of a little postal station somewhere in the middle of Russia.[183] Just how much of all this is pure fiction may never be known. Prokofiev clearly despised Kochno and Kochno may have felt the same way about Prokofiev. Therefore, the radical difference in their accounts of this ballet's genesis should not be that surprising, nor should the fact that the ballet and its music ended up sporting two different titles (Kochno's *Le Fils prodigue* and Prokofiev's *L'Enfant prodigue*).

Distracted by negotiations for two upcoming performing tours in Russia and claiming overwork, Prokofiev tried to evade a commission from the impresario. In a letter dated 21 September 1928, he enumerated the projects that were keeping him busy, and claimed that the time remaining to write a new ballet was insufficient ("two to two and one-half months"); he suggested either setting a ballet to his latest piano pieces, *Choses en soi*, or reviving *Chout*. Prokofiev met with Diaghilev on 22 October to discuss these options as well as the impresario's plan to present a new ballet by a Soviet composer. Prokofiev's friend, Boris Asafyev, who had arrived from Russia for a visit on 8 September, joined these talks. Based on hearing Dmitry Shostakovich's First Piano Sonata and Gavriil Popov's "Vocalise" for high voice and piano in A minor[184] (both played by Prokofiev), the impresario decided to commission Popov. Asafyev was instructed to arrange for him to visit Paris for a month and was provided money for a "third class ticket." As for Prokofiev's ballet, the composer played Diaghilev his two-part *Choses en soi* but he found the music "dry." At their next meeting, Diaghilev and Kochno set forth the plot of the ballet he was to write, "the story of the prodigal son transferred to Russian soil." Prokofiev recorded in his Diary that they "laid it out very convincingly. Asafyev was happy, discovering that Diaghilev had guessed just what I now needed. I liked it. And although I have never wanted to work with Kochno, it seems I will take their plot (Diaghilev put the adaptation into Kochno's mouth, although I am convinced that three-quarters of it is Diaghilev's)."

Prokofiev saw Asafyev off on 29 October, and on 2 November, with the completion of the Scherzo of his Third Symphony, he felt he had "untied" his hands and could now work on the new ballet. That evening he met with Diaghilev at the Grand Hôtel to settle the fee. Once again there was a financial disagreement: Prokofiev asked for 25 000 francs (thinking he could easily get 75 000 from Rubinstein), but Diaghilev "with a sick voice" refused. They parted and Prokofiev worked on other projects. On 6 November Diaghilev offered 20 000, claiming that he "pays Hindemith even less." Prokofiev was dissatisfied and again they took leave without settling the issue. Two days later Prokofiev decided it was pointless to argue over 5000 francs and went to Diaghilev to announce his decision. But the good mood quickly spoiled when the composer told Kochno that he would receive only a one-fifth honorarium from the Society of Composers instead of the usual one third. "Then you will need to find another plot," Kochno retorted. "Well of course," Prokofiev replied. Then Diaghilev asked despondently, "Where? We leave for England the day after tomorrow." Prokofiev believed that since he had made a concession he was justified in standing firm, but short-changing Kochno would set a precedent Diaghilev could not allow. He departed in an angry mood. The next day, believing that the ballet had gone "belly up," he began thinking about two new projects: two more numbers for *Choses en soi* and a four-movement orchestral suite for which he already had two numbers (this would become *Divertissement*, op. 43). A telephone call from Diaghilev interrupted his thoughts; he was now offered an additional 2000 francs, the amount that was in dispute with Kochno. That evening Prokofiev signed the contract and on the morning of 10 November he began composing *L'Enfant prodigue*.

Diaghilev admonished him to write the ballet in a simpler style than that of *Choses en soi*, to which he readily agreed.[185] Composition went quickly and easily. Prokofiev turned to his notebook selecting sketches he had composed in the spring and summer, and also chose several much earlier ones that he considered appropriate (for example, the theme for the second number came from 1925). For the servants' number he planned to recycle "Matelote" which he had composed for Romanov's *Trapèze*. After only one week the composer realized with pleasure that he had already "leapt over half of it," and at this rate he would finish in two weeks. He was trying to complete the short score quickly since he still held hope for a Russian tour starting at the beginning of the year. On 22 November he received in the mail a more detailed libretto from Kochno who was in London with Diaghilev. Prokofiev gleefully noted in his Diary that the ballet was already written in outline: "Excellent. Since the music is written before the arrival of the libretto, then I am not tied to it, especially in the future. Kochno thought up several details, some are stupid."

On 23 November Prokofiev called on Diaghilev at the Grand Hôtel. He had just returned to Paris to attend the opening of Ida Rubinstein's ballet season at the Paris Opéra. When the composer told him that his ballet was almost finished Diaghilev was taken aback, saying "What, already! Then it turned out rather poorly?" This reaction is understandable since not that long ago Prokofiev had claimed that two to two and one-half months was not sufficient time to write a new ballet. At 5 p.m. the impresario stopped by Prokofiev's apartment to hear the ballet. Diaghilev very much liked the first and second numbers, the robbery and awakening and the material for the return, but rather less the seductress's music and her dance with the prodigal son.[186] The Romanov material he recommended tossing out. Diaghilev remarked on the great contrast of musical styles in the ballet, "Now you have so much softness, and then you hammer in nails." The two discussed the finale which had not yet been composed, Prokofiev suggesting he use the theme from his second *Choses en soi*, Diaghilev countering, "it needs to be simpler, more tender and softer." That night the composer went to bed thinking that the closing music should sound as if from "on high" to properly illustrate the gospel theme. At 1 a.m. came epiphany—Prokofiev got up and jotted down two bars of music. Later that morning he worked this idea into the concluding theme of the ballet and felt "on top of the world."

At dinner with Diaghilev and Meyerhold on 26 November Prokofiev made a great show of returning to Kochno his expanded libretto for the ballet, explaining that it had arrived "after the composition of the music," and "therefore it might be more useful to you." The composer did not record Diaghilev's reaction, but he probably flinched. Two weeks earlier when the contract was finally settled Diaghilev had had to lecture his two feuding "children" to be nice to each other for the sake of the ballet. More friction lay ahead which would lead to Prokofiev's and Diaghilev's discord in May and culminate in Kochno's legal action against the composer in June.

On 1 December Diaghilev arrived at Prokofiev's rue Obligado apartment to hear the ballet, this time with Kochno in tow. When Prokofiev reached the third number which introduces the seductress, there was a clash. Contrary to the composer's conception, Diaghilev wanted this character to be presented in a sensual manner and proceeded to describe her, according to Prokofiev, "in his customary manner using a whole string of graphic and indecent expressions." The composer objected, stating that he strove to make the music aquarelle-like, withholding the fact that he was loath to write sensual music. In his Diary Prokofiev recorded that Diaghilev became angry, "What kind of prodigal son is this? All the strength lies in the fact that he became a lecher, repented and his father forgave him. If he had left home and simply become a thief then when he returned he would have not have been received with open arms but would have been beaten." The discussion was suspended for the time being. (Three days later when he ran into Diaghilev after a performance of *Baiser de la fée* Prokofiev announced that he would give the impresario "another woman.") Diaghilev was greatly pleased with the remainder of the ballet that evening, suggesting only that the very end be played even slower to allow the melodies to sing out all the more. Departing he paused in the stairway and announced that he was dreaming of a spring season without any Stravinsky ballets. Prokofiev recorded in his Diary, "Unbelievable! Until now Stravinsky was a deity for Diaghilev and he obviously gave him preference over me. Is this another symptom of the fall of the deity?" Diaghilev's business acumen was apparently stronger than his grudge, however, since he presented four of Stravinsky's ballets in the brief, year-end season at the Paris Opéra. And in lieu of reviving *Chout* he would present a newly choreographed *Renard* in the spring.[187]

By mid-December Prokofiev's planned Russian tour was indefinitely postponed and the pace of composition normalized. He had begun orchestrating the ballet on 7 December, and played the "new woman" and the rest of the ballet for Diaghilev, Kochno and Lifar on 30 December. Ideas for the new fourth number (replacing the borrowed "Matelote") were discussed then as well. Although still incomplete—aside from the fourth, the fifth and sixth numbers existed in outline form only—Diaghilev told Prokofiev that this ballet was one of his best achievements. Balanchine first heard the ballet in the company of Lifar and Kochno on 4 January. The composer's observation: "the comments from Balanchivadze do not attest that he understands the ballet" is telling. By mid-January Prokofiev was at work on the new fourth number, which he perceived as "somewhat Mozart-like" in a "condensed sonata allegro form". Working with a form so atypical of the ballet probably prompted the idea of creating a symphony from the ballet's material (it would be his Fourth).

Prokofiev suffered a bout of composer's block while working on the development section in the fourth number, necessitating his setting the ballet aside for a time. A few weeks later, on 6 February, Diaghilev arrived to hear the newly completed middle numbers. Prokofiev was afraid he would find the new pas de deux insufficiently passionate—but he worried for naught. Diaghilev was pleased, only requesting that it be played slower and therefore needed to be cut slightly. Disagreement arose over what to do on stage during the music for the new fourth number, its secondary theme evoked a female image and there was no desire to introduce another woman at this point (this number lies between the Seductress's entrance and her pas de deux with the Prodigal). Days later Prokofiev drew a schematic of the musical themes ("General education aid") for Diaghilev's benefit but it was quickly stuffed into his pocket and not used. Hearing the fourth number again on 17 February Diaghilev said that with its fast tempo and accents it was really fight music, unsuitable for dancing. He wanted instead a "glittering" piece to show off his "two best dancers," Leon Woizikovsky and Anton Dolin. Prokofiev was convinced that this rejection resulted from Kochno's lack of ideas. Diaghilev advised the composer to "think about it" and in about two weeks "a new number would compose itself." Indeed, on 7 March a new theme was thought up and two days later the final number for the ballet was completed. Diaghilev approved it on 10 March stipulating only one cut. The unused music found its way into Symphony no. 4, which the composer was already working on. The last of the ballet was orchestrated and the piano reduction completed on 14 March. Two days later the composer handed the piano reduction over and received a check for 5000 francs. Diaghilev asked him to sign the score, but instead Prokofiev took the opportunity to dedicate it to Sergey Pavlovich. The impresario was flattered ("rather more so than at the dedications of the earlier ballets" the composer noted) and told him that this was especially dear to him "since L'Enfant prodigue was his favorite" of all Prokofiev's music. He kissed the composer and they parted until rehearsal time in Monte Carlo.

An incident occurred during this period that clearly indicates Prokofiev's changing position regarding his homeland. In the past he had recorded occasional anti-Bolshevik sentiments in his Diary. On 20 February having gone to the Soviet Embassy in Paris to look over their collection of scores by Russian composers he was cornered by an official named Arens who asked him to play at a reception to be held there on 5 March. This invitation caused him much angst and many sleepless nights. As in other times of crisis since 1924 Prokofiev found solace in readings from the Christian Science faith. On the one hand, his Soviet passport had expired and he definitely wanted to return to Russia for future concert engagements but, on the other, he did not want to offend his émigré supporters in Paris. "What if an émigré newspaper abuses me?" he wondered. That evening he wrote in his Dairy "It is necessary, apparently, to choose either Russia or emigration. It is clear, that of the two I choose Russia." He did perform at the recital along with other artists, and the right wing Russian newspaper *Vozrozhdenie* attacked him as he had feared, calling him a "rubber doll." Consolation came from a report by soprano Kubatskaya that Stalin was present at one of his Moscow concerts the previous year and at some point had referred to him as "our Prokofiev." This news provoked a telltale response: "Excellent: I can go to Russia without worries!"

Diaghilev had hoped to engage Matisse for the décor but he eventually declined. Prokofiev knew that he would be difficult to engage, "you can't call on him: he is now the most expensive artist, he paints pictures and puts them in the bank." In early March Diaghilev turned to Georges Rouault whom Prokofiev did not know. Forewarned by the impresario that Rouault was not particularly musical, Prokofiev played through the ballet for him on 10 March. He thought that Rouault had fallen asleep during the closing pages what with his closed eyes and heavy breathing, but at the conclusion the artist spoke about a pink minaret which had come into his mind. Rouault and his daughter accompanied Prokofiev and his wife to Monte Carlo by automobile a short time later. The story goes that he turned out the necessary sketches in one night.[188] With his participation the tone of the production became darker. Apprenticed to a stained-glass maker in his youth, Rouault was noted for his powerful, icon-like portraits, often of Christ, with heavy black outlines that depicted sorrow or suffering. Prokofiev, hoping for a realistic staging with décor of quiet dignity, was very pleased with Rouault's designs and called them "excellent."[189]

Prokofiev planned to spend only three days in Monte Carlo but Linette enjoyed herself so much that they remained a week. There was little for him to do as yet except to work with the rehearsal pianist adjusting tempos. Balanchine was busy choreographing *Le Bal* to Rieti's music; not until the last moment would he hurriedly complete the choreography for *L'Enfant prodigue*, spending no more than a "fortnight" on it. Prokofiev occupied himself with the Fourth Symphony. The Prokofievs returned to Paris on 7 April. There one week later they joined Diaghilev in his loge at a performance of *Prince Igor*. The impresario was in excellent spirits that night with the young Igor Markevitch on his arm.

"Apparently this is an escapade while Lifar is in Monte Carlo," Prokofiev wrote in his Diary, "Markevitch is about 16 and looks like a mouse [he was indeed 16]."[190] In the weeks ahead this "escapade" would, in Prokofiev's opinion, have a detrimental effect on the production of his ballet; shortly after its premier he would record in his Diary "the captain was not onboard ship when he was needed." On 15 April he and Diaghilev began jousting over the honorarium should he elect to conduct the premier. For the time being the fee was jokingly settled at one bottle of champagne.

On 23 April Prokofiev departed for Brussels where the premier of his opera *Gambler* would occur six days later. Diaghilev came to hear it accompanied by Markevitch. "Is this a wedding trip?" Prokofiev mused. Afterwards he couldn't resist asking "Why did you bring Markevitch? To show how one should or one should not write music?" Diaghilev smiled and replied, "Well you see that question is too delicate, allow me not to answer it." Three days later back in Paris they agreed on a 3000 franc honorarium for Prokofiev to conduct the premier of *L'Enfant prodigue*. At that meeting Diaghilev praised parts of the opera, adding "it's not similar to anything else as Markevitch says." Realizing that "the master" was now taking musical advice from the 16-year-old, Prokofiev asked for his opinion. Diaghilev reported that "in the beginning he winced but at the end said 'c'est formidable.'" His Diary entry ends, "that lousy kid knit his brow."

By early May the pace of preparations increased for the next two Prokofiev premiers: Symphony no. 3 to be led by Monteux and the Orchestre symphonique de Paris on 16 May and the ballet to be presented at the Théâtre Sarah-Bernhardt five days later. On 6 May Prokofiev went through the score with Desormière who would would start the orchestral rehearsals four days hence and conduct the remainder of the run after the opening night. When he first heard the ballet played at that rehearsal Prokofiev was very pleased, "it all sounds simple and sure: no corrections [are needed]." Diaghilev had entered the hall and hearing Desormière's deliberately slow tempi joked, "what a ballet—all adagio and melancholy." He also demonstrated his continuing "teeth" for Stravinsky and his defection with *Baiser de la fée*, saying "Look how the cellos sing, and the violins! What would Igor say?" One month earlier he had indirectly derided Stravinsky's latest style by making fun of his critique of *L'Enfant prodigue* (Prokofiev had reluctantly played it for him on 14 March). As relayed by Diaghilev, Stravinsky reported "Prokofiev does not feel modernity: he has baroque melodies in the way of the past, and, by the way, in modern melody there is felt a striving towards classical simplicity of lines." At this point Prokofiev interrupted with, "How dare he criticize my melodies when he cannot compose two melodic bars!" Diaghilev was extremely pleased that Prokofiev's cellos were "singing" and he looked forward to how this would displease the "dry and dogmatic" Stravinsky.

On 14 May Prokofiev had his first opportunity to rehearse with the orchestra. He was grateful that Desormière had only left him 50 minutes, "that was enough for me after a seven year hiatus [from conducting]." He bungled the 5/4 meter number, "The dancers," badly confusing the orchestra. Later Desormière told him the fault was his, prompting him to turn to Koussevitzky for a quick conducting lesson. On 16 May he and Linette dined with the Koussevitzkys after attending Monteux's rehearsal of the new Symphony and the Violin Concerto and before attending the opening of Ida Rubinstein's season at the Opéra. The final number that night was the premier of Ravel's *Bolero*, with, in Prokofiev's words, "a motive repeating 1000 times." He continued "Ravel himself conducted, very amusing, holding the baton like a surgical lancet ... [and] in the end he forgot to press the button to lower the curtain."

The day of his Symphony's premier began with Prokofiev attending a rehearsal of the ballet. "It was time, after all," he recorded in his Diary, "I still had not seen even one dance. Besides it was necessary to coordinate the tempos." He found the rehearsal uninteresting (they were going over problem spots, not extended passages) and soon left, driving over to Koussevitzky's for the aforementioned "conducting lesson." He played him the ballet and the maestro praised it, saying it was one of Prokofiev's best works and "a big jump forward in the sense of technique." The concert that evening was poorly attended for which Prokofiev took some of the blame: he had failed to insure that the necessary announcements in the Russian émigré press were made. Nevertheless, he noted that when several whistles rang out at the end, there were loud shouts of bravo in response. He stood to bow three times. Koussevitzky who sat next to him said it was the best symphony since Chaikovsky's Sixth. Diaghilev attended but did not come to offer congratulations. The next day he would praise the Scherzo and the end of the first movement but, when prodded, object to the over-prominence of strings. Prokofiev thanked Monteux for his excellent direction, keeping to himself that he found his reading earthbound and lacking in line. After the previous day's rehearsal he had recorded in his Diary that Monteux was "musical and conscientious" and worked "very painstakingly," but added "don't expect a flight from this tubby short-armed bourgeois."

The next morning, 18 May, Prokofiev conducted a full rehearsal of the ballet. He was too preoccupied with the orchestra to notice what was transpiring on stage but afterwards his wife told him. The dark cloud that would cast a pall on the final days of Prokofiev's and Diaghilev's 15-year relationship had arrived. In part, she decried the female dances where there was a lot of "indecency that does not tie-in with the biblical plot." Prokofiev quickly became angry, "indeed there is: Diaghilev has been driving about Paris and its outskirts with Markevitch while Kochno and Balanchivadze could not think up anything but indecent gestures, completely going against my music and the décor of Rouault which are very strong and very biblical." (This charge of "going against my music" will be examined in Chapter 5.) Thus for the first time in his collaboration with the Ballets Russes Prokofiev had a violent disagreement over the choreography. He apparently had had no objections to Larionov's and few complaints with

Massine's choreography in *Chout* and *Le Pas d'acier*, respectively, even though their efforts undermined each ballet's success (it was primarily Massine's changes in the first act's narrative to which he objected, not so much the dancing per se). Paradoxically, Prokofiev's complaints arose against the only choreography of his western ballets that would prove to be enduring. As with the ballet's inception, there are radically different positions here as well.

The next afternoon he chased all over Paris and finally, at the fourth hall, came upon the company in rehearsal. Watching the ballet he saw a mass of deficiencies and parts that he felt were not in accord with the music, stylistically or temporally. He approached Balanchine and Kochno and lodged his complaints. Diaghilev came over and tried to mollify the composer by blathering "what is easy [to fix] we will change a little bit but for what is difficult it is too late—the general rehearsal is tomorrow." Prokofiev's complaints, including a request to soften the "indecencies" in the seductress's dance and the appearance of the two women ("they are not like prostitutes of today") fell upon deaf ears. He returned home in a bad mood. It became worse the next day at the general rehearsal. He again approached Diaghilev requesting that he tone down the indecency to which he and Kochno halfheartedly replied, "Yes, yes, it is necessary to think about it ..." Next, Prokofiev buttonholed Rouault and, seeing that he agreed, got him to go to Diaghilev, "he will listen to you since this is your province." The rehearsal began and once again the music commanded his full attention; Prokofiev noticed very little on stage. Diaghilev sat close by and asked him to repeat certain numbers and try different tempi. Afterwards Rouault reported to the composer that his complaint had made no impression on Diaghilev whatsoever. (This is not surprising; it seems Rouault lacked assertiveness. When Prokofiev first met him he described Rouault as "a red-faced man of 55, basically a toad," but nevertheless grew to like him.) They both went to the impresario who snapped, "I really like the naked butts," referring to Rouault's main complaint (the costumes were realized by Vera Soudeikina after sketches by Rouault). He scolded Prokofiev, "the choreographer does not interfere with your music and you should not interfere with his dances." Prokofiev retorted, "I don't write music to Balanchine's choreography, rather Balanchine stages dances to my music. He totally did not understand its spirit and I am reporting this [to you]." Prokofiev's extreme anger then caused him to unleash a word which was not part of his usual vocabulary: "The ballet was staged in your absence and they fucked it up. And now you know that you are defending positions which are impossible to maintain." But Diaghilev parried, "I, thank God, have been the director of a ballet company for 23 years, I clearly see that what is staged is good and therefore I will not be changing anything." Prokofiev realized that there was nothing more to say so he sat down next to Stravinsky and poured out his complaints to him. Stravinsky expressed his sympathy saying he would not touch gospel plots for the theater; but he understandably evaded the topic of "indecent costumes" since they had been designed by his mistress (and future second wife). Later, when Linette, Rouault and Prokofiev were heatedly discussing the ballet's staging, Diaghilev flew in from nowhere and rather irritably said, "This is simply dilettantism on your part!" Prokofiev thought "How is this dilettantism? I am a dilettante because I was discussing a production which was going against the music?" But he answered simply, "Then we have nothing to talk about," and took his leave slamming the door behind him. He reflected upon these events that night in his Diary: "It is bad that there was a scandal. But it is also bad that two shit heads defiled the ballet [more very uncharacteristic language]. And Diaghilev defended them." That evening a private preview of *Renard* was given in the grand salon of the Polignacs' imposing house near the Place du Trocadéro, but the Prokofievs were in no mood to attend.

Although he had yet to see the ballet from beginning to end Prokofiev had seen enough of Balanchine's lean, stylized and symbolic choreography with its grotesque movements borrowed from gymnasts and circus performers. Coupled with Rouault's and Linette's reports he was convinced that the dancing did not fit the biblical subject. Yet an impartial observer, and perhaps Diaghilev as well, would have to admit that Balanchine quite successfully depicted the contrasts of mood in the story—youthful defiance, debauchery and repentance—and that the tone of the choreography rather nicely complemented the tone of the score. The choreographer later recalled with barely concealed enmity, "Prokofiev was passé. He wanted this done in the style of old operas like *Rigoletto*. He wanted real goblets, real wine drinking, and real people with mustaches."[191] Balanchine's comments ring true: when Prokofiev first encountered the Ballets Russes in 1913, his highest praise went to Fokine's melodramatic *Schéhérazade*; he found its staging magnificent and in complete accord with the music. But Prokofiev was apparently not alone in desiring the kind of realism that the Ballets Russes had used in productions 20 years before. Diaghilev's aesthetically conservative regisseur Grigoriev also felt that Balanchine's cool intellectualism was ill-suited to Prokofiev's score and wished that Fokine could have choreographed the ballet instead.[192] Diaghilev may have felt that the plot, the score and the décor did call for more emotion than Balanchine's choreography revealed. Grigoriev recalled that he uncharacteristically urged the dancers to interpret their parts to the full and display all the appropriate emotions: "It was odd to hear Diaghilev extol in this way what for so many years he had been wont to condemn."[193] Satisfied or not, Diaghilev had no choice but to squash Prokofiev's and Rouault's last minute insurrection. In the end, this seemingly mismatched collaboration resulted in one of the greatest successes in the history of the Ballets Russes and made a fitting climax to Prokofiev's association with Diaghilev. Unfortunately it soured a relationship that had been deepening since the premier of *Le Pas d'acier*.

The morning of the ballet's premier, 21 May, Prokofiev was in a foul mood. Replaying the recent events in his mind he agreed that Diaghilev in his 23 years as director had had achievements of genius caliber, but he also felt he had had his share of failures, and the choreography of *L'Enfant prodigue* was one of them. Wisely, he realized that he needed to liquidate his mood by the time of the premier or else "all my work will be lost." He went to his publisher's and chatted with Stravinsky who told him that he too was "en froid" with Diaghilev over *Renard*. Prokofiev returned home, took a nap and by evening his outlook had improved somewhat. He arrived at the theater while the performance of Auric's *Les Fâcheux* was finishing. Backstage he briefly talked with Stravinsky who gave him a copy of *Renard* to follow just before he went out to conduct it. Upon hearing its complicated rhythms Prokofiev stopped worrying about his little dance in 5/4. *Renard*'s success was "good" and as the stage hands began setting up for *L'Enfant prodigue*, Prokofiev went to the green room to look over his score and concentrate on the upcoming task. Stravinsky visited him there, crossed him and kissed him, adding "even though you are a nonbeliever." Prokofiev told him that he was greatly mistaken.

It had been just eight years since he first conducted *Chout* for Diaghilev but the situation was hardly the same. A certain emptiness must have replaced the earlier feeling of excitement and hopefulness. He returned to the stage and saw that the decorations were ready. Suddenly, Diaghilev appeared and said, "Wait, Seryozha, don't go out for a moment yet. Let me get to the loge. I want to see when you come out." Prokofiev did as he was asked, then went out and was greeted by loud applause from the sold out hall. He couldn't help but notice the commanding presence of Rakhmaninov who was seated in the front row just two seats away. The applause died away and Prokofiev lifted his arms to begin his final obligation to Diaghilev. The performance went "not badly" he recalled. He conducted the 5/4 number as precisely as he could but that did not prevent the orchestra from smearing the rhythm. At the end loud applause immediately erupted. Swallowing his anger of recent days for the benefit of the cheering hall he went out on stage, hand in hand with Balanchine and Rouault. Kochno dropped behind—Prokofiev thought, on orders from Diaghilev. Stravinsky and Paichadze were the first to congratulate him. Then his proud publisher Koussevitzky boasted "two blows, the Symphony and now this!" Prokofiev headed to the buffet to drink champagne and greet well-wishers. Diaghilev flashed in, kissed Linette and congratulated Prokofiev adding, "We should sit down together but better at a different time—we're all tired now." Whether or not this was his attempt at rapprochement, it was the last time the two would speak in person. Needless to say, the Prokofievs did not attend Diaghilev's party afterwards at the Capucines restaurant. Only one more telephone conversation lay ahead.

Prokofiev attended performances of *Le Pas d'acier* on 22 and 28 May and of *L'Enfant prodigue* on 23 and 29 May as well as 4 and 6 June. The ballets enjoyed success even though the attendance dropped off. Prokofiev continued to pout about the choreography (though it bothered him not enough to stay away) and he deliberately avoided Diaghilev. The impresario had been invited to dine at the

Koussevitzkys' along with Stravinsky and Prokofiev on 23 May but given the company it is quite understandable that he sent his regrets instead. Prokofiev was not pleased with Desormière's performances of *L'Enfant prodigue*; he thought his tempi incorrect and his direction slack. Friends told him that he had conducted it far better. On 29 May Prokofiev recorded in his Diary "again grief, both from the stage and from the orchestra." For this performance substitutes were in the pit and they made a mess of the 5/4 meter dance and in no. 7 (Robbery, a brisk 6/8 tour de force for three clarinets) they "were playing the devil knows what, came in late, [and even] stopped; Desormière's cursing was audible." Prokofiev went to him at the interval and saw that he was in a rage. The conductor asked Prokofiev to write him an abusive letter so that he could present it to the syndicate of musicians. Prokofiev gladly complied, adding in his Diary, "There are no orchestral musicians more undisciplined than the French." His letter stated, in part: "the number in 5/4 was not together, and the basses were a half measure ahead . . . and the solo for three clarinets? What was it they played? It was incredible! I will not speak to you about many other places where the instruments did not enter or were not together, you know better than I." He continued: "… is the orchestra composed of Conservatory debutantes? … [my guests] explained to me that in New York they play better at café-concerts …" and concluded "… [was it] negligence? unwillingness? I would like to accept neither . . . But what?"[194] The letter must have worked because on 4 June Prokofiev learned that the most egregiously offending clarinetist had been fired and this had made a strong impression on the rest of the orchestra. Prokofiev observed that they played better but still poorly. That night Diaghilev was not in attendance, but Kochno stopped by with a cheery "hello," a rather nervy move in light of what he was about to do. Prokofiev responded "dryly."

Back in early January 1929 when discussing the Société des Auteurs and Compositeurs Dramatiques "Bulletin de Déclaration" Prokofiev had demanded that Kochno acknowledge that he borrowed his plot from the gospels. Kochno rightly surmised that the composer had some ulterior motive. "Simple fairness," Prokofiev responded, "after all it was not you who wrote the parable." In his Diary, however, he admitted that there was a motive: "after all Kochno sent me his libretto after three-fourths of the music was already written, and the majority of directions I followed were not from Kochno but rather from the Bible." Fair enough, but he went on, "In Diaghilev's production Kochno, I admit, played some kind of role, but then we swept him aside." Some weeks later this rationale led Prokofiev to publish the ballet's piano reduction without acknowledging the librettist and with nonequivalent Russian and French titles: *Bludnïy sïn* [Prodigal Son] *L'Enfant prodigue* [Prodigal Child]. *L'Enfant prodigue* was used in lieu of Kochno's French title, *La Parable du fils prodigue*, which had been registered with the Société on 3 January and subsequently shortened to *Le Fils prodigue* before the premier. (Since the focus of this book is on Prokofiev and Diaghilev's Ballets Russes (not just the latter) and also for the sake of consistency, I have decided to make all references to this ballet using Prokofiev's title for the music, *L'Enfant prodigue*, rather than the proper title of the ballet which is, of course, *Le Fils prodigue*.) One thousand copies of the piano score were published thus and in early June Kochno sought an injunction against their distribution. Prokofiev received a subpoena on 6 June as did Gavriil Paichadze, the Paris director of Koussevitzky's publishing firm Édition Russe de musique. The two, accompanied by Stravinsky, went to a lawyer on 10 June where they were told that French law was quite clear: once united as collaborators, one cannot be without the other. Stravinsky was especially interested in this matter, not only because of his recent altercations with Diaghilev and "his love" for his colleague, as he claimed, but also "out of hatred for Kochno."[195] Despite Kochno's subsequent braggadocio to the contrary,[196] the court refused his case and fined him for the legal costs. Diaghilev's nonappearance in this whole matter is telling; Stravinsky was convinced that he was the instigator. That seems unlikely but Prokofiev believed him.

The court's decision came on 13 June. The previous day Prokofiev had his last conversation with Diaghilev. He was angry and pessimistic, convinced he would lose the case. The impresario telephoned to ask if he would conduct the premier of the ballet in London. Prokofiev replied that he was not especially keen to do so, and added that before they talked about this he should be paid his fee for conducting in Paris. For the duration of the call Prokofiev deliberately took a disinterested tone, so much so that his wife became dumbfounded by his attitude. Diaghilev also asked if he was coming to the final performance of *L'Enfant prodigue* that night, perhaps in hopes of having a chance to talk over their differences. Prokofiev only said "I'm not sure." To keep the conversation rolling Diaghilev then tried to give him a possible excuse by saying the performance was sold out and that there may not be any seats. He also turned the London conducting request around making it sound like the composer's presence was not really required since that performance would be sold out anyway. Receiving so little feedback Diaghilev concluded with an invitation to call him tomorrow should Prokofiev change his mind, but not later because he was leaving for Berlin. Prokofiev sealed their estrangement with his concluding words "my decision is rather definite." Afterwards he explained to Lina that he had wanted to remain "aloof ... [so] he would better understand that I am aware of his role." But now he would never know what that role was.

The London premier of *L'Enfant prodigue* followed on 1 July at Covent Garden, the only London theater Diaghilev thought worthy of his company. Also on the bill that night were *The Gods Go A-Begging* and *Aurora's Wedding*. *L'Enfant prodigue* was also given during the company's brief run-out to Berlin between engagements in Paris and London with Ansermet conducting. The composer recalled that the public and press were "most enthusiastic" in Paris (he did not follow the company to Germany or London). He wrote to Myaskovsky, "For a long time none of my works has been so unanimously well-received as this ballet." As was his custom, Diaghilev had prepared the British in a pre-concert interview, calling the score a masterpiece and a great musical event, adding, as usual, a curiously worded tag: "at this moment when we are experiencing such a shortage of real feelings, it seems simply incredible that Prokofiev could have found such musical expressiveness."[197] The audience in Paris had already been alerted to expect something new by the Third Symphony, which critics lauded for its "humane" quality ("a rare virtue in our days") and "original thinking amidst thousands of Parisian influences."[198]

But Prokofiev's new style in *L'Enfant prodigue* still baffled many critics. The British press was generally reserved or curt: the *Observer* reported that the score was, for the most part "good," "nicely balanced" but "impersonal,"[199] while *The Times* said that it "made no great impression at a first hearing . . . [being] surprisingly dull" without the composer's characteristic "bright edge."[200] Some French critics were also ambivalent: Boris de Schlœzer in *La Revue musicale* faulted, among other things, Prokofiev's lack of grandeur at the end, but nevertheless added "quelque invention mélodique ... quelles trouvailles harmoniques [singling out the conclusion of the seductress' dance]."[201] He also added that the performance of the music was wanting, a view shared by the composer. Poor performance of the music aside, charges such as "unobtrusive" or "impersonal" were not usually leveled at Prokofiev's ballet music. Western audiences had grown so accustomed to his boisterous, steely music that the reserve of the new ballet took some time to get used to. Eventually these skeptics come round to bestow favorable remarks about his newly emphasized lyricism and simplicity. From a later perspective the British music commentator Propert reported "the music was sonorous and dignified, and extraordinarily unlike anything of Prokofiev's we had yet heard."[202] But at least one critic at the premier noted that Prokofiev's "old" style was still in evidence (as had Diaghilev — "hammering nails"): "Together with the explosiveness and vibrant energy we have come to expect, he shows us gifts of feeling and simplicity that our public did not expect of him."[203] *L'Enfant prodigue* does indeed maintain the same trenchant style of characterization and sardonic humor of the earlier ballets, while its new emotional depth clearly links it to the ballets of Prokofiev's Soviet period.

Perhaps due to its resonance with the generally more serious, even insecure mood at the end of the decade, the outstanding element of the ballet was Serge Lifar's emotionally intense realization of the Prodigal (see Fig. 14). A British observer wrote:

> It was first and last Lifar's ballet. He was necessarily the dominant figure ... and he ruled the stage ... because he showed such power of emotional acting, such an intense belief in the reality of his sufferings, and such unconditional repentance when, broken and disheveled, he threw himself at his father's feet. There had been nothing parallel to it since Nijinsky first played *Petrouchka*, possibly there had been no opportunity for it.

Indeed, as the Prodigal was embraced by his forgiving father and the curtain fell, many in the audience had tears in their eyes. Still there were the usual complaints from purists about the demise of classical dance in Diaghilev's company, some denouncing the erotic partnering between the Siren and the Prodigal, others, the use of revue-like antics such as the suggestion of a boat journey in "Sharing the Spoils" (no. 9; an admitted bit of choreographic padding). Quite a number of critics had reservations about Balanchine's modern, stylized choreography, one calling his work "uneven," in part "silly and meaningless,"[205] another, quite perceptively, "not always related to Prokofiev's music or the plot."[206] Yet there was really no undermining weak link in *L'Enfant prodigue*. Everything about this ballet—from the simple story, the décor, the music, the successful balance of mime to dance, to the dancers executing their parts—combined to produce a work that from our vantage point at least, can be counted among the handful of major accomplishments in the 20-year history of the Ballets Russes. It is the only ballet Prokofiev wrote for Diaghilev that lives on to this day.[207]

The London season concluded on 26 July and the Ballets Russes went on run-outs until 4 August. Diaghilev saw his company perform for the last time on 24 July at a gala for King Fuad of Egypt. In response to the King's request substitutions were made and two of the company's ballets destined to become classics, *Petrouchka* and *L'Enfant prodigue* were given. The following day Diaghilev departed for Paris, then began a whirlwind tour through Germany, Austria and Italy with Markevitch, arriving in Venice alone on 8 August. Diaghilev died there on 19 August 1929 at the age of 57, quite unexpectedly to most who were unaware of his grave condition caused by unchecked diabetes. Prokofiev heard about Diaghilev's death from Souvtchinsky who on 21 August dropped by at his summer residence, a hilltop château near Culoz ("from furunculosis," he reported). The company's existence came to an abrupt end: "without any garland around it" as one dancer recalled, "it just disappeared into thin air."[208]

Plans for the upcoming 1930 season had included new ballets by Hindemith (to be titled *No. 27*, a ballet about bicycle racing)[209] and by Diaghilev's latest discovery, Markevitch (*L'Habit du roi* after Andersen's *The Emperor's New Clothes*), along with a revival of *Giselle*. Despite the success of Prokofiev's *L'Enfant prodigue* (some 16 performances) and back-to-back revivals of *Le Pas d'acier*, Diaghilev had no immediate plans for another Prokofiev commission. Their relationship terminated after the Kochno lawsuit and the disagreement over Balanchine's choreography. Diaghilev and Stravinsky had been completely estranged for months, on the one hand due to the composer's "disloyalty" in working for Ida Rubinstein on *Le Baiser de la fée*, and on the other to the impresario's less than honorable treatment of the composer's music (specifically, a high-handed cut in *Apollo* initiated sometime during the autumn of 1928). Stravinsky and Prokofiev, however, according to the latter, had mended their differences and were on good terms, and socialized as almost "neighbors" during the summer of 1929.[210] Of all the major players with whom he collaborated in the Ballets Russes, Prokofiev would work again only with Lifar and Larionov.[211] Lifar commissioned and choreographed the composer's next ballet *Na Dnepre (Sur le Borysthène)*, for the Paris Opéra in 1932; Larionov created its décor. Prokofiev had dedicated each of his ballets to Diaghilev, and *Na Dnepre* he dedicated "À la mémoire de Serge de Diaghileff."

After hearing about Diaghilev's death Prokofiev wrote to his friend Asafyev:

> You cannot understand what a terrific impact the news about Diaghilev's death had on me ... . His death stunned me not so much musically, since it seemed to me recently that *Prodigal Son* brought the cycle of our collaboration to an end, nor even personally, since his image is still so clear and vital that I can't picture him gone. Most of all, his death signals the disappearance of an enormous and un-questionably unique figure, whose stature increases as he recedes into history.[212]

His Diary entry is quite similar: with the Kochno affair and their differences over the production of *L'Enfant prodigue* Prokofiev had already sensed the end of their business relations, "but Diaghilev as a director of genius, but Diaghilev as a remarkably interesting personality, as an 'object' ... here is where I feel the loss." The following day he awoke with a "heavy head" (that is, another of his chronic severe headaches) and for three hours walked alone in the hills. In the evening he received a letter from Stravinsky stating that he had heard the news from a telegram. He expressed his regrets that he and the Prokofievs had so recently had a merry time at Diaghilev's expense. On 23 May Prokofiev, Linette and Souvtchinsky visited Stravinsky. The conversation kept returning to the death of Diaghilev, and at one point, perhaps fittingly, Stravinsky received a telegram stating "Décédé sans souffrances."

There is no evidence that Prokofiev ever disputed Diaghilev's judgment regarding his ballet music, although he good naturedly gibed him about his rejection of *Ala i Lolli* in a letter regarding the fate of *Chout* from New York City in 1918.[210] His docile acceptance of *Ala i Lolli*'s rejection in 1915, and his willingness to make major revisions in each of his subsequent ballets shows the respect Prokofiev held for Diaghilev's wisdom in matters musical and theatrical. That Prokofiev almost always chafed at demands for revisions in his later Soviet ballets only reinforces the depth of his esteem. Years later writing from Stalinist Russia, he succinctly and defiantly recorded his judgment of the man who had befriended him for 15 years and brought him more than a fair measure of success while nurturing him into one of history's most respected ballet composers: "Here in Russia his work has not been properly appreciated and many are inclined to regard him as nothing more than an impresario who exploited the talents of artists. Yet his influence on art and his service in popularizing Russian art cannot be overestimated."[214] Although their relationship was shaky at both ends and lacked consistency, it proved to be mutually profitable. Prokofiev indeed owed Diaghilev a great deal: although he possessed an innate theatrical talent, he needed the impresario's uncanny insight and pointed guidance to perfect his balletic craft. And for his part, Prokofiev brought Diaghilev more than mere success — through his art and friendship he revitalized the increasingly weary and jaded impresario and sparked his theatrical lifeblood.

Notes

1. This and most of the details about the composer's life in this book come from *Sergey Prokof'yev Dnevnik 1907–1918* and *Sergey Prokof'yev Dnevnik 1919–1933* (Sergey Prokofiev Diary 1907–1918 and 1919–1933, 2 vols.) a private publication in the original Russian by the Serge Prokofiev Estate, July 2002, Paris. All translations from it are my own.
2. Cherepnin had come to Paris in the hope of conducting again for Diaghilev's company, but nothing came of it and he returned home.
3. Prokofiev did meet the musicologist, critic and Russian music champion Michel-Dimitri Calvocoressi and played for him and pianist Robert Schmitz both of his Piano Concertos. They little understood the Second but promised to try to arrange a performance of the First at a Camille Chevillard concert the following season. Prokofiev ended his Diary entry, "with God's luck, but I don't really believe their promises."
4. Prokofiev's Diary contains enough evidence to support that he was fundamentally a bluenose.
5. *Mir iskusstva* was the westward-looking journal founded by Diaghilev and his circle in 1898; it was edited by him until its demise in 1904. The journal's collaborators, including Alexandre Benois and Léon Bakst, were advocates of art for art's sake, and although they promoted symbolists and postimpressionist painters at the expense of the then prevalent Russian realist school, their tastes ran quite wide — including art from Russia's distant past.
6. The futurist movement, begun in Italy by the poet and dramatist Filippo Tommaso Marinetti in 1909, glorified modern urban society, heavy industry, machinery, speed, youth, and, unfortunately, violence. Most futurist achievements were realized in the visual arts. The primary musical innovation — replacing pitches with systematized noises — was theorized by Francesco Pratella in 1912. Members of the Russian avant-garde, such as Mayakovsky, soon adopted some of the tenets of Italian futurism. It also influenced the Russian Constructivist movement.
7. A *chastushka* is a Russian peasant song with short, rhymed couplets and is musically distinguished by successive recurrences of short, one or two-part melodic figures. At reh. 99 in the Concerto's finale the clarinets, first bassoon and violas initiate a two-bar, repetitive folk-like motive. The soloist states the theme at reh. 100 followed by three character variations. The piano and orchestra then take turns presenting the theme in Glinkaesque changing background fashion.
8. This celebrated example of the impresario's foresight must be tempered somewhat since Stravinsky was apparently the fifth choice for the job of composing *L'Oiseau de feu* after Cherepnin, Lyadov, Glazunov and Sokolov. See Richard Taruskin, *Stravinsky and the Russian Traditions*, 2 vols (Berkeley and Los Angeles, CA, 1996), vol. 1, pp. 574–9.
9. From a letter to Eleanora Damskaya, who had been a fellow student at the St Petersburg Conservatory, dated 25 June 1914 (OS). Harlow Robinson, *Selected Letters of Sergei Prokofiev* (Boston, MA, 1998), p. 16.

10. From a letter to Eleanora Damskaya dated 5 July 1914 (OS) in Robinson, *Selected Letters*, p. 17.
11. A painter without formal musicual education, Russolo nevertheless gave a bold musical voice to the movement.
12. Using music from Rimsky-Korsakov's opera *Snegurochka* (Snow Maiden), *Le Soleil du nuit* was a trial work for the young choreographer Massine, supervised by the painter–stage designer Larionov. Larionov also executed the ballet's designs. It was premiered in Geneva on 20 December 1915.

   Likewise, *Kikimora*, set to Lyadov's music, was choreographed by Massine under Larionov's supervision. The latter again doubled as designer. This ballet was premiered on 28 August 1916. *Kikimora* later became part of the ballet *Les Contes Russes* (1917), a ballet (all choreographed by Massine/Larionov) uniting three Russian folk tales: *Kikimora*, *Bova Korolevich* and *Baba Yaga*.

   The genesis of *Parade*, the ballet which historians traditionally use to date the artistic shift in Diaghilev's company, began in late 1914 with Jean Cocteau's efforts to entice Erik Satie as composer, and then Pablo Picasso as designer for his scenario inspired by popular entertainment. By May 1916 Cocteau had tentatively brought together Satie, Picasso and Diaghilev as collaborators, but only by the following August was Picasso firmly committed to design the ballet. It was premiered on 18 May 1917. See Frank W.D. Ries, *The Dance Theatre of Jean Cocteau*, Theatre and Dramatic Studies, no. 33 (Ann Arbor, MI, 1986), pp. 35–8.
13. Lynn Garafola, *Diaghilev's Ballets Russes* (New York, 1989), pp. 81–2.
14. Ibid., pp. 84–5. Garafola also goes too far in her argument about the subordination of dance: "Beginning in 1915 and continuing throughout the postwar years, design not only supplanted music as the unifying element of Diaghilev's productions, but altered the relationship of choreography to the overall plan of a work. If, before, dance had been an equal, now it became a subordinate of design, with the goal of the choreographer being to enhance the inventions of scene painter and costumer." Dance, even in the era of Fokine, was subordinate to the drama which in turn was inexorably linked with the visual tableau. See Tim Scholl, *From Petipa to Balanchine* (London, 1994), p. 6.
15. Letter to Eleanora Damskaya, dated 21 February 1915 (OS). Robinson, *Selected Letters*, pp. 22–3. Prokofiev makes a humorous reference to an antiquated Russian unit of measure (poltora sazhenia). My thanks to Harlow Robinson for the clarification.
16. This most revealing letter was sent to Stravinsky in Clarens from the Grand Hotel, Rome. It is quoted here from Igor Stravinsky and Robert Craft, *Memories and Commentaries* (Berkeley and Los Angeles, CA, 1981), p. 68. In his biography Harlow Robinson includes a slightly different version, translated from the letter as published in I.S. Zil'bershtein and V.A. Samkov, eds, *Sergey Dyagilev i russkoye iskusstvo* (Moscow, 1982) vol. 2, pp. 124–5. The changes in nuance undoubtedly result from the process of translation. Another version of this letter, printed by Robert Craft, *Stravinsky: Selected Correspondence* 3 vols (New York, 1982) vol. 2, pp. 19–20, is a curiosity. Its differences are both striking and nonsensical: (in sequence) it is the score, not the composer, that is to be left around for two or three months; instead of Cherepnin, it is Gorodetsky who is the *faux avante-gardiste*; and, once again, it is the score, not the composer, that is to be brought to Stravinsky
17. Israel Nestyev, *Prokofiev*, trans. Florence Jonas (Stanford, CA, 1960; reprint edn, 1970), p. 99. Nestyev summarizes the *Tribuna*, *Concordia* and *Giornale d'Italia* and quotes *Il Messaggero*, all from 9 March 1915. The concert also held an Etude from the composer's opus 2 and three excerpts from his *Ten Pieces*, op. 12 (Nos. 1, 3, 7). No encores were given. The composer noted that the reception of the solo

pieces was better than that for the Concerto. The concert opened with Chaikovsky's *Romeo and Juliet Fantasy Overture*, and, after Prokofiev's music, continued with *La Mer* and *Till Eulenspiegel*, all conducted by Molinari.

18. Igor Stravinsky, *An Autobiography* (1936; reprint edn, New York, 1998), pp. 56–7.

19. Letter from Prokofiev to Stravinsky dated 10 December 1919, sent from New York City, reprinted in Vera Stravinsky and Robert Craft, *Stravinsky In Pictures and Documents* (New York, 1978), p. 132. *Pribautki*'s gurgles and twitters were likely influences on Prokofiev's compositional style.

20. In his 1941 autobiography Prokofiev claimed the work they performed was *Petrouchka*. His was not the only memory that played tricks – Cangiullo recalled in his autobiography *Le serate futuriste* that the piece was *L'Oiseau de feu*! (he claimed that Pratella slept through the performance). Excerpt translated in Carolina Tisdall and Angelo Bozzolla, *Futurism* (New York and Toronto, 1978), pp. 117–18.

21. *Shut*, nos 397–9 in A.N. Afanas'yev, *Narodnïye russkiye skazki*, 3 vol. (Moscow, 1855–63; reprint edn., Moscow, 1957), vol. 3, pp. 186–94.

22. While the couple were basking in the success of the Ballets Russes' production of *Le Coq d'or* which featured Goncharova's décor, Larionov was called-up by the Russian army upon the declaration of war with Germany (1 August 1914). They left France and returned to Russia. By early September Larionov was at the front and less than a month later he had been wounded. He was medically discharged in January. Diaghilev then began a series of telegrams inviting the couple to rejoin the Ballets Russes circle. They arrived in Switzerland in mid-July 1915 (Diaghilev was then at Ouchy) and by autumn Larionov was making his first drawings for *Chout*. (chronology from Anthony Parton, *Mikhail Larionov and the Russian Avant-Garde* (Princeton, NJ, 1993), pp. 142, 145, 147.

23. Prokofiev, "Autobiography," p. 252.

24. Letter from Prokofiev to Diaghilev from New York dated 1 October 1918. Robinson, *Selected Letters*, p. 65.

25. Prokofiev, "Autobiography," p. 252.

26. The idea of musically contrasting darkness and light was, of course, hardly novel. Recently Glazunov had made a far less extreme depiction in his *Fantasie*, op. 53, "From Darkness to Light," progressing from B minor to C major. This sort of semitonal motion is a prime feature of Prokofiev's music as is his fondness for the key of C major. Perhaps in deference to Glazunov he made his climactic sunrise in a somewhat uncharacteristic key for him, B-flat.

27. Prokofiev, "Autobiography," p. 254. Another scandal surrounds a nonperformance of the Suite at a Koussevitzky concert the following December. Critic Leonid Sabaneyev's negative review, which included the line "the composer himself conducted with barbaric abandon," was published in the Moscow newspaper, *Novosti sezona* (News of the Season). But Prokofiev's Suite had not been performed as planned, due to the inability to muster the necessary musicians in wartime Moscow.

28. Prokofiev had wanted to stop off in Honolulu for several days to soak up the sun and earn some money for the rest of his trip by playing concerts. However, after disembarking he heard about the lengthy queue for booking passage off of the island on account of the War. He immediately returned to his ship and bought a ticket for its continuation to San Francisco (his cabin had already been sold—he had to settle for lesser accommodations). This left him with only $100 in his pocket. Much to his chagrin he was in Honolulu for only seven hours.

29. Prokofiev had rented a small furnished apartment with two rooms and a bath. To the description in his Diary he added, "and downstairs sits one sad Negro. I even like this." The address comes from a handwritten note on Hotel Manhattan

stationery. Although undated, it was surely written on 7 September; Prokofiev had arrived in New York City the day before. "Cher M. McCormick, je vous remercie pour votre amabilité et je suis à vos orders à tout heure. Mon addresse: 107 W. 109 St. Phone Academy 1611 Ap. 54. En attendant le grand plaisir de vous voir. Votre tout dévoué [Signed] Serge Prokofieff." This letter is held in the Cyrus H. McCormick, Jr. Papers, Correspondence File: Part VI 288 to 289, at the State Historical Society of Wisconsin, Madison, Wisconsin.

30. Translation of the letter was made by an unknown party on 9 July, 1918. The translation and original letter are held in the McCormick, Jr. Papers, Correspondence File, State Historical Society of Wisconsin, Madison, Wisconsin.

31. McCormick forwarded Prokofiev's request with a cover letter to George Bakhmetieff at the Russian Embassy on 12 July. However, it was Baron Th. de Guysberg, Acting Secretary of the Russian Embassy in Washington, DC, who responded that the State Department had taken the necessary steps in a letter dated 31 July. On 6 August 1918 McCormick wrote to Prokofiev at the Tokyo Station Hotel, Tokyo, Japan: "Dear Sir: Your letter of 11 June regarding the visaing of your passport to America, was received by me and I have taken the matter up with Washington, with the result that I am this morning advised that the Department of State have cabled the necessary instructions to the American Ambassador at Tokyo. I trust that this may straighten out the difficulty and that the remainder of your journey may run smoothly. I am, Yours very truly, [Signed] Cyrus H. McCormick." By the time this letter arrived in Tokyo, Prokofiev had departed.

32. Kucheryavy was escorting the Russian pianist Skylarevsky, a Professor at the Saratov Conservatory, to the USA. Skylarevsky was not allowed into the country due to visa problems so he went to Vancouver, British Columbia in Canada, and from there he launched a recital tour.

   On 27 August Kucheryavy took Prokofiev aside and told him that his business was going extremely well and that he was to receive $15 000 upon arrival in New York City. He told him that he would be "happy to share it," and so the composer should not worry about being low on funds nor rush to conclude the first contract that came his way.

   Many years later when visiting Moscow, Prokofiev learned from Kucheryavy's daughter that he had died in March 1932, having been declared a "wrecker." (Since 1928 these early victims of Stalinist purges were exposed in sensational press coverage and show trials. Accused of opposing developing socialism, "wreckers" were actually scapegoats for the many failures in Stalin's Russia.) Prokofiev had visited Kucheryavy in November 1929 during a previous trip to Moscow.

33. On 26 August Prokofiev dropped in on a former rival for the Rubinstein Prize at the Conservatory in the spring of 1914, the pianist A.V. Zelikman, who had opened a modest studio in San Francisco.

34. The pieces probably included the Toccata for piano, op. 11, *Sarcasms*, the Second Sonata, op. 14, Four Etudes, op. 2 and the Ballade, op. 15. Gabrilovich returned the music to McCormick in June 1918 along with a letter stating in part, "To tell the truth I am not greatly impressed by his works,—that sort of music does not appeal to me." Letter held in the McCormick, Jr. Papers, Correspondence File, State Historical Society of Wisconsin, Madison, Wisconsin.

35. *Chicago Herald and Examiner*, 7 December 1918; Boston *Evening Transcript*, 26 October 1918; *New York Times*, 21 November 1918; all from Malcolm H. Brown, "Prokofiev in the United States," *Bericht über das Internationale Symposium "Sergej Prokofjew—Aspekte seines Werkes und der Biographie,"* (Regensburg, 1992), pp. 47, 44, 45, respectively.

36. Prokofiev was not pleased with de Lamarter, calling him "simply no kind of conductor, in addition to not knowing the score he waves God knows how." Prokofiev felt compelled to take the lead during the Concerto rehearsals. During the concert de Lamarter reportedly "fell behind, but did not do any dirty tricks."

37. Prokofiev recorded in his Diary that Campanini decided in favor of *Oranges* "because *Gambler* absolutely demanded Russian artists, and although he dreamed about getting them, even Chaliapin exclusively for a whole series of Russian operas, he was not sure the political situation would allow it, for which I was glad."

38. The translation to French was made by New York acquaintances, the singer Vera Janacopulous and her attorney husband, Aleksey Stal. Why this opera after Gozzi was not done in Italian remains an open question. Benois had given him a copy of the Italian original. Prokofiev was fluent in French and knew only a little Italian; however, that should not have been a factor, since the music was already composed when the translation was made. The day before he left for Europe in April 1920 Prokofiev gave his future wife Lina $150 ostensibly as an advance for an English translation of the libretto for use at Covent Garden, but pragmatically to provide her the means to come and join him in Europe that summer.

39. In its obituary on 20 December, the *Chicago Herald and Examiner* stated that the Chicago Opera's beloved General Director and conductor had been ill for a year. According to this account he had given "special devotion and energy" to plan and prepare the 1919–20 season, and consequently "no change or interruption" was necessary aside from those operas which were canceled. The paper reported that he died without any thought as to his successor. Gino Marinuzzi took charge of artistic affairs until 1921.

40. Prokofiev was also seeing a lot of two other women at different times during this period, both destined to become Hollywood actresses: Dagmar Godowsky (daughter of the famous pianist Leopold Godowsky), whom he met after a New York concert on 17 February 1919, and Stella Adler, whom he met a week later. On 13 February 1920 the latter showed up after six months silence and asked to take piano lessons with him. In his Diary entry for that day he recorded that he must somehow prepare Lina for this. Prokofiev spent considerable time with Dagmar during his 1919–20 trip to the US, including some New Year's Eve revelry under the palm trees in Los Angeles.

41. Prokofiev eventually grew tired of this ongoing project, especially after the Christian Science faith entered his life in June 1924 and gradually distanced him from the subject.

42. Marinuzzi even pointed out two locations for cuts: one each in the second and third acts.

43. "To be accurate," says Barry S. Brook, "the 'd'après Pergolesi' subtitle should be revised to read: 'd'après Pergolesi, Gallo, [?] Parisotti [1853–1913!], Monza, and [?] Count Unico Wilhelm van Wassenaer." See Brook, "Stravinsky's *Pulcinella*, the 'Pergolesi' sources," in *Musiques, signes, images*, ed. Joël-Marie Fauquet (Geneva, 1988), pp. 41–66).

44. Nancy Perloff, *Art and the Everyday* (Oxford, 1991), p. 4.

45. Garafola, p. 344.

46. This was not a piano score, nor a piano reduction, but a true short score using, almost equally, two or three systems. Ideas for instrumentation were frequently included, and the composer freely expanded to four, five, and even six staves to capture fully the intended voicing, texture and harmony.

47. Prokofiev, "Autobiography," p. 268.

48. This was just a one evening affair (14 June 1927) before Romanov and the other dancers departed for America.

49. A 14 April letter to John Alden Carpenter from Royat attests to this: "I am very busy finishing my ballet which opens the season in Paris."

50. Nestyev, *Prokofiev*, p. 181. No date is ascribed to this and the author provides no documentation. Presumably this information came to light during the author's discussions with the composer over the period 1940–47.

51. Letter to Myaskovsky dated 15 July 1924. *Sergey Sergeyevich Prokof'yev i N. Ya. Myaskovskiy Perepiska*, ed. M.G. Kozlova and N.R. Yatsenko (Moscow, 1976), p. 199.

52. A book (or perhaps an opera) could be written about the entire Chicago–*Oranges* affair. Max Pam, Prokofiev's biggest nemesis in this affair, it seems, resigned as chairman of the executive committee but remained with the Chicago Opera Association as a vice-president and board member.

53. An opera-ballet by Cimarosa with new orchestration and recitatives by Respighi. It was premiered in Paris on 27 May 1920.

54. Serge Grigoriev, *The Diaghilev Ballet 1909–1929*, trans. Vera Bowen (London, 1953; reprint edn, Harmondsworth, 1960), p. 168.

55. Ibid., p. 171.

56. Sokolova alternated with Catherine Devillier as the hero's wife.

57. Lydia Sokolova, *Dancing for Diaghilev*, ed. by Richard Buckle (London, 1960; reprint ed., San Francisco, CA, 1989), pp. 176–7.
    After *Chout*, Slavinsky (1901–45) choreographed nothing more for Diaghilev. In 1930, however, he choreographed a ballet designed by Larionov to Prokofiev's "Classical" Symphony that was performed by Michel Benois' Opéra-Ballet at Paris's Théâtre Pigalle.

58. Richard Buckle, *Diaghilev* (New York, 1979), p. 381. The Ballets Russes productions of *Chout* were always given in somewhat cramped quarters.

59. In 1920 Radlov opened the Popular Comedy, a theatre of improvisation, farce and buffoonery in Petrograd. Improvisation there was both verbal and physical, with clowning, acrobatics and pantomime. See Elizabeth Souritz, "The Young Balanchine," *Ballet Review* (Summer 1990), p. 67. This is the same Radlov who would suggest to Prokofiev a ballet on the the subject of *Romeo and Juliet* in late 1934 and collaborate with him on the scenario the following spring.

60. Parton, p. 150.

61. John Drummond, *Speaking of Diaghilev* (London, 1997), p. 168.

62. Boris Kochno, *Diaghilev and the Ballets Russes*, trans. by Adrienne Foulke (New York, 1970), p. 159.

63. Ibid.

64. Grigoriev, p. 173. Their next great choreographer, Bronislava Nijinska, would rejoin the company the following autumn.

65. Vernon Duke [Dukelsky], *Passport to Paris* (Boston and Toronto, 1945), pp. 125–6.

66. *Observer*, 5 June 1921; quoted in Nesta Macdonald, *Diaghilev Observed by Critics in England and the United States 1911–1929* (New York, 1975), p. 262.

67. Parton, p. 183.

68. Ibid., p. 155.

69. Ibid., p. 184.

70. Arnold Haskell, *Balletomania: The Story of an Obsession* (London, 1934), p. 319.

71. Ibid.

72. Cyril W. Beaumont, *Bookseller at the Ballet, memoirs 1891 to 1929* [incorporating *The Diaghilev Ballet in London*, 1951] (London, 1975) p. 190.

73. Larionov's choreographic sketchbook was possibly taken along with countless

sketches, paintings, notebooks, and so on from his and Goncharova's Paris atelier by Russian agents in 1987. At last report this priceless haul sits uncatalogued, in unopened boxes in a Moscow museum depository. See Konstantine Akinsha, Grigorii Kozlov, and Oleg Bebgazov, "The Strange Illegal Journey of the Larionov–Goncharova Archive," *ART News* (March 1997), pp. 80–85.

74. Sokolova, p. 180.
75. B. Shletser, "Dyagilevskiy balet," *Poslednie novosti*, 2 June 1921.
76. Kochno, p. 160. Laloy wrote: "Les mouvements de la danse ... sont l'exacte résultante de la musique et du décor scénique." *Comœdia*, 19 May 1921.
77. Michel Fokine, *Fokine: Memoirs of a Ballet Master*, trans. by Vitale Fokine (Boston, MA, and Toronto, 1961), p. 173.
78. Arnold Haskell and Walter Nouvel, *Diaghileff: His Artistic and Private Life* (New York, 1935; reprint edn, New York, 1978), p. 294.
79. *Le Figaro*, 18 May 1921.
80. *La Revue musicale* (2), 1 July 1921, 63.
81. Pierre Scize in *Bonsoir*, 20 May 1921 and Roland Manuel in *L'Éclair*, 23 May 1921, respectively; both quoted in Robinson, *Sergei Prokofiev*, pp. 163 and 164, respectively.
82. Other performance cuts are marked in the orchestral manuscript Prokofiev and Ansermet conducted from: reh. 196 to reh. 197 in scene 4, one bar at one after reh. 253 in scene 5, and two before reh. 259 to reh. 259 also in scene 5. A cut may have been made at reh. 220 in the fourth entr'acte as well. All of these simply tighten-up the musical discourse.
83. In his Diary Prokofiev added, "Ansermet in general is not a bad musician but he does not have his own opinions and being a creation of Stravinsky, he completely absorbs all his points of view."
84. Grigoriev, p. 243. The stage was 31 feet 10 inches wide and just 31 feet deep.
85. Ibid., p. 175.
86. Buckle, p. 383.
87. According to Cyril Beaumont Larionov "did not suffer from inhibitions. Occasionally, without any preamble, he would indulge in some strange sudden whim; as when walking with friends up Charing Cross Road, he suddenly sat down on the pavement and bade them grasp his legs by the ankle and drag him along as though he formed an improvised sleigh." Beaumont, p. 267.
88. Shortly after he returned to St Brevin, Prokofiev had a bicycle accident which confined him to bed for several days with a bloodied face, a broken tooth and stitched lip.
89. *Observer and The Sunday Times*, both from 12 June 1921.
90. Beaumont, p. 190.
91. *The Times*, 11 June 1921.
92. Letter to Eleanora Damskaya, dated 15 July 1921 in Robinson, *Selected Letters*, p. 39.
93. Letter to Chicago insurance executive Ephraim Gottlieb (a devotee and occasional intermediary) dated 27 July 1921.
94. *Observer*, 11 June 1921.
95. *Observer*, 11 June 1921. In a similar vein *The Times* on 11 June 1921 added: "It is vastly entertaining for a little ... but [it] soon palls." See Chapter 3, "Entr'actes," for a discussion of this "redundancy."
96. Ernest Newman, *The Sunday Times*, 12 June 1921.
97. Hubert Griffith in the *Observer*, 12 June 1921.
98. "To the Editor" under the banner "Music of the Day" in *The Daily Telegraph*, 18 June 1921.

99.   *The Daily Telegraph*, 10 June 1921.

100. Léon Vallas, *Vincent d'Indy*, 2 vols. (Paris, 1946), vol. 2, p. 108.

101. A brief article signed by H.G.H. from an unknown English language newspaper, entitled "The Russian Ballet," dated 10 June 1921, held by the New York Public Library Dance Collection, fond. Classmark *MZGR Chout.

102. Boris de Schlœzer, "Serge Prokofieff," *La Revue musicale*, 2 (1 July 1921), 58. Successful ballet music (in the traditional sense) has a *dansante* quality to it, which is achieved through both melody and rhythm.

103. *Comœdia illustre*, 20 May 1921.

104. Prokofiev, "Autobiography," p. 273. Some time later Stravinsky returned a perjorative "Bach-like" accusation in regards to Prokofiev's Third Piano Concerto. See note 31 in Ch. 5.

105. In a letter to Koussevitzky dated 28 November 1924 Prokofiev wrote, "He [Diaghilev] isn't putting on my *Buffoon* at all: it seems that if someone finds shelter under Koussevitzky's wing, then he also earns Diaghilev's curse." From Robinson, *Selected Letters*, p. 187.

106. The list may be found in Lifar's *Serge Diaghilev: His Life, Work and Legend* (New York, 1940), p. 232.

107. By 1926 Stravinsky would assert that Poulenc was just a "secondary" composer (along with Auric). See the Diary entry for 29 September 1926.

108. Kochno, p. 22.

109. The soloist was Marcel Darrieux, leader of Koussevitzky's orchestra.

110. Prokofiev was forced to reorchestrate the Piano Concerto in 1923 since the full score had been destroyed, probably turned into heating fuel at his old Petrograd apartment during the civil war. Fortunately, the piano reduction of the Concerto (and the full score of the Violin Concerto) were saved and brought from Russia by his mother in 1920.

111. I am grateful to Garafola for sharing these insights during a 1995 telephone conversation.

112. A new overture for a biblical ballet came from Rubinstein in July 1930, but after some preliminary negotiations Prokofiev politely declined, choosing instead the ballet project Lifar proposed that August for the Paris Opéra.

113. Honegger completed a score based on *Judith* in April 1925 for the small Théâtre du Jorat located in the hamlet Mézières, just northeast of Lausanne (the same locale that held the premier of his *Roi David* in 1921). It was premiered there on 13 June. This may have led to Rubinstein's waning interest in the project with Prokofiev, and at the same time drawn her attention to a possible new collaborator. This *Judith* was incidental music with solo vocal parts for the title character and a servant. The initial response was tepid. *L'Impératrice aux rochers*, also incidental music, was composed for Rubinstein between 6 August and 13 November 1925. The premier was finally given at the Paris Opéra in 1927, but, according to Harry Halbreich, it was no great success either. The two's best known collaborative effort was *Jeanne d'Arc au Bûcher*, first performed in Basle in 1938.

114. In his letter of 9 July 1924 Prokofiev explained, "The Mariinsky Theater could produce an excellent ballet with this suite; they'd have to change the plot a little, since there will be some pieces missing, but I have nothing against such a change, especially if the choreographer is sensitive and talented ... In view of my contract with Diaghilev, I can't write any of this officially ..." From Robinson, *Selected Letters*, p. 92.

115. According to Gunhild Oberzaucher-Schüller, *Chout* was not shown in Cologne until May 1927, when it was presented with new choreography by Hellmuth

Zehnpfenning. See "Der Balletkomponist Sergej Prokofjew in der ästhetischen Pflicht seiner Auftraggeber," in *Bericht über das Internationale Symposium "Sergej Prokofjew—Aspekte seines Werkes und der Biographie*," (Regensburg, 1992), note 47, p. 244.

116. On 24 February 1924 the *New York Times* announced that *Chout* would follow an oriental divertissement entitled "The Arab Fantasia," which was set to "authentic folk melodies" assembled by Anis Fuleihan and performed by "native instruments." The two were "antipodal," the *Times* remarked the day following the 6 March premier. *Chout* was called "a gem. In stage setting, costuming, gesture and choreography it followed the cubistic patterns of Prokofieff's music. The salty taste of cynicism made it all the more amusing."

117. The "orchestra" was comprised of two pianos, one violin, a flute, an oboe and percussion; the role of the hero was danced by Albert Carroll.

118. In his autobiography Prokofiev recalled his feelings upon settling in Paris in 1923: "Living in Paris does not make one Parisian, and France having been victorious on the battlefield wanted to be victor in the field of music as well. Hence the exceptional attention showered in the 'Six' …, which the 'Six' did not altogether deserve." Prokofiev, "Autobiography," p. 275.

119. The young American composer George Antheil performed his piano pieces *Sonata Sauvage*, *Mechanisms* and *Airplane Sonata* as part of a Ballets Suédois performance at the Champs-Élysées Théâtre in October 1923. His music nearly caused a riot. According to the composer, "The next morning the Parisian newspapers caricatured me on the front page … [one showed] me dressed in overalls, standing before a piano that had a steam engine attached to it. I was controlling a system of indicators, gauges, and levers substituting for a keyboard. Its caption read: 'Last Night's Music of the Future at the Ballets Suédois.'" George Antheil, *Bad Boy of Music* (Garden City, NY, 1945), p. 134.

120. Robinson, *Sergei Prokofiev*, p. 184.

121. The draft of this rather surreal libretto is in the composer's hand. It reads as follows: 1. Ballerina (theme and variations), 2. Dance of Boors (with the ballerina, 5th variation). It ends with a group (they hug), 3. The Jumpers jump out (they scare the Chinese men with their intensity) (they embrace the ballerina), 4. Challenge to a duel (choreographic roll-call) Fight with a firecracker. They spin. Explosion. 5. They mourn the dead ballerina.

    The ballet at this point had a proposed duration of 14 minutes. Ballet rights (for 1925–26) are stated at the bottom of the page. The document is not dated by the author, but Prokofiev and Romanov signed a contract on 22 June 1924. For a complete history of *Trapèze* see Noëlle Mann's "*Trapèze*: a Forgotten Ballet by Serge Prokofiev and Boris Romanov," in *Three Oranges* 4 (November 2002), pp. 4–9. (*Three Oranges* is the journal of the Serge Prokofiev Association; <http://sprkfv.net>) According to Prokofiev the ballet was also presented in Stuttgart.

122. Romanov's conductor, Efrem Kurtz even suggested some corrections to make in the orchestration of the Quintet, about which Prokofiev recorded, "To my surprise, they are quite small and insignificant."

123. Ballets have been set to the five-movement Quintet, however; for example, *Il Circo* at La Scala in Milan in late 1970 with choreography by Elide Bonagiunta. For details about choreographer Christopher Hampson's new ballet to Prokofiev's complete score, premiered by the English National Ballet on the stage of Sadler's Wells Theatre in April of 2003 see this author's "*Trapèze* reinterpreted," *Three Oranges* 5 (May 2003), pp. 24–7.

124. This company, which had been founded in 1925, was then co-directed by Prince Alexis Zereteli and Colonel W. de Basil. Romanov replaced choreographer Nijinska who left to form her own company. In addition to *Chout* (designed by Léon Zack), Romanov choreographed a new *Pulcinella* and *El amor brujo*. London saw this trio of ballets beginning 27 May at the Lyceum Theatre conducted by Goossens. Local critics remained unimpressed with *Chout*; the *Times* said "... the ballet takes about an hour to play; much too long and most is dismally unfunny. Prokofiev's music is, one must suppose, also a piece of buffoonery, but very wearying to the ears with its blare and reiteration of short phrases."

When *Chout* was revived the following spring in Monte Carlo, the company had been renamed the Ballets Russes de Monte Carlo, a new joint venture between Casino de Monte Carlo ballet organizer René Blum and de Basil. Their London debut under this moniker came in July 1933 at the Alhambra Theatre and an American tour followed on 22 December 1933, but without *Chout* in their repertory.

125. Prokofiev, "Autobiography," p. 277. Late in his career Prokofiev hoped to revise the symphony, but the project was never fulfilled. He did tinker with the score in 1926 before it was sent to his publisher.

126. Ibid.

127. Letter to Myaskovsky dated 4 August 1925. From Robinson, *Selected Letters*, p. 258.

128. Prokofiev added that Diaghilev was not venting his spleen with those words, rather his tone implied that he nevertheless had warm feelings towards Auric's *Les Matelots*.

129. Martinů's ballet *The Revolt*, completed by summer's end 1925, used black notes, white notes, high ones and low ones, some "chubby and bearded, others tall and thin," according to Jaroslav Mihule's liner notes for the Supraphon recording of 1991 (11 1415-2). Apparently such an idea was "in the air" at the time. Martinů's ballet was premiered in Brno in February 1928 with choreography by Ivo Váňa-Psota. This was the same Psota who would be first to choreograph a ballet to Prokofiev's *Romeo and Juliet*, using the music from Suites 1 and 2. It was premiered in Brno in 1938 with the choreographer dancing the role of Romeo.

130. Although the Prologue of *The Red Whirlwind* had workers waving hammers (as a sign of "slavery"), it is the second act that resonates most strongly with *Le Pas d'acier* through its vignette-like scenes purportedly showing the strengthening ties between city and country. It featured black marketeers with sacks over their shoulders, various kinds of riffraff, disheveled members of the former upper class, soldiers and speech makers, as would *Le Pas d'acier*. It also provides other resonances: a dynamic change of scenery, a massive procession and a finale depicting the "union of the peasant and the worker" (compare this with *Le Pas d'acier*'s original scenario given in Chapter 4). See Souritz, *Soviet Choreographers*, pp. 278–84.

131. In the early spring of 1924 a power play occurred between Diaghilev and the director of the Monte Carlo opera house. Referred to as the "Affair Ravel," it climaxed after a brief revival of the composer's ballet *Daphnis et Chloë* (with Anton Dolin) and just prior to the premier of his *L'Enfant et les sortilèges*. Diaghilev had heated words with the composer in the lobby of the Hôtel de Paris, probably about cuts or changes, and being unsuccessful vowed to withdraw his dancers from the production. As a result of his stubbornness and hysterics, Diaghilev lost more than half of his subsidy and the name of the company changed from The Ballets Russes de Monte Carlo back to The Ballets Russes de Serge de Diaghileff. See Garafola, pp. 237ff.

132. Souvtchinsky emigrated to Paris in 1920.

133. Prokofiev, "Autobiography," pp. 277–8.

134. Robert Dézarnaux in *La Liberté*, 9 June 1927.

135. Prokofiev, "Autobiography," p. 278.

136. It is significant that neither a choreographer nor an experienced scenarist took part in the creation of the ballet. Nijinska had left the company in January 1925, and although George Balanchine had been onboard since autumn of 1924 (his first choreographic assignment for the company had been the 1925 restaging of *Le Chant du rossignol*) and Massine returned on an as-needed basis, the Ballets Russes was again without a clearly defined choreographic esthetic.

137. "Badgers" is the name of a gang of misfits—bandits, deserters and disgruntled anti-Bolshevik peasants—who in the wake of the civil war lived in underground hideouts in the woods outside the village Vory.

   At the start the youthful brothers Semyon and Pavel, taken to Moscow from their native village to seek work, go their separate ways, but are reunited years later when the former, a "Badger," surrenders himself to a dreaded Communist commissar who turns out to be the latter. In the novel's third and final part the peasants of Vory led by Semyon rebel against the Bolsheviks' forceable grain requisitions, exemplifying contemporary urban—rural mistrust and misunderstanding. Although the novel ends "correctly" with a sense of "community" it is Semyon who holds the reader's sympathy. Thus *The Badgers* takes a rather skeptical look at contemporary life. Prokofiev's writings make it clear that he did not sympathize with the revolutionaries.

138. Buckle, p. 486. Rothermere was proprietor of the *Daily Mail*.

139. *La Chatte* had music by Henri Sauguet, architectural and sculptural constructions by Naum Gabo and Antoine Pevsner, and choreography by George Balanchine. It also preceded *Le Pas d'acier* during the Paris season by eleven days. Sauguet's unostentatious music provided a pleasant accompaniment, but it had no resonance with the décor and precious little with the story. Prokofiev dismissed the music as "trash."

140. In a letter to Asafyev Prokofiev noted that there had been seven rehearsals and that "it came out more clearly" than the previous year, but added, "there still hasn't been a definitive performance." Robinson, *Selected Letters*, p.107.

141. This excerpt comes from the end of Prokofiev's Diary account of the event, dated 18 May 1926: "the demonstrators began to burrow forward across the parterre. But here something unexpected happened: because this was the premier of an Englishman's music there were many Englishmen in the hall—splendid gentlemen in tuxes and monocles. These gentlemen, not knowing what the demonstration was about, thought that this was a demonstration of some group against the performance of English things. And they stood up for themselves. From my balcony I saw splendid tuxedoed men turning and according to all the rules of boxing, delivering stunning blows on the unfortunate demonstrators. One of them, having gotten one on the cheekbone, sat on the floor and covered his head with his hands, and a décolleté lady flew upon him and struck him several times with her program. The police eventually got them out of the hall and the audience demanded that the ballet begin from the beginning. Then it became clear that the music in and of itself was crap, and especially after *Pulcinella*. The decorations were nice, but as it seemed to me, insignificant. Thus, in essence, the show was not worth a demonstration."

142. By the end of the month, however, Prokofiev recorded that his impression "had noticeably faded upon repetition."

143. John Bowlt, "Constructivism and Russian Stage Design," *Performing Arts Journal*, **1**, no. 3 (Winter 1977), 75–6.

144. Yuriy Elagin, *Temnyi genii: Vsevolod Meierkhol'd* (New York, 1955), pp. 248–9, quoted in Bowlt, p. 80. A color reproduction of Popova's maquette is found in Georgii Kovalenko's "The Constructivist Stage," and a picture from the production accompanies Bowlt's "The Construction of Caprice: The Russian Avant-Garde Onstage," both articles in *Theatre in Revolution: Russian Avant-Garde Stage Design 1913–1935*, ed. Nancy Van Norman Baer (New York, 1991), p. 146 and p. 65, respectively.

145. The sketch is reproduced in Lesley-Anne Sayers, "Sergei Diaghilev's 'Soviet' Ballet: *Le Pas d'acier* and its Relationship to Russian Constructivism," in *Experiment/Eksperiment*, **2** (1996), 119, Fig. 38.

146. Elizabeth Sourits, "Constructivism and Dance," in *Theatre in Revolution: Russian Avant-Garde Stage Design 1913–1935*, ed. Nancy Van Norman Baer (New York, 1991), p. 138.

147. Baba-Yaga and the Crocodile is the subject of a number of late seventeenth and early eighteenth-century Russian *lubki* (woodcuts). Their traditional interpretation is an Old-Believer satire on Peter the Great (or as suggested in Fig. 19b, Empress Catherine). Baba-Yaga, of course, is well-known as the flesh-eating Russian fairy-tale witch of of boney legs and mortar, pestle and broom accouterments. But here in Figs. 19 a and b she is dressed in a foreign costume and headdress, armed with what could be a razor, riding on a cloven-hoofed quadruped, confronting the grandly bearded crocodile (or at least a Russian conception thereof). The opposition of Old Believers and their Antichrist, Peter, is clearly presented. However, a recent reconsideration discounts the Old Believer angle in favor of folk humor and the influence of sorcery in all Russian classes at the time. See Dianne E. Farrell, "Shamanic Elements in Some Early Eighteenth Century Russia Woodcuts," *Slavic Review*, **52**, no. 4 (Winter 1993), 725ff.

    Baba-Yaga and the Crocodile was probably not included in part one of *Le Pas d'acier* ("Stories and Legends of the Countryside") for its underlying political satire, however; it seems highly unlikely that anyone in the audience, émigrés included, would have recognized it, let alone expected it in a ballet about life in Soviet Russia. Massine probably turned to Rovinsky simply for inspiration—much in the same manner as using the characterful drawings in Giorgio Lambranzi's *Theatralische Tantz-Schul* (1716).

148. Oberzaucher-Schüller, p. 226. This begs for further clarification or a source, but has neither.

149. *Observer*, 3 July 1927. This is the same newspaper Diaghilev used in 1921 to try to put a positive spin on the compromised production of *Chout*.

150. Léonid Massine, *My Life in Ballet* (London, 1968), pp. 171–2.

151. Vladimir Kameneff, *Russian Ballet Through Russian Eyes* (London, 1936), p. 35. Although he then lived in the West, the author claims to have attended ballet performances in Moscow and Petrograd both before and after the revolution.

152. Sourits, "The Young Balanchine in Russia" in *Ballet Review*, **18** (Summer 1990), 71.

153. Michael Kirby, *Futurist Performance* (New York, 1971), pp. 93–6.

154. *Daily Express*, 7 July 1927, quoted in Vincente García-Márquez, *Massine* (New York, 1995), p. 196.

155. Massine, pp. 171–2.

156. *Observer*, 3 July 1927. This was a prescient appraisal, politically speaking.

157. Dukelsky, p. 195. On opening night Dukelsky sat with the composer in Diaghilev's box.

158. *Observer*, 10 February 1927.
159. *The Daily Telegraph*, 5 July 1927, and *The Times*, 5 July 1927, respectively.
160. Walter A. Propert, *The Russian Ballet 1921–1929* (London, 1931), pp. 57–8.
161. *Musical America*, 16 July 1927, under the banner, "Survey of European Activities."
162. *Vozrozhdenie* (Paris), "Balet Dyagileva," 10 June 1927, p. 3.
163. *La Revue musicale*, **9** (1 July 1927), 50.
164. Propert, p. 57.
165. *Daily Express*, 5 July 1927, quoted in MacDonald, p. 348.
166. *Musical Times*, **68** (1 August 1927), 744.
167. André George in *Nouvelles Littéraires*, 21 June 1927, as quoted in Robinson, p. 211.
168. *The Times*, 5 July 1927.
169. *The Daily Telegraph*, 5 July 1927.
170. Stravinsky did not congratulate Prokofiev after the premiere. He may have been still smarting from the audience's tepid response to his *Oedipus Rex*. Asked a short time later by a London reporter what he would write next, he answered, "In any case it won't be music with hammers." The crude and rather clumsy hammering on stage was a last minute expedient ordered by Diaghilev, despite his agreement with the composer to have the sounds made in the wings.
171. *The Times*, 5 July 1927.
172. *The Daily Telegraph*, 5 July 1927.
173. *Observer*, 10 July 1927.
174. *Observer*, 3 July 1927; interview with Diaghilev under the heading "The New Ballet."
175. *La Revue musicale*, **9** (1 July 1927), 49.
176. The gala performance was held on 27 December 1927. The performance count by year was: 1927, Paris-5, London-10; 1928, Paris-4, London-4; 1929, Paris-3.
177. The ballet excerpts followed Haydn's Symphony no. 88 in G. The program gave the following titles: "Train of Men carrying Provision Bags," "Sailor with Bracelet and Working Woman," "Reconstruction of the Scenery," "The Factory," "Hammers," and "Final Scene," thus numbers ii, vi, vii, ix, x and xi from the ballet.
178. The American production of *Le Pas d'acier* was presented on 21 and 22 April 1931. Stokowski conducted his Philadelphia Orchestra. In a letter to Myaskovsky Prokofiev wrote, "I hear that the music was brilliantly played, but that the story line and choreography were cut so badly as to be unrecognizable, and therefore unsuccessful. Nonetheless, the hammer and sickle made an appearance, as well as pieces of red fabric and other emblems of Soviet daily life." Robinson, *Selected Letters*, p. 294.

  The ballet was indeed considerably different. It was meant to be a satire on the machine era, on the irony of "speeding up", according to the author of the scenario (and creator of the scenery and costumes), Lee Simonson. The program lists dancers representing steel, iron, and coal; in addition, there were two efficiency experts (the ballet's choreographer Edwin Strawbridge was one of them), a labor leader, clergyman, boy scouts, "Uplift Army" leaders, dowagers, flappers, blue cross nurses, college professors, a financier, soldiers, etc. The fourth scene was entitled "bucolic labor" (with drinking). The ballet was presented as the annual dance production of the League of Composers. Its companion piece on the bill was Stravinsky's *Oedipus Rex*, staged using huge marionettes. See, for instance, *Dance Magazine*, 31 May 1931, pp. 32–3.
179. Richard Taruskin has labeled Diaghilev's ballet a "tawdry example of 'radical chic' before the term was current." Taruskin, "The Anti-literary Man: Diaghilev and Music," in *The Art of Enchantment: Diaghilev's Ballets Russes 1909–1929*, p. 121.
180. Letter to Myaskovsky dated 9 July 1928.
181. Kochno, p. 272.

182. Ibid.

183. Bernard Taper, *Balanchine: A Biography* (New York, 1984), pp. 109–10.

184. Popov composed this piece in July 1926; it was published as his op. 3 in 1927. His second "Vocalise" in F# minor was composed in April 1927 but not premiered until June 1929. The third is just a sketch.

185. The ballet, nevertheless, would demonstrate a familial similarity in thematic content, for example, with the main theme of op. 45a and the Andante of op. 45b. This is not uncommon in neighboring works of Prokofiev's œuvre.

186. The brief outline Prokofiev composed to is presented in Chapter 5. The ballet's numbers are as follows: 1. The departure, 2. Meeting friends, 3. The seductress, 4. The dancers, 5. The prodigal son and the seductress, 6. Drunkenness, 7. Pillage, 8. Awakening and remorse, 9. Sharing the spoils, 10. The return.

187. Prokofiev sensed that *Chout* was not going to be revived when on 17 February Diaghilev stopped by on his way to the circus and asked to borrow his copy of the score to *Renard*.

188. See Kochno, pp. 274–5, for his account of Rouault's procrastination and how Diaghilev finally forced him to produce the sketches in one night. Another version comes from Lifar; both are summarized in Alexander Schouvaloff, *The Art of the Ballets Russes* (New Haven, CT and London, 1997), p. 301.

189. Prokofiev, "Autobiography," p. 287. When he first saw some of Rouault's paintings the day after they met Prokofiev found them gloomy and unpleasant. Nevertheless he thought that Rouault would turn out appropriate décor for a biblical ballet. According to the composer's wife, he grew to appreciate how well they harmonized with the production (that is, his music). The scenery (two backcloths, one with the minaret, the other with the tent) was executed from Rouault's designs by Prince Alexander Schervashidze.

190. Prokofiev was first introduced to Markevitch (born 27 July 1912) by Diaghilev at a Ballets Russes program on 3 January. Prokofiev recorded in his Diary that the impresario called him a "new composer" and added that "he would soon come to my place to play his music." Markevitch had greatly impressed the impresario with his yet-to-be-finished *Sinfonietta*; as a result he received a commission for the Piano Concerto that was premiered during an interval between ballets at Covent Garden on 15 July.

191. Interview with George Balanchine included in the documentary, "Diaghilev: A Portrait," written by Tamara Geva and produced by Peter Adam for BBC Television in association with R.M. Productions of Munich, 1979.

192. Grigoriev, p. 260.

193. Ibid., p. 261.

194. Letter to "Cher Désormière [sic]" dated 30 May 1929.

195. In a letter to Ansermet dated 11 June 1929, Stravinsky provides some of the details along with a hefty dose of sarcasm: "Both … [the director] and Prokofiev are accused of having murdered the 'book,' that masterpiece of literature (in the complaint Kochno calls himself a 'man of letters'), by publishing the titles in a form that renders the meaning of this 'work' completely different from what Kochno had conceived, etc. etc. … There, *mon vieux*, is what's happening with these gallant gents of the Ballets Russes, so genteel, and so devoted to the cause of art!" From Robert Craft, *Stravinsky: Selected Correspondence*, 3 vols. (New York, 1982–5) vol. 1, p. 197.

196. In his book Kochno claimed that Prokofiev was forced to destroy the first edition. Kochno, *Diaghilev and the Ballets Russes*, p. 272.

At about the same time Prokofiev is said to have cheated Balanchine out of a share of the royalties (see Taper, p. 112). That Balanchine was as "impoverished" as Taper claims, however, seems hard to believe in light of dancer Alexandra Danilova's recollection that he could afford to order his suits from Savile Row because Diaghilev paid him two salaries, one as dancer and one as choreographer. Alexandra Danilova, *Choura* (New York, 1986), p. 82.

197. *Observer*, 30 June 1929.
198. Prokofiev, "Autobiography," p. 287.
199. *Sunday Observer*, 7 July 1929.
200. *The Times*, 2 July 1929.
201. *La Revue musicale*, **10**, no. 8 (July 1929), 151.
202. Propert, pp. 74–5.
203. Émile Vuillermoz, *Excelsior*, 23 May 1929, quoted in Robinson, pp. 230–31.
204. Propert, p. 76.
205. *The Times*, 2 July 1929.
206. De Schlœzer in *La Revue musicale* (July 1929), 151.
207. *L'Enfant prodigue* survives today, albeit in altered form. The first revival, with new choreography by David Lichine, was given by de Basil's Ballets Russes de Monte Carlo. It premiered at the Theatre Royal in Sydney on 30 December 1938. Balanchine first revised the ballet as *Prodigal Son* in 1950 when Jerome Robbins danced the title role. Subsequent revivals by Balanchine were for Edward Villella in 1962 and Mikhail Baryshnikov in 1978. See George Balanchine, *Choreography By Balanchine: A Catalogue of Works* for a summary of the variations between productions (ed. F. Mason, reprint edn, New York, 1984), pp. 92–3.
208. Tamara Geva in the documentary, "Diaghilev, A Portrait."
209. Hindemith claimed he was overworked in a 2 January 1929 letter to Diaghilev about the proposed ballet and recommended Martinů as a substitute. When he visited Prokofiev to hear *L'Enfant prodigue* on 6 February, the impresario asked "from whom can one order a ballet in case Hindemith is late?" Who is Martinů? Who is Villa-Lobos?" After some discussion the latter was asked to audition for Diaghilev four days later at Prokofiev's home. After hearing two hours of his music Diaghilev confided to Prokofiev, "He is talented but his taste is not worth a fig." Prokofiev added in his Diary that Villa-Lobos "was nervous and for aplomb he sucked on a cigar which smoked up all the rooms."

The impresario kept after Hindemith, even personally (at Baden Baden in late July 1929, where a performance of his *Lehrstück* was given). Hindemith's controversial comic opera *Neues vom Tage* had had its premier run that June in Berlin. Diaghilev probably needed Hindemith more than Hindemith needed a ballet commission from Diaghilev.
210. Stravinsky was summering nearby at Echarvines by Lac d'Annecy.
211. There are no Diary entries for the year 1931, so it is unknown (but doubtful) whether Prokofiev worked with Romanov on his revival of *Chout* for the Opéra Russes à Paris that spring.
212. Letter from Prokofiev to Asafyev, 29 August 1929. From Robinson, *Selected Letters*, p. 232.
213. Dated 1 October 1918, it reads in part, "Sometime ago you shamelessly rejected the music for my *Ala i Lolli* just as Nouvel did, who later, having heard it in orchestral form made his apologies."
214. Prokofiev, "Autobiography," p. 288.

CHAPTER 2

The path to success: gauging originality versus influence in *Ala i Lolli* and *Chout*

Like Stravinsky before him Prokofiev had never written a ballet when he received his first commission from Diaghilev in 1914. Furthermore, despite his composition of no fewer than five operas, he had never seen a theatrical work of his reach production. By the time *Chout* was presented in 1921, Prokofiev had attained a level of mastery in ballet composition, but his success had come only after two false starts over the course of six years. His initial lack of experience and difficulties in pleasing Diaghilev, combined with his well-documented interest in (and criticism of) Stravinsky's highly successful early ballets beg for an investigation into the degree and nature of possible influence. But Stravinskian influence is only one possibility; it is also necessary to examine how Prokofiev's early ballets relate to their Russian heritage and to western theatrical music in general. In this pursuit it is essential to differentiate between topical influences and those that actually affected Prokofiev's musical style. It stands to reason that Diaghilev, who commissioned these ballets, played a great role in the former, while the agents of the latter remain to be determined.

Prokofiev succumbed to the magic of opera at a very tender age; indeed, some of his earliest childhood compositions were in that genre.[1] In maturity he lavished an incredible amount of time on operas that were either produced without much success or never made it to the stage at all. In fact one, *The Fiery Angel*, was undertaken without a commission or any plans for production — the story's visual possibilities were the only impetus. Just as Stravinsky had promoted his opera *Le Rossignol* before receiving the commission for *L'Oiseau de feu*, Prokofiev tried at his audition to interest Diaghilev in his highly melodramatic opera *Maddalena* or a new one after Dostoevsky's *The Gambler*. But the impresario responded that opera "as a form was dying out, whereas ballet … was flourishing" and asked Prokofiev for a ballet instead. While money was the ostensible reason for deflecting these offers, it is doubtful whether Diaghilev would have been willing to gamble on an opera by an untried composer. With untried ballet composers, however, he would, although he would sometimes "lose." Prokofiev had never considered writing a ballet before,[2] but he knew of Stravinsky's successes and that a ballet for Diaghilev's company guaranteed

116

renown. Without hesitation he temporarily shelved his operatic plans to fulfill the impresario's request. During his career in the West, ballet commissions afforded Prokofiev a source of financial security as well as guaranteed public performances. Yet he still believed that his operas—*The Gambler*, *L'Amour des trois oranges*, and especially *The Fiery Angel*—would be the vehicles for his greatest success.

In his first autobiography Prokofiev mentions his favorite operas and symphonic works during his student years, but remains virtually silent on his impressions of ballet. He briefly mentions having seen *Sleeping Beauty* during his first trip to Moscow in 1900 and recalls that he was unimpressed when he played through Lyadov's composer-autographed score in early 1906, "I did not like all those ballet-style numbers." Ballet was still regarded in academic circles as a lesser endeavor for a composer, Chaikovsky's successes notwithstanding. Even though Rimsky-Korsakov had included ballet in his operas *Mayskaya noch'* (May Night) and *Noch' pered rozhdestvom* (Christmas Eve), and with *Mlada* even resuscitated the hoary opera-ballet complete with traditional miming, he outlined his position against the genre in a letter of 1900:

> 1. it is a 'degenerate art' 2. 'miming is not a full-fledged art form' 3. 'balletic miming is extremely elementary and leads to a naive kind of symbolism' 4. 'the best things in ballets, the dances, are boring since the language of dance and the whole vocabulary of movement is extremely skimpy' 5. there is 'no need for good music in ballet; the necessary rhythms and melodiousness can be found in works of any number of able hacks today,' and that 6. 'ballet music is usually performed in a sloppy manner anyway.'[3]

Nevertheless, his pupil Glazunov managed to be appointed to a faculty position at the St Petersburg Conservatory in 1899 despite his having taken up the balletic torch from Chaikovsky, composing by then three ballets and other balletic compositions.

His apparent indifference notwithstanding, Prokofiev may have come into contact with the ballet fare at the Mariinsky Theatre during his student years in St Petersburg. Aside from the standard works such as *The Humpbacked Horse*, *Paquita*, *Le Corsaire*, *Don Quixote*, *Giselle* and *Coppélia*, the more memorable encounters might have included the Chaikovsky ballets and perhaps the more recent ones by Glazunov, including *Raymonda* (1898) and *The Seasons* (1900) or *Le Pavillon d'Armide* (1907) by Cherepnin. Except for *The Seasons*, all of these are formulaic story ballets with *pas de seul*, *grand pas de deux*, geometric arrangements by an impersonalized female corps, and grand divertissements offering colorful character and national dances, choreographed by, or in emulation of the eminent classicist, Marius Petipa (1818–1910).

As the nineteenth-century drew to a close, a younger generation of Russian dancers and choreographers sought to radically change ballet above and beyond the recent attempts at revitalization brought about by foreign influence.[4]

Encouraged by *Mir iskusstva* ideals, they wished to dispense with ballet's stiff academic style and classical conventions, and strengthen the dramatic aspect through spectacular décor and flowing, more realistic movements. They were inspired by the performing freedom and sheer emotionalism of Isadora Duncan, who first performed in St Petersburg in late 1904. Most of the ballets that Prokofiev saw during his summer visits to western Europe in 1913 and 1914 were choreographed by two such innovators: Mikhail Fokine and Boris Romanov. Without abandoning classical ballet's narrative style or its elaborate spectacle, their ballets diverted from tradition in duration, form, look, vocabulary of movement and spatial design. Many critics of the day praised this style, calling it the "new ballet," and later, "choreographic drama," or simply "choreodrama."[5] This latter term is customarily associated with choreographer/dancer Salvatore Viganò's highly dramatic ballet style at the beginning of the nineteenth century (half mimed, half danced). But the term regained currency a century later, for example, in a 1913 interview Stravinsky declared, "I am an adherent of so-called choreodrama, which is bound to replace the contemporary type of ballet."[6]

Prokofiev mentioned the Ballets Russes productions he saw in his letters home in 1913 and 1914; the works include: *Petrouchka*, *L'Oiseau de feu*, *Daphnis et Chloë*, *Carnaval*, *Schéhérazade*, *La Tragédie de Salomé*, *Le Coq d'or*, *Midas*, *La Légende de Joseph* and *Narcisse et Echo*. From his observations it is obvious that he was hardly swept away by Diaghilev's musical commissions. His comments about the productions suggest an approval of a close relationship between music and movement. All but *Carnaval* (a series of vignettes to orchestrations of Schumann's op. 9) and *Le Coq d'or* (an opera with the roles danced as well as sung) are essentially *ballets d'action*, for which the music illustrates the drama. He favorably reported the perfect union of music and gesture in *Petrouchka* and in a few places in *Le Coq d'or*. His brief criticism of *Daphnis et Chloë*'s dramatic passages, which he called "feeble" and "[unintentionally] funny,"[7] moreover suggest a preference for musical literalism in this genre. He was perhaps most impressed with *Schéhérazade*'s "magnificent staging" and "successful cooperation with the music." Despite his inexperience, the headstrong young composer no doubt departed for home confident that he could outdo all that he had heard and seen.

The extent of Stravinsky's musical influence over Prokofiev as he wrote his first ballets for Diaghilev is often overstated—the composers shared a common heritage and consequently their ballets have a family resemblance. Some reckless comments have been made over the years, claiming that *Ala i Lolli* is "modeled on" or "fashioned after" *Le Sacre du printemps* without specifying whether the reference pertains to musical or nonmusical aspects, or both. Prokofiev's own words can easily mislead: "I had already heard Stravinsky's *Sacre du printemps* but I had not understood it. It is quite possible that I was now searching for the same images in my own way [in *Ala i Lolli*]." But Prokofiev was adamantly his own man during this period—unwilling to borrow or copy. His qualifying "in my own way" must be respected, just as "images" strongly suggests an end not a means. It is true that Prokofiev and Stravinsky were certainly closest ideologically during the period of *Ala i Lolli* and *Chout*, sharing an interest in Russian primitivism and neonationalism by different degrees and for different reasons. But topical resonance does not imply appropriation of compositional style. This distinction has been generally heeded when appraising Prokofiev's acquiescence to contemporary musical trends in *Le Pas d'acier*; the rush to apply "Stravinsky clone" is primarily endemic to the first two ballets, *Chout* and *Ala i Lolli*.

Even though both Stravinsky and Prokofiev studied with Rimsky-Korsakov, their musical backgrounds were quite different. It is hardly surprising that the musically inclined Stravinsky, brought up almost literally in the Mariinsky Theatre where his father was the leading basso, became a musical dilettante while obliging his family with studies in law. In his early twenties he embarked on a cosmopolitan career after a few years of private lessons, without the benefit of a conservatory diploma and concomitant title of "free artist." Prokofiev, on the other hand, had his precocious musical talent nurtured for a while by Rheinhold Glière while growing up in the remote Ukrainian countryside. Upon the urging of Glazunov, his parents enrolled the rather prolific 13-year-old composer in the St Petersburg Conservatory where he stayed for 10 years of training (Fig. 15). Stravinsky lacked such a thorough grounding but he was a far more receptive student. He studied on a private basis with the grand old man himself, and practically became a part of his family. As his prized pupil, Stravinsky also gained admission to the biweekly Wednesday evening musical gatherings held at Rimsky-Korsakov's apartment. The instruction Stravinsky received in private lessons was essentially the same that Prokofiev received at the Conservatory, in other words, "Rimsky's system" (that is, using his harmony textbook *A Practical Course in Harmony*). Prokofiev, by happenstance, had all of his harmony lessons with Anatoly Lyadov, instead. Their mutual indifference and indolence undoubtedly clouded the spirit if not the letter of the requisite course material. Prokofiev's repeated charges of apathy against his teacher must be tempered by his own "frivolous attitude" (in Lyadov's words). The two seemed to deserve each other. Prokofiev's only class with Rimsky-Korsakov was a weekly four-hour orchestration seminar held in an overcrowded classroom. He recalled that he never got to know the man, "he never singled me out" (at least in a positive manner).

Although Rimsky-Korsakov had been a member of Balakirev's *moguchaya kuchka*, and thereby formed a link back to the putative founder of Russian national music, Glinka, the youthful Prokofiev was not at all overawed by him or the heritage he represented. In fact, his behavior in his seminar was, by his own admission, juvenile and offensive. He took great pleasure in annoying the old man, after which he would look around the classroom in triumph, seeking, but not receiving, approval from his far wiser classmates. Stravinsky, by contrast, referred to Rimsky-Korsakov as "master"—greatly appreciative that the elderly composer took him under his wing. Later, however, he would openly criticize his former teacher's music (for political and self-serving reasons), despite copious evidence of stylistic influence in virtually all of his early works. Conversely, while Prokofiev never developed a personal feeling for Rimsky-Korsakov, he liked much of his music, the fairy tale operas in particular. All the while he was being disrespectful or inattentive in his seminar, he would attend the dress rehearsal and three consecutive performances of his professor's latest opera *Skazaniye o nevidimom grade Kitezhe i deve Fevronii* (Legend of the Invisible City of Kitezh and the Maiden Fevroniya) and applaud, in his own words, until his hands ached.[8]

Prokofiev's orchestration seminars with Rimsky-Korsakov lasted two years, during which he recalled learning next to nothing. While he spent more time at the Conservatory in harmony, counterpoint and composition classes with Lyadov (he even took private lessons in his home), the faculty member to whom he felt closest was Cherepnin, who had also been a student of Rimsky-Korsakov at the Conservatory. Cherepnin not only taught Prokofiev score reading and conducting beginning in 1907, but further widened his musical outlook. Cherepnin was employed by Diaghilev as a conductor for his 1909 Paris season of ballet and opera (which included performances of his recent ballet *Le Pavillion d'Armide*), and was later commissioned to write *Narcisse et Echo* for the 1911 Ballets Russes season. Soon dubbed his official "Kapellmeister,"[9] Cherepnin was also Diaghilev's first choice to compose the score for *L'Oiseau de feu* in 1909, and he had begun working on it before falling out with Fokine and withdrawing.[10] Later, Diaghilev would grow tired of Cherepnin's music and deride Prokofiev's affiliation with him. (Cherepnin was dismissed from his position as first conductor in the summer of 1911, and Pierre Monteux took his place.) Cherepnin's sympathetic support was important to Prokofiev during his years at the Conservatory. Aside from his encouragement and that of some of his classmates (Myaskovsky in particular), the traditional St Petersburg Conservatory, in the composer's view, did not leave much of an imprint on his style. However, a closer look at his music says otherwise.

The composer was supported away from the Conservatory by like-minded, anti-academic musicians affiliated with the avant-garde "St Petersburg Evenings of Contemporary Music." There the young Prokofiev heard the music of Ravel, Debussy and Stravinsky, among other modern composers, and performed the music of Schoenberg for the first time in Russia. He recalled his audition for the group's inner circle of Nurok, Nouvel and the critic Karatïgin, "I had never before experienced such immediate enthusiasm [for my music]." He made his public debut as composer at an Evening of Contemporary Music concert on 18 December 1908 (OS), performing seven of his piano pieces including four which subsequently were "polished" and published as his opus 4. Almost overnight he established a reputation as the *enfant terrible* of Russian musical modernism.

Stravinsky as quickly had become the musical sensation of the Ballets Russes' seasons in Paris and London with *L'Oiseau de feu* (1910), *Petrouchka* (1911) and *Le Sacre du printemps* (1913), all the while becoming more and more estranged from the musical life in his homeland. While Stravinsky was heralded by the French critics as a link to the past glories of the *kuchkists* and a purveyor of neonationalism, Prokofiev was viewed by a far more conservative audience in his homeland as an independently minded "radical futurist."[11]

Prokofiev did not take active interest in Stravinsky's music until after *L'Oiseau de feu* had brought him fame in Paris.[12] The first music of his Prokofiev likely heard was the introduction to that very ballet, played by Stravinsky at the piano two months before its public premier. This was at an intimate musical soiree arranged by Nurok in the offices of the journal *Apollon* on 10 April 1910. (Prokofiev performed his First Piano Sonata, "Skazka" from op.3, and a short Etude from op.4.) Never one to withhold his opinion, Prokofiev told Stravinsky that "there was no music in it [the ballet's introduction], and if there was any it was from [Rimsky-Korsakov's] *Sadko*." Not surprisingly the thin-skinned Stravinsky took offense. Robert Craft claims that the two "became friends" at Prokofiev's December 1908 public debut at an Evening for Contemporary Music concert,[13] yet the first mention of Stravinsky in the composer's diary comes on 12 April 1910. Prokofiev seems to have missed the St Petersburg premiers of *L'Oiseau de feu* (in Suite form) at a Ziloti concert in October 1910 and *Petrouchka* (three movements only) at a Koussevitzky concert in January 1913. He first heard *Le Sacre du printemps* at a St Petersburg concert performance led by Koussevitzky in the winter of 1914. He expressed his delight with the work's liveliness in his Diary but also thought that some passages were too loud and in other quiet spots "there was such unrestrained false music that you would be surprised that ... Stravinsky doesn't have a screw loose!"[14] Though he claimed he did not really "understand" *Le Sacre* upon first hearing, his subsequent correspondence reveals that it certainly intrigued him. On the other hand, Prokofiev had criticized both *Petrouchka* and *L'Oiseau de feu* for their lack of substantial and original thematic invention in his letters to Cherepnin and Myaskovsky. In a 1913 letter to Myaskovsky he called the music of *Petrouchka* "dynamic," the orchestration "excellent," but called a large part of it no more than "modernistic filler." To Cherepnin that same year he wrote that he was "exasperated" by its music, "or more truly, by the low level of the author's standards for music," a not uncommon view amongst Russian musicians and critics at the time. Their 1910 encounter and these criticisms illuminate a fundamental difference in the two composers' outlooks: Prokofiev was unusually rigid in his disapproval of using borrowed material, whether for conspicuous display, passing reference, or even as a sign of homage.[15] To him originality was paramount. But he certainly knew the high regard in which Stravinsky was held by Diaghilev and the cognoscenti among the ballet audience in western Europe. He would seek similar success, but without borrowing or imitation.

Diaghilev, ever vigilant for new talent which would enthrall the Paris audience, had tapped the inexperienced young composer in 1914 to write a ballet on some Russian fairy-tale or prehistoric theme. But the impresario expected something in the neonational vein. He apparently did not realize that like Stravinsky, Prokofiev needed to be converted to neonationalism. *Kuchkism* (that is, conspicuous appropriation of Russian folk music) had become passé by the turn of the century in St Petersburg academic circles. Diaghilev was aware, as many were, that Prokofiev's music (and indeed, even his personality[16]) already reflected the Russian vogue for neoprimitivism. In a September 1912 review of the composer's Four Etudes for Piano, op. 2 in *Muzïka*, a critic stated: "Here are works from which gust a primitive strength and freshness."[17] But because of Diaghilev's uncharacteristic lack of close involvement, Prokofiev's first ballet grew into an unsuitable orchestral showpiece that was only partly primitivistic and almost completely lacking in marketable Russian color.

In addition to *Ala i Lolli*'s rather inauspicious beginning, Prokofiev was at a far greater disadvantage than Stravinsky had been when Diaghilev asked him to compose *L'Oiseau de feu* in December 1909. Stravinsky had already worked for Diaghilev, orchestrating two Chopin piano pieces for inclusion in the company's June 1909 production of *Les Sylphides*. Furthermore, he was given a complete, professionally rendered libretto appropriated from well-known fairy tales, and he worked with (actually, for) his choreographer in the closest collaboration possible—improvising at the keyboard as Fokine acted out the scenes. As the junior partner Stravinsky had no choice but to yield to Fokine's direction. Although he later had harsh words to say about him, it is certain that he could not have written the kind of music that Fokine wanted without this intensive "tutorial."

Stravinsky had to forge a new path in order to provide the sort of accompaniment that Fokine's choreodramas required. Fokine had abandoned the conventional French forms like the *grand pas de deux* and stiff movements of the *danse d'école*. He had also dispensed with the traditional vocabulary of explanatory gesticulations, leaving the story to be told by realistic actions, dance and music. The type of fully textured, organic symphonic music Chaikovsky had written for the mimed dialogues in the Prologue of *Sleeping Beauty*, for example, was unspecific and needed the dancers' conventional, exaggerated gestures to relate the events. This music churns on and on symphonically, quite independent from King Florestan's and Catalabutte's argument and distressed gesticulations over the omission of her name from the guest list for Aurora's christening. There is, of course, a dialogue between winds and strings in this passage, but it suggests the nature of the action without controlling or even paralleling it. Petipa's instructions for Chaikovsky did not call for specifics, "When a loud noise is heard—a quite lively movement." Newly composed music for Fokine's choreodramas, on the other hand, was required to actively participate in the narration—it had to help the dancers as they "presented" natural expression rather than just accompany gestural "representations."[18] Lacking any recent precedent in ballet, Stravinsky, according to Taruskin, turned to more familiar ground appropriating from "the old Wagnerian 'music drama'" "a kind of purposely 'formless' instrumental recitative, which derives its coherence strictly from the story line and from the deployment of leitmotifs."[19] He continues: "The mimed 'recitatives' in this most operatic of all ballets [*L'Oiseau de feu*] are constructed mosaic-fashion out of the leitmotifs ... the progress of the music being tied in the most literal way to the detailed and highly anecdotal action."[20] Instead of just facilitating the action, this type of music helped interpret it. When one compares Chaikovsky's accompaniment to the aforementioned gestural dialogue in *Sleeping Beauty* with an excerpt from Ivan's and Kashchey's encounter in *L'Oiseau de feu*, the phrasing alone shows just how much closer the latter's music is tied to the dialogue. Stravinsky also borrowed from opera the convention of using diatonic harmony for human characters and chromatic harmony for fantastical ones, a procedure used by Glinka in *Ruslan and Lyudmila* and exploited by Russian composers ever since. By using the operatic model Stravinsky was able to provide sufficiently explicit music that helped narrate the ballet's story.

It is logical that he would have turned to known operatic models. In some respects, however, these models were themselves indebted to early nineteenth-century ballet, and, of course, Grand Opera. Highly descriptive, dramatic music, or "presentational" music as I would like to call it (in lieu of more traditional labels such as onomatopoetic or mimetic),[21] was a major component of the realistic ballet-pantomimes that graced the stage of the Paris Opéra in the 1830s. This music was, as Marian Smith observes:

> characterized by frequent changes of meter and key, stop-and-start phrasing narrative sounding snippets and occasional pregnant pauses ... [it] was designed to follow the action closely; in it, events, motion, moods and personality all found some sort of musical expression. It is with this sort of music that composers ... endeavored to help audiences understand the plot.[22]

This music was, in turn, partly rooted in the less *auguste mélodrame* of the Parisian boulevard theaters. So too, Fokine's choreodrama. We shall see that Prokofiev took up this presentational technique to a point of excess in his first version of *Chout*, leading Diaghilev to order a revised score that harked back to symphonic style.

Overview of the similarities and dissimilarities between Prokofiev's and Stravinsky's early ballets

Despite the fact that both *Le Sacre du printemps* and *Ala i Lolli* deal with prehistoric subjects, involve deity worship, sacrifice and abduction, neither the "plots" nor the music inspired by them are all that similar. Each composer began with a musical concept for a neoprimitive ballet, then collaborated with a respected authority in the field of letters: Roerich for Stravinsky and Gorodetsky for Prokofiev. However, quite unlike Stravinsky's and Roerich's ethnologically researched, yet timeless ritual, Gorodetsky and Prokofiev settled for a traditional story ballet. They both seemed eager to tackle a ballet about the Scythians, but neither had had any experience writing a ballet scenario. The result is a generic story about power, abduction and rescue transposed to prehistoric times. In this regard *Ala i Lolli* is actually more akin to *L'Oiseau de feu* than to the impersonal presentation of the ancient rite in Stravinsky's later ballet. Both *L'Oiseau de feu* and *Ala i Lolli* contain a struggle between good and evil: the mortal heroes Ivan Tsarevich/Lolli try to rescue the captive princess/Ala from the evil Kashchey/Chuzhbog, and are themselves rescued/transformed by the Firebird/Veles. Diaghilev recognized the ordinariness of Gorodetsky's scenario and dismissed it as a "Petersburg trifle appropriate for the Mariinsky Theatre ten years ago... ." Prokofiev, thoroughly absorbed by Gorodetsky's (and his own) primitivistic imagery, had not.

The designated choreographer, Romanov, who had recently collaborated with the Ballets Russes on Stravinsky's *Le Rossignol*, was busy working on experimental ballets as well as staging conventional ones for operas at the Mariinsky Theatre. He did meet with Prokofiev to hear about the new ballet on 27 October 1914 (OS) and on 1 December there *may* have been a meeting with Gorodetsky present. Regardless, it is extremely doubtful whether Romanov had any influence on the project. Gorodetsky's inexperience with the genre and Romanov's non-contribution may account for such incongruities as having the principal female character onstage alone tied to a tree and killing off her rescuer before they had a chance to dance together. Some of the ballet's most fantastical elements originated with Prokofiev, who demonstrated his ideas for Gorodetsky at the piano—a turnabout from the Fokine–Stravinsky collaboration on *L'Oiseau de feu*.[23] As Prokofiev became engrossed in making *Ala i Lolli* an orchestral tour de force, the story and balletic intent became ancillary. Such a departure would not have occurred had the ballet been written under Diaghilev's usual close supervision. After Nurok and Nouvel advised the impresario what Prokofiev was doing, Diaghilev quickly summoned him to Italy. This spelled the end of *Ala i Lolli* as a ballet.

Prokofiev admitted being inspired by Stravinsky's *Le Sacre du printemps* as he wrote his first ballet but claimed not to have been influenced by it: "it is quite possible that I was now searching for the same images *in my own way* [emphasis added]" Rather than technical specifics it was undoubtedly *Le Sacre*'s generalized, primitivistic sound that fascinated him. The proof lies in the comparison of the two scores: they are alike only in the most superficial way. That Prokofiev was following the vogue of primitivism in his characterizations of Veles and Chuzhbog, a style that came quite naturally to him, to be sure, is a fair statement to make (elsewhere, however, primitivism is forsaken for voluptuousness, wittiness or orchestral effects). That the young composer was obviously taken by the way Stravinsky made his orchestra sound and was fired to go one better is also certain. But parallels like these are not what we are seeking—they are precompositional inspirations that could, but do not necessarily dictate musical style.

The difference in musical style between the *Scythian Suite* and *Le Sacre du printemps* is readily apparent. The usually charitable Russian critic and composer Asafyev (under his nom de plume, Glebov) pointed out the "metric monotony" of Prokofiev's score straightway in a 1916 *Muzïka* article,[24] an accusation that has probably never been leveled at Stravinsky's kaleidoscopic score. Consider Monteux's 17 orchestral rehearsals in preparation for the premier of *Le Sacre* in 1913 ("we kept our eyes glued to his baton" one oboist recalled) and the fact that this score remains today a conductor's rite of passage. Compare this with the *Scythian Suite*'s being performed by the conductorless Russian orchestra Persimfans (PERvyi SIMFonicheskii ANSambl', First Symphonic Ensemble) in December 1925. To cite but one example, Chuzhbog's dance and "Ritual of the Rival Tribes" may be logically compared in that they deal with displays of prowess and their geneses come from not dissimilar rhythmic cells (Exx. 2.1 and 2.2). Both even have contrasting lyrical passages and interruptive brass outbursts evoking some sort of primal savage cry (trombones in measures 7 and 10, and horns and trombone 4 before the end, respectively). Prokofiev, like Stravinsky, extends and elides phrases in constant variation and changes to triple meter for the quieter contrasting sections. Both examples are governed by a steady pulse. But what sets the two examples apart is their metric groupings and lyrical style. Stravinsky makes nearly hypnotic repetitions and permutations of his rhythmic cell against a foreground of metric irregularity. His doubling of the theme at the third suggests to Taruskin its progeny in a specific genre of Russian dance song.[25] Stephen Walsh believes that Stravinsky, "perhaps following the instinctive practice of the peasant singer, lets the bar line fall, not according to a rhythmic schema, but as dictated by added or subtracted melodic values."[26] Prokofiev's steady meter, on the other hand, does evoke a sense of elemental power, but, characteristically, the main interest is lyrical—his cell is an arresting head motive of an evolving theme. This example, and others,[27] gives lie to claims (proceeding from Communist Party mouthpiece Tikhon Khrennikov) such as "Prokofiev squandered his native gifts to imitate Stravinsky's several styles." The composer did not "imitate" nor did he, as the author of a widely circulated textbook claims, "choke off his ... melodic gift."[28] Furthermore, by the time of *Le Sacre du*

Ex. 2.1   Opening of "Chuzhbog's dance," 2nd movement, *Scythian Suite*

printemps and the subsequent works of his "Russian period," Stravinsky had undergone a major stylistic metamorphosis, appropriating the essence of Russian folk music to make the foundation of his new musical language. When he composed *Ala i Lolli* Prokofiev had yet to be converted to neonationalism. Apart from a slight reminder of *Night on Bald Mountain* (compare, for example, reh. 25 with m. 130 in Rimsky's version of the score) and perhaps *L'Oiseau de feu* (compare reh. 27 with reh. 133 in Stravinsky's ballet), Prokofiev's music has no distinctive Russian character. (It is generally accepted that nonnative audiences discern "Russianness" by association, that is, through comparison with known paradigms.[29])

Colorful Russian character abounds in Prokofiev's next ballet, however—the result of Diaghilev's and Stravinsky's reorientation process. In consequence, discussions of *Chout* often include mention of *L'Oiseau de feu* or *Petrouchka*, even *Le Sacre*. All of them use presentational music in varying degrees to illuminate the narrative. Both *Chout* and *L'Oiseau de feu* are based on Russian fairy-tales, and both rely heavily on conventions of the Russian theatre. But Prokofiev was more selective and furthermore compelled to personalize his *kuchkist* stimuli. The traditional harmonic polarity between real characters (diatonicism) and fantastic ones (chromaticism) which Stravinsky exploited in both of his first two ballets was not particularly amenable to *Chout*: its adversaries are all quasi-fantastic characters (that is, clever buffoons preying on gullible ones) until the introduction of the "real" merchant in the second half of

Ex. 2.2 *Le sacre du printemps*, "Ritual of the Rival Tribes," reh. 57–9

the ballet.[30] Prokofiev probably felt no obligation to exploit this traditional antithesis because he could make trenchant characterizations through other means. When both composers did draw on the same tradition, for example the use of the *khorovod* (discussed below), the results reflect individuality far more than a shared *neokuchkist* style.

Prokofiev's tuneful, Russian folk-inspired music along with Larionov's colorful *lubok*-inspired designs and some puppet-like antics for the dancers, might recall *Petrouchka*.[31] But Prokofiev faced a far different task setting *Chout's* lengthy narrative than Stravinsky did painting atmospheric tableaux in *Petrouchka*. And although Prokofiev wrote music suggestive of Russian folk music for his ballet, he stopped short of Stravinsky's outright quotations and conspicuous use of popular tunes. Furthermore, the ballets' respective décors present two different worlds: Larionov's farcical stage action and cubist-distorted décor are wholly unlike the realism Benois brought to the retrospective *Petrouchka*. Nor did *Chout* share *Petrouchka*'s convincing synthesis of dance, design and music. Although both ballets had the choreography added last, Fokine's (and Nijinsky's) efforts were perfectly tailored to the music and the story. Larionov's cubist/futurist staging, on the other hand, provided a degree of discontinuity with Prokofiev's predominantly lyrical music (a feature not uncommon in modern dance productions).

Having introduced some general areas of musical and nonmusical similarities and differences between Prokofiev's and Stravinsky's early ballets and beyond, we can more closely and systematically examine Prokofiev's use of folk material, formal procedures, and techniques of characterization in his first two ballets, weighing the degree of influence against originality. The result will show that Prokofiev did not rely upon Stravinsky's ballets as models, but instead used them—as he used the traditions of theatrical music, Russian and otherwise— more as an inspiration in creating his own, highly personal music.

A surrogate for *Ala i Lolli*

Prokofiev's *Skifskaya Syuita* (Scythian Suite) must serve in place of the composer's unfinished short score of *Ala i Lolli* which was performed for Diaghilev in 1915 but is almost certainly lost. After making the Suite from the rejected ballet Prokofiev might have discarded or at least not valued highly what remained. He carried the Suite, his First Piano Concerto and other solo piano works with him when he left for his American tour in 1918. Aside from the manuscripts which had been deposited with the publisher Gutheil before he left and those which his mother managed to carry with her when she left Russia in 1920, his music was lost during the revolution, probably as a result of the party decree which reassigned and divided up living quarters. This loss notwithstanding, we have a fairly good idea what Prokofiev's first ballet was like. According to the composer, the Suite and ballet are quite similar. As he looked over what he had completed for *Ala i Lolli* he discovered that "if a few uninteresting passages were deleted the rest of the music was well worth saving. A slight revision here and there resulted in a four movement *Scythian Suite* with the material laid out in approximately the same order as the ballet."[32] Understandably, Prokofiev provided no stage instructions in the Suite and no synopsis accompanied the score published for Gutheil by Breitkopf und Härtel in 1923. But there exists a hastily written summary of the action in the composer's hand (full of strikeouts) that was probably intended as program notes for the Suite's Petrograd premier on 16 January 1916 (OS). Until the composer's Diary was made available, this was perhaps the only surviving primary source related to *Ala i Lolli*'s scenario. It was no easy matter to align the extant bits of the story with the music of the Suite:

I. Worship to the Sun—Veles (first theme) and to the beloved wooden idol Ala (~~middle~~ (second theme, slow).
II. Chuzhbog ~~and dance of devil miraculous~~ ... summons the seven snakes and he dances surrounded by them. He abducts Ala
III. Night. Ala chained to a tree in captivity at Chuzhbog's. But as soon as he wants to approach, ~~her~~ the moon's rays fall on her and the god of darkness cannot attack her in the light.
IV. Folk hero Lolli sets out to free Ala. He is to be killed in the unequal battle against Chuzhbog. But the Sun-Veles rises and strikes Chuzhbog with his rays.

At the top of the document on which this outline appears, there is a brief resumé of the compositional process: "~~This music~~ in 1914 first sketches ... for the ballet of the Scyths ... ~~(in 1914)~~, but in the next year reworked into Scythian Suite ...."[33] Nestyev's undocumented account of the action of the Suite in his biography differs in a few important details as do the program notes written by Felix Borowski for the first performance of the work outside Russia (by the Chicago Symphony Orchestra on 6 December 1918, conducted by the composer). The primary discrepancy involves Chuzhbog's abduction of Ala, which, according to the handwritten summary alone occurs at the end of the second movement.

Any attempt to recreate the ballet scenario from the Suite's programs was impeded first of all by the discrepancy in number of movements: the ballet had five. The scenario for the latter which Prokofiev recorded in his Diary on the evening of 9 October 1914 (OS) after he and Gorodetsky had concocted it in just one hour is no Rosetta stone, however. Many details of this *ballet d'action* remain unknown. Nevertheless, the draft scenario, quoted below, helps us in the attempt to recreate the original role of the music of the Suite.

First scene: The god Veles (the sun) has a daughter, the happy goddess Ala. The foreign dark god Tar wants to abduct her, but he is powerless against the light of the sun (Veles). The sun goes down. Tar steals Ala. Then a simple mortal, singer [*pevets*] rushes into the chase in order to save her for he has fallen in love with her.

Second scene: Evening. The episode of the chase. The singer succeeds in getting Ala but the dark god gets her back again.

Third scene: In a northern fjord. Ala is in chains [a captive of] Tar. Night. Tar wants to take hold of her [*obladet'*], but every time at that moment the moon comes from behind the clouds. In the moon's rays appear moon maidens. Against the light Tar is powerless and the moon maidens defend Ala.

Fourth scene: Dawn. The singer again overtakes Tar. Battle. The mortal one is killed. In the sky go the Bovidae, all kinds of demons and the sun rises—Veles, who has come out to look for his daughter. He defeats Tar and at that moment the chains fall from Ala. She loved the singer and is hurt by his death.

Fifth scene: The stage decoration of the first scene. Veles by means of burning transforms the brave defender of his daughter into godhood. Ala throws herself into the fire after the body of her beloved and the reverse happens—she becomes a mortal. Alas, they are different again.

Prokofiev saw the ending as somewhat humorous, but Gorodetsky stood firm by it.[34] At their next meeting two days later Prokofiev became upset with Gorodetsky because he offered only static tableaux, ignoring the requisite action for a ballet. He had thrown out the second scene and forgotten the composer's demand for movement as the curtain rose. After a bout of peevishness ("I explained, 'I don't like any of it' and lay down, very upset, on the sofa") Prokofiev was once again actively working with his collaborator. He restated his desire to have the people laying face down as the curtain rose, and came up with a new plan for the second scene. He created the idea of alternating moon rays and clouds in the third scene and also the procedure of transforming the singer into an idol by use of a curtain. By the end of the meeting "the ballet flashed into our imaginations, we were both satisfied and excited." By 16 October Prokofiev was busily working on the music for the first, second and third scenes. "I mobilized all the sketches and themes [I had] composed in the spring and summer, [and] written on scraps of paper." He confessed, "sometimes it is confusing [trying] to find these scraps, they are scattered everywhere ... ." He used one of them to illustrate the moon maidens, whom he envisioned as "cold, tender and mysterious, not from this world."

Trying to settle the action in first scene proved to be the biggest impediment to progress on the ballet. As he started to compose, all Prokofiev had to work with was his idea of people lying face down at the opening and the abduction of Ala at the end (by 20 October he began referring to the evil god as Chuzhbog in his Diary). He wanted something that would interest the audience in the singer (or "poet" as he once referred to him) and he also wanted bold action at the start, "all these rites." He shared with Gorodetsky his idea of having "a magnificent funeral procession with the body of a hero. The priests are summoned, [then] Ala resurrects him. Exultation. Chuzhbog snatches Ala, the grateful knight rushes to save her." But Gorodetsky protested that the act of resurrecting the dead was not characteristic of old Slavic pagan beliefs. He promised to come up with something; a month later he finally did.

The composer's Diary entries from this period help to clarify some of the action of the original scenario. For example, Chuzhbog makes three passionate approaches towards Ala in the third scene, each stronger than the last,[35] and at the end of this action there is a short conclusion. Ala's dance before Veles after she is freed in the following scene unfolds in four parts: "an upsurge of joy upon gaining her freedom, some kind of mystical ritual, somewhat affected gratitude, a joyful dance." On 28 October Prokofiev recorded his conception for the conclusion of the fourth scene, "Ala over the corpse of the singer does not give way to grief or despair, she is too otherworldly for that. Perplexity and dismay ... tenderness towards her prostrate friend—these are her feelings." Also in regards to this scene he wrote: "the sunrise ... is not a phenomenon of nature, but rather like a procession of heavenly forces, concluding with the appearance of the Sun-god." Since the fourth scene was the only one he finished before being summoned to Italy by Diaghilev, it may be safe to assume that these are his final thoughts and that this is reflected in the music. Prokofiev played the fourth part for Gorodetsky on 18 November, after which the writer exclaimed "picturesque, fresh, wild!" That same evening the action of the first scene was at last finalized (the opening music for "the priestesses" had already been composed by then), except for the details of sunset, something Gorodetsky never provided.

It appears that Prokofiev never got around to the final movement of the ballet—there is no mention of his composing anything for it. It would have been a daunting task to make the concluding conflagration sound climactic in the wake of the stunning, fourth scene sunrise. When summoned by Diaghilev the first two movements were "half done," the third "almost done," and only the fourth was completed. He had begun orchestrating the music on 2 December but three days later got bogged down with the many-layered music of the sunrise. By 9 December he was energetically working on its conclusion (the part that drove Glazunov away at the premier), but acknowledged that "it crawls very slowly. It is all counterpoint. But it will sound splendidly." He put great stock in the orchestration of his first ballet. Earlier he remarked about the defeat of Chuzhbog, "on the piano it is nothing special, but in the orchestra ... it will be stunning."[36] By 4 January he was dividing his time between the ballet's first scene and practicing for the upcoming performance of his Second Piano Concerto at the Russian Music Society on 24 January. On 1 February (OS) he set out by train on the long journey to Italy.

When comparing the original ballet draft with the four movements of the Suite ("Worship of Veles and Ala," "Chuzhbog and the dance of the evil spirits," "Night," "Lolli's march and the procession of the sun"), it is apparent that they follow the same general dramatic sequence but differ in the number of events depicted. The first movement of the Suite undoubtedly omits the concluding action in the first scene of the ballet: the abduction of Ala by Chuzhbog, and the appearance of Lolli. It is virtually impossible to place the abduction in the existing music of the Suite. It seems likely that Prokofiev would have created a substantial representational passage for this; recall that he considered Ravel's efforts feeble in the tangentially similar passage in *Daphnis et Chloë*, and also that he approved of the congruity of music and action in *Schéhérazade*. But there is no obvious place where such a dramatic event could have taken place amidst the first movement's glorification of Veles and Ala, even though both parts are nicely sectional as befitting ballet music. The softly stated return of Veles's theme at reh. 16 (muted horns) amidst the ongoing volupté of Ala's music and the protracted dimenuendo surely must accompany the sunset. Since the Suite ends there, the ensuing abduction and appearance of Lolli must be some of the "uninteresting" bits that were dropped from the ballet, that is, unless they were relocated to another part of the Suite. Given Prokofiev's desire for an arresting start, *Ala i Lolli* probably opened just like the Suite with the Scythian ritual dance music glorifying Veles, perhaps even with the masses prostrate. Ala's subsequent slower, lyrical music could also accompany either mime or dance. Borowski's program notes add that this middle section is intended to be a "sacrifice" to the "well beloved idol, Ala," daughter of Veles, which may or may not have been part of the ballet.

We do not have the revised scheme Prokofiev used for the ballet's second scene, but it is possible that the action and music of the Suite's second movement correspond to it completely, or nearly so. An ongoing series of dances performed by the evil Chuzhbog and his cronies makes far more balletic sense than the originally planned chase episode. The composer's program for the Suite states that Chuzhbog summons the snakes and *he* dances surrounded by them. Borowski's notes corroborate this but Nestyev has everyone dancing, which is more dramatically apt, and all but demanded by the sectional music. The different Suite summaries have conflicting information about the participants of the dance, one calling them "seven pagan monsters," the other, "seven loathsome subterranean monsters," but these are mere details. The composer's placement of the abduction of Ala in his program notes for this movement is either a mistake or it might suggest that some of this music may have originally been used in scene one of the ballet for that very purpose. Neither Nestyev nor Borowski places the abduction here, but they did not know the original score. The only omission from the ballet in this movement may have been some mimetic music involving Lolli and Chuzhbog, perhaps at both ends.

The action in the third scene of the ballet is matched by that of the Suite's third movement: Chuzhbog steals in at night to assault the captive Ala who is chained to a tree, but the moon's rays fall on her and protect her. The music opens with a wonderful evocation of a moonlit night, complete with high, shimmering *pianissimo* strings. Two of Chuzhbog's three entrances are easily located, the first being the foreboding, low Bs (and stopped French horns) at reh. 35, and the final attack is clearly signaled in the music at reh. 43. Each time his theme is gradually "overpowered" by the music of the moon maidens, their eight-bar theme is first heard at reh. 38. It seems likely that the second attack was cut in the process of making the Suite.[37] Prokofiev remarked in his Diary that each of the three subsequent attacks should be stronger, but that presented a problem of how to overpower the last one's *fortissimo* climax. He achieved this through a montage effect at reh. 48, with a precipitous drop in dynamics allowing the muted trumpet signal to cut through "all the chaos," as he called it. After hearing the Suite's Paris premier in May 1921, Prokofiev revised the third and fourth movements. Although he dismissed the surgery as "minor" in a 15 May 1922 letter to officials of the Concerts Populaires in Brussels where the Suite was to be performed in a month ("... ce ne sont que quelques petits corrections j'ai fait en publiant la Suite."), he was most anxious to hear from Koussevitzky about the revised score's success under his baton. In the third movement he cut ten bars between reh. 37 and 38, that is, shortening the first attack. He also removed the flute doubling of the harp at the very opening and rewrote the flute lines at reh. 41 and after reh. 48.

At first glance the fourth movement seems to parallel the ballet as far as it goes. The Scythian folk hero Lolli arrives to free Ala who is still held captive by Chuzhbog. Lolli battles the evil god but perishes. The sun-god Veles rises, banishing the night and Chuzhbog with it. The beginning of the sunrise is easy to spot at reh. 69, as it recalls Veles's music from the opening movement. What comes before is problematic, however. After the opening *tempestuoso*, march-like section, most of the music seems to be anything but heroic (beginning at reh. 53). And there is nothing to suggest battle music, except in the most abstract sense. Chuzhbog's rhythm does steal in softly at reh. 56 in the clarinets but the music never comes close to his established character. The bouncy tune that follows surely cannot represent a fight to the death, even when restated *fortissimo* (reh. 62). And it would be a stretch to consider the music before the sunrise as accompanying Lolli in the throes of death, although we do encounter chromatic runs in hairpin dynamics as at the start of the movement. The anapestic rising second-falling third motive beginning at reh. 67 might represent Chuzhbog since it is not vanquished until six bars before the end. Without further evidence we are left to speculate. However, it does seem likely that material from the ballet's fourth scene was omitted from the middle part of the Suite's last movement. In addition, rearrangement of material seems likely (more anon). Even though he had not completed the ballet Prokofiev realized that he had ample material for a Suite, and that the stunning musical sunrise would make a logical conclusion. Ala's subsequent dance and lament was superfluous to the Suite, although in the ballet it provided a necessary dramatic contrast and a bridge to the final scene.[38]

Most of the sections of the ballet's story that are missing in the Suite rely upon mime: music for Ala's abduction, the music for Lolli as he resolves to save her, her "perplexity" over his death, and the battle between Lolli and Chuzhbog. This is wholly consistent with the normal procedure in making a ballet suite. But according to Nestyev, Prokofiev was keen to create "terrifying, barbaric images ... that would stun his audience."[39] The music for the abduction and battle would seem to fit this description. In that light it is difficult to dismiss them as "uninteresting passages," unless, of course, their thematic material had already been displayed during the Suite's second movement, Chuzhbog's dance.

Without more evidence it is impossible to know exactly how much is missing from *Ala i Lolli*, and therefore lost. The dramatic cohesiveness of the ballet may have been undermined by the Suite in regards to recollection motives (Veles' music excepted). The music of the Suite nevertheless unfolds as if in service to a ballet narrative, being comprised primarily of brief and usually contrastive sections. This does not discount the possibility of some manipulation to make more satisfying musical forms for the concert hall. But the music of the Suite likely represents much of the original idea.

The scenario Prokofiev and Gorodetsky worked out for *Ala i Lolli* was set in ancient times and had traditional types of roles: hero, villain, damsel in distress, and benevolent protector. To clearly distinguish the two powerful antagonists, one from the realm of light (Veles), the other from the realm of darkness (Chuzhbog), Prokofiev relied on conventional means for the former but used an extremely forceful, nearly crude musical style for the latter. This was quite in keeping with the prevailing fashion of primitivism but without an obvious musical precedent in the theatre.[40] The evil and powerful god Chuzhbog in *Ala i Lolli* is dramatically akin to other fantastical characters such as Chernomor in Glinka's *Ruslan and Lyudmila* and Chernobog in Rimsky-Korsakov's *Mlada*, and also to Kashchey from this same opera, Rimsky's opera *Kashchey bessmertnïy* (Kashchey the Deathless) and Stravinsky's *L'Oiseau de feu*. A comparison between Stravinsky's "Infernal Dance of All Kashchey's Subjects" from the latter (itself a descendent from Rimsky's "Infernal Kolo" in *Mlada*) and Prokofiev's second movement, "Chuzhbog and the Dance of the Evil Spirits" does reveal similarities in formal outline, instrumentation, and thematic character. Yet, Prokofiev ignores Russian harmonic tradition in making his characterization. He is justified in doing so because Chuzhbog is no Kashchey: the former is a barbarian, the latter an evil sorcerer. Prokofiev's hypnotically driving rhythms in the opening of Chuzhbog's dance bludgeon the listener, and, along with the fortissimo dynamic level and clear tonal center on pitch E, they bespeak earthy brutality. On the other hand, Stravinsky's more variegated writing—unarticulated downbeats and mercurial phrasing—aptly suggests Kashchey's magical air. Aside from a few very casual similarities (rhythmic figures, pedals) Rimsky-Korsakov's Chernobog is no real model either; the two characterizations are really quite different (to start with, Chernobog has a voice, courtesy of 12–16 unison basses, whereas Chuzhbog can only dance). Rimsky's demonic writing pales in comparison to Prokofiev's savage sounds. In his quest to musically differentiate Chuzhbog from Veles, Prokofiev painted in uncommonly bold strokes and thus became, in Taruskin's words, "the Scythian composer par excellence, emphatically recognized as such [in] his own day."[41]

Some of the characterful music in the Suite's finale also seems nontraditional, but for the opposite reason—it sounds alien to the nature of the ballet. Presumably the bold, sweeping music at the outset of the fourth movement (*tempestuoso*) accompanies Lolli as he marches in to rescue Ala from Chuzhbog. The French horns' "short-long" *forte* outbursts and the trumpet's motive with three crotchets and accented double semiquavers do suggest defiance and determination (and also point to the Prodigal's similar characterization at the opening of *L'Enfant prodigue*). But if the subsequent ironic and witty music at reh. 53—a veritable menagerie of sounds, with buffoonish playful leaps, chattering winds and comically loud outbursts—is meant to characterize Lolli, then he is more neurotic than noble, a none too distant relation to the emasculated hypochondriac *Prince in L'Amour des trois oranges*.[42] This would not be the last time Prokofiev provides an unexpectedly bizarre characterization in his ballets for Diaghilev. But a more likely solution is at hand: vermin. Twice Prokofiev mentions them in his Diary, once calling his music for them "amusing," another time describing their role: "the vermin which led Ala," presumably onto the scene after Veles has defeated Chuzhbog in scene four (perhaps they had led her to captivity as well). The abrupt change in style and tone at reh. 53 (or at least two bars thereafter) and again at reh. 56 suggest that this section in the Suite came from the end of the ballet scene. The role for the rest of the music in the middle of the Suite's finale, however, remains conjecture.

The heroine Lolli intends to rescue is no mere mortal, to be sure. For her musical portrait Prokofiev relies upon the theatrical tradition of the "exotic heroine," an especially common figure in romantic ballet. But her music is also foreshadowed in one of the composer's non-theatrical works, namely the third movement of Piano Concerto no. 2 (reh. 70). Perhaps Prokofiev was recalling a passage Diaghilev had especially enjoyed in 1914, or else this could just be another example of the composer's stylistic stability (which, along with his remarkable constancy of characterization, will be discussed in Chapter 5). With the music that is at the same time alluring yet slightly distant, Ala becomes the prototype for future ballet heroines such as the ouvrière in *Le Pas d'acier*, the seductress in *L'Enfant prodigue*, Natasha in *Na Dnepre*, and so forth. Both here and in the Suite's third movement there is an air of *volupté* that contradicts the primitivistic setting. Ala is first depicted by an archaic sounding melody built from a five-note scale played by flutes (reh. 8 in the first movement), but 20 bars later by chromatically inflected diatonicism in the violins.[43] Her seductiveness comes in part from the melodic decorations, the hypnotic accompaniment, and the exoticism of the harmony. But all this is tempered by the cool flute sonority. The music for the composer's first ballet heroine thus sounds distinctively Prokofievian and it is nicely adaptable besides.

It is not known whether Veles, the sun-god, was intended to be represented on stage or meant to be an unseen spirit. Nevertheless, his musical characterization is clearly in the Russian tradition of theatrical heroes. The "Worship of Veles" features a ten-bar theme screamed *molto pesante* by three trumpets (primarily from e^2 to a^2, doubled at the fifth and octave; 1 after reh. 2) against a busy, multi-layered ostinato accompaniment. This march certainly evokes either the requisite physical strength for a corporal representation or the power for an omnipotent one. Veles "reappears" at the end of the Suite in the form of a sunrise to a not completely dissimilar melody, borne again by the trumpets. The tempo is slower and the meter changed to 6/4—the inherent lilt of this meter perhaps meant to suggest the radiating waves emanating from the sun. Veles' might is illuminated by a superbly protracted textural and dynamic crescendo achieved by dynamic shading and judiciously delayed entries of the eight horns and four trombones. Aside from mutual exploitation of obvious descriptive elements (pedals, tremolos, and so forth), the sunrise in Prokofiev's ballet—the Suite's musical and dramatic climax—is, not surprisingly, quite unlike the more transient, motivically generated "Daybreak" section in *L'Oiseau de feu*. It was probably Veles' portrait that prompted the Soviet musicologist Boganova to note the heroic tenor of Prokofiev's score.[44] Others already had done so, in 1916 Asafyev had likened the effect of this music to Borodin's *Polovtsian Dances*.[45]

Prokofiev's finished Suite indicates that *Ala i Lolli* would have made a serviceable ballet, at least from a musical standpoint. Indeed, it has been so used since 1927. Prokofiev had hoped to have the Suite performed as a ballet by Ida Rubinstein at the Paris Opéra in the spring of 1926, but its first appropriation was by Max Terpis for his *Die Erlöste* (The Saved), an allegorical ballet on a theme by Dante, which was premiered at the Berlin Staatsoper on May 7, 1927. Prokofiev attended the first performance incognito, but was not overwhelmed ("a very stupid production," he wrote Myaskovsky). Later that year Nijinska choreographed a ballet to the Suite which was premiered on 11 October at the Teatro Colón in Buenos Aires. The Suite's vivid orchestral colors and tremendous power (woodwinds in fours, eight horns, five trumpets, and four trombones) make up for some of the less inspired passages that seem little more than note spinning.[46] Obviously what Diaghilev heard in 1915—an incomplete first draft performed at the piano—sounded pallid by comparison. Based upon our knowledge of the published Suite, the impresario's dismissal of the ballet as "just music, and very bad," seems unduly harsh and says more about his expectations than Prokofiev's music.

Ala i Lolli lacks the strong national color and perceptible folk song-like style which Diaghilev well-knew guaranteed success in the West. But this was just half the complaint: the impresario also considered the ballet old-fashioned in plot and style. It was hard not to sound passé in the wake of *Le Sacre du printemps*, in which Stravinsky had successfully (although somewhat anachronistically) wed modernism, primitivism and Russianness into a timeless ritual. Without having heard the score's best characteristic, its orchestration, he was probably justified in calling *Ala i Lolli* "a St Petersburg fabrication ... good for the Mariinsky Theater ten years ago": its evocations are ultimately generic, its primitivism is unspecific and inconsistent, and its style is nothing new—though it did amplify musical primitivism. Russian color or ethnological purity had been of no concern to Prokofiev, nor was there any attempt to imitate Stravinsky's advanced style. Diaghilev felt that neither the ballet's music nor the plot, which he considered "trite," was worth salvaging. Despite having condescended to Bakst's weakness for ballets on Grecian themes in the past (*Narcisse* and *Daphnis et Chloë*), and allowing *Papillons* to follow *Carnaval* (both using music by Schumann), the impresario did not like to repeat himself. *Ala i Lolli* was old news: its dramatic core recalled *Daphnis et Chloë*, its primitivism was overshadowed by the milestone *Le Sacre* and it was redundant next to the ever popular *Polovtsian Dances*.[47] Diaghilev's interests now lay with futurism although he still anxiously awaited Stravinsky's neonational *Les Noces*. With the arrival in 1914 of the Moscow futurist/neoprimitivist stage designers Goncharova and Larionov and the moldable young dancer Massine, he set out on a new aesthetic course.

In this context *Ala i Lolli* stood no chance. In sizing up the situation in the spring of 1915, Diaghilev probably decided that Prokofiev was not going to outdo Stravinsky on the modernist front, but he could at least improve the Russian sound, that is, marketability, of his music. Despite his care to start *Ala i Lolli*'s replacement out on the right foot, he created a new problem in his demand for more than just music (see Chapter 3). Thus the rejection of *Ala i Lolli* set up the rejection of Prokofiev's next ballet, as well. Still *Ala i Lolli* was an important step in Prokofiev's development as a ballet composer. Hence, the surviving music of the Suite remains an invaluable, though not completely revealing source for examination.

Presentation of folk elements

It is not surprising that the *Scythian Suite* lacks overt Russianness given the composer's inherent disinterest in national sources and his well-documented dislike of borrowed material and stylistic imitation. Nevertheless, some of Prokofiev's early music does reveal an innate folk-like quality. Diaghilev thought that the second theme in the Second Piano Concerto's finale suggested a Pan-like creature when he first heard it in 1914, and this prompted a passing notion to use the Concerto as music for a *ballet d'action*. He may also have viewed this *kuchkist*-sounding, *chastushka*-like theme and its Glinkaesque changing background treatment as proof that Prokofiev could write in the national style that so pleased the Parisian audiences, thus his uncharacteristic lack of involvement with this new ballet on "some Russian theme." Much earlier when the young Prokofiev was under Glière's tutelage between 1902 and 1903, the short piano "ditties" he composed did contain folk-like elements. Glière surmised that the songs sung by the Ukrainian villagers near the Prokofiev estate must have had a strong effect on the boy.[48] But the composer himself recalled that the songs he heard as a youth did not make an indelible impression. Once after Glière had improvised upon an Ukrainian folk theme in front of guests, Prokofiev took his turn but insisted upon using his own theme. His own words from his biography best sum up this insistence upon originality:

This proclivity toward working with my own materials has stayed with me ever since, and when it came to my own improvisations or compositions, I would bypass the folklore and use my own melodies.

I had the same attitude toward the folk songs they sang at Sontsovka [his boyhood village]. On Saturday nights and Sundays I often heard the village girls 'singing.'

But for whatever reason—whether because the Sontsovka region was lacking in good folk singers or because I was annoyed by the 'squawking' of the village singers—I never listened closely to the songs and didn't remember a single one. It is possible, of course, that subconsciously I absorbed those songs despite all that. At any rate, some twenty-four years later when I *first* tried to make my music Russian [in *Chout*; emphasis added], the material—my own, but in the Russian mood—came easily and naturally.[49]

These are hardly the sentiments of a fervent neonationalist.

When called upon in 1915 to help Prokofiev make his second ballet "truly Russian," Stravinsky was writing in a new national style inspired by the sounds and rhythms of spoken Russian. It is unlikely that the tight-lipped Stravinsky would have been willing to open his sketchbook and share the details of his newly found compositional technique, nor would Prokofiev necessarily have been receptive, despite his delight in some of his colleague's latest works.[50] Although Stravinsky had abandoned the kuchkist manner of setting folk songs, he might have pointed out his folk borrowings in *L'Oiseau de feu* and *Petrouchka* to his younger colleague, and perhaps other pieces as well. He also probably reminded Prokofiev of the standard sources—the Balakirev collection of 1866, and the Rimsky-Korsakov of 1877—and perhaps even recommended some recent ethnographic editions. However, considering his pained recollection of folk singing ("squawking") in his native Ukrainian village, it is doubtful whether Prokofiev would have shared Stravinsky's enthusiasm for Linyova's ethnologically correct polyphonic transcriptions made from phonograph recordings.[51]

Prokofiev was quite outspoken against lack of originality (that is, borrowing) and lack of "music" (that is, melody), as his correspondence and occasional reviews and articles for the journal *Muzïka* demonstrate. He approved of using simple, traditional material only when new "piquant" harmonies were added, thus combining the "artlessly simple" with a "complex accompaniment."[52] He admired Stravinsky's *Three Little Songs* (1913) because of the composer's "ear-pricking" harmonizations despite the rather banal folk tunes.[53] Prokofiev believed that outright borrowing, however, indicated a lack of talent. In 1913 he chastised Stravinsky for stealing from Rimsky-Korsakov's *Sadko* for the opening of *L'Oiseau de feu*. (Years later Prokofiev claimed that he stole *Le Sacre*'s "figure" from Glazunov's *Sten'ka Razin*.)[54] In correspondence with Myaskovsky about *Petrouchka* Prokofiev called Stravinsky "musically bankrupt," criticizing his use of "remplissage" (filler), and common tunes, which he called "odna truka" (nothing but trash).[55] Now, despite Stravinsky's guidance and Diaghilev's coercion to make *Chout* "truly Russian," Prokofiev was understandably still loath to parody. Although he used borrowed material in his Soviet period works, at this stage of his career he relied on music of his own invention (his 1919 *Overture On Hebrew Themes* being an exception). He declared as much when he wrote to Stravinsky after their meeting in Italy, "thumbing through Russian folk songs showed to me lots of interesting possibilities." One exception aside, the "interesting possibilities" led to his own folk-like creations, to which he added his own "piquancies."

Earlier Stravinsky had been equally amenable to both outright appropriation from folk sources as well as free invention. As he developed his modern neonational style he reached a point where having gone through so many folk sources he could "probably think them up faster than looking them up."[56] Prokofiev would have been more receptive to Stravinsky's newly composed folk-themes, like the *protyazhnaya* (melismatic, lyrical folk song) for Ivan Tsarevich in *L'Oiseau de feu* (reh. 12, 45, 71), than the conspicuous borrowings from the Rimsky collection, used in, for example, the "Ronde des Princesses" and the coronation finale in the same ballet.[57] His reference to "interesting *possibilities* [emphasis added] among the folk songs he had seen suggests that he might have been amenable to the practice of crafting a new entity from certain features of a given model.

Indeed, Prokofiev's primary theme in *Chout*—not just the main character's identifying tune, but one that permeates much of the score in leitmotivic fashion—is probably his own invention but cannot be ruled out as his abstraction of a model (Ex. 2.3) Unfortunately we do not have the composer's sketchbooks to enable us to recreate the compositional process of *Chout* as Stravinsky scholars have done for *Le Sacre*. This hypothesis is therefore based solely on the casual, Gestalt-like resemblance to a possible model, perhaps the quintessential (to western audiences, anyway) Russian folk song, "Vo pole beryozïnka stoyala" (In the Field Stood a Little Birch Tree; Ex. 2.4). This song appeared in the pioneering Lvov and Pratsch collection of Russian folk tunes of 1790 and was reharmonized by Rimsky-Korsakov for his collection of 1877. "Little Birch Tree" is widely known in slightly altered guise as the second theme in the finale of Chaikovsky's Fourth Symphony (Ex. 2.5) and to more serious Russofiles in Balakirev's *Overture On Three Russian Themes*, in Glinka's "Tarantella" in A minor for piano and in Grechaninov's *Russian Folk Dances*. It even appears in a

Ex. 2.3   Hero's main theme from *Chout*

Ex. 2.4   **"In the forest stood a little birch tree" from Rimsky-Korsakov's**
           ***One Hundred Russian Folk Songs* (1877)**

Ex. 2.5   **Theme two, finale of Chaikovsky's Symphony no. 4 (mm. 10–17)**

St Petersburg singspiel that predates the Lvov and Pratsch collection.[58] Whether this influence was merely subliminal, part of a deliberate transformation, or whether the similarity is just a happy coincidence, Prokofiev's main theme sounds as genuinely Russian. Though Prokofiev's theme lacks the harmonic closure and repetition of the folk song, it shares both the typically Russian descending line from the fifth degree to the tonic and a bipartite form with not dissimilar rhythmic profiles in each part. If Prokofiev's first three measures were reordered from: 1, 2, 3 to: 2, 3, 1, as the composer does for variety's sake during the course of the ballet, the resultant succession of measure-long rhythmic patterns matches the Chaikovsky arrangement of the folk song (see below). In a similarly manipulative manner, Prokofiev's consequent phrase could be seen as an extended rearrangement of the folk song's second half. Certain features of *Chout's* main theme like the irregular meter and the *peremennost* (that is, tonics ending lower than they began) sideslip from A to G# at the close even suggest more fidelity to Russian folk song practice than seen in Rimsky-Korsakov's harmonization. Although this similarity is not exact, it does exemplify the composer's method of thematic variation (as we will see later in his treatment of a borrowed factory song refrain at the opening of *Le Pas d'acier*). And the coloristic quartal chords in the consequent phrase, for example, demonstrate his interest in the modern aspects of Russian national style.

    In an interview with the *Observer* Diaghilev called *Chout* characteristically Russian but without any of its themes being derived from folklore. His qualifier may not be too significant as he was prone to hyperbole and condescension in his posturing encounters with the British press. It may have been nothing more than an acknowledgment of an original effort in light of the company's spate of pastiche scores as well as an attempt to gain some (well-deserved) distance from the 11-year-old *L'Oiseau de feu* and 10-year-old *Petrouchka*. At least one French critic had already noted that the score featured "quelques thèmes populaires russes, fortement déformés."[59] After the ballet's unauthorized United States premier by the Neighborhood Playhouse, a *New York Times* critic observed that the composer took "a Russian theme on which he has imposed his own characteristic dissonances."[60] Prokofiev admitted that he was unsure what powers affected him as he "settled down to compose the thematic material for *Chout*, trying to make it as truly Russian as possible." He acknowledged that childhood memories may have affected him subconsciously because the Russian national idiom" came quite easily. Whatever the impetus, the main theme of *Chout* went a long way towards providing the marketable Russian sound Diaghilev sought. It is unfortunate, however, that this delightful theme is heard too frequently during the course of the ballet (see "Entr'actes," Chapter 3).

Prokofiev evoked a typically Russian sonority by traditional means as well, for example using *protyazhnaya* style themes for the merchant and Molodukha, and imitating the *gusli*—one of the native folk instruments used by wandering minstrels, a type of psaltery—in both themes (reh. 153 and reh. 194, respectively) and the balalaika in the latter as well (1 after reh. 155). Despite the composer's typical distortions such as disjunct contour and octave displacement (not to mention piquantly mutated harmonic accompaniments), the fundamental folk-like quality in these themes remains clear. A *khorovod* is all but called for in the scene where the merchant enters and the seven daughters file past for his inspection. Prokofiev fashioned his own (unlike Stravinsky who borrowed his for *L'Oiseau de feu*) but diluted its identity by having it serve a dual function: it is first heard when the merchant enters with his matchmakers (reh. 194), and later in augmented form (reh. 199) the themes becomes the daughters' *khorovod* (where it is so labeled in the 1915 holograph). When accompanying the young ladies Prokofiev raises the theme two octaves and reduces the dynamic level to *pianissimo*. He also drops the previous folk instrument-like accompaniment in favor of one of his typical, delicate lattices of arpeggiated chords. While this does not belie the *khorovod's* repetitive character, it does suggest that the dramatic concept was more important than the integrity of his folk-inspired dance.

Not all the Russian folk elements found in *Chout* were prefigured in Stravinsky's early ballets. Prokofiev's framing introduction heard at the outset and just prior to all but the last two tableaux suggests a Rimspky-Korsakovian *priskazka* (or "Once upon a time ...") as found in *Skazka o Tsare Saltane* (The Tale of Tsar Sultan), *Zolotoy petushok* (The Golden Cockerel) and, perhaps most famously, *Schéhérazade*. Prokofiev never explained the purpose of his introductory passage, although he was quite proud of it, claiming that it sounded to him like "the dust being wiped off of the orchestra before the performance." While this is a description and not a statement of intent, it does resonate with the fantastic nature and the role of a *priskazka*.

Prokofiev fulfilled Diaghilev's demand that *Chout* be something "truly Russian," but he did so, quite characteristically, on his own terms. Given the political bias against *Chout* in Soviet Russia, it is understandable why Nestyev went no further than acknowledging that the main theme is "in a Russian national vein." With its frivolous buffoonery laced with undertones of malevolent mockery and ridicule, *Chout* flew in the face of the Soviet agenda for art, that is, uplifting Socialist Realism. Against his repeated criticism of Prokofiev's willful caricature of folk style in *Chout*, Nestyev's admission that the main theme has a "warm, human quality and its harmonies are exquisitely beautiful and expressive" may be as close to an admission of kinship that he felt comfortable making.[61] Although *Chout* uses some of the same traditional folk elements as *L'Oiseau de feu* and *Petrouchka* it is certainly not modeled after them. Unlike Stravinsky, Prokofiev did not borrow folk tunes, rather he used the well-known collections as a point of departure. He personalized and modernized his folk-like themes by making their melodic lines disjunct and mutating their simple, reiterative harmonies. He could evoke a typically Russian sonority as well as Stravinsky but chose to do so only if it served his dramatic concept. He used what seems to be a Rimsky-Korsakovian *priskazka* but characteristically flattered himself by referring only to the music's novelty. Stravinsky's assistance at the behest of Diaghilev in 1915 may not have provided much more than conviviality and reassurance. There is none of Stravinsky's latest style in *Chout*. Whereas Stravinsky took the essence of folk music to forge his new, distinctive style, Prokofiev modernized selected kuchkist procedures. Of the earlier Stravinsky there is not so much an influence as a shared heritage. *L'Oiseau de feu*, *Petrouchka* and *Chout* all reveal an assimilation of traditional techniques, but the independence of their composer's personal styles yielded quite different results.

Formal procedures

Chout weaves an elaborate web of organic motives, a procedure Prokofiev would rely upon later to unify *L'Enfant prodigue* and the longer Soviet period ballets. All the scenes in *Chout* contain music derived from or related to the main character's primary theme (the main character is henceforth referred to as the hero). Prokofiev probably heard and may have been duly impressed by Stravinsky's partially completed ballet *Les Noces* during their 1915 encounter, but *Chout*'s deployment of one quintessentially Russian theme is hardly equivalent to the former's dependence upon a tightly knit web of ethnographically derived motives. The nature and treatment of primary material affords further evidence of the fundamental difference in their compositional styles: Stravinsky, beginning with *Petrouchka*, built musical mosaics using tiny repeating melodic cells as his building blocks whereas Prokofiev adhered to

Fig. 1   Sergey Pavlovich Diaghilev (1872–1929)

Fig. 2   Contemporary British caricature of some violent acts in *Chout*

Fig. 3   Prokofiev in New York, 1918–19 season

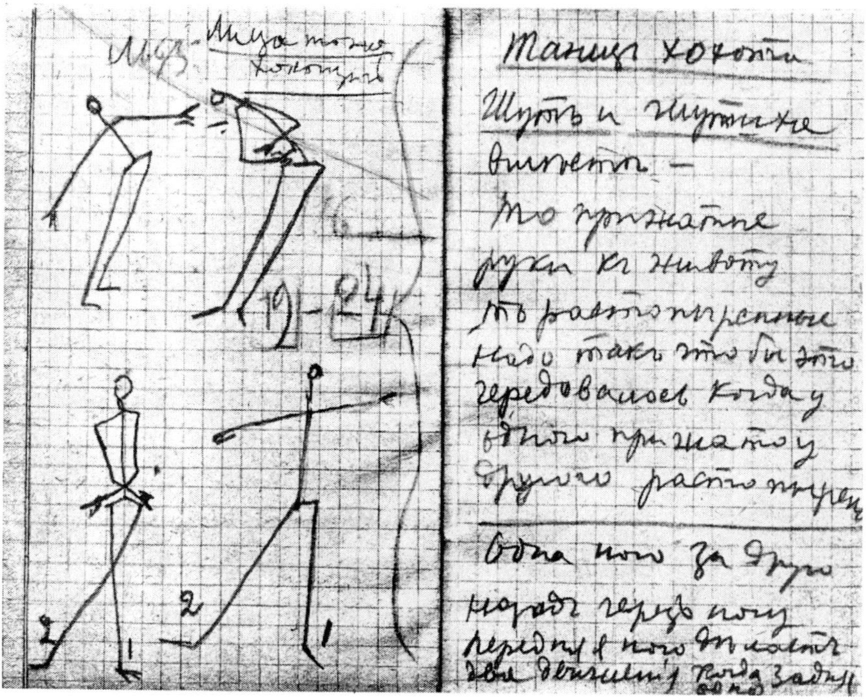

Fig. 4   Larionov's sketchbook for *Chout*, opened to sketches and
descriptions for the "Danse du rire"

Portrait de Larionow, par Juan Gris.

Fig. 5 **Pencil sketch of Larionov by Juan Gris for the Paris 1921 Ballets Russes program book**

Fig. 6   Larionov's later, cubist-inspired design for *Chout* scene 1: the hero
sits atop the stove hatching his plan

Fig. 7   Larionov's cubist/*lubok* design for *Chout* scene 5, the merchant's
bedroom, in the Paris 1921 Ballets Russes program book

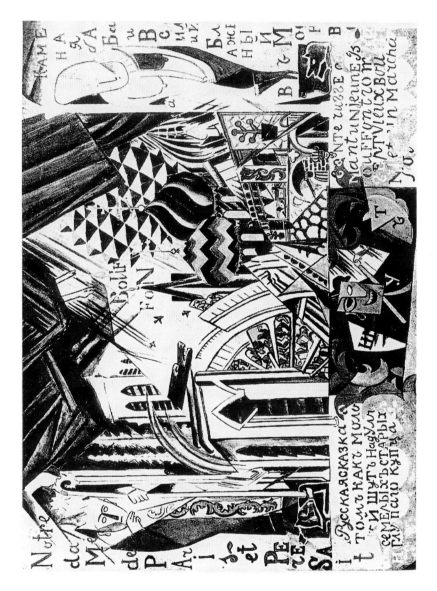

Fig. 8 Larionov's curtain for *Chout*

Fig. 9   The hero buffoon (Slavinsky) and his wife (Sokolova)

Fig. 10   Modish costumes from *Le Pas d'acier*. From left to right:
Tchernicheva, Lifar, Danilova, Massine

I

LE PAS D'ACIER

1920
(CREATION)

Ballet en deux tableaux de SERGE PROKOFIEFF et GEORGES IAKOULOFF
Musique de SERGE PROKOFIEFF
Constructions et Costumes d'après les Maquettes de GEORGES IAKOULOFF
Chorégraphie de L. MASSINE
Les Costumes sont exécutés sous la Direction de Mmes N. IAKOULOFF et A. YOUKINE
Les Constructions exécutées dans l'atelier de M. D. KAMISCHOFF, à Paris

*Les deux tableaux de ce ballet présentent une suite de scènes résumant deux aspects de la vie russe :
les légendes du village et le mécanisme de l'usine.*

PREMIER TABLEAU

I. Bataille de Baba-Yaga avec le Crocodile

Mlle Vera Petrova,
MM. Tcherkas, Efimow, Domansky, Kochanovsky,
Petrakevitch, Borovsky, Gaubier

II. Le Camelot et les Comtesses

M. Léon Woizikovsky
Mlles Thamar Gevergeva, Dora Vadimova,
Henriette Maikerska, Sophie Orlova
MM. Lissanevitch, Pavlow, Hoyer, Ladré, Ciéplinsky,
Ignatow, Strechnew, Hoyer II, Romow.

III. Le Matelot et les trois Diables

M. Léonide Massine
MM. Jazvinsky, Fedorow, Winter
MM. Tcherkas, Efimow, Domansky Kochanovsky,
Petrakevitch, Borovsky, Gaubier

IV. Le Chat, la Chatte et les Souris

Mlle Vera Petrova   M. Thadée Slavinsky
Mlles Savina, Markova, Miklachevska, Kouchetovska,
Evina, Jasevitch.
MM. Lissanevitch, Pavlow, Hoyer, Ladré, Cieplinsky,
Ignatow, Strechnew, Hoyer II, Romow

V. La Légende des Buveurs

Mr Léon Woizikovsky, Nicolas Efimov, Constantin Tcherkas.
MM. Domansky, Kochanovsky, Petrakevitch,
Borovsky, Gaubier.

VI. L'Ouvrière et le Matelot

Mlle Alexandra Danilova   M. Léonide Massine

VII. Ensemble

Par tous les Artistes

DEUXIÈME TABLEAU

VIII. Le Béguin

Mme Lubov Tchernicheva   M. Serge Lifar

IX. Passage des Ouvriers

M. Lissanevitch, Pavlow, Hoyer, Ignatow, Strechnew, Hoyer II

X, XI, XII. L'Usine

Mmes Alexandra Danilova, Lubov Tchernicheva, Vera Petrova.
MM. Léonide Massine, Léon Woizikovsky, Serge Lifar,
Thadée Slavinsky.
Les Ouvrières : Mlles Thamar Gevergeva, Dora Vadimova,
Henriette Maikerska, Sophie Orlova.
Mlles Savina, Soumarokova, Branitska, Chamié, Markova,
Fedorova, Zarina, Klemetska. Miklachevska, Kouchetovska,
Slavinska, Obidennaia, Barash, Evina, Matveeva, Jasevitch.
Les Ouvriers : MM. Tcherkas, Efimov, Domansky,
Kremnew, Jazvinsky, Fedorov, Winter, Lissanevitch,
Pavlow, Kochanovsky, Hoyer, Cieplinsky, Petrakevitch,
Ladré, Borovsky, Hoyer II, Ignatow, Strechnew,
Gaubier, Romow.

Fig. 11   **Excerpt from the Paris 1927 20th season Ballets Russes program
book**

225. Драка Бабы Яги съ крокодиломъ.

224. Драка Бабы Яги съ крокодиломъ.

Fig. 12   Baba-Yaga and the crocodile

Fig. 13   Tchernicheva and Lifar with hammers in the factory finale

Fig. 14 Closing scene of *L'Enfant prodigue*: Lifar crawls to his father

Fig. 15 Nikolay Rimsky-Korsakov (1844–1908), Anatoly Lyadov (1855–1914) and Alexander Glazunov (1865–1936). Glazunov welcomed the thirteen-year-old Prokofiev to the St Petersburg Conservatory. There he studied orchestration with Rimsky-Korsakov and composition with Lyadov

Fig. 16 Doubrovska as the Seductress in *L'Enfant prodigue*

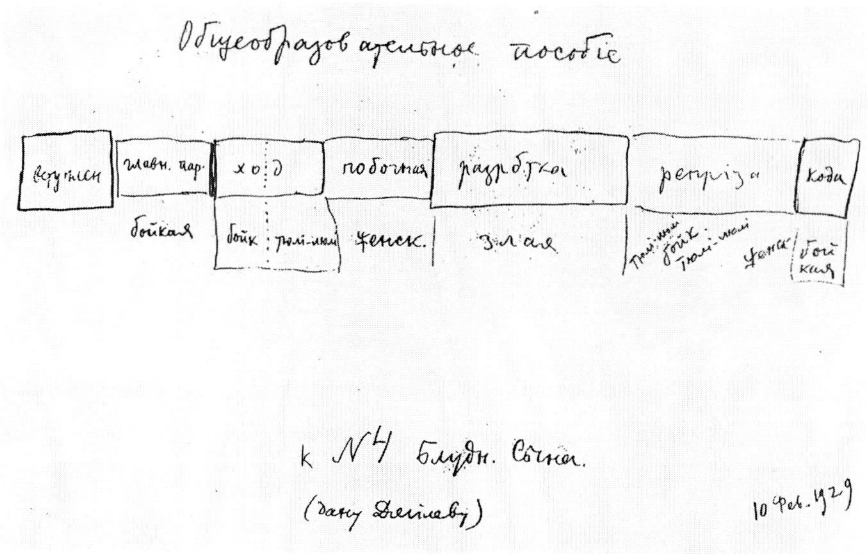

Fig. 17 Prokofiev's "General Aid" for *L'Enfant prodigue*'s original
number 4, the male servant's dance. In the boxes from left to
right: "Introduction; main part/animated; procession/animated;
secondary/fem.; development/evil [or angry]; reprise/animated;
coda/animated" [at the bottom] "(given to Diaghilev)"

Fig. 18 **The portrait of Diaghilev that hung above Prokofiev's desk in his Moscow apartment**

traditional methods of growth based on variation of the lyrical phrase. While passages with a "repetitive intensity of melodic figures,"[62] to use the composer's own description, occur in both *Ala i Lolli* and *Chout*, they hold only passing prominence before reverting to accompanimental ostinati in a lyrical context.

Given *Chout*'s long, detailed scenario in which the hero is either present or else controlling the course of events in absentia, Prokofiev needed a network of thematic or motivic recurrences in order to help tell the story of the ballet through the orchestra. Since his cartoonish buffoons undergo little character transformation—they merely act and react—they do not need to metamorphose. The hero's triumph is presumed from the outset. In this regard the motivic network in *Chout* lacks the dramatic significance of those deployed in *L'Enfant prodigue* and the later Soviet ballets. Here the music evolves almost exclusively for variety's sake. It grows through outright repetiton (reh. 5 material repeats at reh. 9), modified repetition (for example, through sequence and change of instrumentation as seen in the first two statements of the hero's theme), extension and organicism. We can understand this best by following the transformations of the hero's primary theme in scenes one and six (where he appears undisguised), and observe how it is related to other motives and themes in the middle scenes. The treatment of the primary theme in the more symphonic entr'actes will be considered separately.

In scenes one and six Prokofiev varies and transforms the hero's theme (designated as AB) through manipulation of its motivic components as seen in Ex. 2.6 (the A section comprising measures a1, a2, a3; the B section, b1–b4). Most motivic transformations are made from the first three measures, either individually or as a unit. In particular a2 will become an important unifying element in the ballet. These motivic variations and transformations either adjoin the original theme or serve as counterpoints to others. In the latter case they can serve to remind the listener of the hero's predominance. Some variations are obvious, like the extension of a1's quaver figure (bar 1 of Ex. 2.7) , the extension of an inverted a1 (bar 5 of Ex. 2.7), and the imitative treatment of A (bar 9 of Ex. 2.7).

The next motivic variant of the main theme is an important one, thus it is given its own designation R; it emerges during the elongated close of a theme that I refer to as "urging." This theme (reh. 13) itself is the second part of a section begun at reh. 11 in which the hero enthusiastically explains his plan about the magic whip to his wife. It started with an expansion of the "jumping down from the stove" music heard 20 bars before. The appellation "urging" is chosen because of the dramatic context, the emphatic nature of the opening melodic notes (rising a sixth to the accented b^2 then falling a seventh, in the 1915 scored marked *espressivo*), the rising and falling chromatic lines underneath (with hairpin dynamics) and the subsequent appoggiaturas (see Ex. 2.8). Quite typically this is repeated with modification eight bars later, but soon elides into the new motivic variant of the main theme, R, formed by appending a new repeated note figure (perhaps meant

Ex. 2.6   Hero's primary theme labeled for this discussion

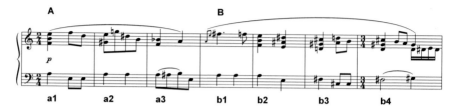

Ex. 2.7   Four before reh. 5 to reh. 7

Ex. 2.8   To his wife, hero enthusiastically explains his plan

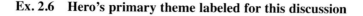

to recall the duplet quavers in AB's accompaniment) as an anacrusis to a2 (see one after reh. 15, Ex. 2.9). This section concludes with a *diminuendo* repetition of a four-note variant of R. As you would expect, this music returns when the seven neighbors arrive and the hero's scheme is put into practice. Before that happens the hero and his wife dance for joy celebrating his clever plan to music that will be discussed below. Repetitions of R now fitted into a triple meter context serve as a four bar link between the dance and its repeat (reh. 21). After the neighbors arrive the plan is enacted and we see R's notes being rhythmically altered, the value of its third and fourth notes doubled and an extra note at the end. It is used during the staged display the hero and his wife put on for their seven visitors, before the "violence" erupts (see Ex. 2.10, one after reh. 30). Thus instead of

Ex. 2.9 Introduction of variant "R"

Ex. 2.10 Variant of "R" 1 after reh. 30

repeating the plan music exactly, Prokofiev's music grows along with the unfolding drama. Once again Prokofiev repeats this (reh. 32) before eliding into a closing section in preparation for the "Quelle fictive."

The "revival" music at reh. 42 heard after the hero has "killed" his wife and struck her three times with the magic whip, is closely related to R, in turn. Back in duple meter, it is appended by a dramatically protracted half close suggesting the indecision and tentativeness of the freshly reanimated wife (see Ex. 2.11). However, soon she is busy setting the table to repetitions of R (*Allegro marcato*, reh. 43) with a new two bar tag. Though the violence is over, R reminds us that the plan is still unfolding. This section, too, is repeated (reh. 45) taking us up to the next event, the seven fools gathering to hold council.

At the beginning of scene three before he disguises himself as his sister (Molodukha), the hero is briefly seen running about trying to avoid the seven, now enraged (and widowed) buffoons. An augmentation of R is heard briefly amidst the commotion and general hubbub (see Ex. 2.12, 3 before reh. 133).

The undisguised hero returns in the final scene leading a band of seven soldiers to the strains of an aggressive march. As the whole story is retold for the benefit of the soldiers Prokofiev offers a truncated variant of the main theme (reh. 289) made by combining R with b3 and b4 (see Ex. 2.13) with note values doubled. The moment of the hero's triumph over the merchant is made

Ex. 2.11   "Premiers pas indécis" at reh. 42

Ex. 2.12   Scene 3, 3 before reh. 133

Ex. 2.13   Scene 6, reh. 289

abundantly clear a short time later by a resounding statement of A also in augmentation (*Adagio pesante*; reh. 299, Ex. 2.14).

Two other important themes that accompany the hero's antics are direct descendants of his primary theme: "La Danse du rire" in the opening scene and the music accompanying his victorious, first "jumps of joy" (as so labeled on the 1915 score) in the finale. The opening of the former is related to the accompaniment in a1 and a2 (see Ex. 2.15, reh. 19–20). The relationship is bolstered by the aforementioned use of R as a closing motive before the repeat of the dance (reh. 21). The "jumps of joy" theme is related to the entire primary theme, measure by measure: the first three being reshuffled and the last four being inverted (see Ex. 2.16). Prokofiev's typically jagged line contains a falling octave and a fourth between measures three and four—a strong closing gesture that is exploited for the remainder of the ballet. As the secondary theme in the final dance, "jumps of joy" is featured prominently. The ballet ends with a *fortissimo, meno mosso* statement of the A-like part of this theme, thereby proving both unification and closure (see Ex. 2.17, end of the ballet).

Ex. 2.14   Scene 6, reh. 299

Ex. 2.15   "Danse du rire," reh. 19–20

Ex. 2.16   Scene 6, "Jumps for Joy" theme, reh. 305

Aside from the aforementioned brief appearance in scene three, the hero only appears in disguise during the middle scenes of the ballet; hence, his music is not heard. Nevertheless, his control over the course of events is suggested by rhythmic or melodic similarities with his principle theme, a2 in particular. In scene two the "Dance of the Buffoons' Wives" reveals this kinship when the theme is varied after its first statement, resulting in an approximation of A and B

Ex. 2.17 *Chout*'s revised ending

(see Ex. 2.18). The rhythm of the bracketed area, the contour of the four quavers, their anacrusis and the downward resolution to the crotchet suggest an intervallically altered A. The repeating falling fourth dactyls at the close suggest an affinity to B. Fittingly, the wives' dance is related to their daughters' *khorovod* (which also serves as the merchant's theme) in scene four: the seven-beat

Ex. 2.18   **Scene 2, reh. 83–4**

melodic head motives seem to be variants of each other (compare the first two measures of Ex. 2.18 and Ex. 2.19). The daughter's *khorovod*/merchant's theme also shares with the main theme the use of a falling fourth at the close, here a falling d^2 to a^1 (bracketed in the example). Later in this scene when the merchant selects Molodukha as his bride, the seven buffoons react in stunned horror to music which recalls the descending close of her theme (reh. 154) while also resonating with the hero's theme part A (rhythmically) and its descending line from B (granted, spanning different quality of sevenths; reh. 209). After the hero/Molodukha has replaced himself with a goat during the chaotic sequence of events leading up to the "Danse rituelle" in scene five, an augmented statement of the opening of this theme briefly reminds us of his supremacy (reh. 257). Furthermore, the beginning of this section (reh. 255, *moderato*, *con agitazione*) relates back to scene one's "Danse du rire": each ends its opening four-bar phrase with a wedge formed by contrary motion scales.

In the entr'actes the hero's main theme is also employed as a unifying device. Each of the first four entr'actes opens with a full statement of AB before proceeding with a thematic recollection from the preceding scene (the fifth breaks off after the second measure to exploit a2). Because the context is symphonic rather than dramatic, one might expect more far-reaching development than in the ballet proper. But partly due to the entr'actes' brevity (from about one and half minutes to just over three), and perhaps because the composer did not want to belabor the theme in a non dramatic context, the variations are actually rather conservative. Prokofiev treats either the whole theme or isolated motives to brief sequential repetitions, simple embellishments, augmentation, diminution, and reordering. When he rearranges the sequence of the opening three measures to a2–a1–a3, as at rehearsal 66 in the first entr'acte, the result recalls Chaikovsky's rendition of "Little Birch Tree" (see Ex. 2.20, oboe solo). Two felicitous examples of thematic manipulation result from variation of the consequent phrase B. At rehearsal 118 in the second entr'acte (Ex. 2.21), Prokofiev interrupts the statement of the primary theme after b1, and continues with the reordered version of the opening theme just mentioned (a2–a1–a3), though the accompaniment follows the normal sequence as it did above in Ex 2.20. Prokofiev continues to feature permutations of the preemptive a2 in nearly every bar until the next theme takes over (at reh. 124). More

Ex. 2.19   Scene 4, reh. 194–5

Ex. 2.20   First entr'acte, reh. 66

Ex. 2.21   Second entr'acte, reh. 118

impressive, however, is the treatment in the fourth entr'acte where the relationship between the merchant's theme and the primary motive is made even stronger, though the entr'acte was composed long afterwards (see Ex. 2.22). Again Prokofiev interrupts AB after b1, this time unobtrusively appending four measures of the merchant's theme in lieu of b2–b4 (reh. 221). This is followed by a reshuffled statement of "A": a2–a1–a3 (oboe solo), and a restatement of the merchant's theme with its first notes inverted (reh. 222).

Ex. 2.22   Fourth entr'acte

Understandably the hero's theme is given the greatest prominence, yet Prokofiev repeated other characters' themes to signal their reappearance on stage. The seven buffoons' entry and exit music, their "council" music (heard whenever they gather to the side for collective thought), Molodukha's theme, and the merchant's theme are all used in this manner. Important events often occur during the closing, two-measure octave descent of Molodukha's theme (reh. 154): she is beaten by the seven who have just seized her in scene three, the seven are horrified by the merchant's selection of her as his bride in scene four, and the merchant lowers her out the window after she feigns illness in scene five.

As victims of the hero's schemes the seven and the merchant portray a wider range of moods. However, Prokofiev chose not to alter the merchant's identifying theme. Instead he used different themes to mirror his varying emotional states: his entry and exit doubles as the daughters' *khorovod*, when he thinks of his beloved Molodukha he does so to her theme, he caresses her to a new theme, and he buries her (actually, the goat) to music derived from the seven wives' funeral.

The changing moods and various encounters of the seven buffoons, on the other hand, are portrayed through transformations of their entrance/exit music (Ex. 2.23). In scene one it remains unchanged, but when the seven arrive home in scene two with the newly acquired magic whip in hand, they make a less demonstrative entrance: the former heavy tread (three trumpets, three horns, piano and Glockenspiel playing the ostinato; full strings playing the theme) is replaced by lighter instrumentation (upper strings, clarinets, two horns, piano and bells playing the ostinato; two muted trumpets playing a discontinuous version of the theme). In scene three the seven enter "enraged" (*più mosso prestissimo tempestoso*) since the magic whip has just failed them and they are seeking revenge (reh. 140). Prokofiev emphasizes the chase by replacing their ominous,

Ex. 2.23 Seven buffoons' entrée in scene 1, *Chout*

ascending disjunct bass line with a more nimble walking bass played by the strings. He represents their fury by "gusts" of ascending chromatic quavers in the winds marked *feroce*. Their entrance in scene four is for once clearly incidental: the main activity is the seven daughters' preparing for the arrival of the merchant and matchmakers. When their fathers enter just the bass line of their theme is heard (solo tuba, *mezzo forte*) as an harmonically unobtrusive counterpoint to the ongoing theme and ostinato (reh. 180). Later in this scene their entrance theme (minus the ostinato) is used in a broadly humorous vein as the seven pompously puff themselves up to greet the visiting merchant (*Andante gravissimo*, *fortissimo*, *pesante*; reh. 192). Here Prokofiev gives the theme its weightiest and slowest presentation, appending it with an absurd, blaring (*Marcatissimo*) and dissonantly layered fanfare complete with trilling woodwinds (one after reh. 192). For their last entrance—jumping out from behind the hedge to mock and grimace at the grieving merchant in the finale (reh. 275)—Prokofiev appends the ascending seesawing theme of the entrance motive onto their other calling card, the collective thinking music first heard at reh. 46 in scene one (Ex. 2.24; see Ex 2.32 below for the original "council music"). After providing ample opportunity for mocking and grimacing (represented by a shrill clarinet solo *a due*, chordal equivalent of the "raspberries" in the brass and cascades of "laughter" in the flutes and xylophone), Prokofiev reintroduces the combined motives, signaling the last hurrah for the seven before the arrival of the authorities.

While by no means exhaustive, this survey reveals Prokofiev's use of recurrent themes to achieve both dramatic coherence and musical variety in *Chout*. Given the prolix nature of the story and the composer's lyrical inclination, their use was probably self-evident. Russian tradition, not Stravinsky, was the

Ex. 2.24   Seven buffoons' council theme elided with their entrée theme, scene 6, *Chout*

guide for this modularity and the use of a controlling main theme. The use of recurring themes is certainly not as systematic nor as detailed as Chaikovsky's in *Swan Lake* and *Sleeping Beauty*, nor as the composer himself would do later in *L'Enfant prodigue*, *Romeo and Juliet*, *Cinderella* and *Tale of the Stone Flower*. Nevertheless, their use in *Chout* does demonstrate a concern for theatrical unity. And the additive manipulation of the hero's theme provides further resonance with Russian folk music style.

But one is left with a nagging doubt that perhaps the composer went too far in response to Diaghilev's request for a symphonic approach in revising *Chout*. As we will soon see, Prokofiev also went overboard with highly descriptive music in the first version of the ballet in an effort to counter the impresario's charge of writing "just music." The revised score of *Chout* does display Prokofiev's solid craftsmanship and skill at maintaining unity across a wide canvas. But perhaps it is too much of a good thing. Harping about redundancy in music intended to accompany the dance is not altogether fair, but critics at the premier also noticed this fault in the score, even amidst all the distractions on stage. Even though *Chout* is a masterful score and a sign of compositional maturity, it nevertheless betrays the composer's youthful over-anxiousness to acquiesce and to please.

Harmonic, textural and rhythmic characteristics

As Prokofiev's audience we are not alone in finding a strong dose of irony in his harmonic style. When the composer rehearsed his Third Piano Concerto with Alfred Hertz and the San Francisco Symphony in February 1930 he noted that the conductor was "good-naturedly laughing into his beard in those spots that seemed dissonant to him." Allegedly one of the composer's sons once remarked that his father writes normal music, then he "Prokofievizes it." Prokofiev's music definitely has a distinctive sound, spiced, as it is, by what have become almost affectionately dubbed "wrong notes." The question of how to approach these "wrong notes" in a meaningful manner has the present generation of music theorists busy. One view has these "unexpected dissonances" absolutely integral to the musical structure, hence only pitch-class set analysis will give them their full due. In this light the inveterate notion of consonance and dissonance is eschewed, perhaps somewhat idealistically. Another approach hears these notes as surface ornaments in a diatonic context, thus allowing the use of traditional tonal theory and modified Schenkerian principles. At its worst this sort of analysis can give the impression of sleight of hand. A rational approach would seem to take advantage of both. No attempt to enter the fray is made in these pages, nothing less than a book-length discussion would do the topic justice.[63] What follows then is a cursory and eclectic overview of Prokofiev's harmonic practice in his first ballets for Diaghilev.

The harmony in the *Scythian Suite* and *Chout* is tonal, but not in the traditional sense. Rather, this practice must be termed expanded tonality, a result of Prokofiev's penchant for added tones, chromatic inflections, implied tonics, enriched dominants and dominant substitutes—all of which can veil the diatonic appearance, if not the sound of his music. Prokofiev claimed that his highly personal style of harmony grew from an incident in his youth. The prolific 11-year-old composer had been deeply offended by the composer Sergey Taneyev, who, having played though Prokofiev's first symphonic draft, laughed as he remarked about the simple harmony, "mostly I, IV and V." This incident impelled the composer to develop, in his words, a more "experimental" harmonic style. Some years later when he again auditioned his music before Taneyev, Prokofiev was proud to have earned his censure: "Far too many wrong notes."[64]

Even with the embellishments and substitutions, Prokofiev's harmony remains broadly functional. He thrives on dominant–tonic motion, making great sport of obscuring the chords and confusing their roles. Prokofiev's notorious sudden, mid-phrase semitonal displacements are part of this scheme which allows chords and their mutations to coexist. A section's overriding tonality can be quite readily determined from the ostinati and the final cadence, but at the local level his music can be quite tricky to analyze because of its heavy chromaticism and independently moving voices. However, his harmonic texture is not always dense or obtuse—the opening phrases of "La Danse du rire" from scene one of *Chout*, for example, reveal the composer's fondness for music "on the white keys only." Examples like this become more and more plentiful in his subsequent ballets. Except for the occasional use of quartal chords as local color (see the hero's main theme) the music is tertian. C major is his favorite key, and despite varying degrees of ambiguity along the way, it is usually C that triumphs at the end, though sometimes backlighted with added tones as if to make a musical chiaroscuro. One of the most distinctive features of Prokofiev's music is its juxtaposition of plainest consonance and extreme dissonance. These features can also be superimposed: a simple diatonic melody moving in rhythmic simultaneity with a highly chromatic background, as for example, Veles's opening theme of the *Scythian Suite*. But even when the surface is at its most clangorous, as Taruskin observes, "it is utterly characteristic of Prokofiev that beneath ... there always lay a simple harmonic design and a stereotypical formal pattern straight out of a textbook."[65] Even though chromaticism and pedals can be said to be the very basis of Prokofiev's music, no one overriding harmonic scheme governs the *Scythian Suite* and *Chout*.

In *Chout* Prokofiev did not exploit the established arsenal of Russian "fantastic harmonies"—octatonicism (the scale alternating tones and semitones), pentatonicism, and the whole tone scale—to the extent one might expect, even in obviously "fantastic" situations (Glazunov and Skryabin, two early influences, also used strict octatonicism sparingly). He did use that defining characteristic of Stravinsky's music, octatonicism, to highlight some frightening and mystical aspects of *They Are Seven*, and to portray the cabalistic setting as the sorceress Fata Morgana and the magical Tchelio rise from the ground at the opening of scene two in *L'Amour des trois oranges*. However, the first calling card of the fantastical seven buffoons in *Chout*, their entry/exit music (Ex. 2.31), achieves its distinction through a lopsided ostinato, willful orchestration and eccentric melodic line. Its octatonicism seems almost ancillary. The symmetrical pitch structure D#–E–F#–G in the disjunct melodic line suggests it, baldly-stated, though Prokofiev's passing A-flat, and embellishing D and B lie outside the only plausible collection. Indeed, this example is not all about tritones, rather it is an oscillation of sonorities in which (not surprisingly) a tonic and a dominant (G and D) take precedence out of a chromatic context. This is not to imply that tritones do not have a strong role in Prokofiev's early ballet music, however. But they function as a tool not as a panacea. Unlike Stravinsky's early ballets or Rimsky-Korsakov's later scores where octatonicism forms the very basis of their harmonic language, Prokofiev used this "fantastic harmony" as the young Rimsky-Korsakov had done (for example, in *Musical Picture-Sadko*), that is, as isolated, dramatic splashes of color.

Prokofiev used pentatonicism in brief passages, for example the melody in the second phrase of wives' dance in scene two of *Chout* (see Ex. 2.18, 5 after reh. 83). As it is not endemic to Russian music (though it is certainly heard there), the pentatonicism adds a slightly exotic character to the gentle, yet seductive dance, thereby characterizing these ladies not unlike Ala or the seductress in *L'Enfant prodigue*. He also used whole tone collections at times, for example, in *Chout* to underscore the merchant's fright when his beloved has turned into a goat, the aforementioned wedge at one before reh. 256 (see Ex. 2.25).[66]

Prokofiev relied upon modalism rather frequently in his first ballets: in *Ala i Lolli* to suggest archaic sounds and in *Chout* to evoke a Russian folk character. A clear-cut example of modality is the third movement, "Night" in the *Scythian Suite*. It opens in A-Aeolian and even uses a gapped scale to further foster an archaic sound. But Prokofiev's use of modes was not always so straightforward, his rather simple modal themes sometimes cohabit, not surprisingly, with "piquant harmonies." Ala's music in the first movement of the *Scythian Suite* (reh.8) is played by the flutes in D-Dorian (what Balakirev called the "Russian minor" because of its prominence), but the celesta, harp and piano provide a

Ex. 2.25 Whole-tone arpeggio, 1 before reh. 256

vibrant whole-tone harmonic setting below. Similarly, Molodukha's theme in A-Aeolian unfolds above oscillations of a mutated dominant pedal (reh.152). Prokofiev's modalism can seem ambiguous on occasion, for example the Merchant's love music at the opening of scene five is in G-Mixolydian, although a case could be made for D-Dorian. Earlier the Merchant's entrée theme was presented in A-Aeolian against a background harmony that plays with one's expectations regarding dominant and tonic chords. These examples demonstrate the composer's penchant for setting simple melodies with obfuscated harmony. Despite the mix of chromaticism and modality, Prokofiev's invented folk-like themes in *Chout* bespeak authentic folk intonations.

Prokofiev's chromaticism is largely a result of his predilection for added tones, altered tones, layering, and chordal sideslipping or substitutions. This chromatic style had already appeared in his previous works, but in the ballets it often serves dramatic ends. Dissonant counterpoints or doubling of melodic lines are used to portray violence, power or anger in both *Chout* and the *Scythian Suite*. Like his use of "fantastic' harmonies, chromaticism is sometimes used in passing as decoration or as accompaniment, for example, the swelling and subsiding semiquaver sextuplets that animate the opening *tempestuoso* of the last movement of the Suite, the ascending notes over a tremolo that set the mysterious tone at the introduction of the whip in scene one of *Chout*, or the descending staccato eighths that seem to depict laughter during the mocking scene in *Chout*'s finale (see Exx. 2.26–28). This is really nothing new: one need only turn to Rimsky-Korsakov's "Mount Triglav" section of *Mlada*, for example (a source of inspiration for both of his students mentioned in these pages), to see similar decorative figuration and sweeping chromatic scales. Other examples, however, demonstrate the fundamental importance of chromaticism to Prokofiev's vocabulary. For example, the use of both D and D#, A and A#, and B and B-flat in the opening of the hero's primary theme are typical of a Prokofievian chromatic melody (see Ex 2.3), or what Malcolm Brown calls his "variable scales": "He took whatever pitches he needed to construct his melodies and harmonies, consequently the pitch set for a passage may range from a few to as many as 10 or 11. Having selected a particular pitch set he felt no qualms about changing it at will, so with a note unaltered one moment and altered the next."[67] In spite of the flux the music's centricity is clear, due in no small part to its simple tonic-dominant motion.

Prokofiev's music for the most part is vertically conceived—a likely consequence of his composing at the piano. *Chout* contains many examples of layered textures: oscillating figures in the bass with chromatic or simple folk-like diatonic tunes above. This stratification is often emphasized by the orchestration. Although the layers may occasionally blend into one sonority (for example, in cadential passages) or merge at closure, they are heard as essentially separate entities. For example, consider the passage accompanying the seven buffoons as they mock the grieving merchant in scene six (Ex 2.29). The piano reduction

Ex. 2.26 *Scythian Suite*, opening of the fourth movement: typical chromatic ebb and flow

Ex. 2.27 Tone setting chromaticism during the introduction of the whip

Ex. 2.28   Descending chromatic "laughter"

Ex. 2.29   Use of dissonant, planar style to accompany the seven buffoons as they mock the grieving merchant in scene 6

facilitates recognition of three planes: the top line descending from E-flat (flutes, oboes, piano), which at reh. 278 descends chromatically in quavers (xylophone added); the brass chords which help articulate the beginning of each phrase and oscillate in and out of consonance with the bass; and the bass which centers on E (strings). Measure one might suggest passing bitonality (E-flat and E), however, "third flips" are an integral part of Prokofiev's music (inverting a triad around its third; customarily heard in progression) whereas polytonality is not (even the well-known example with two key signatures in *Sarcasms* is centered on one pitch). That is not to deny passing ambiguity from competing tonal centers, but sections generally end with a single resolution. Taken as a whole the passage can be considered as planar music with Prokofiev's characteristic chromaticism and pedal point. A less complex example occurs at the end of scene four where the composer exploits the sonority of one dissonant pedal on E (E A#

D) under permutations of one chord (G# B D#) to accompany the violence on stage (the seven buffoons beat the matchmakers, Ex 2.30). Though all but the A# are relatable to E, Prokofiev's orchestration suggests otherwise: he separates the two sonorities by pitting trumpets and woodwinds against the rest of the orchestra. Layered music such as this was not uncommon at the time. Stravinsky had used it, for example, in *L'Oiseau de feu*'s "Berceuse" where the C-naturals at the start of the oboe's chromatically descending motive suggest a passing separate layer notwithstanding the context of dominant ninth harmony (2 before reh. 184). Bartok would even provide some examples in his veritable compendium of contemporary style, *Mikrokosmos*. But in service to *Chout*'s maliciousness and fantasy Prokofiev used layered texture with perhaps unprecedented frequency.

Prokofiev's melodic doublings are generally consonant and closely spaced (for example, when the seven buffoons beat the matchmakers, reh. 217) although stratospheric open octaves do occur, most often in amorous contexts (for example, the Merchant's theme, reh. 223). With or without contrasting planes or ostinati, they, along with the exploitation of the brass instruments, give a strident quality to many passages in these two works. The maximization of primitivism in Chuzhbog's music, power in Veles' and the brutality of the "Querelle fictive" in scene one of *Chout* (reh. 35), are all achieved in part through consonant, textural heft. Infrequently Prokofiev will thicken the texture by adding motivic counterpoints to the melody that are not strictly parallel. Although this might suggest an attempt to imitate Russian folk polyphony (*podgoloschnaya*, or heterophonic "free parallelism"), his documented dislike of an ethnographically correct vocal style leads one to believe that he developed his style quite independently.

Prokofiev's music in these two works is largely homophonic. The plentiful

Ex. 2.30   The seven buffoons beat the matchmakers at the end of scene 4

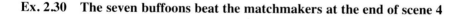

ostinati supplant imitative writing (similarly, variational procedures are used in lieu of motivic development). As his friend and colleague Nabokov observed, Prokofiev seems to have had a "particular dislike for the style of imitative counterpoint, and used to make fun of certain of his contemporaries for writing fugues and fugatos."[68] A remarkable exception in his ballets, and indeed in ballet music in general, occurs in *Chout* where the imitative entries and stretto of a wild fugato heighten the suspense as the seven buffoons decide to kill their wives in scene two (reh. 95). The brief subject is taken from the opening theme of the scene (reh. 74). Like most of his chromaticism, doublings, "fantastic" harmonies, and so forth, this fugato serves a theatrical purpose. Even more striking than its appearance, perhaps, is the highly personalized rendering, for example, with most entries at the minor second.

Shared harmonic practice aside, there are some cosmetic similarities in Prokofiev's and Stravinsky's orchestration and use of ostinati. Only the former can be documented as an influence. Prokofiev was always interested in this aspect of other composers' music—often it was the only critique he would make about it (aside from whether or not there was any "music" to be found). Despite their differences, Prokofiev always admired Stravinsky's orchestration. How exactly the general sound of Stravinsky's *Le Sacre du printemps* fired Prokofiev's orchestrational imagination while he composed *Ala i Lolli* is not known. Using virtually the same instruments (Prokofiev adds harps, piano and celesta), and depicting similar subjects, the *Scythian Suite* and *Le Sacre du printemps* quite naturally make similar kinds of sounds: for example, suggestions of ancient pipes and drumming. Both were influenced to a degree by the so-called French "impressionist" school but the results are once again distinctive. Certain passages in *Le Sacre* suggest that Debussy remained an important influence (for example, the opening to part two), but without detracting from the work's archaic Russian character. Prokofiev's impressionistic foray in the third movement of the *Scythian Suite* on the other hand overwhelms through its "onomatopoeia." Brown summarizes this nicely: "Rapid trills and pizzicati in muted strings, low growling tones in the brasses, and hushed vibrating figuration in harps and celesta imitate the actual noises of night—buzzing insects, rustling leaves, animal grunts, and perhaps even oriental wind bells brushed by nocturnal breezes."[69] The characteristic figuration, tremoli, divisi strings, use of harmonics (and even a motive that sounds reminiscent of *Daphnis et Chloë* at reh. 36) all contribute to an impressionistic sheen wherein primitivism all but disappears. Prokofiev's use of two harps adds a nice antiquarian touch at the start, but elsewhere their glissandi sound anachronistically voluptuous. The sounds of the celesta, perhaps another debt to Ravel's ballet,[70] also belie primitivism. Nevertheless, when compared to Stravinsky's even more detailed string writing, warmer wind timbre, and more flexible rhythmic style in the aforementioned opening, Prokofiev's impressionistic nocturne seems to have a decidedly Nordic chill about it, as befitting a northern fjord.

Prokofiev's rhythms and phrasing in the *Scythian Suite* and *Chout* are for the most part unremarkable and conventional. The *Scythian Suite* was censured as far back as 1916 by Asafyev for its squareness. In this light the first movement's use of a 10-bar theme and the opening of Chuzhbog's dance stand out. In the latter Prokofiev extends his theme by two beats at measure 12, yielding two consecutive 3½ bar phrases in a context of 3's, which itself is rare (the movement starts with a 4-bar vamp, and 4-bar phrasing takes over after the repeat of the theme). *Chout*'s introduction is a 6-bar phrase (4 + 2) and the hero's theme that follows is in seven bars (3 + 4), both of which alert us that the phrasing will be somewhat less regular than in the previous work. It remains fairly predictable nevertheless.

Prokofiev overwhelmingly favors duple meter in both works although he has a penchant for ending phrases with a bar in triple meter (see the main theme in *Chout* and the opening phrase in the *Scythian Suite*). Only two extended passages in triple meter occur in each work. In a letter to Nicolas Slonimsky in 1931 the composer acknowledged this shortcoming which also appears in other contemporaneous works: "This latest period [of my music] doesn't have that 'absolute predominance' of measures in 4/4 meter, something for which you pricked me in passing."[71] When triple meter occurs for any duration in these two works, it provides either variety within a larger section of duple meter or it helps to underscore a dramatic contrast, for instance, the execution of the plan—as opposed to its description—in scene one of *Chout*. Surprisingly, he does not exploit 5/4 meter in *Chout*, even though it is strongly associated with Russian folk music, the wedding dance repertory specifically. One brief passage of 7/4 meter stands out in scene two as all hope of reviving the seven wives winds down (reh. 109). Rapid Stravinskian shifts of meter are nowhere to be found.

About all one can say about the rhythms in these works is that they aptly propel the music. According to Nabokov, "Prokofiev always used to say that his chief interest lay not in rhythm but in the invention of good theme."[72] Obviously far less captivating than the innovative rhythms of *Le Sacre*, they seem unadventuresome even next to *L'Oiseau de feu*. His use of syncopation is really no more advanced than Beethoven's. Prokofiev does occasionally use hemiola (three beats against two) perhaps to underscore the drama as for instance during Chuzhbog's attempted attack on Ala in the Suite's third movement. In later ballets he would approach Stravinsky's intricate rhythmic style only in the quest of dramatic effect, for example, the uncharacteristic syncopation and use of hocket in the fight between the stepsisters and stepfather in *Cinderella* (reh 34). His use of rather pedestrian rhythms in his early ballets is not helped by the foursquare and predictable phrasing. Prokofiev had been far more rhythmically daring and experimental in his early piano works.[73] But this is not to imply that the rhythms are in any way deficient—we find, after all, eminently danceable music with plenty of variety. Lyrical flow was obviously more important than rhythmic intricacy. When called for by the drama he could rise to the occasion and provide unusual and apt rhythmic characterization, like the lopsided gait in the seven buffoons' entrée (also used for the "Fata Morgana" motive in *Oranges*). That this example recalls Musorgsky's gnome in *Pictures At an Exhibition*, only reinforces the unprogressive nature of Prokofiev's rhythmic vocabulary.

The most basic similarity between the *Scythian Suite* and *Le Sacre du printemps*, aside from use of an extreme dynamic range, is the incessant rhythmic drive. But Prokofiev did not borrow this technique from Stravinsky — rhythmic ostinati and repeated accompanimental figurations had been a feature of his early piano music as well as his Piano Concerto no. 1 and especially Piano Concerto No. 2, and have earlier Russian precedents, besides. The composer considered the "toccata" or "motor line" a key component of his style from early on, compelled by a powerful impression of Schumann's *Toccata*, op. 7. He generally used ostinati in a traditional, unadventuresome manner: as repeated entities linked like a wallpaper pattern end to end to help propel the music. The elemental force in the *Scythian Suite* comes in part from this simple repetiton. Stravinsky, however, used ostinati as a vehicle for a whole new concept, shifting juxtapositions of smaller, contrasting fragments or cells which produced vibrant musical mosaics.[74]

The only conclusion to be drawn after searching for stylistic influences on Prokofiev's first ballets is one that corroborates the hypothesis: the composer, though inexperienced in the genre, copied no models, rather he relied foremost upon his own intuition and established style. Prokofiev's variegated harmonic palette is quite his own, although the components are not, of course, his invention. His rhythms and phrasing certainly owe nothing to modern trends. His staunch adherence to lyricism sets him apart from Stravinsky's latest works. Harmonic practice aside, only secondarily did he draw from others, for example, some pointers on orchestration from Stravinsky, some coloristic writing from the impressionist school and his teachers and mentors, character delineation by keys and the like from theatrical tradition, modularity in lieu of organic development from Russian tradition, and selective use of of Rimsky-Korsakov's "fantastic" harmonies for coloristic purposes.

Means and style of characterization in *Chout*, part one

Like Musorgsky, Lyadov and Rimsky-Korsakov, Prokofiev had a keen, innate sense for musical caricature. His vivid orchestral portrayals of the grotesque and the absurd, with their poster-like display of bright, primary colors, and bold, yet finely wrought gestures, were especially successful. Less colorful, but equally trenchant, were his almost sneering, sarcastic musical portraits. Prokofiev's penchant for highly individualized characterization can be traced all the way back to his youthful, grandiose and action-packed operas such as *The Giant* and

Desert Islands. It can also be seen in his youthful lists of favorite composers and works, which included such items as Grieg's humorous trolls, Rimsky-Korsakov's fantastic images and clever, toy-like processions, and Wagner's realistic portrayals and larger-than-life characters.[75] It is not surprising that the bold staging of *Schéhérazade* made the strongest impression during his introduction to the Ballets Russes ("It is staged in grandeur, in perfect harmony with the music," he wrote to Myaskovsky in June 1913). While his talent for characterization was demonstrated in some early piano pieces as well as the opera *Maddalena*, the early ballets, *Chout* especially, reveal his talent at the fullest. His biting caricatures and some of the characterizations stand apart from theatrical tradition, and his naturalistic accompaniments for *ballet d'action* go beyond Stravinsky's "presentations" in *L'Oiseau de feu* and *Petrouchka*. Much like his obsession with orchestration and orchestral effects in *Ala i Lolli*, Prokofiev became so engrossed with the mimetic passages in his first version of *Chout* that the ballet as a whole suffered. But that is an issue for the next chapter. For now we seek influences on Prokofiev's means and style of characterization, first examining the dramatic personae, then the *ballet d'action*.

His characterizations for *Ala i Lolli* discussed above may be satisfying, but those in *Chout* are brilliant. Given the detailed scenario about a bunch of colorful, grotesque buffoons—some guileful, others gullible—he was able to display his talent for caricature. The success of *Chout*'s characterizations and descriptive music is measured by the fact that one can easily visualize the absurd movements and pratfalls of this odd lot just by understanding the plot and hearing the music. Prokofiev's musical portraits are made with the broadest of strokes, yet the results are highly distinctive.

Jesters and buffoons, descendants of the traveling *skomorokhi*, had frequently appeared in Russian theatrical works over the latter half of the nineteenth century. Buffoons or fools appeared as comic relief in such works as Serov's opera *Rogenda* (1865), Ostrovsky's play *Snegurochka* (The Snow Maiden, for which Chaikovsky composed incidental music in 1873, and Rimsky-Korsakov an opera in 1881), Borodin's *Prince Igor* (the drunks Skula and Yeroshka), in Rimsky-Korsakov's *Sadko* (1896) and as a court jester in the latter's *Tale of Tsar Sultan* (1900). Examples are less plentiful in contemporary ballet but two buffoons appear briefly in the fourth tableau of *Petrouchka*, dressed as a pig and a goat. Even Cherepnin's French retrospective ballet, *Le Pavillion d'Armide*, first presented by the Ballets Russes in 1909, had a dance of the buffoons. Buffoon music was typically simple and folk-like, with occasional uses of theatrical comic clichés. Often it was not that distinguishable from the larger body of orchestral scherzos, witness Rimsky-Korsakov's popular "Dance of the Buffoons" from *The Snow Maiden*. But Prokofiev's buffoons—the seven dupes, their wives, and the hero buffoon and his wife—were not merely decorative elements in an opera, ballet or play, they were the main characters. And their musical portraits are wholly unlike those of any of their predecessors.

Chout's sense of the preposterous, like that of the near contemporary *L'Amour des trois Oranges*, paralleled a trend in the modernized Meyerholdian theatre. Its pervasive cruelty and mocking sarcasm, however, set it apart. Fairy tales are like that some times; Rimsky-Korsakov's fairy-tale opera *Le Coq d'or* was even bloodier. Though *Chout* certainly shares a sarcastic edge with *Le Coq d'or* it lacks its fundamental political satire. The hero's malice coupled with the tone of Prokofiev's music makes the roles of Kashchey, Carabosse, or Chernomor seem almost tame by comparison. Despite its appropriation from Russian folk tales, *Chout* is also akin to the *commedia dell'arte* tradition, specifically, the knockabout clowning of Pulcinella (or Punch to English audiences, Petrushka to Russians). Prokofiev's main buffoon is far closer to the classic Petrushka than is Stravinsky's tragic Pierrot-like puppet. There is no record of Prokofiev's encountering a glove-puppet street theater in Russia (it was a rather lower-class entertainment), but one suspects that he would have enjoyed the physical humor.[76] Intentionally or not, Prokofiev accentuated the genuine (that is, non-Symbolist) Petrushka-like character of the story.

Even though *Chout*'s story is pure fantasy, its viability hinges on the characterizations of the protagonists: the hero buffoon must be convincing in his superior craftiness—his ability to trick seven buffoons and the wealthy merchant. The seven neighbors must be perceived as sufficiently gullible and simpleminded to believe in the powers of a magic whip which brings the dead back to life. By most accounts Larionov's exaggerated portrayal of the seven left no doubts as to their true character, but Prokofiev's music went a long way by itself.

We first encounter the seven as they enter the hero buffoon's home. As if to represent their oafish tread and spasmodic movements, the music is made deliberately boisterous and grotesque. Prokofiev uses a rhythmically lopsided ostinato that alternates between two sonorities (Ex. 2.23). The wide leaps (mostly major sevenths) in the chromatically rising, seesawing theme played by the strings bolster the character's eccentricity, while the harmonic repetiton and accentuation of the tonic (the G's) perhaps suggest their doltishness. The entrée becomes an important calling card, recurring at least in part whenever the seven arrive or depart. It is not too dissimilar from the victory motive of an equally fantastic character, the sorceress Fata Morgana in *L'Amour des trois oranges*. (Ex. 2.31). Not surprisingly then, the entrée later acquires a darker, more sinister side: its disjunct, ascending line accompanies the hero as he pretends to murder his wife in scene one and as the seven literally murder theirs in scene two. Rimsky-Korsakov also used processionals and fanfares for important entrances in his fantastic operas such as *Le Coq d'or* and *Tale of Tsar Sultan*, but with a big difference in tone. Whereas Rimsky's have been termed "toy-like" due to their machine-like precision and scale, Prokofiev's entrée is larger than life and ludicrous, in a word, "buffoonish."

While the entrance music depicts the seven buffoons as noisy, uncouth and

Ex. 2.31 Hemiola effect in Fata Morgana's triumphal music, beginning 3 after reh. 84, Act I, *L'Amour des trois oranges*

perhaps prone to violence, their collective slow-wittedness is fully demonstrated by Prokofiev's trenchant "council music" or "thinking music," another calling card first used when they gather to hold council (Ex. 2.32). He combines a droll, repetitive and tonically anchored "tune" grunted out by three bassoons with

Ex. 2.32 Seven buffoons' "council" music, *Chout*

wandering chromatic arpeggios marked *penseroso* for two solo clarinets (one a bass clarinet). This cleverly captures the obviously limited and unfocused mental acuity of the seven as they engage in collective thought. While examples of humor portrayed through bassoons are plentiful in western music, it is fair to say, without implying any indebtedness, that Prokofiev admirably continues the Russian preeminence in this skill.

His original portrait of the seven wives (1915) was more consistent and humorous than in the published version of the score. Both open with them sitting by seven tables awaiting the return of their husbands. Prokofiev's leaden, downward thrusting theme implies that these are indeed robust, earthy Russian peasant women. Once the husbands arrive home the two versions differ. The composer originally provided a possible incentive for outrage (if not murder) by having the wives heartily (disgustingly?) dig into their supper one at a time, cleverly accompanied by seven imitative entries of the weighty downward thrusting theme (Ex. 2.33). In the revised score, however, after the seven husbands enter, the wives dance to a new number in a completely contrasting character: a solo clarinet plays a soft, smoothly gliding theme over harp and string accompaniment. Although the dance tune does feature downward motivic motion in its pentatonic consequent phrase, it is otherwise dissimilar from the opening heavily orchestrated, foot-dragging theme. This presents a conflicting characterization that the choreographer might have exploited: gross women dancing to sensuous music. Quite unlike any previous portrayals of native peasant women in the Russian musical theater, *Chout* demanded that the seven wives be seen as comic annoyances, whose sacrifice was necessary for the development of the story. After their husbands give up all hope of reviving them with the magic whip, they are dispatched in a 12-bar funeral procession as the curtain falls—a variant of their opening theme—their cruel fates having been fulfilled.

The musical portraits of both Molodukha and the bride-seeking merchant are warmer and more lyrical, closer to the traditional folk style characterizations common in nineteenth-century Russian theater. The merchant, of course, is not a fellow buffoon, but rather a "mortal," and a wealthy one at that. His musical characterization is less extravagant, more "humane." For example, he expresses

Ex. 2.33   Opening of the scene 2 fugato in the revised version of *Chout*

his feelings of love for Molodukha (opening of scene five) in traditional Glinkaesque manner, with a simple, modal, folk-like theme. Still, he is just another victim of the hero buffoon's guile. When he grieves for the dead goat he mistakenly believes is Molodukha, or when he is forced to pay a 300-ruble settlement for the hero's "dead sister," he looks just as ridiculous as the seven duped buffoons did trying to revive their murdered wives with a useless "magic" whip. But even here the merchant's portrayal remains lyrical and relatively consonant. In the first instance Prokofiev exploits the lamenting cliché of the falling second and in the latter, a loud, protracted thematic statement of the hero's theme. Tradition is doubly served by the merchant's comeuppance at the hands of a wily, mischievous Russian peasant and by his depiction through conventional harmonic means.

Quite unlike the other characters in *Chout*, the hero is a picture of consistent confidence, mirthfully manipulating the course of events. His national character is presented immediately by his theme's folk-like quality. His cruel mischievousness and utter lack of conscience are fully revealed before the end of the first scene by music that is at once lighthearted and aggressive. We have already seen how his theme asserts itself in the opening scene, generates other motives, and how his alter ego theme resounds when he wins the merchant's hand in scene four, and when he triumphs monetarily in the final scene forcing the merchant's humiliated withdrawal. Even when he finds himself in a difficult predicament, being led into the amorous merchant's bedroom in scene five, the music suggests that he remains calm and rational. While the merchant passionately caresses Molodukha to continuing strains of the love theme, the cool-headed hero plans his next prank. His "thinking music"—a measure and a half of steadily ticking quavers followed by what seems like a weighing out of the possibilities in the alternating downward and upward motivic inflections—is quite the opposite of the seven buffoons' unfocused council music (reh. 240). By the end of the ballet, having been indirectly responsible for the deaths of seven women and one goat, the buffoon performs a gloating victory dance with his wife, brandishing a purse full of extorted rubles. We are left with no doubt about the malicious and manipulative nature of this relative of Til, Pulcinella and countless other rogues. No small measure is due to Prokofiev's vivid characterizations.

When it came to mimetic music, Prokofiev, the born literalist, was on his mettle. Using largely traditional means, he represented in meticulous detail the physical actions of the story. Some examples associated with characterizations, for example, thinking music, grotesque eating music, bizarre entrance music have already been introduced. Prokofiev had demonstrated this ability earlier in his student opera *Maddalena*, with its hackneyed, melodramatic *coups de théâtre*, including well-timed flashes of lightening and peals of thunder and a climactic duel to death. Later proof of this literal inclination is found in the stage instructions of the 1915 manuscript for *Chout*, where the composer insisted upon the use of a real goat in scene five: above rehearsal 178 he instructs, "In the window, in place of the bride, appears a she-goat." In parenthesis below he added: "Absolutely, a real one, a live one" (one hopes that he would not have also insisted upon the poor animal's actual demise on stage).

During his 1915 meeting with Stravinsky, Prokofiev was quite taken by his colleague's near literal depiction of a drunk emptying his bottle in the song "Kornilo" (Uncle Armand), later claiming, "you express drunkenness through your clarinet with the skill of a real drunkard." At that time Stravinsky was gestating what would become *Renard*, like *Chout*, based on texts from Afanasyev, but otherwise wholly different in its use of the sounds of the words as a formative part of the music. The seven gullible buffoons in *Chout*, however, are not too dissimilar from the cock (or even the fox when he forsakes his tail) in *Renard*. Nor are the composers' fixations on representing violence (the *salto motale* and gruesome demise of the fox on the one hand, the murders and beatings on the other). But this is surely fortuitous. Many years away from his own animalistic morality tale, *Peter and the Wolf*, as well as from the mandates of Socialist Realism, Prokofiev had already established a fondness for near-literal musical representations, including Stravinsky's emptying bottle. The latter, along with his musical "illustration of the tiniest features of what is happening on stage"[77] in *Petrouchka* may be that composer's strongest influence on Prokofiev's early ballets, though they are more motivational than stylistic. Although Prokofiev became carried away with this kind of music in his first version of *Chout*, this talent served him well in later works, especially those for the cinema. Sergey Eisenstein, the famous film director with whom Prokofiev collaborated on *Alexander Nevsky* and *Ivan the Terrible* spoke of the composer's "highly developed faculty for 'hearing' the plastic image, a faculty that enables him to create amazingly exact sound equivalents for the images that come within his range of vision."[78] The pianist Sviatoslav Richter would later say of him, "He could write music about anything: the chair here, or the table, or even this nail."[79]

In *Chout*, with all its highly detailed action—fighting, beating, sobbing, laughing, howling, running, whip cracking, goat chasing, rope (or drape) lowering, and so forth—there is ample opportunity for detailed musical presentation. This is accomplished mostly through traditional musical clichés, though exact antecedents are not easily recalled. It is uncertain why Prokofiev felt the need for so much highly presentational music as he sat down to compose *Chout* upon his return from Italy in 1915. He either wanted or felt obligated to depict all the action in the music. Perhaps Diaghilev's passing consideration of a ballet pantomime set to his Second Piano Concerto coupled with the considerable amount of *ballet d'action* Prokofiev had seen in the Ballets Russes' productions of *Schéhérazade*, *La Légende de Joseph*, *L'Oiseau de feu* and *Petrouchka* were still in his mind. The latter certainly set precedents for realistic depictions in ballet (for example, the tambourine drop as Petrushka "dies"), and for many years long stretches of character music had been used (for example, the battle sounds in Act I of *Nutcracker*), but never so much detail for so long—at least in the ballets that Prokofiev and his contemporaries would have known. And despite their many presentational sections Stravinsky's ballets seldom preclude the dance. A likely rationale came from Musorgsky's experimental dialogue opera *Zhenit'ba* (The Marriage), which Prokofiev heard in 1909 (its musical presentations include water splashing, boot dropping, sneezing, and so forth). Taruskin has pointed out that this "recitative opera" affected the composer's subsequent operas,[80] but it may have served *Chout* as well, at least in regards to concerns with stagecraft. Meyerhold and Larionov also seem to be plausible candidates for influence but significant contact with them came later (Prokofiev did not meet the latter until October 1916).[81] Perhaps even staged pantomime might also be a model for the first version of *Chout*, though this seems less likely given the composer's lack of contact with it.[82] Whatever the reason, Prokofiev, without the ready collaboration of a choreographer, turned his first version of *Chout* into a tour de force of presentational music much as he had turned *Ala i Lolli* into an orchestral showpiece. Consultations with Diaghilev in 1920, however, resulted in the abandonment and reduction of much of this literal, fussy mimetic music. After all, dancers could succinctly and clearly dispatch most physical gestures with or without illuminative music. An element of humor was lost, but as a result of the revision *Chout* gained a more successful dramatic pace. From the start Prokofiev's music was energized by the felicitous match between his own temperament and the story's sardonic tone. Significantly, the best of his original inspiration—the brilliant characterizations and caricatures—remained in the revised score.

Diaghilev's influence on Prokofiev

I have argued that Prokofiev did not directly model his early ballet music after that of Stravinsky or any other composer, and though he partook of elements from the heritage of Russian and western theatrical music, and from the latest in Rimsky-Korsakovian harmony, he manipulated these elements to suit his own style. The music of the *Scythian Suite* and *Chout* document his belief in originality and disdain for parody. Although in many respects fresh and even original, these two scores broke no new stylistic ground for ballet music. Nevertheless, this music reveals a composer keenly attuned to theatrical effects and bold characterizations. What is more Prokofiev provided a rich variety of highly *dansante* material in spite of *Chout*'s dramatic requirements.

But Prokofiev's successful ballet career did not begin smoothly. Between 1914 and 1920 Diaghilev provided needed direction on three occasions. Before *Ala i Lolli* Prokofiev had not considered writing a ballet. Before *Chout* he had not composed in an explicitly Russian style. Before *Chout* was produced, Diaghilev would again work closely with the composer, culling the wheat from the chaff, explaining the essence of ballet music. By the time *Chout* was premiered in 1921, Prokofiev had harnessed his estimable talents in the service of ballet. The greatest influence at the start of his ballet career, then, was not any composer's or school's musical style or techniques, rather it was the knowledge of how music should function in a successful ballet. This is clearly demonstrated by comparing the two versions of *Chout*—the subject of the next chapter.

Notes

1. Prokofiev began composing operas in 1900 after visiting Moscow with his mother. There he saw the operas *Faust* by Gounod and *Prince Igor* by Borodin. The result of those encounters was "The Giant, An opera in three acts," comprising 12 pages, begun after his return (he was eight years old). "On Desert Islands" followed later in 1900. At age 12 he composed "A Feast in Time of Plague" (after Pushkin) with guidance from his private tutor, Glière. *Undine* was begun in 1904, but abandoned in 1907. He had played its Overture and some of its first act at his audition to enter the St Petersburg Conservatory. His hoped his fifth opera, *Maddalena* (1911–13) would be staged at the Conservatory, but he never completed it.
2. Prokofiev had included a short section of ballet in his opera *Undine*. Then in 1908 Nurok had asked him to compose the music for a pantomime he had written. This intrigued the composer, but he had reservations about music's "secondary role" in the genre. His participation came to nothing. In November 1912 he wrote to a friend: "I have heard something of Stravinsky's ballets, but for the moment the idea of writing my own does not interest me." (Letter quoted in Harlow Robinson, *Sergei Prokofiev A Biography* (New York, 1987), p. 66).
3. Cited by Richard Taruskin in "From *Firebird to The Rite*: Folk Elements in Stravinsky's Scores," *Ballet Review*, **10** (Summer 1982), 75.
4. Revitalization came about through cross-fertilization with imported genres (for example, *ballet-féerie*) and dance techniques, as well as from a new emphasis on unity and interest in the past. All of these trends are evident in Petipa's 1890 production of *Sleeping Beauty*. See Tim Scholl, *From Petipa to Balanchine* (London, 1994), pp. 17–20 and 33. This renewal, it should be noted, did not require anything radically different from the ballet composer.
5. Regarding the "new ballet" see Scholl, p. 55.
6. Quoted by Richrd Taruskin in *Stravinsky and the Russian Traditions*, vol. 2 (Berkeley and Los Angeles, CA, 1966), p. 982, note 26.
7. Prokofiev probably refers, at least in part, to the scene which some early critics also derided: Chloë's abduction by pirates in the brief span of six bars.
8. Prokofiev recorded in his first autobiography that he was also very fond of Rimsky's operas *Sadko*, *Snow Maiden* and *Tale of Tsar Saltan*.
9. Taruskin, *Stravinsky and the Russian Traditions*, vol. 1, p. 450.
10. Ibid., vol. 1, p. 575. The music survives as *Le Royaume enchanté*, op. 39.
11. Malcolm H. Brown, "Stravinsky and Prokofiev: Sizing Up the Competition," in *Confronting Stravinsky: Man, Musician and Modernist*, ed. Jann Pasler (Berkeley and Los Angeles, CA, and London, 1986), p. 39. As a perjorative label, "futurist" was often used willy-nilly by musical conservatives.
12. Prokofiev was rather absorbed in Conservatory activities at that time; the outside composer he was most interested in then was Skryabin.

The first public performance of Stravinsky's music was on 27 December 1907 (OS) at a St Petersburg Evenings of Contemporary Music concert. It is virtually certain that Prokofiev did not attend this concert. His "introduction" to this organization by his old theory tutor Mikhail Chernov occurred not too much later, perhaps the following spring, and his own public debut followed that December. It is very unlikely that Prokofiev attended any of Stravinsky's premiers in 1908 and 1909.

13. Vera Stravinsky and Robert Craft, *Stravinsky in Pictures and Documents* (New York, 1978), p. 310.

14. His Diary account from 12 February 1914 (OS) continues: "In the audience were many who applauded strongly, but the majority were lost ... [some] were looking from side to side mockingly as if to say this is the kind of filth that the futurists write."

15. This outlook would change by the time he began his last ballet, *Tale of the Stone Flower*, during the summer of 1948. He was impelled to make emulative quotations and references to Russian musical classics for political reasons in the wake of the February 1948 Central Committee Resolution that denounced him for "formalism," "elitism," and so forth.

16. Taruskin provides an unflattering but apparently accurate appraisal of the young composer's personality: "Even before he wrote his *Scythian Suite* (1915) ... the rude, gangling prodigy was looked upon with bemusement as a veritable Scythe in his person as in his work." *Stravinsky and the Russian Traditions*, vol. 1, p. 856.

17. Quoted in Brown, "Stravinsky and Prokofiev," p. 42. During this "craze for the savage, the primitive" as Korney Chukovsky called it in his book *The Futurists* (1922), advocates undoubtedly were quite eager to appropriate grist for their mill.

18. Taruskin uses "representational" and "presentational" in reference to miming, but the distinction works just as well to distinguish the type of music used for traditional pantomime from that of the choreodrama. *Stravinsky and the Russian Traditions*, vol. 1, p. 587. Also see note 20 below.

19. Ibid.

20. Ibid., vol. 1, p. 610.

21. I will use Taruskin's term "presentational" here and below to describe highly descriptive ballet music. My intention is to convey the meaning of both onomatopoetic and mimetic, and, moreover, to emphasize the extraordinary nature of this music. In his discussion of the *ballet d'action* in *L'Oiseau de feu*, Taruskin uses "presentational" to describe the more natural and emotional movements in Fokine's choreodramas, as opposed to the stiff, stylized "representational" gestures of nineteenth-century ballet (see note 16 above). But the term also works quite well to describe ballet music that actively participates in, or even controls, the narration of events, such as much of the music in the 1915 version of *Chout*, as we shall see.

22. Marian Smith, "Music For the Ballet-Pantomime at the Paris Opéra, 1825–1850" PhD dissertation (Yale University, 1988), p. 77.

23. Gorodetsky's brief, rather poetic account of his collaboration with Prokofiev may be found in V.P. Yenisherlova, *Sergey Gorodetskiy, zhizn' neukrotimaya: stat'i, ocherki, vospominaniya* (Moscow, 1984), pp. 72–4.

24. Igor Glebov (Boris Asafyev), "Iz nedavno perezhitogo," *Muzïka*, no. 249 (12 March 1916), 168.

25. Taruskin, *Stravinsky and the Russian Traditions*, vol. 1, pp. 923–4.

26. Stephen Walsh, *The Music of Stravinsky* (New York, Toronto, Oxford, 1993), p. 46.

27. Another illustrative comparison can be made between the conclusion of Veles' theme in the first movement (reh. 4) and Stravinsky's notorious "Procession of the Sage" (at reh. 70). Taruskin has noted, only a glance at the two pages is needed to realize

the vast stylistic gulf that separates the two composer's music (Taruskin, *Stravinsky and the Russian Traditions*, vol. 2, p. 1421). This is quite true, compared to Stravinsky's riot of polyrhythms and polymeters, Prokofiev's theme and his entire accompanimental complex move in rhythmic lockstep to the 4/4 meter. But there is a simple reason. Despite the density of sound, it is, once again, primarily lyrical music. Retrospectively Prokofiev recognized that from his twenty-third or twenty-fourth year he had formed his "dictionary of idioms," that is, his stylistic palette. He had already composed a considerable amount of music by then besides. He deserves better than to be labeled an epigone: the simplicity of his rhythm and regularity of the downbeat here strongly suggest to me that no parody was intended.

28. Both comments are by William Austin, *Music in the Twentieth Century* (New York, 1966), pp. 461 and 462, respectively. In the first citation Austin is supporting Khrennikov's politically charged claim regarding all of Prokofiev's ballets for Diaghilev.

29. An excellent article for further reading in this area is Michael Beckerman, "In Search of Czechness in Music," *Nineteenth-Century Music*, **10**, no. 1 (1986), 61–73.

30. It is closer in this regard to *Le Coq d'or* where Rimsky-Korsakov integrates the two styles because everything in it is unreal.

31. It apparently did for Austin, who claims that *Chout* is "modeled on *Petrouchka*." Austin, *Music in the Twentieth Century*, p. 462.

32. Prokofiev, "Autobiography," p. 252.

33. Reproductions of the front side of this page can be found in many sources, for instance, in Natalia Savkina's *Prokofiev: His Life and Times*, trans. Catherine Young (Neptune City, NJ, 1984), p. 62. My thanks to Natalia Savkina for locating this document and sharing the contents of its reverse side.

34. In his Diary Prokofiev added, "I laughed that this ending reminded me of the joke about two friends, an elevator and stairs ... never managing to meet each other."

35. Prokofiev liked to do things in three's at this early stage of his balletic career. See Chapter 3 for more "three's" in the first version of *Chout*. Diaghilev would cure him of his tendency towards redundancy.

36. It is not for nothing that he never made a piano transcription of this ballet/Suite.

37. Another possibility would join the beginning of the second attack to the conclusion of the third.

38. It would seem more dramatically apt to have scene four end with Ala's dance, relocating her mourning to the finale. The composer's audition of this music before Diaghilev apparently ended with the latter. Perhaps this music depicting "perplexity" helped to induce the impresario's ensuing tirade (see Chapter 1).

39. Nestyev, *Prokofiev*, p. 91.

40. *Le Sacre du printemps* is probably the benchmark of primitivism, but the style does not serve to distinguish a specific character.

    A precedent from outside the theater is the opening allegro of Vladimir Senilov's tone poem *Skifi* (1912), "Theme of the Scyths." The melodic profile, metric groupings, narrow range and emphasis on tonic chords bring to mind Prokofiev's music for Chuzhbog (a brief musical excerpt of the Senilov may be found in Taruskin, *Stravinsky and the Russian Traditions*, vol. 1, p. 857, ex. 12.1b). Senilov's metric grouping at the start has one bar each of 2/4, 3/4, 4/4, which is not that dissimilar from Prokofiev's expansion of the basic three-bar phrasing at mm. 8–19.

41. Taruskin, *Stravinsky and the Russian Traditions*, vol. 1, p. 856. Taruskin defines Scythianism, as "rendering primitive antiquity in a shockingly coarse and brutal manner."

42. This section (reh. 32) begins 33 seconds into the movement in Abbado's Chicago Symphony Orchestra recording.

43. It is certainly possible that this musical change parallels something dramatic, such as the presentation of offerings.

44. Boganova views the heroic style of the *Scythian Suite* as a forerunner to Prokofiev's mature (read Soviet) national style (Tat'yana Boganova, *Natsional'no-russkiye traditsii v muzïke S. S. Prokof'yeva* [Moscow, 1961], p. 29).

45. Igor Glebov (Boris Asafyev), "Iz nedavno perezhitogo," in *Muzïka*, no. 249 (12 March 1916) p. 168. In a 1932 letter Prokofiev wrote to Asafyev thanking him for again mentioning his Suite in the same breath as works by the revered *kuchkists*, "You flattered me when you referred to my *Scythian Suite* while talking about Borodin and Rimsky; I felt like a child seated at the table with adults." From Harlow Robinson, *Selected Letters of Sergei Prokofiev* (Boston, MA, 1998), p. 124.

46. One spot that comes to mind is the transitional modulating passage through *ad nauseam* triplets at reh. 22 in Chuzhbog's dance, possibly a holdover from some dramatic idea. The asymmetrical accents here seem rather feeble next to passages in part one of Stravinsky's *Le Sacre du printemps*, for example, "Les Augures printaniers" and "Jeu de rapt."

47. In 1920 Diaghilev greeted Milhaud's audition of his primitivistic tour de force, *L'Homme et son désir*, with icy silence.

48. Glière further stated that he tried to encourage this interest by introducing the folk song collections of Rimsky-Korsakov, Lyadov and Balakirev (in S.I. Shlifshteyn, ed., *S. Prokofiev, Autobiography, Articles, Reminiscences*, trans. Rose Prokofieva (Moscow, n.d.), p. 148). This reminiscence from the mid-1950s surely has a political rationale — an attempt to rebuild Prokofiev's reputation in the wake of Stalin's (and the composer's) passing.

49. Prokofiev's recollection here (from Sergey Prokofiev, *Prokofiev By Prokofiev: A Composer's Memoir*, trans. by Guy Daniel, ed. by David Appel (Garden City, NY, 1979), pp. 47–8) differs slightly from the one in his short autobiography.

50. Taruskin claims that "Stravinsky always guarded his technical advances and innovations as trade secrets." Richard Taruskin, "Chernomor to Kashchey: Harmonic Sorcery; or, Stravinsky's 'Angle,'" *Journal of the American Musicological Society*, **38** (1985), 77.

51. Prokofiev did consult such sources much later in his career, and made his own collections of Russian folk songs (opp. 104 and 106 of 1945).

52. Nestyev, *Prokofiev*, p. 66. This is demonstrated in his own music when he joins simple diatonic melodies with colorful harmonies, as in, for example, Molodukha's theme (discussed below).

53. Prokofiev, "Igor' Stravinskiy, Tri pesenki ... dlya golosa i fortepiano," *Muzïka*, no. 226 (October 1915), 390. Reproduced in V.P. Varunts, *Prokof'yev o Prokof'yeve: stat'i i interv'yu* (Moscow, 1991), p. 17.

54. Prokofiev, *Dnevnik 1907–1933*, p. 657. No clarification of "figure" is given.

55. This latter opinion was shared by many in Russian musical circles.

56. Taruskin, *Stravinsky and the Russian Traditions*, vol. 2, p. 1370.

57. Stravinsky acknowledged using three folk songs in *L'Oiseau de feu*. Only the two from Rimsky's collection have been identified thus far. Presumably the theme for Ivan Tsarevich was the composer's invention.

58. *Yamshchiki na podstave* (Postal Coachmen At the Relay Station), 1787, text by Lvov and music by Y.I. Fomin. Discussed in Taruskin, *Defining Russia* Musically, p. 7.

59. *La Revue musicale*, 1 July 1921, p. 57.

60. *New York Times*, Sunday, 24 February 1924.

61. Nestyev, *Prokofiev*, p. 185 and 186. The eminent Soviet folk music specialist Tatyana Boganova similarly acknowledged the Russianness of *Chout* but quickly added the

requisite qualifying political spin: Prokofiev failed to properly portray genuine Russian character as he later did in such Soviet period works as *Alexander Nevsky*, *War and Peace* and *Tale of the Stone Flower*. She added that the tradition of Rimsky-Korsakov and Lyadov was "distorted" by his "pseudo-Russian modernism." Boganova, pp. 22 and 26.

62. These are his own words describing the toccata, or "'motor' line" aspect of his style. "Autobiography", Prokofiev, p. 248.

63. Recent investigations include Richard Bass, "Prokofiev's Technique of Chromatic Displacement," *Music Analysis*, 7 no. 2 (1988), 197–214; Neil Minturn *The Music of Sergei Prokofiev* (New Haven, 1997); and two recent doctoral theses: Deborah Rifkin, "Tonal Coherence in Prokofiev's Music," PhD dissertation (University of Rochester, Eastman School of Music, 2000); Daniel Zimmerman, "Collections Without Clusters," PhD dissertation (University of Chicago, 2002).

64. Prokofiev, "Autobiography", p. 232.

65. Taruskin, *Defining Russia Musically*, p. 86.

66. Cadential wedges, though not overused, seem to be one of the composer's favorite devices. Another memorable example can be found in *L'Enfant prodigue* no. 6, L'ivresse (reh. 125; beginning at 1:33 in Järvi's recording) leading to C-major, but immediately eliding to the next passage with an insolent sounding A-flat in the bassoons and third trombone.

67. Malcolm Hamrick Brown, "The Symphonies of Sergei Prokofiev," PhD dissertation (Florida State University, 1967), p. 498.

68. Nicholas Nabokov, *Old Friends and New Music* (Boston, MA, 1951), pp. 169–70.

69. Brown, "Symphonies," p. 173.

70. There are other parallels as well, for example, the falling octaves at reh. 48 during Ala's distress and the falling sixths as Chloë is led in by her captors, 2 before reh. 131. Perhaps Ravel's score had made a memorable musical impression on Prokofiev, despite his criticisms (see Chapter 1).

71. Letter dated 28 May 1931, from Robinson, *Selected Letters*, p. 169.

72. Nabokov, p. 168.

73. See, for example, the polymeters in his Etudes for piano op. 2 no. 2 and the frequently changing meters in *Sarcasms* no. 5.

74. Stephen Walsh speaks of Stravinsky's "reintroduction of the old idea of rhythm as material," this is, "rhythmic essences" becoming primary musical material in *Le Sacre du printemps*. See Walsh, pp. 44–5.

75. Prokofiev admitted having a passing fascination with Wagner. Possibly the mythical world of the latter fired the imagination of the former. Prokofiev attended the complete *Ring* cycle for three seasons in a row beginning in 1908. It is not surprising that the strongest impressions came from bold, physical actions: "In *Siegfried* I adored the forging of the sword ... In *Götterdämmerung* I especially liked the part where Siegfried journeys down the Rhine with the sound of the horns and shouts coming from the bank: that wild whirlwind captivated me ... . All I can say is that Wagner had a tremendous influence on me at that time." Prokofiev, *Prokofiev By Prokofiev*, p. 246.

76. Whereas Meyerhold, according to Catriona Kelly, apparently took every opportunity to go to the fairground and sneak into the circus, Prokofiev is reported to have attended the circus once in Moscow at age 12 and found it "boring" (*Prokofiev By Prokofiev*, p. 81). His attitude probably remained unfavorable in adulthood: after hearing Auric's *La Pastorale*, he wrote in his Diary, "the music stinks of the circus." The puppet theater is, of course, quite another world. Catriona Kelly, *Petrushka: The Russian Carnival Puppet Theater* (Cambridge, MA and New York, 1990), p. 145.

Prokofiev was, however, well acquainted with the Russian tradition of grotesque comedy known as the *kapustnik*, skits which mocked and ridiculed, having been involved in some during his conservatory days. This according to Michael V. Pisani, "A Kapustnik in the American Opera House: Modernism and Prokofiev's *Love for Three Oranges*," *Musical Quarterly* (Winter, 1997), pp. 487–9.

77. Prokofiev's observation in a letter to Myaskovsky from London, 24 June 1913, from Robinson, *Selected Letters*, p. 235.

78. Sergey Eisenstein, "P-R-K-F-V," in *S. Prokofiev: Autobiography, Articles, Reminiscences*, ed. by S.I. Shlifshteyn, trans. by Rose Prokofieva (Moscow, *c.* 1958), p. 258.

79. From Natalia Savkina, "Back in the USSR," *Three Oranges* 1 (January 2001), p. 13.

80. See Taruskin, "Tone, Style, and Form in Prokofiev's Soviet Operas: Some Preliminary Observations," in *Studies in the History of Music*, vol. 2 (1988). Nicolas Nabokov, whom he knew since the mid-1920s, claimed he remembered "whole scenes" from it. Nabokov, p. 163.

81. In regards to Larionov, influence came, in typical Ballets Russes fashion, *after* the music had been composed. Prokofiev did stop by to see him in Moscow while returning from his 1915 Italian sojourn. He relayed Diaghilev's invitation to come to Switzerland and design *Chout*. We do not know if Larionov had any advice regarding the music Prokofiev was about to compose, but it is doubtful whether he would have been a factor in the score's highly mimetic nature. At that time Larionov's theatrical experience was minimal (see Anthony Parton, *Mikhail Larionov and the Russian Avant-Garde* (Princeton, NJ, 1993), p. 150). The only comment Prokofiev made in his Diary about this meeting with both Larionov and Goncharova was, "I love talented people!"

It seems that Prokofiev first met Meyerhold on 1 October 1916 (OS) at conductor Albert Coates's home when an informal run-through of *Gambler* was given. Influence from Meyerhold's controversial avant-garde productions at the Mariinsky Theater may or may not have preceded this meeting; however, Prokofiev did not mention the director's name in his Diary until the day after their introduction.

82. Max Reinhardt's massively produced and emotively mimed plays were on the boards throughout Europe at the time. His *Oedipus Rex* was performed in St Petersburg in both 1911 and 1912, and his production of Gozzi's *Turandot* was given in a Russian version in Moscow in 1912. Yet it is not known whether Prokofiev was attracted by such fare.

CHAPTER 3

The two versions of *Chout* and the Suite

The first draft of *Chout* reveals Prokofiev's great skill for trenchant musical characterization in the manner of Musorgsky, Rimsky-Korsakov and Lyadov, but it also demonstrates the composer's failure to understand the special needs of ballet and practical theater. Until he revised the score with Diaghilev in 1920, Prokofiev had not received the sort of education Stravinsky obtained by working with Fokine on *L'Oiseau de feu*, nor by then had he seen any of his theatrical works—three operas and two ballets—brought to life on stage.[1] *Chout* would be the first to be produced, but only after Diaghilev directed its revision, harnessing Prokofiev's innate talents to better serve the dramaturgy and the dance. Aside from signaling Diaghilev's conception of ballet music, the two versions of *Chout* document Prokofiev's development as a ballet composer, a story as yet unrecorded despite the accessibility of the 1915 holograph to scholars since 1972.

The 1915 manuscript

The 1915 holograph short score, rebound by its present owner to include pages added in 1920, is now held at the Pierpont Morgan Library in New York.[2] The 1915 portion comprises 25 sheets of two-sided, 24-stave paper of two watermarks, both from Jurgenson of Moscow. It is notated by the composer in black ink. The music appears on pages numbered 1 through 49, except that 32 and 40 were left blank in order to continue a pattern of starting each new scene on the recto side of a leaf. The back side of page 49 is unmarked. Two leaves of slightly shorter 24-stave manuscript paper, numbered 51–53, hold the revised final dance composed in 1920. Although some pages reveal a hastier pen or squeezed-in afterthoughts, the original layer of the score is very neat and easy to read. Prokofiev no doubt ensured that this, his second attempted ballet for Diaghilev was fully comprehensible. The layers of corrections, additions, instructions, strikeouts and lightly penciled-in substitutions in blank spaces and staves above or below the music undoubtedly date from June 1920 when Prokofiev retook possession of his score. All the stage instructions seem to be in the composer's hand, but because of the varying manner in which they were placed with respect to the music, it is difficult to tell exactly when they were added. Since Prokofiev was unable to personally present his new ballet to Diaghilev, it seems most likely that he would have wanted to show the correspondence between action and music in the original score. Their 1915 provenance is supported by the substantial number of stage instructions that do not correspond with those in the published piano score of 1922 and by those that fell under the large "X's" of crossed-out passages during the revision process.

Prokofiev composed the 1915 short score using, almost equally, two or three systems. Ideas for instrumentation were frequently included (both in 1915 and during the revision), and the composer freely expanded to four, five, and even six staves to capture fully the intended voicing, texture and harmony. Consequently this score probably represents at least the second layer of composition. A nine-stave single leaf manuscript containing a sketch for the added wives' dance held at the Pierpont Morgan Library provides an example of Prokofiev's incipient stage of composition as do the more hastily written drafts, exclusively on two staves, for the fifth entr'acte and the revised final dance that appended the 1915 score. The original holograph included suggestions for cuts and timings by the composer for each scene (7, 4, 4, 5, $4^1/_2$, $4^1/_2$ minutes, respectively), making the first version of *Chout* a 29-minute ballet in 6 separate scenes (compared to the revised score's duration of just under an hour including the entr'actes).

The history of *Chout*'s revisions

Diaghilev returned the bound manuscript to Prokofiev in London during the company's season there in June 1920. After taking a day to reacquaint himself with a score he had not seen for five years, the composer played through *Chout* at the piano for the impresario, Massine and Ansermet. The following day he played it again, this time before Diaghilev's entire circle. The impresario then gave his "cautious speech," saying that the music followed the action too closely and had too many details. The illustrative parts needed to be replaced by the development of themes. In other words, Prokofiev was instructed to abandon the approach Stravinsky had pioneered for *L'Oiseau de feu* and *Petrouchka*, whereby presentational music helped describe the action, and hark back to the Chaikovsky style of symphonic ballet music. Over the course of three meetings he and Diaghilev sat down to go over the score in detail, deciding on exactly what needed to be reworked and what should be cut. Diaghilev maintained that each scene needed to be different from the others and cited *Petrouchka* as an example. Prokofiev deflected this demanding request by pointing out that buffoons in different situations were the sole content of his ballet, and that to make each three to four minute scene distinctive would create unnecessary diversity—maybe even damage the humorous impression. Ironically, Diaghilev's request for entr'actes to connect the six scenes coupled with his call for the use of symphonic style would compound the repetitiousness he was hinting at. Since it was too late for such a major revision, the talks moved on to monetary issues.

Prokofiev returned to France and by 20 July had settled into his summer digs at a rented villa in Mantes-sur-Seine about an hour west-northwest of Paris. He spent the rest of the summer revising the score to follow Diaghilev's suggestions and to suit his own more mature artistic taste. The composer recorded in his Diary:

> Once I had moved to Mantes, I settled down to *Chout*; quite quickly and with pleasure I reworked the first four scenes, inserting two new dances [sic] in a major key (Diaghilev complained that the whole ballet was in the minor) ... then I did the first entr'acte and worked on the full score [orchestration], which went along pleasantly though not very quickly; three to five pages a day. I played the piano for one to two hours a day, or more often in the evening, in preparation for my program in America.

By 1 October when he returned to Paris to prepare for his upcoming transatlantic voyage Prokofiev had finished revising the last two scenes, composing the final dance anew. He had completed the entr'actes and the orchestration up to the beginning of the fifth scene. He would make the piano reduction of the ballet while onboard ship to the USA, and finish the full score when he returned to Europe in the early spring of 1921. Prokofiev played *Chout* for Stravinsky during his two-week stay in Paris and asked his opinion of its orchestration. Stravinsky liked the score very much and suggested only a few changes. Diaghilev arrived on his way from Venice to London and applauded the revisions. He even had a recording made of Prokofiev playing the ballet at the piano. The composer wrote in his diary that Stravinsky's and Diaghilev's praise "made me very excited and I was proud."

The quantity and scope of the revisions Prokofiev penciled into the 1915 score at Diaghilev's behest is quite remarkable. After the composer made these corrections and additions it became more difficult to follow: some pages hold a confusing array of cross-outs, arrows, and squeezed-in revisions. Furthermore, original rehearsal numbers have been written over and new ones added with a resulting lack of continuity in places. Another *Chout* manuscript with the first four tableaux, presently unavailable, probably holds the next and perhaps the last layer of revisions. Auctioned from Sergey Lifar's estate by Sotheby's of London in May 1984, it is described by the house annotator as containing:

> the first four tableaux, lacking entr'actes ... with corrections to the music in Prokofiev's hand, in blue ink and pencil, together with details of the scenario (not always corresponding exactly to the text in the published version), with a few markings in green pencil possibly in the hand of Diaghilev, some annotations in other hands in pencil, the whole manuscript notated in blue ink on up to twelve staves per page ... c. 110 pages, folio ...[3]

Since it contains annotations dealing with the scenario and cuts entered by both Prokofiev and Larionov it was probably used for rehearsals in Monte Carlo while the composer was completing the orchestration of the last two scenes at Royat in mid-April. The piano reduction Prokofiev sent to Diaghilev for use in rehearsals is as yet unaccounted for. Also unaccounted for is the manuscript with the altered fifth and sixth tableaux which must certainly have been made, since the 1915 score does not contain all of the revisions. While many of the shorter additions were squeezed onto blank staves, the longer replacement sections for the last two tableaux were sketched elsewhere. Two leaves (numbered 51–53) appending the 1915 score as presently bound are headed in the composer's hand, "Concluding dance from *Chout*," with "unfinished draft" added below in parenthesis. Although written onto two staves throughout, and in a hastier hand that includes mark outs and notes squeezed together at the end in order to make them all fit, the dance is actually, save one repeat, complete and in final form.

At their June 1920 meetings Diaghilev asked Prokofiev for entr'actes to connect each of the six scenes in order to make a continuous ballet. Why Prokofiev did not come to see their need in 1915 is difficult to imagine, the contract had stipulated the ballet to be "in six *combined* acts ... [emphasis added]" Prokofiev sketched the fifth entr'acte right into the 1915 manuscript. Being the shortest of all, it appears entirely on page 40, fortuitously left blank in 1915 between the end of scene five and the beginning of scene six. Aside from a change in meter from 4/4 to 2/4, the two-stave sketch is otherwise identical with the published version. It was probably meant for the composer's and perhaps copyist's eyes only, as it is not so neatly written as the 1915 manuscript. Prokofiev had also left page 32, between scenes four and five, blank in 1915; but he did not utilize this space for the appropriate entr'acte sketch, perhaps knowing the music would not fit. Although the remaining entr'acte drafts were made elsewhere,[4] the changes they necessitated at the ends of the first three scenes were written on the blank staves at the bottom of the respective pages. The original scene-ending double bars have been either scratched out (scenes i and iii) or a segue begun across them (scene ii) to facilitate a transition to the entr'actes. These transitions, however, were later partially (scene ii) or completely (scene iii) crossed out.

Comparison of the 1915 score with the published score

According to the composer, Diaghilev pointed out a number of places in the score that needed to be rewritten, to which he readily agreed. Prokofiev later recalled that, "In rewriting the ballet I endeavored to replace the unsuccessful parts with development of the music of the other parts. Here and there some new music had to be composed, and the final dance entirely rewritten."[5] This is precisely what he did; however, the scope and nature of these revisions have never been properly addressed. The difference between the 1915 score and the published ballet is striking. In response to the impresario's command, over 40 percent of the former was deleted or rewritten (not counting the added entr'actes). The litany of penciled-in directions and crossed-out passages (also in pencil) extending from one measure to several (even the entire page 26) in the 1915 manuscript surely dates from this June 1920 encounter. From all this one can only conclude that Prokofiev learned how to write successful ballet music under Diaghilev's guidance.

Apart from his desire to make the ballet continuous Diaghilev had two main objections with the 1915 score: there was too little opportunity for dancing, and the excessive attention to details in the plot bogged down the ballet's dramatic pace. Both faults stemmed from Prokofiev's curious overdependence on highly descriptive music. His characterizations were brilliant (indeed they remained largely intact in the revised score), but he had become carried away with literal depictions, or presentations, of the characters' actions. This fussy attention to inessential mime not only resulted in excessive sectionalization of the music but also undermined the choreographer's role. When the revisions were being discussed that June, Diaghilev surely intended to assign the ballet to Massine, the company's acclaimed (and sole) choreographer, although there is no evidence that he participated in the revision process.[6] Massine's artistic freedom would have been severely limited by the original score—music that insisted on telling the story almost by itself. Furthermore, while pantomime laden story ballets were a feature of the early years of the Ballets Russes and continued to be box office draws, they had by this time become objects of derision to Diaghilev.[7] In his first version of *Chout* Prokofiev had not only given too little consideration for the proper pacing of the story but failed to provide the sort of music that a ballet requires. Diaghilev directed Prokofiev to reduce the role of mime by eliminating unnecessary details in the narrative and provide more continuous, danceable music.

Following his direction Prokofiev penciled instructions onto the pages of the 1915 score, such as: "try to add previous theme," "[insert] major dance," "cut-to...," "break into dance," "extend," "not necessary," "introduce theme," "don't repeat," "end with this," "add a little something," and even an occasional "good." Major deletions and condensations occurred in nearly every scene—lengthy mimed passages were replaced by music less enslaved to the details of the narrative. Further opportunities for dance were provided by adding a new number and expanding existing ones. Examination of some of the revisions will show how the ballet was improved by eliminating unessential details in the narrative, while others suggest that Prokofiev was persuaded that the dancers, too, can tell the story (these categories, which overlap and share examples, are introduced merely to facilitate discussion). A study of the largely rewritten finale (scene six) reveals both types of changes as well as demonstrating how Prokofiev created a new, far more theatrically successful climax using his original themes.

Improving the dramatic pacing

Aside from a large cut and some changes in the accompanying narrative,[8] the revised version of scene one is the same as the original up to the entrance of the seven buffoons—not surprising since much of this music is seminal. Prokofiev introduces four individual musical ideas for the not-so-distinct segments of the narrative: the hero's main theme at the curtain, music for hatching the plan (distinguished by its downward octave leaps, doubly announced at reh. 8 and 11), another for sharing it with his wife (with its distinctive "urging" motive, reh. 13), and a brief celebratory dance (reh. 19). Variations of the hero's theme recur in between as a connective or linking theme. Prokofiev was aware that he may have written more music than necessary and like a true ballet specialist wrote, "possibly one or two cuts," connected with an arrow to just after reh. 13 (the hero explaining the plan). Indeed, 18 bars were removed from the original (more than he had indicated). What is more, they were replaced by two bars that succinctly capture their essence: just one dotted quaver-semiquaver pair is added to the continuing ostinato and melodic motive in place of eight bars worth.[9] Despite the disjunctions (reh. 8, 11, 13) and the generosity of thematic material, the music heretofore had flown by of a piece. But when the seven gullible neighbor buffoons arrive on stage, Prokofiev began his niggling attention to dramatic detail that undermined the scene's continuity.

He probably saw nothing wrong with his original, protracted music for the staged argument, fight and demonstration of the whip's "magic" power since the action was critical to the story and the seven observers were supposed to be thickheaded. Diaghilev, however, thought otherwise, convincing Prokofiev that his penchant for building tension (and humor) through repetition undermined the dramatic pace (see Charts 3.1–3.3). First to go was the section in which the hero's wife stubbornly refused her husband's demand to set the table not once, not twice, but *three* times. Her resistance is depicted by firm and steady woodwind passages, while her husband's rage increases (ascending cascades of *fortissimo* semiquavers, marked *precipitato*; enclosed area, Chart 3.1). Although not without its humor, Diaghilev apparently saw this musically sectionalized pantomime as redundant and instructed Prokofiev to get on to the fight and "murder," which the composer duly noted on the bottom of the page ("develop and get to [rehearsal number] 26"). Diaghilev's concern with dramatic pacing notwithstanding, this passage, along with all the other dramatic redundancies in the original *Chout*, demonstrates the composer's knowledge of the true character of the Russian *skazka*; it features not only multiple characters, but also repetitive, ritualized actions. If from no other source he would have known this from Rimsky-Korsakov's *Tale of Tsar Sultan* with its three wishes, three wonders and three bee stings.[10] Nevertheless, the presentational passage was replaced by a more symphonic one that restates themes in leitmotivic fashion. Prokofiev reused the same theme ("sharing the plan," with its "urging" motive) but appended it

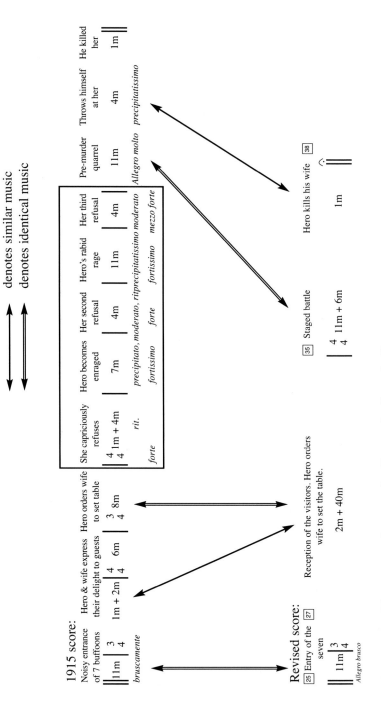

Chart 3.1 *Chout*, scene 1, events leading to the "murder"

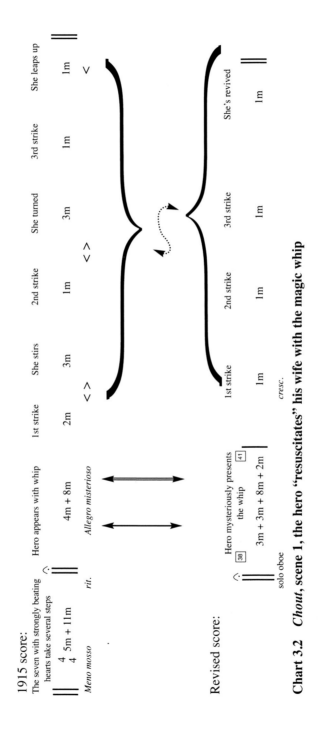

Chart 3.2 *Chout*, scene 1, the hero "resuscitates" his wife with the magic whip

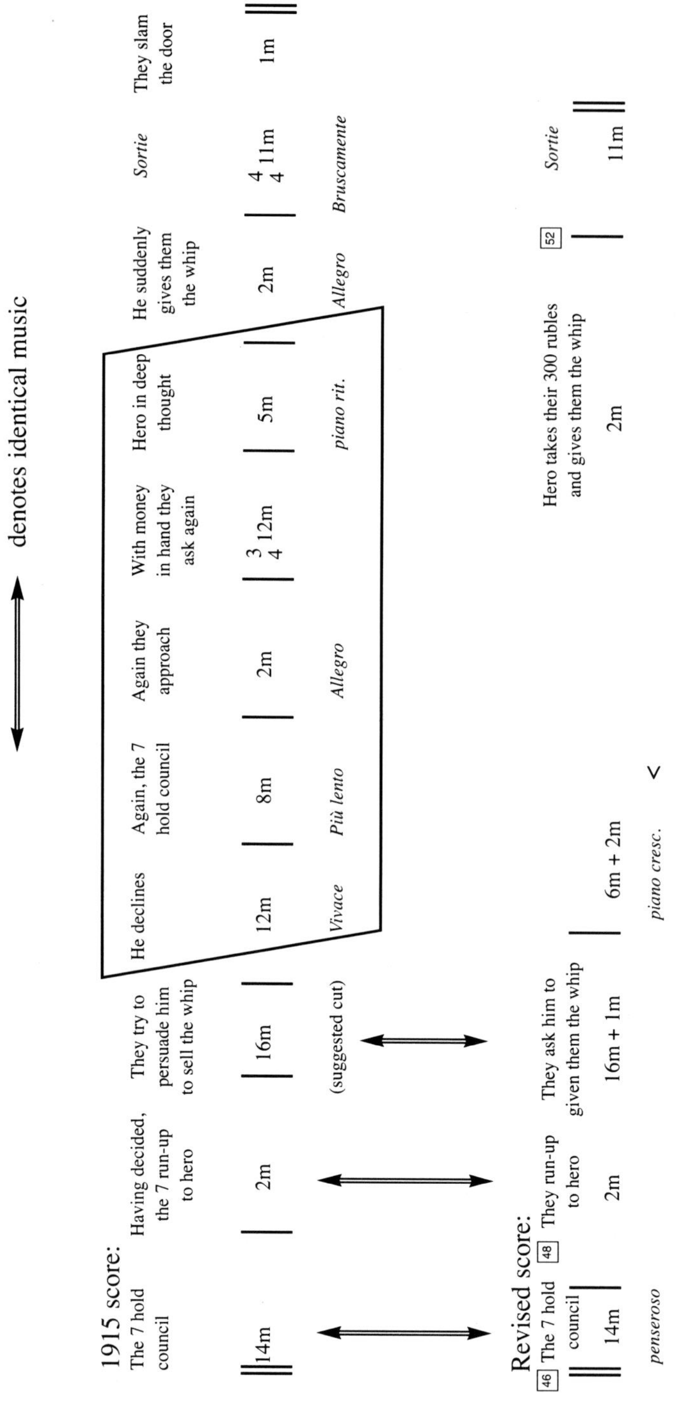

↕ denotes identical music

1915 score:

The 7 hold council	Having decided, the 7 run-up to hero	They try to persuade him to sell the whip	He declines	Again, the 7 hold council	Again they approach	With money in hand they ask again	Hero in deep thought	He suddenly gives them the whip	*Sortie*	They slam the door
14m	2m	16m	12m	8m	2m	3/4 12m	5m	2m	4/4 11m	1m
		(suggested cut)	*Vivace*	*Più lento*	*Allegro*		*piano rit.*	*Allegro*	*Bruscamente*	

Revised score:

46 The 7 hold council	48 They run-up to hero	They ask him to given them the whip			Hero takes their 300 rubles and gives them the whip		52 *Sortie*
14m	2m	16m + 1m	6m + 2m		2m		11m
penseroso			*piano cresc.*	∨			

Chart 3.3   *Chout*, scene 1, the seven buffoons purchase the magic whip

with a varied repetition, brief statements of the hero's main theme, and disjunct ascending bass line (*bruscamente*) associated with violence. The result is not appreciably shorter but it is definitely more continuous.

After the hero "murders" his wife, the stunned guests "with strongly beating hearts take several steps" over the course of 16 measures. Though the string tremolos, tolling bass drum and halting, muted brass chords aptly depict their fear, Diaghilev apparently felt that it was dramatically unwise to mark time for so long. This section was therefore crossed out in favor of the immediate introduction of the whip.

The original version of the wife's revival was also protracted. In between three musically represented lashes of the whip, Prokofiev added suspenseful, rising chromatic scales, hairpin crescendos and tremolos to correspond to his stage instructions: "she stirred," "she turned," and "she leaps up" (see enclosed area, Chart 3.2). While retaining the same musical ideas (short, accented notes preceded by grace notes for the whip strokes and ascending chromatic lines with crescendos for building suspense), the eleven measure section was condensed to four, with one whip stroke per bar and no intervening stage instructions.

The last major dramatic reduction in this scene occurs after the seven buffoons hold council and decide to buy the whip (Chart 3.3). As with the wife's threefold refusal to set the table, Prokofiev prolonged and musically sectionalized the encounter. Throughout the original score there are many repetitions of the seven buffoons' characterizing themes: their crude and gaudy entrance/exit music and their hilarious "council music," heard whenever this slow-witted group gathers to make decisions. Prokofiev may have intended the latter as a running gag as he included it in each scene the seven appear. Diaghilev, on the other hand, considered it just another impediment to the dramatic flow since this and two of the subsequent appearances were dropped from the ballet.[11] Originally, after 14 bars of council music the seven buffoons, having made a decision, run up to the hero (two bars of Allegro, *fortissimo*) and "tenderly and persuasively" ask him to sell the whip (16 bars, *espressivo*). But the hero "with a frivolous expression" refuses their request over the course of the next 12 bars (*Vivace*; playfully rising anapests). Forced to hold another council (*più lento che la prima volta*, eight bars), the seven return to the hero (to the same two bars of *Allegro* traveling music as before) and repeat their request, this time with money in hand (12 bars; now with a triangle marking nearly every beat). The hero is given four measures to mull the decision over ("in deep thought," softly, with a ritard) before suddenly giving them the whip (*Allegro, fortissimo*). Prokofiev did suggest a possible cut in this passage,[12] but Diaghilev wanted the transaction even tauter. The revised score settles the deal after the first request. Prokofiev retained the first two sections (the first approach and request) then jumped to the close, which was expanded slightly for better dramatic effect. All of these examples from scene one demonstrate how the original score's sectionalization and redundancy gave way to a tighter, more dramatic symphonic sweep in the revision.

Similar deletions or reductions were made in the following scenes. In the second both the council and the act of dragging the corpses to the proscenium arch were excised, and the attempted revival and funeral cortege were abridged. In scene three the important introduction of Molodukha's theme was originally buried in a busy, lengthy bit of *ballet d'action* ("Molodukha plays a trick"): the seven now enraged buffoons rush off to search the hero's house (with cartoon-like bustling music that grows softer as they leave center stage) and finding nothing, rush back (the music grows louder as they return). They confront Molodukha who feigns innocence (introduction of her theme), show displeasure with her "babbling," and run off to the side to hold council. Deemed inconsequential, the passage was streamlined into two consecutive, more symphonic sections, the first supporting the seven's rage, the second for an uninterrupted presentation of Molodukha's theme. Also deleted were two brief passages of alternating clarinet and flute *fioritura* that were probably intended to evoke the disguised hero's magical powers over the seven.[13] In scene four Prokofiev had undermined the culminating sweep of the drama with a disjunctive section of very prosaic ("solemn" in his words) exit music for the merchant and his chosen bride, Molodukha, complete with a calculated grand pause at the end. Instructed to "use the merchant theme" instead (penciled-in note), the revised conclusion became more concise and ongoing.

Two sections of fussy detail occur in scene five: the lowering of the sheet[14] and the protracted introduction of the goat. The former was truncated and incorporated into the musical flow while the latter was eliminated in deference to the choreographer's resources. He or she would have had no choice but to slavishly follow the separate, immutable segments in the original score. With each stage instruction the character of the music (tempo, texture, rhythm, dynamics, and so forth) abruptly changes: "something gives a tug" (one bar), the merchant "drags up the sheet" (four bars), "in the window appears a she-goat" (five bars), the merchant "draws back" (four bars), "he drops his wardrobe [*svalil shkap*]" (one bar; *fortissimo* chord complete with bass drum thwack), "at the noise the servants begin to gather" (two bars), "merchant" (one bar), "servant" (two bars), "Merchant" (two bars), and so forth. It seems that in addition to an inability to focus on only the salient features of the story, Prokofiev also had failed to grasp, or was unwilling to allow, that the choreographer was his collaborator—that his or her talent and resources could, at times, more efficiently and effectively convey the essence of the story.

Making the music a collaborative part of the ballet

Without a choreographer's guidance, Prokofiev loaded the original *Chout* with highly specific stage instructions and corresponding music, thus highlighting pantomime at the expense of dance. Diaghilev's dismissal of *Ala i Lolli* as "just music" may provide some justification, although *Chout*'s curious dependence on melodramatic theatricality has no precedence in Prokofiev's work, certainly not to this degree, nor is it so prominent a feature in any other ballet score newly composed for Diaghilev. (I use the term melodramatic here and elsewhere to mean extravagant, not to imply a dramatic form.) There are some parallels between *Chout* and the opera *Gambler*, conceived earlier but not composed until after the ballet's completion in 1915. Both works encountered similar postponements and underwent similar major revisions prior to their much delayed premiers. *Chout*'s highly detailed musical narrative is similar in some respects to the declamatory nature of the opera, one which was modeled on the patterns of conversational speech without altogether forsaking the composer's lyrical style. Similar "literary" approaches had been taken by Dargomïzhsky in his experimental opera *Kamennïy gost'* (The Stone Guest) and to an even greater extent by Musorgsky in *The Marriage*. In both *Chout* and *Gambler* the rebellious composer rejected traditions of the immediate past, and both reveal the composer's interest in effects. However, the interruptive sections of mime in *Chout* are quite different from the "ongoing scenic action" in the *Gambler*.[15]

Perhaps Prokofiev used the highly detailed, fairy-tale inspired plot as a point of departure to show off his representational skills. He clearly distorted the traditional view of ballet music—that it must remain subservient to dance, only coming to the fore to illuminate passages of pantomime—to his own purpose. Defiantly an enemy of tired nineteenth-century operatic conventions, Prokofiev took a decidedly backwards glance in 1915, harking back to the likes of Rameau and Gluck, eighteenth-century composers who also wrote such dramatically charged ballet music that it essentially described the dance by itself. Like them, Prokofiev assumed total control over the dramatic aspect of his ballet. To this end he summoned an eclectic array of obvious theatrical clichés, which, paradoxically, had been exploited in much conventional nineteenth-century theatrical fare. The result at times seems more appropriate for pantomime or a puppet play than a ballet, or, closer to home, one of Fokine's emotive choreodramas. Prokofiev may have remembered the high percentage of mime in the calculated spectacle *La Légende de Joseph* without understanding that its use of non-dancers was exceptional and that the Joseph (Massine in his solo debut) lacked the experience and virtuosity for a true *danseur*'s role. He probably felt that dancing was adequately served by *Chout*'s many *dansante* dramatic passages. But when he reviewed the score with Diaghilev in 1920, the impresario persuaded him to change the music into a more collaborative vehicle, one more conducive to choreographic exhibition. These changes were of two basic types: the addition or expansion of danced sections and the replacement of pantomime by dance.

Originally scene one had only two brief opportunities for dancing unencumbered by the exposition of the narrative. The first was a 14-measure regularly phrased dance (a truncated close interrupts the regularity) to accompany the hero and his wife as they celebrate their newly devised plan to deceive their neighbors with a magic whip ("satisfied … they laugh" and dance). After the seven buffoons have departed with their newly purchased whip the scene ends with a 19-measure reprise appending a representation of laughter ("left alone the buffoon and his wife burst out with uncontrollable laughter"). Diaghilev probably suggested expanding these sections since this was the hero's only chance to dance with his wife, unencumbered by the ongoing event in the plot, until the ballet's finale. At the end of the first appearance of the dance Prokofiev penciled-in "extend," and by the second, "almost double it." In revising the score he duly doubled the length of both the dance and its reprise using traditional modular techniques of the specialist composers: in the former he simply inserted a new half-cadencing phrase to add a first ending and in the latter he rounded the dance by adding the original opening at the end.

Although scene two is not without opportunities for dancing, Diaghilev wanted a self-contained dance in a major key for the seven wives to be inserted between their husbands' return home and their decision to try out the whip. Over the grand pause at the conclusion of the seven buffoons' entry music, Prokofiev penciled-in "major [mazhor] dance" with a downward pointing arrow. Important characters in a ballet are obviously supposed to dance; without the addition the seven wives might just as well have been non-dancing extras. Originally a seven-voice fugato followed the husbands' entrée, each entry corresponding to the seven wives, in turn, heartily digging into her supper. Apparently this action was supposed to be so repulsive that it prompted the seven buffoons to hold council and decide to kill them; afterwards they would try out the magic whip. On account of their uncouth eating habits, these unfortunate women were murdered less than five minutes after they appeared on stage. At least with the added dance, the choreographer had the opportunity to provide a stronger motivation, one using whole bodies in motion, not just mimes' arms and mouths.

Prokofiev's dance for the wives is a fairly regular rondo in D major with a twice-recurring refrain and a coda that serves as a dramatic link to the next action. Its gliding, almost ethereal refrain paints a character quite inconsistent with the lumpishness and earthiness established at the opening of the scene, however ("The seven wives behind seven tables wait for their husbands. Scene of everyday life"). But the rondo's two episodes reestablish the ladies' grotesque character and familial relation by recalling the leaping sevenths from their husbands' entrée in the first and reusing the weighty, downward thrusting scene-opening music for the second. The first episode also foreshadows the mayhem to come since this music originally accompanied the seven buffoons' negotiations to buy the whip in scene one. The wives' dance is thus a typical example of a Prokofiev ballet rondo: the refrain is newly composed, the episodes are flashbacks and the coda serves as a dramatic segue. With its addition the fugato lost its association with eating (Prokofiev penciled onto his manuscript: "long fugue directly to murder"). Expanded by added entries and a stretto, the revised fugato now served to generate suspense leading up to the act of murder.

Further opportunities for dancing in the revised score came from turning sectionalized passages into continuous dance music. At Diaghilev's request a brief, interrupted dance for the seven buffoons' daughters in scene four was expanded and made continuous (the penciled-in note reads: "break into dance").[16] Originally the dance tune was just an incidental part of a closely controlled stage action in A–B–A' form with temporal and harmonic closure at its junctures: "Daughters are in a state of agitation thinking that a suitor is coming" (part "A," 12 measures *un poco agitato*, crotchet = 184). "They calm down" (part "B," 9 measures *Allegretto*, crotchet = 152), lastly "Molodukha sees that the merchant is coming. Commotion" (5 measure reprise of the opening "A", now *Vivace*, minim = 100). The "A" part comprised two musical sections: one sporting a new fleet tune, the other integrating the new material with brief recalls of the scene opening music ("the seven daughters 'doll' themselves up"). The slower "B" was a shortened version of that very theme. In making the revision Prokofiev dropped the "B" and expanded his "A" into a two-episode rondo, another example of this favored form. Enlarged and made continuous, this "Danse des filles des bouffonnes" allowed the choreographer a rare opportunity to actually lay out a dance number (although it goes by in less than a minute), one that still serves a dramatic function. A similar situation occurred later in the same scene: Prokofiev had the merchant show passing interest in one of the daughters, resulting in an interruption of their flowing *khorovod*. This five-bar *ballet d'action* ("her father bows deeply," *ritard*; "no, she won't do," *a tempo*) rated a penciled-in "*ne nado*" (not necessary) during the score's review.

A more successful finale

Another deficiency appears at the end of the last scene of the 1915 score: stretches of dull, uninspired music that may have resulted from haste. Along with the sectionalized passages of tedious mime that Diaghilev wanted removed, these changes mandated revision of nearly the last two-thirds of the scene (see Chart 3.4). The opening part, however, needed only minor adjustments. Several measures into the goat's funeral march (*tristemente*) Prokofiev had added a new, softly stated motive with the accompanying stage instructions: "from behind a fence the faces of the [seven] fools can be seen." Five bars later they jumped out (*Allegro moderato, fortissimo*) and began mocking the grieving merchant, their council theme (without the *penseroso* clarinets) silencing the funeral music. Diaghilev considered the fence peeping unnecessary and the funeral too long: a heavy, vertical pencil mark mid-phrase—between the eleventh and twelfth measures—probably indicates where he wanted the latter to stop. But instead of just lopping off the remaining bars and jumping ahead, Prokofiev took the opportunity to rephrase the march and fashion a new close. Its new beguiling irregularity gave it more of a Russian quality. Two more cuts helped fine tune the length of the section, and the addition of their disjunct entrée theme and a shrill sounding clarinet solo (*a due*) improved the representation of mocking.

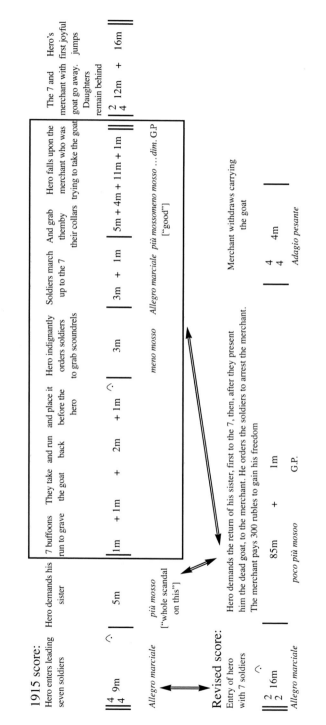

Chart 3.4 *Chout*, scene 6, a resolution of the drama

With the entry of the hero and seven soldiers, the story reaches its point of resolution: the hero demands the return of his "sister" (Molodukha, that is, himself), and when the seven produce the dead goat instead, he demands their arrest and compensation from the merchant. Prokofiev once again tried to explain every detail through the music, and the result was another lengthy sectionalized pantomime (Chart 3.4). The revised score presents an entirely different, much improved concept from this point onward, despite its reuse of four themes. Although the first of its two parts still has a narrative function, it utilized ongoing music eminently suitable for either dance or mime.

First, a discussion of the original version. Prokofiev began promisingly with a bracing nine-bar *allegro marziale* fanfare for the entry of the hero and the soldiers, followed by another new theme (hereafter referred to as the "*più mosso* theme") that is related to the original "hatching the plan" music from scene one. The latter accompanies the hero's demand for the return of his "sister." But after only five measures Prokofiev abandoned this lyrical, danceable style for melodramatic pantomime music (enclosed area Chart 3.4). Prokofiev's stage instructions state: "The buffoons run to the grave" (first measure), "They take the goat" (second measure), "They run back with it" (third measure), and "place it before the buffoon" (fourth measure). At least all of the foregoing had been continuous, but now Prokofiev adds a dramatic pause presumably to allow for the hero's reaction. Then at a slower tempo and with the physical action presented in the music, the "hero indignantly orders the soldiers to grab the scoundrels" (a three and one-half octave *glissando*). To a repeat of the *allegro marziale* theme, the soldiers "march up to them" and "grab them by the collar," Prokofiev connecting this last instruction by arrow to the specific note. The mime continues with the hero "falling upon the merchant who was trying to take the goat." This fracas opens to a transitory reappearance of the *più mosso* theme but quickly degenerates into churning semiquavers and sequences of a motive suggestive of scuffling. After receiving money from the merchant during a calculated grand pause, the hero releases him and orders the soldiers to release the seven buffoons. The dumb show ends with the soldiers "taking several steps and releasing them" (to a third statement of the *allegro marziale* theme) and the merchant departing with the dead goat. A lengthy transition ensues with more churning semiquavers and demi-semiquavers before Prokofiev finally returns to the realm of the dance with a new theme accompanying the hero's "first jumps of joy." It is closely related to the hero's main theme from scene one. The climactic dance follows 16 bars later.

Apart from the excessive detail and sectionalization, the dramatic resolution is not as satisfying as it could have been because the music and events never join in a resounding climax. Furthermore, too much time elapses between the culmination of events and the hero's celebration. The *allegro marziale* fanfare certainly provides bold underscoring for the release of the merchant and the seven buffoons but it is an odd choice for what should surely be a dramatic climax. Then to have the seven defeated buffoons and the merchant exit to nondescript transitional music is also dramatically inept. Since 12 bars go by before the "first jumps of joy" theme begins, they could amble off at leisure. Meanwhile the soldiers remain on stage as they are to partner the seven daughters, and the hero has nothing essential to do except mark time until his theme emerges from the climax-inducing note-spinning. After 26 anticipatory measures the concluding dance, *scherzando*, finally appears, but a climax is again thwarted due to the precipitous drop in texture and dynamics at its start ("hero dances with the purse," violin solo with simple ostinato accompaniment, *piano*).

Effective though it might have been, Prokofiev's presentational music here is, at best, pedestrian. Neither the running music nor the motivic music accompanying the buffoon's attack on the merchant is on a very high level. On the other hand, his two new themes are typically characterful and eminently danceable. But they amount to no more than brief, inconsequential respites amidst the descriptive music. In reviewing the score with Diaghilev, Prokofiev penciled-in "whole scandal on this" next to the first entry of the first theme and "good" by the second. Henceforth, musical themes were to be the basis for Prokofiev's ballets.

The original concluding dance began with a new eight-bar theme that featured a highly decorated solo violin line, evoking the folk-like strains of a village fiddler. But Prokofiev abandoned the dance tune after one repetition. And instead of reintroducing previous themes as episodes or secondary ideas, he fell back on uninspired, perhaps hastily conceived closing pattern work. A tirade of churning, ever accelerating semiquavers whose outline vaguely resembles the dance theme is followed by an unmemorable idea that goes nowhere, but at least it does so quickly (*presto*). Prokofiev desperately stokes the fire with some syncopation (reh. 229) before ending the ballet on tired, flat feet (see Ex. 3.1; compare with the motivically generated revised ending, Ex. 2.17). Even the closing gesture sounds as much like a halfhearted nod towards the conclusion of *Le Sacre du printemps* as an echo of the the ballets opening whip motive. Not only was the original finale too short by almost half, but its last three pages recall Diaghilev's epithet for *Ala i Lolli*: "just music." This manufactured, generic climax was unbefitting such a thematically rich ballet. Three penciled-in comments directed the necessary revisions: twice Prokofiev wrote "introduce theme," and under the passage of empty syncopations, he wrote "add a little something."

Unlike the original version, the revised finale is fresh and theatrically sound. All traces of sectionalized mime were removed (enclosed area chart 3.4). Retaining his themes, Prokofiev refashioned the narrative and dance sections into a sweeping dramatic culmination. All the stage instructions were placed at the beginning of the climactic section, freeing the choreographer to express the details through a flowing combination of gesture and dance. Instead of being a throwaway for a superfluous bit of mime, the *più mosso* theme formalizes the

Ex. 3.1 **Original ending of** *Chout*

dramatic resolution, an apt usage since it is related to the "hatching the plan theme" from scene one (reh. 13). It leads off the series of brief musical flashbacks—the sheet-lowering music, the goat-revival music, the hero's main theme and the merchant's love theme, and so forth—wherein the story is retold for the benefit of the authorities. The occasional restatements of the *marziale* fanfare suggest the soldiers' attempts to keep this finger-pointing mob in order. All of this builds to a grand pause and a climatic *adagio pesante, ben tenuto* statement of the hero's theme, which accompanies the forlorn merchant as he withdraws carrying the dead goat.

The final dance starts as it did in the original score with only minor changes. At the point where Prokofiev's inspiration flagged in 1915, the hero's "first jumps of joy" is introduced as a contrasting theme. Both themes and their variants alternate until near the end where Prokofiev combines them in true *kuchkist* fashion. He makes a transition to the closing section with a characteristic seesawing bass ostinato (reh. 318). He still uses syncopation to build tension but this time it propels a theme (reh. 320, 326). After a climax-inducing stretto the ballet ends with an augmented statement of the "jump for joy" theme thus affording both musical and dramatic unification (Ex. 2.16). Diaghilev had but one suggestion for this revised final dance which Prokofiev added onto his working short score: "from here [reh. 313] ... more massive." The composer dutifully obliged.

Diaghilev had perhaps overcompensated for his lack of specifics when commissioning Prokofiev's first ballet. *Chout*'s story was lengthy and overburdened with fine points from the start. It needed an experienced ballet scenarist to ferret out its essence. Working from the Diaghilev approved scenario, however, Prokofiev fashioned a ballet that was detailed to a fault. Ironically, the added freedom in the revised score compounded the task for the inexperienced Larionov when he replaced Massine as choreographer in 1921. In light of his complaints about the lack of details, he probably would have preferred the original.

Diaghilev knew that *Chout* was certainly worth saving—indeed, many of its best features appear in the first draft. Except for some slight revisions in accompanimental figuration, re-slurrings and added rhythmic propulsiveness, the opening pages remained unchanged. Prokofiev's *priskazka*, the folk-derived motives, almost all of the themes, and the system of motivic permutation and recall discussed in Chapter 2 were original concepts. Prokofiev was not completely ignorant of the duties of the ballet composer, either: for example, he had suggested locations for possible cuts and he even appears to have adopted the traditional ballet-specialist practice of including some padding. Excising all his suggested cuts, however, would not have solved the problem. The original score needed improved continuity and a reorientation towards dance. What the two versions of *Chout* tell us then is that Prokofiev possessed an innate *dansante* lyricism, a fair share of theatrical sensibility and an individualized Russian soul, but that, understandably, he needed to be taught, as Stravinsky had been by Fokine, that choreographers and dancers were capable of equally important contributions towards the realization of a story ballet, and for that they need flexible support, not rigid direction. It also tells us that Diaghilev had abandoned the presentational style of *L'Oiseau de feu* and *Petrouchka* for a more traditional "symphonic" ballet.

The entr'actes

More than any logistical reason it was Diaghilev's desire for a continuous ballet that gave rise to the entr'actes. *Chout*'s scene changes were probably dispatched relatively quickly since few props were used and only Larionov's backdrops and probably the lighting needed to be changed. The hero's costume changes to and from the attire of Molodukha were undoubtedly made easier with the entr'actes but they did not mandate them. The entr'actes are quite brief: the first and third are slightly over two minutes each, the last is not even a minute and a half, though the second and fourth are both more intricate and longer at around three minutes each. Diaghilev probably dictated their duration and perhaps suggested their content as well. At the top of the page holding the sketch for the last entr'acte Prokofiev had penciled-in "very short entr'acte," followed by "40 seconds" with "45" written over it (or vice versa, it is difficult to tell). The penciled instruction continues: "to previous theme and lead to" with an arrow drawn to the top of the next page, the beginning of scene six.

The five entr'actes are fashioned from the music of the ballet proper. Each is an ongoing collage of themes introduced in their respective preceding scenes. Music from the more mimetic passages is not used. Prokofiev unified the entr'actes by having each open with the hero's main theme and close with either the *priskazka* (the first three) or the same reordered variant of the main theme (four and five). The entr'actes and the ballet proper are stylistically identical. This is amply demonstrated by the composer's ability to skip freely back and forth between the two when he constructed the second movement of the ballet suite in 1922. This was done to avoid presentational music and to pass by a theme that was to be featured later. The thematic material from each representative scene, if changed at all, is manipulated by variation (for example, diminution or motivic reordering) or fragmentation (with sequencing), and in cases of rejuxtaposition, given new closing phrases. A brief example from the second entr'acte shows a simple variation of the music that accompanied the seven buffoons' desperate whip lashes, stated amidst repetitions of the ubiquitous "a2" (compare Exx. 3.2 and 3.3). The ensuing recall of the seven wives' dance (reh. 121) after statements of the whip motive demonstrates Prokofiev's disinterest in maintaining the original chronology in the entr'actes. Another example, a similar intermingling of motives, occurs near the end of the same entr'acte when the grace note adorned first note of the *priskazka* appends statements of "A" in anticipation of the entire

Ex. 3.2   "Coups de fouet desordonnés," scene 2

Ex. 3.3   Simple variant of Ex. 3.2 at 2 before 121 in the ensuing entr'acte

priskazka which follows. Despite passages such as these, more is literally repeated than refashioned. The longest example of of the latter practice—a 30 measure section based on Molodukha's theme in the third entr'acte—resulted from the dearth of other exploitable, lyrical material in the preceding scene. Aside from the second entr'acte's episodic-like restatements of the opening theme, and the fourth's and fifth's rounding with it, all of the entr'actes are through-composed. They do reveal, however, introductory, middle and closing sections. An examination of the fourth will illuminate most of these features.

The new themes in scene four are the "daughters' waiting theme" (heard while they await the arrival of the merchant and his matchmakers), the "Danse des filles des bouffons," and the merchant's entrée (which also serves as the daughters' *khorovod* when doubly augmented). All appear in the entr'acte but not in the original order. As in the other entr'actes, the introductory section opens with the hero's seven bar theme in the original key after which variants follow. First the opening notes are rewritten in dotted rhythm and the mode is changed to major (this particular variant had already appeared in the middle of the first entr'acte). After one repetition Prokofiev moves on to clever juxtapositions of the hero's theme and the merchant's entrée music as discussed in Chapter 2 (see Ex. 2.22). The main body of the entr'acte recalls all three new themes. Apart from a change in barring from 4/4 to 2/4, the first 32 measures come directly from the *khorovod*. Following without pauses are, in turn, the original eight measure "daughters' waiting theme" (reh. 227), and the "Danse des filles des bouffons" in a new formal scheme, with lengthened contrasting episodes (reh. 228). But before reaching its original close Prokofiev smoothly elides into the last part of the entr'acte (see Ex. 3.4), appropriating the dance's rising chromatic lines as an ostinato accompaniment to an augmented statement of the hero's main

Ex. 3.4   Conclusion of entr'acte no. 4

theme in its reordered guise (a2–a1–a3 + B). He makes one last flashback to the merchant's arrival theme (reh. 237) before ending with the reordered main theme and its original accompaniment (reh. 238).

This and the other entr'actes present, in organic fashion, music that was originally sectionalized and unconnected. They sum up the ballet's non-mimetic music so well that Prokofiev appropriated all or part of the second, third and fifth when he made the ballet suite. In light of the composer's system of motivic recall in the ballet proper (discussed in Chapter 2), the additional recurrences of the hero's theme in its various versions throughout the entr'actes leads to an unfortunate degree of tedium, as noted by early critics. Presumably this would not be as noticeable in the theater as in the concert hall. But this does not mean that the less repetitious Suite should be the only version used in the latter venue. Conductor Gennady Rozhdestvensky cuts the first three entr'actes from the full ballet for concert presentation without a narrator.[17] This eliminates a great deal of the redundancy and it allows the seven buffoons' entire entrée theme to be heard as well as their delightful council music, neither of which is included in the Suite. In the light of audience expectations for concert performances of entire ballets, this version is not too lengthy (*c.* 49 minutes). On the other hand, the composer voiced concern that the 12-part Suite from *Chout* was too much for one sitting, implying too much for a suite: "I did not intend all of them [the movements] to go into one program; five or eight numbers .... is quite enough"[18] (all 12 movements take about 35 minutes to perform). Regardless, both the thematic redundancy and the entr'actes themselves were born of dramatic necessity. And, intentionally or not, this formal repetition reinforced *Chout*'s link with the Russian fairy-tale tradition.

Conclusion

Diaghilev's dissatisfaction with Prokofiev's first ballet, *Ala i Lolli*, had provided the impetus for enrolling the composer in a practical course of study. The first lesson involved commercial appeal, that is, developing a recognizably Russian sound. The 1915 version of *Chout* clearly fulfilled this need. The second lesson, concerning the special requirements of the genre, was delayed until 1920. With Diaghilev's help and his own more mature artistic outlook, Prokofiev made the revised score of *Chout* tighter in its discourse, and, with enhanced continuity from the added entr'actes, more symphonic in its sweep. The ballet also became more traditional, providing greater opportunity for choreographic freedom. As with Musorgsky and his experimental opera *The Marriage*, Prokofiev's over reliance on presentational realism became a passing phase. With its reconciliation of music and dance, the 1920 version of *Chout* represents the source of Prokofiev's mature ballet style.

The *Chout* Suite

Writing from his home in Ettal (Germany) on 4 September 1922, Prokofiev apologized to the conductor Albert Coates for the delay in producing a concert suite from *Chout*. He claimed difficulty in obtaining the score from Diaghilev[19] but reported that it was now at hand, and he promised that the Suite would be ready by November. This was a bit premature. Although he completed his emendations by

December the score was not printed until almost a year later. The Suite was premiered on 15 January 1924 in Brussels, under the direction of Frans Rühlmann.

In a letter dated 21 September 1922, Prokofiev gave his instructions to the German music publishing firm Breitkopf and Härtel for extracting a 12 movement suite from his ballet score.[20] I have annotated these instructions below in brackets, identifying the excerpts' locations in the ballet and providing the titles of each movements as found in the published score.

Gentlemen,

I am forwarding to you under a separate cover (insured) the orchestra score of my ballet "Chout."

A symphonic suite is to be extracted from this ballet. I am enclosing a list showing which parts of the ballet will constitute the suite and in which order they have to be taken. Please make your copiers copy the music for the suite according to this list, and then send me back both the manuscript of the ballet and the copy of the suite, so that I can correct it. Thereafter, I will return the suite for engraving.

… Please start this work right away, as the score of the ballet might be soon needed for its production in Paris This work, however, must not interfere with the preparation of the material for "The Love etc. [for Three Oranges]" as the latter must not be delayed either. Kindly inform me when you expect to finish copying the suite of the ballet, and acknowledge receipt of the manuscript.

Very truly yours,

SP.

List showing which parts of the *Ballet* "Chout" will constitute the *Suite* of the same ballet. The Suite is in 12 movements.

1.

From the beginning to [reh.] 8; then from 11 to 23 and from 58 to 60.
["The Buffoon and His Wife"]
[1–8: opening of the ballet through the introduction of the hero's theme and its variations; 11–23: the hero shares his plan with his wife, followed by their "danse du rire"; 58–60: the last 12 bars of scene 1, which is the end of the reprised dance. The entire encounter with the seven neighbor buffoons is omitted: their entry, greetings, hero and wife quarrel, "murder," her "revival," purchase of the whip, the seven exit.]

2.

73–79; 116–127; 85–93. Leave an empty page for conclusion which I will write myself.
["Dance of the Wives"]
[73–79: opening of scene 2, the seven wives await the return of their husbands; 116–127: this is from the the middle of the second entr'acte but rebarred from 2/4 to 4/4, it restates mm. 88–91 from the middle of the 7 wives' dance; 85–93: the wives' dance from the second statement of the refrain to the conclusion, thus repeating 12 bars just heard]

3.

95–114. Leave an empty page for conclusion
["The Buffoons Kill Their Wives (Fugue)"]
[in scene 2: the seven decide to kill their wives (fugato), the murder, attempted resuscitation, funeral cortege, to the end of the scene]

4.

152–167. Empty page for conclusion
["The Buffoon As a Young Woman"]
[begins midway through scene 3: the first appearance of the hero as Molodukha, the seven seize and beat her, continues to the end of the scene]

5.

167–177.
["Third Entr'acte"]
[all of the third entr'acte up to the repetition of the *priskazka* at the close (the middle part is built on Molodukha's music but changed to triple meter); although brief, this number is essentially redundant and thus a candidate for omission if performance time is critical]

6. from 178 till 2 bars after 181; then 185–191 and a page free for concl.
["Dance of the Buffoons' Daughters"]
[178 to 2 after 181: the opening of scene 4—the seven daughters waiting for the merchant (stops before their maltreatment of Molodukha); 185–191: the daughters' dance minus its original conclusion]

7. 192–203; 206–214. & pge for concl.
["Entry of the Merchant and His Welcome"]
[1 after 192–203: scene 4 continued, the seven buffoons go to greet the merchant (the disjunct theme of their scene 1 entrée), the merchant's entrée, the daughters' *khorovod*; 206–214: the merchant falls in love with the cook (Molodukha's theme from movement 4) and he leads her away]

8. Leave to [sic] empty bars in the beginning; then 239–246
["In the Merchant's Bedroom"]
[two bar vamp, then the opening of scene 5, the merchant and the cook, the former in love, the latter thinking how to escape (stops before the cook feigns illness)]

9. 255–268
["The Young Woman Becomes a Goat"]
[the concluding music of scene 5: the merchant pulls up the drape and finds that his beloved cook has turned into a goat, commotion, the goat dies; at the ninth bar the Merchant's theme is stated; Diaghilev's London cut came after 20 bars, following the second scalar wedge]

10. 268–275. Page for concl.
["Fifth Entr'acte and the Goat's Burial"]

[the full last entr'acte and the opening of scene 6, the merchant buries the goat]

11. 283–299
["The Buffoon and the Merchant Quarrel"]
[in scene 6: the hero arrives with seven soldiers to the *allegro marziale* theme (where Diaghilev's London cut ended); ends at the Grand Pause after the seven produce the dead goat instead of the hero's "sister"]

12. from 299 to the end.[21]
["Final Dance"]
[continues from no. 11 to the end of the ballet: the merchant withdraws with the goat as "A" of the main theme is stated *Adagio pesante*, followed by the *Danse finale* in which the hero and his wife dance while brandishing their purse of extorted rubles, and the seven soldiers partner the seven daughters]

Though it might seem somewhat impersonal, this was Prokofiev's customary procedure for creating a suite. Someone at his publisher's copied the music according to these instructions. The composer then sat down and added new conclusions for each number. He also had to correct the copyist's work: in his diary he complained "195 pages of small writing . . . like all copyists [he] sometimes fantasizes." The new closing sections are generally four bars (but the second movement's is six, and the third's, just two). Prokofiev had second thoughts about the sixth movement: it is considerably longer than originally planned, continuing with music from the fourth entr'acte, reh. 227–230 and reh. 232 to 4 before 235, leading to a new 14-bar close. Except for the use of entr'acte excerpts in the second and sixth movements, the music proceeds in the same order as in the ballet. Understandably, some of the loud and dissonant passages accompanying acts of violence (for example, the end of scene 4) were passed over in creating this concert fare. Surely the most regrettable omissions are the seven buffoons' humorous calling cards: their "council" music and their bizarre entrée/sortie, both introduced in scene one of the ballet. The disjunct melodic line of the latter does appear briefly in no. 6 and at the start of no. 7, but without its humorous, lopsided ostinato.

A ballet could be produced using the music of the Suite, indeed, Prokofiev promoted this idea in his correspondence with the Mariinsky Theater and Boris Asafyev during the summer of 1924 and Diaghilev planned to use it for the 1929 revival (see Chapter 1). A staging using the full original ballet score, however, would be an even more welcome endeavor. In the meantime, we will have to be content with the all-too-infrequent concert performances of the Suite. Prokofiev was justifiably proud of *Chout*; surely it deserves to be performed more often than it is.

Notes

1. All of Prokofiev's early operas (discounting juvenilia) failed to garner timely productions: a hoped for student production of *Maddalena* at the Conservatory came to naught, *The Gambler* was not premiered until 1929, and *L'Amour des trois oranges* suffered repeated delays that pushed its premier back to December 1921.

2. The 1915 *Chout* holograph is part of the Robert Owen Lehman Collection on deposit in the Pierpont Morgan Library, New York.

3. Sotheby's of London catalog, *Ballet Material and Manuscripts from the Sergey Lifar Collection*, May 1984, item no. 198, p. 201. The full score Ansermet and Prokofiev conducted from is also a holograph, but it is relatively correction and annotation free.

4. These drafts have yet to be located.

5. Sergey Sergeyevich Prokofiev, "Autobiography," trans. and ed. by Oleg Prokofiev; assoc. ed. Christopher Palmer, in *Sergei Prokofiev Soviet Diary 1927 and other Writings* (Boston, MA, 1992), p. 268.

6. Even though Massine, along with the company's conductor Ansermet, did attend Prokofiev's performance of the ballet at the piano, Diaghilev needed no assistance for the task at hand. Besides, his opinions in matters musical were authoritative. Still, both Massine and Diaghilev were probably of like mind regarding the score's shortcomings. Whereas Ansermet was vocal in his praise, both Diaghilev and Massine were guarded, but agreed nevertheless that there were many "beautiful and Russian scenes."

   In his autobiography Massine did not mention any discussion with Prokofiev regarding *Chout*. The two had spent time together in Italy during the spring of 1915, and according the Massine, enjoyed each other's company. By 1920 Massine's choreographic accomplishments ranged from the cubist/futurist *Parade* (1917) to the highly successful, exotic story ballet *Le Chapeau tricorne* (1919).

7. The company's early, melodramatic pantomime ballet, *Schéhérazade*, had become high camp to Diaghilev by 1920, yet audiences still enjoyed it. Its final presentation in Paris was in 1922, but it lasted longer elsewhere. See Richard Buckle, p. 292 and p. 516. According to Lifar, during a performance of *Schéhérazade* in Monte Carlo in the spring of 1928 Diaghilev "watching this ... somewhat antiquated ballet ... burst into such uproarious laughter that two aisle seats crashed under him." Serge Lifar, *Serge Diaghilev, His Life, His Work, His Legend, An Intimate Biography* (New York, 1940), p. 331.

8. From the outset Prokofiev's stage instructions demonstrate his close attention to detail. He originally intended that the hero explain his plan at reh. 13, having jumped off the stove to do so at reh. 12. Prior to that he was making such "despairing" noises while working it out in his head that they forced his wife to stop her housework (from reh. 8 to 9). These details, like most that follow, were simplified or eliminated in the revised score: the hero jumped down at reh. 8 and shared his plan at reh. 11. Now the choreographer would decide what to do at the introduction of the new theme at reh. 13, and the musical disjunction at reh. 9.

9. Prokofiev may have been composing directly onto the manuscript by the second and third system on page 3 where the bulk of the cut was made since his hand becomes comparatively rushed. Perhaps he was anxious to set down a new idea for expanding the passage rather than copying from his sketches.

10. This succinct summary comes from Richard Taruskin, "Rimsky-Korsakov. Opera." *New Grove Dictionary Online*, ed. L Macy, <http://www.grovemusic.com>

11. In addition to the deletion from the scene at hand, the sevens' "council music" was excised from scene two (deciding whether to kill their wives), and scene three

(deciding to take Molodukha as a hostage and making her their cook). Brief appearances of this music were retained at the end of scene of scene four (enraged at the turn of events the seven decide to beat-up the matchmakers) and in the finale (enjoined with the entrée theme, see Chapter 2). The seven do not appear in scene five.

12. Prokofiev wrote sideways on the score just after the first council session: "Of course, a possible cut here to [rehearsal] 43 [the seven's second approach to the hero], but I'd be sorry to lose 38 [the seven 'affectionately ask the hero to sell the whip'] to 40 ['the hero declines their request']." Prokofiev's favored passage survives.

13. They are vaguely reminiscent of the magician's cascading notes in *Petrouchka* (reh. 31).

14. Peter would lower the lasso onto the wolf to a similar motive in *Peter and the Wolf*, at reh. 34.

15. Regarding the latter, see Richard Taruskin, "Tone, Style and Form in Prokofiev's Soviet Operas: Some Preliminary Observations," in *Studies in the History of Music*; vol. 2, "Music and Drama" (New York, 1988), pp. 216–22.

16. This is the second dance referred to by the composer in his diary account of the revisions (see Chapter 1): "I added two new dances in a major key ..." Clearly it is not new, rather it is an expansion of an existing tune. And despite his claim, this dance is in A minor (albeit with touches of C Major).

17. Rozhdestvensky presented *Chout* in this manner with the Boston Symphony Orchestra at Symphony Hall, Boston, in April 2003.

18. Prokofiev, "Autobiography," p. 274.

19. For a while the score was unavailable due to the ballet's revival at Paris's Théâtre Mogador, which ran from 20 June through 1 July 1922.

20. Since 1917 Prokofiev's music was published by Gutheil, a firm acquired by Koussevitzky in 1914. Since 1901 Breitkopf and Härtel of Leipzig had acted as agent for Gutheil, and jointly published their titles. Gutheil was then taken over by Boosey and Hawkes of London in 1949.

21. This is the handwritten draft of the letter, written by the composer in English.

CHAPTER 4

Topical appropriations and a "new simplicity" in *Le Pas d'acier*

Each of Prokofiev's ballets for Diaghilev mirrors not only the specifics of its commission but the changing aesthetics of the company as it sought to oblige the prevailing temperament of its Parisian and London audiences. With the appearance of competitors such as Rolf de Maré's Ballets Suédois in the early 1920s, Diaghilev's company was no longer perceived as being the leader of Parisian theatrical modernism. By tapping his own enormous wealth de Maré was able to introduce more experimental fare inspired by cubo-futurism, jazz, Dadaism and surrealism. *Chout* had been the Ballets Russes's only counter. After its financial crisis in late 1922 and early 1923 Diaghilev's company was forced into a chameleon-like existence, dependent upon the whims of wealthy French and British patrons, in turn. The result was a spate of fashionable ballets by Auric, Milhaud and Poulenc in 1924–25, followed by two decidedly British works with music by Lord Berners (Gerald Tyrwhitt-Wilson) and Handel (arranged by Beecham), respectively. When the fad for contemporary ballets about the lifestyles of the wealthy leisure class began to wane, a ballet on contemporary Soviet life in a futurist and constructivist setting became the sequel. *Le Pas d'acier* marked the return to bankable Russian exoticism, and its topicality was still very much à la mode. It, no less than the other works of this period, provides a rough barometer of the audience's changing taste over the course of the decade. Though Prokofiev's ballets for Diaghilev were carefully calculated to assure fame and success, his music made far fewer concessions to fashion than did design or plot. Still, *Le Pas d'acier* marks the height of Parisian influence on Prokofiev's style.

Prokofiev's career in Western Europe began promisingly with performances of the *Scythian Suite* and *Chout* in 1920[1] and 1921, but after some initial success his popularity began to wane, in part due to the perception that he had nothing new to offer. With one exception each of his western premiers from 1922 to 1924 was a work he had written or at least begun before leaving Russia. These include the Third Piano Concerto presented in Paris and London in April 1922 (a work with an especially long gestation, dating back to 1911), the Paris premier of Violin Concerto no. 1 (composed in 1916–17) in October 1923, the Second Piano Concerto (originally composed in 1912–13), and *They Are Seven* (composed in 1917–18), the last two presented at separate concerts in May 1924. His

Symphony no. 1 , the "Classical" (composed 1916–17), was given its European premier at Prince's Theatre in London on 11 June 1921 as an intermission feature preceding a presentation of *Chout*. The Fifth Piano Sonata was his first completely new work to be premiered in Europe since 1921 (Paris, March 1924), yet it was not a great success. Prokofiev still sought his share of fame, but it was difficult to hold the limelight of Parisian musical life. He laboriously reorchestrated and refined his surviving piano score of the Second Piano Concerto for a 1923 Koussevitzky concert perhaps with the hope that he could repeat Diaghilev's favorable impression, if not the work's scandalous premier. Unfortunately the Concerto had to share the bill with the first performance of Honegger's fresh, immediately acclaimed *Pacific 231*, and suffered by comparison. Boris de Schlœzer wrote in *La Revue musicale* that the Second Concerto, despite some inspired moments, was too dense and tedious and was therefore inferior to the Third. By comparison, André George's review of *Pacific 231* on the preceding page of that journal was an unqualified rave.[2] Similarly, the First Violin Concerto must have sounded dated next to its program companion, Stravinsky's neoclassical tocsin, the *Octour*. For the most part contemptuous of what Les Six was producing, Prokofiev nevertheless sought success on Parisian terms. He responded to the futurist trend, raising the ante of strident dissonance and textural activity in a symphony "made of iron and steel." But his plan backfired: he made the symphony too complex—it bewildered the audience at its premier in June 1925. The chagrined composer admitted that he had overloaded its textures. With uncharacteristic resignation he observed that the Parisian public "are apt to be too easily bored. Having taken up with one composer they quickly tire of him and in a year or two are searching for a new sensation. I was evidently no longer a sensation."[3] Prokofiev desperately needed a big success if he was to regain his former status. Diaghilev would soon provide the means with a commission for a ballet on a contemporary theme.

Life in Russia was daily front-page news in Paris and London in 1925. Westerners were captivated by reports and rumors about a wide range of topics: deprivation and rebirth, gradual economic stabilization under the New Economic Policy, the power struggle in the wake of Lenin's death, and word of a thriving cultural life despite increasing censorship. Through his correspondence with colleagues in Russia, Prokofiev heard about the high level of audience receptiveness and the growing interest in his music. The critical failure of his Second Symphony at its Parisian premier may have bolstered his interest in visiting his homeland. His friend and colleague, Myaskovsky, professor of composition at the Moscow Conservatory, considered the new symphony "excellent," and blamed the poor reception on the Paris audience, adding that it would be appreciated in Moscow. Diaghilev, too, followed Russian affairs and maintained close contact with Soviet artists, especially Meyerhold. Though certainly no Communist, Diaghilev was interested in bold revolutionary ideas. At various times during this period he would be spurred into considering a trip to

Russia upon hearing an intriguing report about the latest artistic trends there. Perhaps tiring of the company's recent concentration on lightweight French ballets that glorified fashionable lifestyles, he became interested in developing a ballet about the dynamism of life in Soviet Russia. He heard the 6 June premier of Prokofiev's Symphony no. 2 and was probably struck by its forcefulness and serious tone. At the very least it stood in stark contrast to the Ballets Russes' current fare of *Le Matelots*, *Les Biches*, *Le Train bleu* and so forth. Less than three weeks later Diaghilev commissioned Prokofiev to compose the music for his pet project.

Prokofiev received Diaghilev's proposal with enthusiasm and after working out the scenario with Yakulov in late July and early August he composed the music at great speed. He finished the short score by the end of the summer and played it for Diaghilev in early October. Anticipating a spring 1926 Parisian premier, Prokofiev orchestrated much of the score during his winter concert tour of the USA (often on board trains—nicely befitting the ballet's futurist subject). The production was ultimately postponed and Massine, who had returned to the company as a contract choreographer, created its dance in the spring of 1927.

Prokofiev acknowledged a change in style beginning with this ballet, placing more emphasis on diatonicism and lyricism, and utilizing a contemporary, as opposed to a fantastical, Russian musical idiom. However, these harmonic and melodic simplifications and concomitant thinner textures were far more noticeable in *L'Enfant prodigue* and the ballets that followed. Along with brief sections in the new, simpler style, Prokofiev still gave his audience what they expected in *Le Pas d'acier* in response to the futurist subject and constructivist décor. He even added a touch of jazz for good measure. The visceral finale with Prokofiev's musical representation of the sounds of a factory at full operation understandably made the strongest impression. Widespread recognition of his redirection towards lyricism would have to wait for music with a less topical basis.

Le Pas d'acier: collaboration and context

Although the title would come from Massine and the combination futurist-constructivist setting[4] from Yakulov, the concept of a ballet depicting modern Soviet life was Diaghilev's alone. No doubt inspired by what he heard of the latest trends in Soviet theaters and saw at the exhibitions of avant-garde Soviet visual art, Diaghilev envisioned a ballet that would be at the same time topical, authentic and exotic. He claimed he did not want it to be partisan. In response to Prokofiev's challenge that it would be impossible not to be so, Diaghilev waxed on about the 20 million young people in Russia, their sexual desires, their different way of laughing, living and dancing, and that this was characteristic of modern Russia. He concluded emphatically, "we don't need politics!" This was likely meant as balm for the queasy composer; surely he must have realized that a political reading would be inevitable despite the best intentions. His enthusiasm for the subject may well have been bolstered by the prospect of a *scandale*. As Serge Radlov's "circus comedies" were reflected in *Chout*, so too the constructivism, futurism and poster-like agitprop of the contemporary Soviet theater would be transplanted to Paris and London through *Le Pas d'acier*. This new ballet would also have a bit of the circus in it as well, in keeping with its lineage. In asking Prokofiev to write the music Diaghilev essentially acknowledged the composer's role as the company's "Russian specialist."[5]

When he received Diaghilev's commission Prokofiev was not unaware of the Futurist Movement nor without interest in the artistic innovations in his homeland. He had been introduced to the music of the Italian futurists when he traveled to Milan for consultations with Diaghilev on *Ala i Lolli* in 1915. Along with Diaghilev and Stravinsky, he attended a demonstration of a "noise orchestra" made up of eight or nine *intonarumori* (noise intoners) at Marinetti's studio.[6] Although these instruments emitted machine-like noises, their inventor, Luigi Russolo, envisaged them as the source for a new type of music, not just mere imitation.[7] Prokofiev reported his impressions in an article he wrote for the journal *Muzïka*, "Muzkal'nïye instrumentï futuristov" (Musical instruments of futurism).[8] He dutifully described the instruments, their operating procedures and the sounds they produced. His writing reflects an inquisitive and occasionally enthusiastic tone throughout, and despite his conclusion that the instruments were technically too primitive to be used by themselves, he suggested that they could add curious colors to the sound of the contemporary symphony orchestra. Although he acknowledged that Marinetti's theories "passed way over my head," a subsequent letter to a friend reveals that he was not unsympathetic towards them.[9] Little did he know that one day he would be called upon to create his own futurist-inspired music for a Diaghilev ballet. But by that time these musically primitive efforts had been eclipsed by Edgard Varèse's nonrepresentational experiments in sonority on the one hand, and voguish composers' attempts to integrate and/or represent machine-age sounds in a traditional instrumental context on the other. The more modern aspects of Prokofiev's musical style already resonated with the music of the latter group, and the requirements of *Le Pas d'acier* would reinforce the connection.

Music inspired by futurism became a conspicuous part of London concert life once Russolo opened a series of futuristic concerts with his *intonarumori* at the London Coliseum on 15 June 1914 (their introduction to Paris would have to wait until after the war). These "turns" at a music hall were presented in conjunction with an ongoing futurist exhibit at the Dore Gallery. Although Prokofiev was in London to meet Diaghilev at the time, it is not known if he went to a performance. The impresario did go, and became even more attracted to the futurist movement. Russolo's opening selections, "The Awakening of a Great City" and "A Meeting of Motor-cars and Aeroplanes," set the trend, if not always the tone, for subsequent futurist-inspired music regardless of the performance medium. The Dada movement, born in 1916, along with the Great War itself undoubtedly took a bit of wind from the futurists' sails. Early futurist compositions that used new mechanistic devices alongside traditional instruments were few and far between due to technical limits of the former. The most notorious examples were the opera *L'Aviatore Dro* by Marinetti's musical spokesperson Francesco Pratella (1915, premiered 1920) which used *intonarumori* to suggest the sounds of an airplane and an automobile,[10] and George Antheil's casually titled *Ballet méchanique* with its siren and airplane propeller obbligato (1926).[11] Most often composers used traditional instruments alone: such as Leo Ornstein's "Suicide in an Airplane" for solo piano (*c*. 1915), Emerson Whithorne's "The Aeroplane" also for solo piano (1921; later orchestrated), Antheil's *Airplane Sonata and Mechanisms* for piano (October 1923) and Honegger's immediately acclaimed *Pacific 231* (May 1924). Some emotionally cool, toccata-like antecedents for solo piano by Prokofiev (such as, the more clangorous and motoric of his piano pieces, opp. 2 and 17) anticipate these works but lack appropriate programmatic titles and intent. Indeed, musically speaking, this sort of representational futurism had been foreshadowed by such pieces as Charles Alkan's piano etude *Le Chemin de fer* of 1844. Clearly, when seeking futurist inspiration (or constructivist for that matter) in music of traditional means, the title and composer's intent are every bit as important as the musical style. For example, Milhaud's *Machines Agricoles* (1919), a suite for voice and seven instruments whose text derives from descriptions of farm machinery (a reaper, a binder, plows, a harvester, and so forth) taken from an exhibition catalog certainly bespeaks futurism, but the subtitle, "Pastorales," and the lyrical nature of the music do not. The composer's intent, to celebrate the beauty of machines, ultimately tips the scales. Prokofiev's factory music in *Le Pas d'acier* is not that stylistically dissimilar from the primitive sounding passages in the *Scythian Suite* or the more forceful passages in *Chout* or Symphony no. 2 (such as, the end of variation vi in the second movement). It is the ballet's title and setting that insure its inclusion on putative lists of fashionable, futurist-inspired works.

Although Pratella's second futuristic piece, *La Guerre, Tre Danze per Orchestra* (1913) was intended for dancing, ballet was slower than opera in adopting futurism.[12] In 1917, however, a distinctively French offshoot of futurism, the lighthearted "Ballet réaliste" *Parade* appeared promoting the esthetic of the everyday life, in part through its typewriter, revolver shots, siren, roulette wheel, and so forth. In Russia futuristic concepts made an impact in the avant-garde theatres of Moscow through the works of Meyerhold, Tairov and others during the highly experimental period between 1922 and 1923.[13] The earliest futurist-inspired ballet of renown in the West was *Skating Rink*, premiered in Paris by the Ballets Suédois on 20 January 1922.[14] Its setting not only provided a convincing backdrop for contemporary urban violence, but also a typically futurist glorification of speed. In a characteristically formalized score, Honegger successfully presented the ballet's basic idea of roller skating as a metaphor for modern life: incessant, almost hypnotic speed (established in the rhythmic introduction and maintained thereafter by an unrelieved 6/4 meter and rhythmic ostinati in the outer sections) and disturbing human characterization (leitmotivic use of themes for the crowd, the madman and his female victim).[15] Honegger's "motoristic" ostinato—rapidly ascending and descending sextuplets—suggests the noise created by roller skates on a track, thus affording a nice futuristic touch. But the inclusion of human conflict in *Skating Rink* (expressionistically presented) and subsequent futurist-inspired ballets, *Le Pas d'acier* among them, marks a departure from the tenets of Marinetti's movement, in which the individual has no identity. Although mass activity is important and the featured couples are faceless in both Honegger's and Prokofiev's ballets, they can at best be called "futurist-inspired," certainly not true representatives of the futurist movement.

There is no evidence that Prokofiev ever saw *Skating Rink* or even perused Honegger's score; given the ballet's novelty and success, however, it is likely that he would have been at least aware of it. He did know about one other futurist-inspired ballet whose composition was nearly contemporary with *Le Pas d'acier*, one whose concept was known to Diaghilev long before he tapped Prokofiev for this commission. That ballet is *Skyscrapers* by John Alden Carpenter, Prokofiev's friend from his days in Chicago. As both ballets are often spoken of in the same breath, questions of influence will be considered below.

After writer Ilya Ehrenburg's false start, Diaghilev allowed his former *Mir iskusstva* associate Georgy Yakulov to create the scenario for the proposed ballet on contemporary Soviet life in collaboration with Prokofiev. Yakulov, a colorful Georgian painter and theater designer, had almost all the right credentials: in 1914 he had contributed to the *First Russian Futurist Journal* and from 1918 he was associated with the experimental Kamerny Theater in Moscow. He came to Paris in June 1925 to participate in the International Exhibit of Industrial and Decorative Arts and to arrange a personal exhibit (he brought with him hundreds of his works). Among the items he had on display at the Exhibit was his maquette for Alexander Tairov's 1922 Moscow Chamber Theatre production of *Girofle-Girofla*, already known by those who attended performances of it in Paris in 1923. Diaghilev had been at the Théâtre des Champs-Élysées for each performance by Tairov's company that year, "watching every detail eagerly and jealously."[16] Yakulov was well known in Paris avant-garde artistic circles for his "Yakulovization" of the Moscow theater, in which the artist's background in cabaret and burlesque and his preference for crazy, chaotic spectacles came to the fore.[17] This last aspect of his art makes him a rather curious choice for a politically risky task: developing a ballet for western audiences that depicted life in Soviet Russia. But even there the early theater was often more entertaining than politically edifying.

Russian theatrical precedents existed for Diaghilev's planned ballet, the closest being the second "process" or act (the breakdown of the old order) from the first Soviet ballet, *Krasnïy vikhr'* (Red Whirlwind), choreographed by Lopukhov. Despite receiving only one performance (at the State Academic Theatre for Opera and Ballet in Leningrad on 29 October 1924), the ballet gained instant notoriety. Surely Diaghilev and Yakulov knew of it. Musically there was nothing worth emulating, but the ballet's action, choreography and décor offered a clear model. What Yakulov envisioned for the first scene of his new ballet was much like the second act of *Red Whirlwind*, both depicting the colorful, real-life activity on the streets of revolutionary Russia, including the potentially entertaining antics of society's dregs.

Yakulov, Lopukhov and their music-hall predecessors knew well that portraying low-lifes was far easier than properly characterizing the "positive" figures of the new society. This led to a problem: as the decade advanced an increasing number of fundamentalist Soviets found such "entertainment" improper in a work recalling the early days of their glorious revolution. But in 1925 Yakulov and Prokofiev had no way of anticipating that development. On the other hand they apparently decided to ignore the feelings of the growing ranks of Russian émigrés who might also find such fare distasteful.

After the wealth of activity in the opening act, which was to be set near the platform of a provincial railroad station, the second part of Prokofiev's new ballet would present unambiguously a positive social image using a Soviet factory setting. The story was roughed-out beneath Yakulov's sketches for the constructivist décor which included platforms, ladders, flywheels, pulleys, transmission belts, and flashing lights which could all be set into motion along with dancers mimicking their motions. He had already made a similar construction for Tairov's 1922 Moscow Chamber Theater production of the mirthful, circus-like *Girofle-Girofla*. The machine dances which Yakulov envisioned had been in use since the mid-1910s by Italian futurists and were further developed by the experimental stage director Nikolay Foregger at his Moscow studio in late 1922. There the dancer/acrobats depicted trains, transmissions, saws, sheets of iron, pistons and hammers. Foregger set these dances to a futuristic "noise orchestra" comprised of sirens, whistles and rattles so as to evoke the sound of a modern factory as well as the bustle of urban streets.[18] These machine dances became extremely popular and quickly spread to America although for the time being they bypassed France.[19]

It is important that *Le Pas d'acier* was conceived from Yakulov's visual image alone, no scenarist or choreographer collaborated. The difficult task of organizing all this "rather haphazard material" (as Prokofiev called it) into a theatrically culminating narrative fell to the composer. On 2 August 1925 he sent Diaghilev an extremely detailed typewritten scenario (in Russian) based on the ideas that he and Yakulov had worked out. It was accompanied by a musical plan (with projected timings, as usual), a list of characters for the prologue, the first act and entr'acte, and some sketches by Yakulov. The musical plan was headed by the title Yakulov had suggested, "Ursin'ol," which he derived from URSS (Union des républiques socialistes soviétiques). The draft for the second act and finale were sent a short time later because certain details had yet to be worked out. The musical plan reads as follows:

Prologue	1.	Marching by of silhouettes 1 and ½ minutes
First act,	2.	The arrival of the train and bartering 2 minutes
train station	3.	The entrance of commissars and dispersal of crowd 1 minute
and square	4.	The appearance of petty thieves, theft and chase 2 minutes
	5.	Dance of the orator 1 minute
	6.	Entrance of sailors and dance of sailors with one worker 3 minutes
	7.	Commissars, firemen, dispersal of the crowd 1 minute
Entr'acte	8.	Change of Décor 2 and ½ minutes

Based on a verbal presentation of the plot Prokofiev had already received Diaghilev's tentative approval before the latter departed for Venice. Two days after he sent the typescript Prokofiev wrote Myaskovsky that he would start composing the music "any day now." Although their titles would change somewhat, the numbers in the musical plan for act one correspond with those in the published score except for the separate number to disperse the crowd just before the entr'acte (no. 7). All of the proposed timings are shorter than the customary performing times of the finished score, some considerably so, suggesting that either Prokofiev himself became aware of their inadequacy once he began to compose or that Diaghilev asked for the music to be expanded when he heard it in October. It is likely that Diaghilev directed Prokofiev to recast the "Entrance of the Sailors and Dance of the Sailors with a Female Worker" (no. 6) into a pas de deux for the two soloists, now known as "Matelot à bracelets et ouvrière." As a result of that change the sailors enter during the previous number (see below) and the crowd clears the stage before the duet, eliminating the need for number seven. When the ballet was in rehearsal in the spring of 1927 Diaghilev asked Prokofiev to include an additional number to provide more time between acts, one he particularly admired in the chamber ballet *Trapèze* composed for Romanov. In return Prokofiev gained performing rights for *Le Pas d'acier* in Russia beginning in January 1928. He duly orchestrated the interpolation ("crudely," he later observed), one of two late additions Romanov had requested. Not published as part of either score, it survives with new orchestration as the opening number of the *Divertissement*, op. 43, a work Prokofiev put together in 1929.

The scenario that Prokofiev used when he composed *Le Pas d'acier*, the one he and Yakulov devised and the composer fleshed out, differs significantly from that of the production. Since it has not been published, I have translated it but otherwise kept it in its original format, identifying the correlating parts from the score in square brackets when known or probable.

/Pastorale/

[i. Entrée des personages]

Prologue. March past of silhouettes from left to right: 1. Sailors in a military-like run, having cocked their hats, holding their rifles below and at-the-ready, with jackets on [just] one shoulder; 2. male and female toffy vendors and male and female cigarette vendors galloping and spinning with boxes of toffy and cigarettes; 3. the orator with one determined step forward and two small ones backwards, moving in a spiral [and] pointing in a book; 4. a frightened woman running through with a nervous gait, opening and closing an umbrella; 5. commissars with awareness of their self-worth suddenly listening, jumping side-to-side, then resume their crossing in an important stride; they disappear in a jump; 6. the bandit-petty thieves jump on their toes, then crawl, then jump some more; 7. the peddlers [*menshchechniki*] staggering under the weight of their sacks, fall, throwing their sacks over their heads, then they, in turn, fall over the sacks.

[ii. Train des paysans-ravitailleurs]

Act 1: The stage is illuminated. The train approaches (from the right) and the peddlers pour out; from the opposite side come the hungry townsfolk with their things to barter (among them two women in lamp shades [added by an unknown hand]). Dance of barter: woman with a sack and man with an arm chair, nouveau-riche person with a piglet and a woman holding a morning coat on a stick like a flag; in a background of general commotion. The male and female toffy vendors and male and female cigarette vendors are circling about ingratiatingly with their trays.

[iii. Les Commissaires] Three commissars appear (two male and one female [added by an unknown hand]) in various colored service jackets and begin to press the crowd. The crowd dissipates by three-quarters. [iv. Les Petits camelots? (vivace)] Two petty thieves sneak up and rob a commissar. Three commissars chase after the petty thieves. The petty thieves escape by climbing the stairs and throw themselves by a rope onto the center platform, they slide along the board below and disappear into the wings. The commissars follow after them by the same route and also disappear. [v. L'Orateur] Part of the barterers press close in horror. From among them the orator stands apart, giving his indignant speech/dance/. Some people listen, among them an attractive worker

[v. at reh. 74?], to whom the orator stresses his point. Five sailors enter [v. 4 after reh. 76?], well dressed, free and easy. Four scatter on the stage buying goods and flinging money widely. The fifth, the main one, becomes interested in the scene between the female worker and the orator, and wanting to defend her, places himself between them. The orator continues his speech, but in anger throws his book. The book [is] on a rubber band [and it] returns to him. The orator indignantly withdraws. [vi. Matelot à bracelets et ouvrière] The first affected acquaintance of the sailor and the female worker: they dance together but do not touch. Called by his comrades, the sailor bows to her and leaves. The female worker disappears to the opposite side. Commissars return with firemen and clear the marketplace.

[interpolated movement from *Trapèze*]
[vii. Changement de décors]

Entr'acte: firemen /ballet dancers/ with plastique movements to the music rearrange the scene changing it into a factory.

Content of the Second Act

The previous scene of the train station is turned into a factory by the firemen towards the end of the musical entr'acte. [viii. Le Matelot devient un ouvrier] The firemen dance off while the main sailor, who decided to become a worker, appears on stage. Short solo dance with the dancer changed into the garb of a factory worker.

[ix. L'Usine?] Four workers enter and together with the ex-sailor begin to work the first machine which is located around or near the left wing (see drawing 1). A little later, on the most distant and tallest platform, five workers begin to work, among them the heroine. This work on the rolling machine behind the netting is visible in silhouette fashion (see drawing 2). Hero (ex-sailor), catching sight of his sweetheart, strives towards her, but along the way he falls onto the big platform located in the middle of the stage between the machine on which he was working and the platform on which the female workers are working. Thus in this way the empty space and net divide him from his sweetheart. The hero is in dismay that he cannot get to her. [x. Les Marteaux] On his platform five new workers with small and large hammers come up, and having begun to work on this platform, they pull-up the hero. The work with the hammers is exclusively ballet work without noise. Meanwhile, the work at the first machine and on the farther platform with the heroine is finished-off with lighting effects. But then a group of workers, including the heroine, begin to work at a new machine at the right wing (see drawing 3). The heroine from the height of the small platform at the last machine notices the hero working with a hammer on the middle platform: their mime scene from various platforms. Both run below to the first level and with this is marked the beginning of the finale.

Finale

[ix. Finale]: The two soloists dance below on the pedal apparatus, and at the same time the whole factory starts in motion. The pedal apparatus is built on the principle of a lathe or leg-operated sewing machine. The ballet caper concludes with a blow on the pedal which starts in motion a not large system of wheels. The first blow on the pedal is the starting point of the movement of the whole factory: again the work on the first machine at the left wing begins and also on the highest, furthest platform (rolling work) and the work on the machine at the right wing continues. From the center platform where the soundless hammering took place, two workers come down with gigantic hammers, wooden with hollow centers, and they begin to loudly strike them in conformity with instructions in the score: other workers with smaller hammers remain on the middle platform and also strike them rhythmically. From the top a complex pulley system is lowered and set into motion. During the whole finale which lasts from three to four minutes, lighted signs flash in various parts of the stage.

The ballet composer Vladimir Dukelsky, a good friend of Prokofiev's, once passed along valuable advice to would-be ballet scenarists: "keep your ballet story to five or six lines and stay away from literature or editorializing of any kind; the simpler and more direct the scenario the happier the composer and choreographer, the more pleased the audience."[20] Sound advice, but obviously far from Prokofiev's mind as he created this prolix narrative. He seems to have forgotten the lessons learned from the overly explicit scenario for *Chout* in 1915.

Yakulov was urgently summoned by Diaghilev to help ferret out its essence once the impresario decided to mount the ballet in February 1927, but he was engaged in theatrical work in Tiflis and did not arrive until 21 May, by which time the choreography had essentially been set. But in early April Prokofiev came to the choreographer's aid, and, in the composer's words, "got the ball rolling." Despite his efforts and Massine's revisions, audiences were unable to make much sense out of the first act of *Le Pas d'acier*. This is hardly surprising: Massine was not content to simply hone this long-winded narrative into something understandable through dance and mime, instead (with Diaghilev's apparent blessing) he replaced a great deal with movements inspired by unrelated bits from "national legends" (the fight of Baba Yaga and the crocodile, and so forth). This all but guaranteed audience befuddlement.

Much of Yakulov's and Prokofiev's symbolism remains elusive, and while some of the composer's music has character, it is often difficult to overlay the scenario onto the score with any sense of accuracy. Furthermore, distinctive music was not necessary for every action described (such as the leave-taking of the sailor and the female worker). The whereabouts of the presumably annotated holograph short score is presently unknown and neither the published orchestral score nor the piano reduction contain any stage instructions. Prokofiev's prologue opens with the *moderato* refrain of a "well known" factory song (probably performed with the curtain closed, though this is not indicated in the published score), followed by a transition marked *allegro, ma non troppo*, and one theme restated with slight variations of character. Except for a possible correlation at the concluding *meno mosso* with the peddlers stumbling under the weight of their sacks, there is no clear musical delineation of the characters as they, in turn, march across the stage. The slower 18 bars in the middle would seem to suit the commissars' pomposity and perhaps the crawling petty thieves, but this does not fit temporally with the music as published. Since each section of the prologue returns in the finale, and because there is no factory worker in the opening procession, it is probably safe to assume that Prokofiev did not intend any characterization in his prologue.

Given the great amount of activity and the large number of characters introduced in the first act, Prokofiev wisely elected to portray only the most important ones. And demonstrating the knowledge he gained working with Diaghilev on the revision of *Chout*, Prokofiev left his highly representational style of music behind (as the published score demonstrates). Hence the choreographer would be free to stage the activity of no. 2, "The Arrival of the Train and Bartering," an ongoing two-episode rondo, as he or she saw fit. But the music is certainly not without character: the opening theme aptly suggests the sound of a moving train by using the musical cliché of repeated dactyls in a fast tempo, while the incessant quaver pulse and frequent syncopation convey the idea of commotion at the square. Though *Le Pas d'acier* is essentially a divertissement, Prokofiev nevertheless demonstrates his concern with overall unity by building a network of remembrance themes; the theme of the second episode in this number reappears at the opening of "L'Orateur" and is related (intervallicly and rhythmically) to the main theme of "Les Commissaires." His response to the libretto thus far has been eminently danceable music that facilitates rather than dictates the choreographic movement.

The bipartite nature of the third number demonstrates this facilitation. Prokofiev introduces the commissars with a dignified, stately theme (foreshadowed in the previous number), using unambiguous "almost white" harmony. The second part switches to *più mosso (allegro)* and reintroduces the "B" theme from number two, perhaps corresponding to the commissars' "pressing the crowd." Prokofiev builds intensity through dynamic gradation and repetition. The commissars' success ("the crowd dissipates by three-quarters") is noted in the music by a reduction in texture, and a *diminuendo* and protracted *decrescendo* at the end. He obviously had not lost his flair for highly descriptive music—music that tells the story by itself.

The next number accompanying the pickpocketing and chase scene is similarly characterful without restrictive representation. This running 6/8 scherzo anticipates "Pillage" in *L'Enfant prodigue* by its instrumentation, rhythm, and melodic character. Both scherzos are genuinely successful at depicting the appropriate mood while leaving the details of the action to the choreographer. The renaming of this number from "The Appearance of Petty Thieves, theft and Chase" in the scenario above to "Les Petits camelots" (street vendors) in the published score ("Toffy and cigarette vendors" is its Russian title) suggests that Diaghilev did not approve of such shenanigans in his ballet, or that this was one more detail that fell by the wayside as Massine constructed the choreography. No pickpocketing episode is mentioned in any performance reviews thus far encountered. Prokofiev certainly provided a distinct sound for the next number, spotlighting the presumably austere orator in a most ironical manner—giving it the jazziest sound of the whole ballet (perhaps signifying that his oratory fell largely upon deaf ears). The characteristic Prokofievian heroine music at reh. 74 probably corresponds to spotlighting the "attractive female worker" in the crowd, while the most jazz-like section in the whole ballet (4 after reh. 76), surely announces the arrival of the five spendthrift sailors.

There were places in this scenario that could have become quite comical had they been subjected to the composer's trenchant representationalism: such as the orator's gait and bluster, his boomeranging book, and pickpocketing of the commissar by the the thieves. By using bold satirical scenes to characterize old Russia, Yakulov had followed Soviet precedents. As dance historian Elizabeth Souritz notes, "negative types were easier to translate into theatrical terms. All sorts of 'former people,' black marketeers, hooligans, and riffraff–all these real life opponents of the new order reached the vaudeville stage, and then operetta and ballet, as far back as the early 1920s."[21] This might explain why Yakulov and Prokofiev wanted the witty and mischievous Larionov to stage the ballet. In his brief letter accompanying the scenario draft, Prokofiev implored that Diaghilev not select a stage director until they had a chance to meet in September (that is, after the impresario returned from his customary summer holiday in Italy). Had Larionov been chosen the tone undoubtedly would have been altogether different. Diaghilev, however, may not have wanted to risk any misunderstanding. As a result, Yakulov's occasionally cryptic symbolism was acceptable—but the tone would remain serious. Prokofiev, too, trod carefully—his sarcastic tendency was held largely in check.

Conceived as a well-rounded, all-Soviet collaboration, *Le Pas d'acier* suffered from many compromises, a fate that befell Prokofiev's previous two efforts for the Ballets Russes as well. As with other postwar productions the visual element predominated while dance in the traditional sense was relegated to a secondary status (there was precious little room for it!). Aside from Yakulov's plans for machine dances—dancers mimicking the wheels of the train at the outset and their interaction with the machines in the factory finale—little to no consideration was given to dancing. It should be noted, however, that classical dance was considered to be outdated and had been replaced by gymnastics and a "lot of marching about" in contemporary Soviet ballets.[22] Apparently Yakulov was not troubled by the likelihood that the proposed set would greatly restrict the choreographer's spatial design (Larionov had been similarly unconcerned about his impractical costumes inhibiting the dancers' mobility in *Chout*). Perhaps Prokofiev and Yakulov counted on the participation of a Soviet choreographer experienced in the constructivist idiom to ensure a logical continuity of style. The initial lack of choreographic input may not have troubled Diaghilev either, since Prokofiev had demonstrated his understanding of the genre in his revised *Chout*. But the narrative he received from Prokofiev, as overloaded as *Chout*'s and flimsy besides, surely gave Diaghilev pause. Prokofiev recalled that before he began composing the music he had obtained from the impresario no more than a halfhearted approval of the scenario. Diaghilev may have had further doubts, knowing that the acclaimed choreographer Lopukhov had only a *succès d'estime* with his single public performance of the *Red Whirlwind*. He may have hoped that Yakulov's planned scenic spectacular and Prokofiev's music would carry the production, no matter who the choreographer might be.

Le Pas d'acier would not be the first western ballet to convey the futuristic spirit or to wed constructivist décor with futurist machine dances and music. But for Prokofiev it provided the vehicle for success that he had sought for so long. Once again his skill in writing highly descriptive music served him well, but unlike the dance-thwarting presentational passages in the original *Chout* this music was ongoing and *plastique*. His onomatopoeic factory music, and, in particular, the protracted orchestral crescendo in the finale helped turn the production into a stunning, memorable event. He had already provided a similar crescendo for the conclusion of his *Scythian Suite* cum *Ala i Lolli*, but the obvious inspirations from futurism and the ballet's use of jazz-like rhythms and harmony suggest a closer examination into the sources and the degree of topical influence.

Although Prokofiev shared the younger generation of French composers' rejection of late romantic aesthetics and ornate impressionism, and their advocacy of simple, direct music of everyday life resonated with his recent turn to heightened clarity and accessibility, his disparaging comments about their means to this end preclude anything approaching stylistic influence. The composer Nicholas Nabokov recalled a conversation in which Prokofiev criticized his admiration for French music, saying,

> There hasn't been a first-rate French composer since the time of ... Chabrier and Bizet. Because the French composers have been busy entertaining and 'tickling the ears' of their princesses, countesses and marquises." He continued, "I know ... you like everything French. You even like that old crank Satie. And I know what you think about his followers. You think they are important. Well they are not. They're pure mush. The only one in France who knows what he's doing is Ravel. All the rest are hopeless.[23]

Prokofiev's respect for Ravel's music runs like a leitmotif through his writings, culminating in the 1000 word obituary/appreciation for *Sovetskoye iskusstvo* in January 1938. As for the rest, Nabokov does not mention what prompted this tirade; Prokofiev's ongoing difficulty in pleasing Parisian audiences. was no doubt a factor. On other occasions he was more charitable about the "followers of Satie," that unhomogeneous "group," dubbed Les Six. Prokofiev was on friendly terms with most of them, even socializing with Auric and Poulenc (and, far less often, with Milhaud and Honegger), yet he held their more facile works—ballets such as Poulenc's *Les Biches* and Milhaud's deliberately Offenbachish *Le Train bleu*—in highest contempt. Poulenc's 1924 hit ballet had echoes of Stravinsky, Mozart and even his own music, and probably for that reason alone Prokofiev found it "greatly disappointing" and dismissed it as "nonsense." *Le Train bleu* he considered just plain vulgar. On the other hand he liked bits of Auric's *Pastorale* and called his *Les Matelots* "very witty." He generally found favor with the more substantial works of Honegger; after hearing *Roi David* in March 1924 Prokofiev noted "this is something to study." He was captivated by *Pacific 231*, returning to it for days on end in the pages of his diary. The following year he recorded his partial approval of that composer's 1925 *Concertino for Piano* (Prokofiev seldom gave unreserved endorsement to anyone else's music). But just as Prokofiev was at his closest ideologically to Stravinsky during the creation of *Chout* in 1915 without imitating his style, so too in 1925 he heeded the Parisian musical avant-garde without corrupting his highly personal expression. This includes his modest appropriation from jazz.

Jazz quickly became such a major part of Parisian night life in the 1920s that it even began to encroach on the world of ballet. We must remember that the term was used rather indiscriminatebly at the time—distinctions between jazz and its progenitor ragtime were especially blurred. Almost any music that suggested the rhythmic, harmonic or performing forces of jazz, ragtime or blues would be called jazz by laypeople and critics alike. The vast spectrum of jazz styles in this period compounded the issue: ranging from the music of white society dance bands to "Tin Pan Alley jazz" to authentic jazz played by combos generally heard only in nightclubs in the poorer sections of a metropolis. Embryonic symphonic jazz, and the earliest "jazz ballets" were actually closer to the ragtime heritage than to jazz since the music was performed as written (lacking the improvisatory style and swing of real jazz), and without wholly authentic instrumentation. Ragtime rhythms had appeared in ballet as far back as Debussy's *La Boîte à joujoux* (written in 1913 but not premiered until 1919) and Satie's *Parade* (1917). Though Taruskin has presented a convincing revisionist view that Stravinsky's theatrical piece with dancing, *L'Histoire du soldat*, has little to do with jazz, the fact that such a leading composer should entitle one of its dances "Ragtime" was in itself undoubtedly influential.[24] Ragtime rhythms continued to be exploited to varying degrees in later ballets such as Cole Porter's eclectic *Within the Quota* (1923) and Satie's *Mercure* (1924). But not until Milhaud's *La Création du monde* (1923) did the rhythmic, instrumental and harmonic borrowings become more clearly indebted to jazz. This ballet was a result of Milhaud's infatuation with Harlem jazz during his 1922 tour of the USA. Prokofiev never appropriated ragtime or jazz idioms anywhere near the degree of Stravinsky or Milhaud. Yet it would be as hard to escape the sounds of this enormously popular music in Paris in the 1920s as it would be to ignore its coloristic possibility in "serious" theatre music with an intended topicality.

Prokofiev is known to have enjoyed jazz, frequenting the fashionable Parisian cabaret La Bœuf sur le toit with its jazz pianists Jean Wiener and Clément Doucet,[25] and over the years collecting "at least a hundred" jazz recordings which he played "very often."[26] Much later while residing in the Soviet Union, Prokofiev included a brief defense of jazz in an article entitled "Musical America" for the 1939 World's Fair issue of *Internatsional'naya literatura*:

> Many serious musicians are repelled by jazz. Others are interested in it. I think it all depends on which element in jazz one stresses: if it is the element of vulgarity, then jazz is tiresome and even repulsive; if, however, one chooses what is best in rhythm, melody and instrumentation, one may come across great riches. The many orchestral effects which we find in the best jazz music are particularly interesting. Moreover, some of the performers in a jazz orchestra, as for instance those who play the trumpets, trombones, clarinets and percussion instruments, have developed a technique of which corresponding musicians in a symphony orchestra have not even dreamed. To listen to those masters of the jazz band is interesting and useful not only for composers, but for performers as well ...[27]

In 1928 Prokofiev heard a performance of Gershwin's Piano Concerto in F at the Paris Opéra and was sufficiently intrigued to invite the composer to his apartment to play more of his music. He later told Dukelsky that he did not care that much for the Concerto ("32 bar choruses ineptly bridged together") but he did like Gershwin's tunes and his embellishments.[28] Undoubtedly Prokofiev had at least as many opportunities to hear jazz during his 20-plus months in New York and Chicago from 1918 to 1922 as Milhaud had during his visit to the USA in 1922. Prokofiev did not record any of his impressions of jazz during this period, but his subsequent interest is documented. His friendship with jazz enthusiast and fellow-composer John Alden Carpenter might have led to some encounters with authentic jazz during his trips to Chicago.[29] When Prokofiev was busily preparing for the premier of *L'Amour des trois oranges* in 1921, he took a break from the endless rehearsals to attend a concert performance on 24 December by the Chicago Symphony of Carpenter's new ballet *Krazy Kat, A Jazz Pantomime* after George Herriman's comic strip character. This was the first jazz-inspired ballet and the first appearance of the word jazz in an art music title."[30] The premier of the music with dance followed on 20 and 21 January in New York with Prokofiev's friend Adolphe Bolm in the title role. Prokofiev may have attended this performance as well since he arrived in New York a few days earlier for the local premiers of his Third Piano Concerto on 26 January and of *Oranges* on 14 February. Though as R.D. Darrel rightly points out, Carpenter's ballet music is more characteristic of the "Jazz Age" than of jazz itself,[31] *Krazy Kat* does use ragtime rhythms, including a syncopated fox trot, and its small orchestra features a saxophone, "wa-wa" trumpet and trombone, the latter performing an occasional glissando. Perhaps in deference to this trend, Ravel, no early convert to the jazz idiom, reflected the style of Tin Pan Alley by way of the Parisian café in *L'Enfant et les sortilèges* which was premiered in 1925.[32] Prokofiev, who generally admired Ravel's music, saw the opera just about the time he received his commission from Diaghilev for a contemporary Soviet ballet.

Prokofiev must have thought that jazzy rhythms and harmony would help characterize such a ballet and would ensure its topicality, and thus success with western European audiences. Besides, jazz had already been used in a futuristic setting. In 1922 Valentin Parnakh had "acquainted Muscovites with jazz ... and at the same time, came out with a new dance ... [whose] rhythmical structure was prompted by the music, and its movements ... imitated the movements of a machine."[33] By the time *Le Pas d'acier* was first presented in Paris jazz had also made inroads into the more mainstream Russian theaters: even Glière's nearly contemporary *Krasnïy mak* (Red Poppy) entertained Moscow audiences at the Bolshoy Theatre with its Charleston and other numbers with jazz-like rhythms.

The jazz inflections in *Le Pas d'acier* —an unprecedented amount of syncopated rhythms and one baldly stated blue-note cadence—are nearly unique in Prokofiev's oeuvre. Although there is some precedent in such pieces as the

Second Symphony and the Act IV chase in *Oranges*, never before and never again would Prokofiev use so much syncopation in his music. Even the smoothly running machines in the factory finale and the train suggested in no. 2 are not immune from occasional interruptions of syncopations. Most outstanding is the main theme of the fifth scene, "L'Orateur" whose second measure reveals one of the most stereotypical ragtime syncopations (see Ex. 4.1, three after reh. 73), the same one used by Satie in his "Petit fille américaine" movement in *Parade* (for example, reh. 21). Further tied and untied syncopations across agogic stresses are used in the third and sixth measures of the theme as well. With over one third of its measures syncopated, "L'Orateur" strongly suggests ragtime influence, since syncopation was perceived as the defining feature of the genre at the time. And given the blurred distinctions on the Parisian scene between ragtime and jazz, audiences would have probably regarded the theme as being influenced by contemporary jazz. Together with an especially remarkable 12-bar passage of tied and untied syncopation later in the scene (three before reh. 77), this theme succeeds in dating and localizing the ballet every bit as much as the décor (see Ex. 4.2). In the latter passage Prokofiev even seems to evoke the peculiar tone-color of a jazz band through his scoring for reeds, muted trumpet, piano and percussion (snare and bass drum).

Traditional types of syncopation are used throughout the ballet as well, such as: offbeat propulsive rhythms in the train scene (such as, reh. 21), rhythmic displacement to create cross-rhythms at the ends of sections (such as, reh. 11) or to accentuate thematic material (low brass three after reh. 44), and syncopated melodic and rhythmic counterpoints (such as, reh. 88). Some more traditional examples of syncopation suggest contemporaneity without necessarily aping ragtime, such as the offbeat repetitions in the trumpet theme in no. 9 and the exploitation on weak beat stress in the theme and varied restatements of "Le Matelot devient un ouvrier" (such as, reh. 115). Although syncopation occurs in every movement it is not evenly distributed throughout the ballet. In addition to scenes two and five mentioned above, it is also especially prominent in scenes seven through nine, helping to provide a modish air to both the factory workers and the factory.

Ex. 4.1   Ragtime rhythmic cliché 4 after reh. 73 in "L'Orateur"

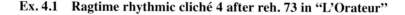

Ex. 4.2 Jazz-inspired passage in "L'Orateur"

   Prokofiev's single, conspicuous blue note passage makes a fitting close to the most jazz-inspired movement in the ballet, "L'Orateur." The usage sounds traditional: a downward half-step motion F#–F–E (doubled at the major second and fourth below) like a bluesy manipulation of pitch common in jazz horn work (Ex. 4.3). Prokofiev's harmonic palette already included similar inflections, but the context and possibly the instrumentation (horns and cor anglais) insures the reference. Indeed, this is quite a startling moment in Prokofiev's music. Still triteness is averted by the subsequent embellished suspension of the fifth and seventh of the V^{11} chord (first and second oboes), and the fact that the terminus of the top voice in this blues-like glide is not a chord tone but an added sixth. Through his doubling and prolonged resolution Prokofiev personalizes his appropriation from jazz.

   Diaghilev had a well known horror for jazz, seeing its propagation as a sign of moral decay. But Prokofiev's one blue note in his half-hour long ballet was

Ex. 4.3   Blues glide at the end of "L'Orateur"

nothing compared with the profusion of them in such pieces as Gershwin's 1924 classic *Rhapsody in Blue*. Ignoring current fashion and almost certain financial gain the impresario fended off suggestions that the Ballets Russes create a Gershwin ballet. *Rhapsody in Blue* did not impress Diaghilev when the composer played it for him at a meeting arranged by Cole Porter during the early spring of 1928. Despite Porter's encouragement, Diaghilev merely responded with a polite offer to "think about it." However, in late May, after the loss of Lord Rothermere's backing, Diaghilev was so short of funds that he actively sought an American tour and Gershwin's permission to use his recent *American in Paris* for a ballet. (The impresario despised travel on the water and America.)[34] Gershwin, who had already promised the first performance to Walter Damrosch, now turned the tables on Diaghilev and put him off. Lord Rothermere reopened his check-book in July, thus ending the crisis, consideration of the tour, and the idea of a Gershwin ballet.[35]

The syncopation and one telling blue note in *Le Pas d'acier* were hardly noticed at the time. In fact, Diaghilev boastfully appropriated Prokofiev's score on behalf of his opposition to jazz in another one of his curiously worded, sermonizing interviews with the *Observer*: "a great feature of [this] music is that its monotonous rhythm [!] is absolutely in opposition to the present day jazz."[36] Contemporary critics took no notice of the ballet's jazz references, though one did call it an "exercise in rhythm."[37] In his Second Symphony (variations ii, v and vi in the second movement) Prokofiev had already exploited syncopated rhythms as part of a similar quest for topical sensation. Off-the-beat repetitions, weak beat stress and tied syncopations, and cross-rhythms all appear but without ragtime or jazz clichés (reh. 92–94, one after reh. 128, and, such as two before reh. 153, respectively). However, the rhythm at the fifth variation's final cadence is suggestive of Tin Pan Alley. The increased use of stylish syncopation and ragtime patterns as well as the blues harmony in the ballet reflect Prokofiev's intention, if not to make *le dernier mot*, then at least to be *au courant*.

Besides this understandable acknowledgment of jazz, the futuristic concept behind Carpenter's *Skyscrapers* would seem to have been a more specific influence. Over a meal sometime during July 1923 Diaghilev asked Carpenter who was visiting Paris at the time, "Why don't you Americans write a genuine American ballet?" Diaghilev began to improvise on the spot, first envisioning a ballet with skyscrapers, automobiles and so forth, then becoming more specific with one that contrasted bustling contemporary American urban life with the lawlessness that would occur during a policemen's strike, the sort that did occur in September 1919 in Boston. Back home in Chicago Carpenter became inspired by Diaghilev's ideas; he changed the story into one contrasting Americans at work and at play, thus allowing for the exploitation of two fashionable trends: futurism and jazz. He was apparently unaware of the impresario's aversion to jazz to say nothing of his dislike of American music in general. He also seemed oblivious to the fact that he had not actually received a commission. Carpenter returned to Diaghilev the following summer to play his completed score. Diaghilev was greatly embarrassed that Carpenter had gone to all the trouble and felt obliged to give it a listen. Afterwards, the impresario mumbled some vague promise of a Monte Carlo premier the following spring. With nothing more than that, Carpenter carried out Diaghilev's recommended revisions and gave the ballet a working title of *Le Chant des gratte-ciel*. He announced to *Musical America* that the ballet would be mounted in March 1925 by the Ballets Russes, describing it as "an endeavor to fix the sound of American activity, the sound of industry," adding that in writing the ballet "it has been impossible to escape jazz."[38] Diaghilev did use his association with Carpenter as a bargaining chip in negotiations for a Ballets Russes American tour, but nothing ever came of the tour nor of his vague promise to produce the ballet. Diaghilev put the score away and had forgotten all about it until one day in the early spring of 1925 a messenger from the composer appeared inquiring whether the Ballets Russes was ever going to stage the ballet. Diaghilev asked Dukelsky, who was in Monte Carlo attending rehearsals for his new ballet *Zéphyr et Flora*, to look over the score for him. When he rejected it the impresario returned Carpenter's score.

Carpenter entered negotiations with the Metropolitan Opera in New York City in April 1925, and it is there that the ballet was premiered on 19 February 1926. Opening and closing with construction workers building a skyscraper, it beat the factory scene in *Le Pas d'acier* to the stage by 15 months. *Musical America*'s reviewer described the scene with blinking red lights at either side of the stage representing traffic signals—"symbols of restlessness," and the backdrop with the abstraction of a skyscraper and a maze of girders. Workmen in overalls went through the motions of "violent labor" to music depicting the rhythms of industry, interrupted by suggestions of the fox trot to accompany the shadows of passersby. At the sound of a factory whistle each worker grabbed a girl and departed to "play" at an amusement park resembling Coney Island, crowded with flappers, sailors, minstrel show players, policemen and other colorful characters.[39]

Prokofiev attended the dress rehearsal for this production on 18 February while he was in town at the end of his American tour. In his diary he remarked that Dukelsky had been correct in his judgment regarding Carpenter's score. "The decorations were amusing, the dancing weak, rather they ran. The music was excellently orchestrated, 'modernist,' but empty. Echoes of *Petrouchka* and the French." By then Prokofiev had finished composing his own futurist-inspired ballet but was still orchestrating it. Nevertheless, it is possible that *Skyscrapers* made at least a subliminal impact on the inception of its sister work, *Le Pas d'acier*. Diaghilev wrote to Kochno in July 1924 that Carpenter had asked for a "Russian Bolshevik painter" to do the décor because "in his ballet, he [says he] is 'not that far away from Bolshevism.' I find this notion amusing." Amusing to be sure, but likely thought provoking as well. The impresario continued his letter along this same line, "The Bolsheviks are wooing me, by the way. The catalogue of their exhibition here starts with my name."[40] It is clear that life and art in Soviet Russia were on his mind in this period. Although Diaghilev rejected Carpenter's score he would seem to have appropriated his basic concepts: futurism, constructivism and exoticism—substituting Soviet Russia for the wild, wild West. However there is no parody here: *Le Pas d'acier*'s futurism and constructivism came from Yakulov, only its exoticism and contemporaneity might be credited to Carpenter. That the two productions ended up having so many parallels only shows how much they were products of their time. In changing the locale Diaghilev was able to capitalize on the topicality of Soviet Russia whose government had recently been recognized by the French. And with Prokofiev he had a proven Russanist composer. Given the politically sensitive theme and the latter's uncompromising music Diaghilev was assured at the very least a *succès de scandale*. Prokofiev's well known surprised reaction to Diaghilev's ballet proposal may not have been so much due to the subject as to his knowledge that its real source lay with his friend and colleague.[41]

As futuristic ballets *Le Pas d'acier and Skyscrapers* do have similarities, most noticeably the resonance between the factory in the one and the construction site in the other. Yet the ballet scores differ in style and sound, and there is no trace of musical influence. In contrast to *Le Pas d'acier*'s overriding lyricism and series of musical tableaux, Carpenter's music is suggestive of a cinematic montage, restlessly panning a vast swatch of Americana. Like *Parade* it uses "freezes" between sections. Prokofiev's use of montage technique in his ballets does begin in the factory scene of *Le Pas d'acier*, but this is minor compared to his later exploitation of the technique. The musical similarities between *Le Pas d'acier* and *Skyscrapers* occur primarily in the robotic and cacophonous industrial depictions. Elsewhere distinctive national coloring—American and Russian, respectively—sets them apart, although Prokofiev, and to a lesser extent Carpenter, reveal an affinity for contemporary French idioms. Prokofiev's factory music is (characteristically) far more representational, and it lacks Carpenter's restless juxtaposition of material and much stronger jazz inspiration. Prokofiev's focus is the factory, whereas Carpenter's is on capturing the contemporary lifestyle of urban American. Carpenter's use of three saxophones and a banjo is pragmatic; despite his flirtation with jazz in *Le Pas d'acier*, Prokofiev did not make use of the saxophone.

Prokofiev's and Carpenter's music reflects a stylistic trend. Like Honegger's climactic, lyrical evocation of the speeding train in *Pacific 231*, both composers use similarly grand, brass-intoned motto themes over restless rhythmic activity (such as, four before reh. 3 in *Skyscrapers*, and reh. 156 in *Le Pas d'acier*). The resemblance at the beginning, between the opening figures in Prokofiev's borrowed Russian factory song refrain and Carpenter's presumed original invention, may be due to a rather small pool of melodic turns that characterize western urban work songs (compare Exx. 4.4 and 4.5). Both scores successfully evoke the din and frenetic pace of modern industry through loud dynamics, rhythmic drive and dissonance.

But there is a vast difference in musical style. Both ballets have been compared with Stravinsky's cool, mosaic-like music in *Les Noces* (premiered in 1923),[42] but as Prokofiev observed, *Skyscrapers* more strongly resonates with *Petrouchka*. The parallels range from the opposition of F# and C to the quotation of popular tunes; the scene with the mechanical dolls (reh. 16) and the brawl (reh. 37) are especially reminiscent. Carpenter's metric fluctuation is far closer to Stravinsky's than is Prokofiev's (nevertheless it should be pointed out that the latter's score demonstrates a marked improvement over *Chout* and the *Scythian Suite* in regards to metric variety). Furthermore, Carpenter's industrial noises are only vaguely suggestive. Beyond the exploitation of extremes of range in the winds and percussive writing for the piano and strings, he suggests generic metallic sounds through tubular bells and Glockenspiel and the pounding and other pervasive "thuds" of a construction site by the bass drum.[43] The air whistle which summons the workers back to the job ("1 compressed air whistle in F-

Ex. 4.4   Opening of Prokofiev's *Le Pas d'acier* based on a borrowed factory song refrain

Ex. 4.5   Opening of Carpenter's "Song of the Skyscrapers," 4 before reh. 3

natural, off stage") and the rhythmically "performed" traffic signals on either side of the stage are his only concession to literalness.

By contrast, Prokofiev authenticated his factory "presentations" through greater musical details rendered by traditional symphonic instruments. From the start Yakulov and Prokofiev had envisioned close correspondence between the music, the operating constructivist set and the dancers' machine-like movements. Massine's choreographic realization cannot be far from Yakulov's and Prokofiev's original concept:

> In the terrible noise of a roaring forge, with turning pulleys, panting pistons and falling hammers, the male and female dancers first execute movements that imitate labor: they lift, they tear apart, they carry, they hammer. And then gradually they themselves become machines; groups of them move back and forth, like pistons and rods, they circle in and out, engage each other, like gears. The odd and even numbers of women standing in a row alternately rise and bend, as if controlled by a camshaft. There are lines of dancers which represent various valves, others are bobbins, and others still are cogwheels. Silhouettes of blacksmiths appear behind the scrim, as if the the factory were full of clouds of steam and smoke. The mouvements keep accelerating and become more and more energetic. *Crescendo, agitato.* Cardboard wheels spin, under the blows of hammers the platform trembles.[44]

Although some of these machine and work movements were more subjective than presentational, each of them could be heard in the music—from the effortful upstroke and and impact of the hammers to the metallic din from the various pistons, levers, gears, camshafts and turning wheels—as well as seen. Prokofiev opened the factory scene with an evocation of steady hum emitted by factory machines and perhaps even of electrical current itself through softly stated rhythmic ostinati and repetition of G–G#–A–G#–G triplets (spanning 196 to 220 Hz). Other "noises" are added: *col legno* double stops in the cellos, heavier accentuations of beats, wider ranged triplet ostinati, and so forth. Nevertheless, Prokofiev's lyricism elevates this music beyond such largely representational exercises as Mosolov's *Zavod* (known in the West as *Iron Foundry*) or Meytus's *Dnieper Dams*. Two themes stated by the oboes and brass, respectively, rise above the din to convey lyrically the character of the movement. They are contrasted with varied restatements of the sailor's and female worker's love theme. This demonstrates once again that Prokofiev learned his lesson well from the rejection of the overly representational version of *Chout*.

Similarly, the wonderfully presentational hammers at the outset of the next number quickly yield to a long-breathed theme. Hammers, of course, only make a sound upon impact. However, Prokofiev goes beyond the ordinary (such as Carpenter's accented bass drum strokes) giving at least a temporal suggestion of the operator's effortful upstroke as well as the musical equivalent of the quick "swish" downward and the forceful impact. A new industrial sound, suggesting perhaps a piston or a lever, is represented at reh. 143 through hairpin dynamics and an oscillation of pitches in the main voice (oboe and first trumpet). But after eight measures Prokofiev returns lyricism to the fore, reshaping the opening hammer material into the movement's secondary theme (reh. 145). The noisy finale does not completely eschew lyricism either: it reintroduces the factory refrain and main theme from the opening number of the ballet and the last mentioned theme from "Les Marteaux." More metallic and percussive sounds are added—such as piano and xylophone glissandi, additional percussion instruments—and the decibel level and degree of dissonance are raised to depict the factory at peak operation. Near the end the music becomes so layered with activity that it almost becomes sheer noise, albeit rhythmically driven noise. Repeated four-octave *fortissimo* piano glissandi add to the already thick sound of the cadential reiterations, enhanced by minor seconds on nearly every chord tone (the ballet ends on the pitch A, sounded from the tuba's AA to the piccolo's a⁵). Though the factory may run on and on, the ballet must end and Prokofiev does so exploiting the rising flourish from the secondary "Les Marteaux" theme. Whereas the workers were the "heroes" in *Skyscrapers*, the factory as futurist and constructivist entity is clearly the victor in *Le Pas d'acier*.

Prokofiev's presentational style is closer to that of *Pacific 231* than to Carpenter's. Despite Honegger's intention "not ... to imitate the noises of a locomotive but rather to express in terms of music a visual impression ... the calm respiration of the machine at rest, the effort at the start, the gradual increase of speed, ultimately attaining the lyric stage, the pathos of a train 300 tons in weight thundering through the dark of night at 120 [kilometers] per hour,"[45] he crafts many descriptive passages with extreme finesse. Yet it is difficult to compare a work that is above all an organic piece of absolute music with music that has a theatrical basis. Furthermore, each composer viewed his futurist subject differently: Honegger saw an inherent beauty in his machine whereas Prokofiev celebrated the cold, brutish power of his.

While both scores deal with mass and speed, Prokofiev's factory machines obviously lack the temporal interest of Honegger's accelerating and decelerating locomotive.[46] Even when his train reaches its cruising speed, Honegger's score has a contrapuntal and rhythmic clarity that is more akin to the music of Stravinsky. Prokofiev's theatrical music is necessarily less consistently ongoing and distinguishes itself through thematic interplay and garish harmonies. Though his factory ("L'Usine," no. 9) operates on a steady crotchet pulse throughout, duple meter yields to triple for a second flashback of the love theme. Furthermore, Prokofiev depicts the contemporaneity of his factory and train (no. 2) through the use of syncopation. Elsewhere Prokofiev's train theme relies on the cliché of repeated dactyls—something Honegger managed to avoid.

Dynamic shading is understandably important in both scores as are characteristic onomatopoetic noises. Honegger's exacting depiction of the train's wheels on the tracks at the outset (*pianissimo* bass and cymbal tremolos and divisi strings playing harmonics *sforzando* on the bridge) are even more finely wrought than Prokofiev's hammers. The metallic noises in *Le Pas d'acier* (usually upward glissandi on piano, xylophone, flute and piccolo, such as reh. 164) are just vaguely suggestive of some factory sound. Both works, like *Skyscrapers*, evoke power through cantus firmus-like brass themes against busy ostinati, and both build to grand climaxes through additive layering: compare Honegger's theme at reh. 14 with Prokofiev's finale. Prokofiev was undoubtedly impressed with Honegger's carefully detailed score, but he wrote his own style of machine music—music that eschewed Gallic elegance for gritty Russian realism.

Russian dance scholar Souritz considers *Le Pas d'acier* the most "Constructivist" of the 1920s ballets.[47] Certainly its music makes an essential contribution to the overall effect. It is incorrect, however, to credit Prokofiev's score as sole progenitor to the numerous machine-age works that followed. Honegger's *Pacific 231* is surely the more famous piece in this field.[48] Futurist-inspired composition in the West peaked the year before *Le Pas d'acier* received its premier, with such works as *Ballet méchanique* and *Skyscrapers*. That same year a much uglier side of the new industrial age was revealed in Fritz Lang's film *Metropolis*, and at least one critic saw *Le Pas d'acier* in the same light.[49] While not at the vanguard, Prokofiev's ballet was still timely. The fact that it was conceived before Stalin's first Five Year Plan makes it prophetic of that era's agitprop. Most émigrés and their supporters in the audience did dismiss the ballet as Bolshevist propaganda: Prince Sergey Volkonskiy wrote in *Posliedniya novosti*: "Let's be honest. It's not pretty, almost utterly ugly and in parts unbearably vulgar."[50] *Le Pas d'acier* nevertheless enjoyed great box-office success, fueled by its headline-fresh exoticism and perhaps even by the euphoria surrounding Charles Lindbergh's momentous arrival in Paris piloting the "Spirit of St. Louis" just two and one-half weeks earlier.

Although a Suite from the ballet was made in 1926 and Koussevitzky and the Boston Symphony initiated the practice of performing various excerpts from the full ballet in November 1927, *Le Pas d'acier* is rarely heard today. The Suite was first performed in Russia in 1928 where the musical aspect of the fad survived the longest. Meyerhold became keenly interested in staging the ballet at the Moscow Bolshoy Theatre (with new choreography), but the production was blocked by the ultra-nationalist Russian Association of Proletarian Musicians (RAPM) after an encounter with the composer in November 1929.[51] Ironically, one of *Le Pas d'acier*'s staunch opponents in Russia was Goleyzovsky, Diaghilev's first choice for choreographer back in 1925. Goleyzovsky claimed (certainly being not the first nor the last to do so) that Prokofiev's ballet music was undanceable.[52] As Souritz notes, although constructivist productions were already anachronistic in Russia by 1929, Meyerhold's staging coupled with Prokofiev's would have made a more consistent realization than Diaghilev's compromised production.[53] It would have also extended the life span of this, Prokofiev's least timeless ballet score.

Prokofiev's redirection of style

The most enduring trait in *Le Pas d'acier* was the composer's "new simplicity," that is, his redirection towards greater lyricism, thinner textures and less strident harmony. In light of the ballet's notorious "mechanistic drive and sheer mass of sound,"[54] however, this retreat from modernism all but passed unnoticed— lyricism and simplicity clearly were not the most immediately characterizing elements of *Le Pas d'acier*. Nor had they been in *Ala i Lolli* and *Chout*, either, although examples of emotive lyrical writing were present there as well. One critic took note of Prokofiev's lyrical inclination in *Chout*, citing his "floraison de mélodies telle qu'on n'en trouve pas semblable dans la musique moderne."[55] Despite its aura of impenetrable complexity, Symphony no. 2, the symphony of "iron and steel," also revealed the composer's lyrical affinity: by returning to the serene diatonic variation subject at the end (in the manner of Beethoven's op. 109 or Bach's "Goldberg Variations") Prokofiev made a prophetic epithet, "lyricism transcends all." But in his quest for success on Parisian terms, lyricism necessarily yielded to more modern tendencies. Then in the wake of the Second Symphony's nonsuccess, Prokofiev conceded that audacious modernism was no longer his guiding principle. His self-proclaimed "radical" redirection in *Le Pas d'acier* included two parts: "a turn towards [a] Russian musical idiom, this time not the idiom of Afanasyev's fairy tales, but one that could convey the spirit of modern times … [and a change] from the chromatic to the diatonic: this ballet … was in large measure diatonic and many of the themes were composed on the white keys only."[56] In the most topical work he ever penned for the vogue conscious Parisians, Prokofiev gave new emphasis to his profound lyrical gift.

Long-breathed lyricism and simple harmony prevail in no. 3, "Les Commissaires" ("almost white," the composer boasted), and no. 6, "Matelots à bracelets et ouvrière." There are other examples as well that do not last that long or else became diluted by the context. The opening diatonic factory song refrain is stated in simple unison for eight bars but is then subjected to a typical chromatically dense closing phrase. Similarly the rondo, "Changement de décors" contrasts "white key" diatonicism in its refrains with highly dissonant planar music in its two episodes. The first episode of the rondo, "Train des paysans-ravitailleurs," has a simple, folk-like quality to it but its eight bars pass by quickly. The lyricism in both of these rondos is muted by rhythmical devices, dynamics and rather thick textures.

Prokofiev's romantic dance for Danilova and Massine in *Le Pas d'acier* clearly foreshadows such numbers as young Juliet's theme or Cinderella's arrival at the ball which followed years later. He imbued Matelot à bracelets et ouvrière" with a humanistic warmth that had been missing (rightly so) in the dance of the hero buffoon and his wife in *Chout*. Though not in traditional form, this number is Prokofiev's first romantic pas de deux; in writing it he opened an outlet for some of his most poignant expression. Cast in the composer's favorite key of C major, it is nevertheless not harmonically simplistic (Ex. 4.6). After the textbook opening progression from IV to I through a secondary dominant it introduces some ambiguity by immediately moving to A minor then on to the Lydian mode on F. Nicholas Slonimsky's term "pandiatonicism" is suitable in this case, although most of the music remains within the widely inclusive tonic complex of C (that is, C major in a Prokofievian sense). As in many of his later love duets, emotion and poignancy are depicted by a protracted and chromatic cadential progression that is resolved in a clear and victorious resolution (reh. 96 to the end). Prokofiev's theatrical use of cadential dissonance was an important stylistic trait, used as late as the last page of his final ballet, *Tale of the Stone Flower*. At the beginning of "Matelots à bracelets et ouvrière" the contrasts in texture, rhythm and tempo suggest the couple's initial awkward and hesitant flirtations. The delicate theme introduced in the middle section is an example of the composer's characterizational consistency—its register, instrumentation, dynamics and melodic turns of phrase are similar to other feminine love themes in his theatrical works (Ex. 4.7). When the consequent phrase repeats at reh. 94 it is accompanied by two flutes ethereally weaving arpeggios from a¹ to b³ much like the first violins and violas do at the end of "Love Dance" in *Romeo and Juliet* (and the flutes at the end of the First Violin Concerto, to add a non-theatrical example). As if his "new simplicity" were not already obvious, Prokofiev separates the two statements of this theme with the quintessential nineteenth-century pas de deux addition, a violin solo, singing the opening theme in augmentation.[57] As part of a futuristic and constructivist work about life in the new Soviet Russia written for Paris and London audiences in the mid-1920s, this number certainly demonstrates Prokofiev's fulfillment of Diaghilev's admonition: "write in your own style."

Prokofiev's second professed change, to a modern Russian musical idiom, is

Ex. 4.6   Opening theme in "Matelots à bracelets et ouvrière," reh. 82–3

Ex. 4.7   Middle section of "Matelots à bracelets et ouvrière," reh. 88–9

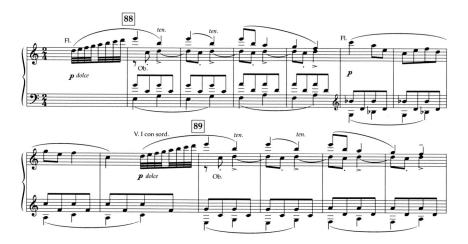

far less momentous than his redirection towards a new simplicity. In fact, this statement from *c.* 1940 smacks of political expediency. Prokofiev had already been converted by Diaghilev to an overtly Russian style and encouraged by Stravinsky to survey native folk music for inspiration. *Chout* demonstrated the composer's personal adaptation and modernization of *kuchkist* practices. The music of the new Soviet Russian society, that is, the great proletariat, was not appreciably different from genteelized Russian folk music that was so revered as source material by the *kuchkists*. Both have a simple, accessible style and share similar intonations. The important difference between Russian musical influences in *Le Pas d'acier* and *Chout* is not a question of style so much as it is the composer's new method of appropriation. For the first time in his ballets but not the last, Prokofiev resorted to quotation. The model, a "well known" factory song refrain, is shown next to Prokofiev's altered version in Exx. 4.8 and 4.9. Typically, the composer personalizes the tune almost beyond recognition, adjusting the rhythm to suit his lyrical style and adding characterful, folk-like acciaccaturas and a more interesting melodic contour. He de-emphasizes the original's tonic-dominant stasis through harmonic ambiguity and open-endedness. The new song-like cantilena at the start as well as the ensuing disjunction to a high register and addition of minor seconds in the cadential progression are all hallmarks of the composer's style. Elsewhere there is further proof that Prokofiev freely drew upon his country's musical heritage. His use of Russian *chastushki* style—that is, simple, lively peasant dance songs distinguished by repetition of short melodic figures as in the first episode of "Train" (reh. 26)—was welcomed by Asafyev in a newspaper article in 1928.[59] But despite the inclusion of a contemporary Russian work song and use of authentic folk style, most in the Ballets Russes audience probably took the

Ex. 4.8 **"Well-known" factory song refrain as presented by Nestyev (1973)**

Ex. 4.9 **Prokofiev's version of the "well-known" factory song refrain, with appended close**

score's harmonic brashness and clangorous factory presentations to be the sound of the new Russia. *Le Pas d'acier* satiated the Parisian taste for *le dernier mot* in bold music; but it also announced *sotto voce* Prokofiev's path for the future.

Le Pas d'acier was successful enough to be be revived in subsequent seasons. Perhaps Diaghilev's biggest disappointment was that its premier caused less of a *scandale* than anticipated. Its weakest point was the first act narrative, its most memorable, the factory finale with its powerful synergy of music, décor and dance. The music splendidly accomplished what it was supposed to do. For Prokofiev *Le Pas d'acier* provided the Parisian success that had eluded him for so long. Nabokov called it Prokofiev's greatest success there."[60] It was successful in London as well: the *Daily Express* noted "judging by the tempestuous reception it received last night, it will become a regular feature of the Russian Ballet program."[61] The *Observer* called Prokofiev's effort "good stage music," while *The Times* remarked that "Prokofiev certainly gets from the orchestra an extraordinarily vivid impression of the hum and roar of machines."[62] This, rather than the new simplicity, was the music's lasting impression. *Le Pas d'acier* reinforced the public's perception of his balletic style: highly skillful in characterization and presentations, and aggressively modernist. After extracting the four-movement Suite from the ballet in 1926,[63] Prokofiev's interest in topicality held on for one more work, Overture in B-flat for Seventeen Musicians ("American"), op. 42, before disappearing altogether.[64] Expedience would force its reappearance in the late 1930s when the composer went to great lengths to gain acceptance in Stalinist Russia.

Although Diaghilev's commission for a ballet about contemporary Russian life was welcome news after the poor reception of Symphony no. 2, its futurist-constructivist concept was a less than ideal vehicle to demonstrate his newly redirected style. Diaghilev's and Yakulov's ideas, the venue and need for success forced Prokofiev to be Janus-faced in composing *Le Pas d'acier*. Despite the evidence of his new simplicity, the composer's topical appropriations and continued use of a great deal of aggressive modern style (such as glaring dissonance and rhythmic intensity) demonstrate that he still believed in Paris as the arbiter of European taste, and was willing to accede to its terms. The overriding musical character in this ballet was hardly avoidable. But with its success behind him Prokofiev quickly lost interest in this "keeping up with the Joneses." Given a highly suitable vehicle, he demonstrated even more of his new simplicity in *L'Enfant prodigue*. Notwithstanding the trend of Stravinskian neoclassicism and the changing social climate, the public did not immediately warm to this style. But Prokofiev's self-esteem and personal convictions were stronger in 1928 than they were in 1925. By then he had conquered Paris as best he could and was thinking of working in his homeland more often. Ironically, he believed that that was the place where he could compose music on his terms alone.

Notes

1. Conductor Albert Coates had presented the *Scythian Suite* to London on 1 November in concert with the London Symphony Orchestra.
2. *La Revue musicale*, 1 June 1924, pp. 247–8.
3. Sergey Sergeyevich Prokofiev, "Autobiography," trans. and ed. by Oleg Prokofiev; assoc. ed. Christopher Palmer, in Sergei Prokofiev Society Diary, 1927 and Other Writings (Boston, MA, 1992), p. 277.
4. The terms futurism and constructivism both apply to *Le Pas d'acier*: the décor and some of the choreography was constructivist (e.g. gear and piston dances) while the subject of the ballet was inspired by futurism. Whereas futurism has an established association with music, constructivism does not. Truly "constructivist music"—that is, music wholly utilitarian and completely unostentatious—would necessarily be abstract, untheatrical and probably unsophisticated (Satie's and Milhaud's *Musique d'ameublement* of 1920 fits this description). Consequently, the music of *Le Pas d'acier* will not be referred to as being "futurist-constructivist," rather "futurist inspired" or "futurist."
5. By this time another Russian "son," Vladimir Dukelsky (Vernon Duke), had joined the Ballets Russes circle. Though he composed the ballet *Zéphyr et Flora* (1925) imitating classical Russian style, it is unlikely that Diaghilev would have commissioned him for this project since he had already been given a follow-up assignment: a ballet to a libretto by Kochno, eventually entitled "Three Seasons" (Diaghilev did not care for autumn). Some music was composed but the ballet never materialized.

6. Some of futurist poet Francesco Cangiullo's account of this demonstration is included in Rodney J. Payton, "The Music of Futurism: Concerts and Polemics," *The Musical Quarterly*, **62**, no. 1 (January 1976), pp. 28–30.

7. Ibid., p. 41. For many, futurism conjures up the notion of representational music despite Russolo's protestations and Francesco Pratella's clear statements of purpose. As the movement spread after the war, the term futurism obviously grew to encompass more than its founders intended. The term had been misappropriated even earlier than that, often being used as a handy label for especially unpleasant modern music (for example, at the 1913 premier of Prokofiev's Second Piano Concerto in Pavlovsk.

8. S.S. Prokof'yev, "Muzïkal'nïye instrumentï futuristov," *Muzïka*, no. 219 (18 April 1915) [OS], 255–6. The article is reproduced in V.P. Varunts, ed., *Prokof'yev o Prokof'yeva: stat'i i interv'yu* (Moscow, 1991), pp. 16–17.

9. Excerpts from the 19 August 1915 (OS) letter to Ye. Zvyagintseva may be found in Varunts, p. 17. Prokofiev disagreed with his friend's negative opinion of futurism.

10. Although it was not presented beyond the composer's hometown of Lugo, Italy, Pratella's opera garnered reviews by London's *Musical Times* (1 November 1920, p. 777) and Paris's *La Revue musicale* (1 November 1920, p. 73). Whereas the story was certainly contemporary ("très *futuriste*" claimed *La Revue musicale*), the music was considered nothing new ("technically stale" said the *Musical Times*, and "très *passéiste* … (On y sent l'influence de Mascagni [Pratella's teacher])" reported *La Revue*. Russolo's *intonarumori* were probably employed as a result of Marinetti's persuasion. But Pratella did not use them in the abstract manner the inventor had envisioned, except, perhaps, for the sounding of a primal wail at the opera's close. See Payton, "The Futurist Musicians," pp. 86–7.

11. Antheil's oft-discussed *Ballet mécanique* (which was not a ballet) was begun in response to his notorious concert performance opening for the Ballets Suédois on 4 October 1923. Originally planned as film music, it was completed in early 1925 and received its public premier on 19 June 1926 at the Théâtre Champs-Élysées led by Vladimir Golschmann. Despite the composer's claim that the piece has nothing to do with actual descriptions of sounds, instead being more a "mechanistic dance of life," it is clearly a product of the machine-age aesthetic. His use of the sound of an airplane propeller as a pedal point near the end is a case in point. Antheil never suffered from lack of modesty: after the 1923 concerts he called himself "the leading young composer of Paris," but he went too far when he implied that composers such as Prokofiev were following him (with *Le Pas d'acier*). Competing with him, possibly. Satie's ballet with film, *Relâche* (Theatre Closed; premiered by the Ballets Suédois in December 1925), however, does somewhat substantiate his claim. See Antheil, *Bad Boy of Music*, (Garden City, NY, 1945) pp. 135–9.

12. Payton, "The Futurist Musicians," PhD dissertation, University of Chiacago, 1974, p. 84. Diaghilev's desire to simulate an aircraft passing silently over the set of *Jeux* bespeaks contemporaneity more than futurism, given the ballet's overwhelming humanistic focus.

13. See Elizabeth Souritz, "The Young Balanchine in Russia," *Ballet Review*, **18** (Summer 1990), 66–7.

14. Its interactive cubist designs by Fernand Léger owed much to Larionov's for *Chout* (and likewise prompted some criticism for their alleged incompatibility with the music). See Émile Vuillermoz in *Excelsior*, 22 January 1922.

15. This concept was hardly novel, witness Charlie Chaplin's film, "The Rink" of 1916.

16. Arnold Haskell and Walter Nouvel, *Diaghileff: His Artistic and Private Life* (reprint edn, New York, 1978), p. 127.

17. John Bowlt, "When Life Was a Cabaret," *ART News*, December 1984, p. 126.

18. Elizabeth Souritz, "Soviet Ballet of the 1920s and the Influence of Constructivism," in *Soviet Union/Soviétique Union*, 7 (1980), pp. 120–2.

19. Elizabeth Souritz, "Constructivism and Dance," in *Theatre in Revolution: Russian Avant-Garde Stage Design 1913–1925*, ed. by Nancy van Nanman Baer (New York, 1991), pp. 137–9.

20. Vernon Duke (Vladimir Dukelsky), *Passport to Paris* (Boston, MA, 1945), p. 12.

21. Elizabeth Souritz, *Soviet Choreographers in the 1920s*, trans by Lynn Visson, ed. and additional trans. by Sally Banes (Durham, NC, 1990), p. 213.

22. Ibid., p. 280.

23. Nicholas Nabokov, *Old Friends and New Music* (Boston, MA, 1951), p. 144.

24. Taruskin points out that the ensemble of *L'Histoire du soldat* is more like an East European village band than a jazz combo *c*. 1917–8. And unlike the shifting meters in Stravinsky's piece, jazz at this time had a steady beat. Nevertheless, the percussion rhythm at reh. 33 in "Ragtime" is highly representative.

25. Arbie Orenstein, *Ravel: Man and Musician* (New York, 1975), pp. 83–4.

26. His son Oleg called this collection of pre-1936/38 jazz phonograph records, "truly well-chosen." Oleg Prokofiev, "My Father, His Music and I," trans. Andrei Navrozov, *The Yale Literary Magazine*, **148**, no. 2 (September 1979), 19.

27. This was not that risky or naive a venture on Prokofiev's part: there had been a jazz revival in Russia in the 1930s following the demise of the conservative, anti-West RAPM (Russian Association of Proletariat Musicians). Serge Prokofieff, "Musical America," *International Literature*, no. 4–5, World's Fair Issue, 1939 [English language version, published in Moscow], p. 200.

28. Duke, p. 209.

29. Regarding Chicago-based Carpenter's interest in jazz see Howard Pollack, *Skyscraper Lullaby: The Life and Music of John Alden Carpenter* (Washington, DC, and London, 1995), pp. 198–9. In an interview with *Musical America* in 1924 Carpenter stated, "I have always felt keenly for jazz. I have loved it and felt a great value in it. It is the first really spontaneous American musical expression." "New Carpenter Ballet for Monte Carlo Delineates Industrial Activity in U. S.," *Musical America*, 16 August 1924, p. 27.

30. Pollack, pp. 195, 203.

31. R.D. Darrell, program notes for Carpenter's *Krazy Kat* included with New World Records compact disc 80228-2 (New York, 1977).

32. Orenstein rightly calls the dialogue between the Wedgwood teapot and the Chinese cup (reh. 28) a pastiche of Tin Pan Alley "complete with piano, sliding trombone, xylophone, wood block, and cheese grater," but perhaps overstates the connection with jazz (Orenstein, p. 194). Ravel's syncopated rhythms clearly derive from ragtime, thus *L'Enfant et les sortilèges* may be considered an example of contemporary jazz only because of imprecise terminology used at the time.

33. Souritz, "Soviet Ballet of the 1920s," p. 120.

34. Diaghilev was always loathe to go the USA. "America is a barbaric country," he once told dancer Tamara Geva as she was about to leave the company, "They know nothing about art! . . . They are cave people!" Tamara Geva, *Split Seconds*, a remembrance (New York, 1984), p. 349.

35. Also see Lynn Garafola, *Diaghilev's Ballets Russes* (New York, 1989) pp. 243–4. Anton Dolin, who danced off and on with the Ballets Russes, did choreograph a ballet to *Rhapsody in Blue*, entitled *Le Rapsodie en bleu*. It was premiered in mid April 1928 at the Théâtre des Champs-Élysées. Dolin danced the role "Le Jazz." There was also a role entitled "La musique classique" (danced by Vera Nemchinova), thus giving some idea of the ballet's action.

36. *Observer*, 3 July 1927.

37. Propert, *The Russian Ballet in Western Europe 1921–1929*, 59.

38. *Musical America*, 16 August 1924, p. 27.

39. Oscar Thompson, "Modern American Life Symbolized in 'Skyscrapers.'" *Musical America*, 27 February 1926, pp. 1 and 5.

40. Quoted in R. Buckle, *Diaghilev* (New York, 1979), p. 437.

41. Prokofiev had visited both Diaghilev and Dukelsky in Monte Carlo during late March 1925, probably not long after the latter's rejection of Carpenter's score. There is no record of any conversation about this ballet in Prokofiev's diary, but considering their mutual friendship (Dukelsky had courted Carpenter's daughter when he lived in New York City) it stands to reason Prokofiev would have heard about it then, if not earlier.

42. Nestyev's musical assessment is uncharacteristically vague (perhaps out of political necessity): "The music of [*Le Pas d'acier*] is written in a thoroughly constructivist style closely related to that of Stravinsky's *Rite of Spring* and *The Wedding*." Nestyev, *Prokofiev*, p. 224. Carpenter biographer Pollack claims that *Skyscrapers'* "dense, organic construction plausibly owes something to *Les Noces*." Pollack, p. 224. Carpenter had been quite taken by Stravinsky's ballet, which he saw at its premier.

43. It is difficult to accept Pollack's claim that the bass drum part is "particularly effective in suggesting hard, manual labor," since Carpenter's dynamic markings for the instrument are surely ill-considered (often *pp*, just occasionally *mf* against *ff* tutti woodwinds, strings and two pianos).

44. Robert Dézarnaux, "La Musique; Théâtre Sarah-Bernhardt," *La Liberté*, 9 June 1927.

45. Excerpt from an interview with the composer in the Geneva magazine, *Dissonances*, reproduced in the pocket score (Editions Salabert, Paris, 1924).

46. Near the end of his career Prokofiev wrote a children's suite for orchestra, *Winter Bonfire*, op. 122, that opens and closes with an imaginary train trip. His thematic representation of the train is as hackneyed as a cartoon soundtrack, but it serves the purpose. At the very end he slows his train to a stop through a simple *ritenuto*. Similarly, *Le Pas d'acier*'s train comes to a halt via four *pesante* closing bars.

47. Souritz, "Soviet Ballets of the 1920s," p. 119.

48. Musically speaking, the most influential futurist-inspired mechanistic orchestral works were probably *Pacific 231* and *Skyscrapers*, the first of which was by far the more widely known if for no other reasons than its brevity and its genre of orchestral tone poem. Carlos Chavez's 1926–27 ballet *Caballos de vapor*, also known as *H.P.*, closely paralleled *Skyscrapers*. The automobile became a subject again in 1926 with Frederick Converse's *Flivver Ten Million*. Mosolov's *Zavod* (The Foundry, 1926–28), part of a projected ballet entitled *Stal'* (Steel), Deshevov's brief *Rel'si* (Rails) for piano (1926) and opera *Lyod i stal'* (Ice and Steel, 1930), and Meytus's *Na Dneprostoye* (On the Dnieper Dam) for percussion are probably the best known Russian examples, at least by reputation. Shostakovich's *Bolt* (The Bolt, 1931) brought some welcome (and intentional) comic relief to the category. A far less well known, but early and particularly ambitious example by Arseny Avraamov premiered in Baku on 7 November 1922 to honor the fifth anniversary of the Soviet Republic. It was written for "several choruses with spectators participating, cannons, foghorns of the entire Caspian flotilla, 2 batteries of artillery guns, many full infantry regiments including a machine gun division, hydroplanes and all of Baku's factory sirens. A central steam whistle machine sounded out "The Internationale" and "La Marseillaise." The performers were led by pistol-armed conductors who stood on

specially built towers. This monster concert was repeated in central Moscow (without Baku's flotilla, of course) on 7 November 1923. See Marina Lobanova, "Avraamov, Arseny Mikhaylovich," in *The New Grove Dictionary of Music Online* ed. L. Macy, <http://www.grovemusic.com> and S. Rumyantsev, "Kommunisticheskiye kolokola," *Sovetskaya musïka* (1984), pp. 54–63.

49. See Chapter 1, p. 75.

50. *Posliedniya novosti*, 14 June 1927, p. 3.

51. At an informal reception for the composer at the Bolshoy Theatre on 14 November 1929, members of the powerful RAPM asked Prokofiev politically charged questions about the ballet. He responded in a rather rude and arrogant manner, perhaps unaware of the power this group now wielded. (Stalin's first Five-Year Plan had begun in 1928 and with it came massive reprisals against "enemies of the Revolution." This atmosphere along with the Party's "hands-off" policy towards the arts and its tacit support allowed the RAPM to empower themselves to such a point that they could dictate musical policy.) The RAPM fought back in articles of such vehemence — condemning the composer's "unprovoked" boorishness, his "anti-musical, formalistic "stunts" and "tricks," the "wrong-headed" production, and so forth — that the rehearsals for *Stal'noy skok* were interrupted. The production was finally canceled.

One goal of Prokofiev's during this trip to Russia had been to "look around," in serious consideration of relocating to his homeland. His encounter with the RAPM, however, provided a rude awakening to the increasingly conservative political climate in Stalin's Soviet Russia. In an article which appeared there in 1931 he was even branded a fascist. Prokofiev did not return until December 1932. By then the RAPM had been abolished by Party decree which ended all independent artistic societies in a move towards centralization of power. See Malcolm H. Brown's summary in "The Symphonies of Sergei Prokofiev," PhD dissertation, Florida State University, 1967, pp. 377–9.

52. Souritz, "Soviet Ballet of the 1920s," p. 123.

53. Ibid., p.124.

54. A description by Brown, p. 274.

55. Boris de Schlœzer, "Prokofiev's 'Classical' Symphony," *La Revue musicale* (June 1923), p. 158.

56. Prokofiev, "Autobiography," p. 278.

57. In 1938 Prokofiev wrote to Jascha Heifetz suggesting he use this number as a violin solo, "I think [it] would come out well on the violin. In any case I've wanted to arrange it for violin [and piano, presumably] for a long time now." Robinson, *Selected Letters*, p. 170.

58. The example is taken from Israel Nestyev, Zhiznÿ Sergeya Prokof'yeva (Moscow 1973) p. 278. Perhaps Nestyev considers the tune so "well known" that its identification is unnecessary. It is the sort of tune that when played for native Russians it generates a response such as, "Oh, I've heard that," without any clarification.

59. Igor Glebov [Asafyev], "Stal'noy skok Sergeya Prokof'yeva," *Krasnaya gazeta*, 30 September 1928; cited by Nestyev, Zhiznÿ Sergeya Prokof'yeva, p. 277.

60. Nicholas Nabokov, "Sergei Prokofiev," *Atlantic Monthly* (July 1942), p. 68

61. *Daily Express*, 5 July 1927; quoted in Neste Macdonald, *Diaghilev Observed by Cities in England and the United States 1911–1929* (New York, NY, 1975), p. 384.

62. *Observer*, 10 July 1927 and *The Times*, 5 July 1927; both quoted in Macdonald, p. 349 and p. 350, respectively.

63. The Suite's four movements are titled: 1. Entry of the People; 2. Commissars,

Orators and Citizens; 3. Sailor and Factory-worker; 4. The factory. The first movement corresponds exactly to the first number in the ballet. The second movement combines the first 60 bars of no. iii (Les Commissaires), the first 73 bars of no. ii (Train des paysans-ravitailleurs), 38 bars beginning at reh. 74 from no. v (L'Orateur), and ends with the last 20 bars of no. ii. The third movement is the same as no.6 in the ballet, the pas de deux for the sailor and female worker. The finale combines excerpts from the last three movements. Three numbers from the ballet, "Les Petits camelots," "Changement de décors," and "Le Matelot devient un ouvrier," are not included in the Suite.

64. This transitional work, written for the Aeolian (piano roll) Company of New York, will be discussed in the following chapter.

CHAPTER 5

L'Enfant prodigue and the end of a fruitful collaboration

Whereas Prokofiev's exploitation of the more aggressive aspects of his style indicates a desire to be at the forefront of Parisian avant-garde, his stylistic redirection reflects a sense of arrival. By 1928 Prokofiev had attained a degree of financial security concomitant with a growing audience. He no longer felt obligated to astonish his listeners, striving to outdo the competition (or himself) in order to sustain the early success of *Chout* and the *Scythian Suite*. He had enjoyed a warm, enthusiastic reception back in his homeland in early 1927 and as a result began to consider spending more time in the USSR where a vast receptive audience already held his music in highest esteem. That his musical style was affected by this trip can be measured by the traces of typically Russian melancholia found in his subsequent works. He had achieved his long-sought Parisian success with *Le Pas d'acier*, royalties became steadier, and his domestic responsibilities grew with the addition of a second son at year's end. He was now middle-aged.

Coincidentally, the wave of modernism in Paris had crested: constructivism and futurism were on the wane, surrealism succeeded dadaism, there was renewed interest in *danse d'école* as well as an acceptance of neoclassicism in music for the ballet. In an interview with the *New York Times* in February 1930 Prokofiev stated: "I think we have gone as far as we are likely to go in the direction of size, or dissonance, or complexity in music." His sloganeering seems aimed at his more conservative Soviet critics, yet a barely veiled censure of the recent competitive, often frenetic Parisian venue comes through: "We want a simpler and more melodic style for music, a simpler less complicated emotional state, and dissonance again relegated to its proper place as one element of music."[1] Diaghilev was, as ever, attuned to the changing times. Despite the success of *Le Pas d'acier* he wanted Prokofiev's next ballet to be something less complex and more timeless.

Still it was somewhat uncharacteristic of Diaghilev to be interested in an old-fashioned story ballet like *L'Enfant prodigue* at this time. That perennial audience favorite *Schéhérazade* had been dropped from the Parisian repertory after 1922. The company's previous religious ballets (*La Légend de Joseph* in 1914 and *Liturgie*, abandoned in 1915) had straddled its entry into its most experimental period. The former was a heavily mimed, sumptuous theatrical event whereas the latter was essentially a modernist experiment. But the turn to a humane theme in the late 1920s was not much of a gamble; Diaghilev must have sensed that his audience was ready for such a departure from the company's recent fare. He too had changed over the years: he was now often unwell, suffering from boils due to his diabetes, and was increasingly distracted by his interest in book collecting. Most striking was his disinterest with some of the company's new productions; he delegated more and more responsibility to his young secretary Boris Kochno. Yet Diaghilev remained ever loathe to rest on past laurels, and strove to remain in the vanguard.

As with *Le Pas d'acier*, the initial idea for *L'Enfant prodigue* may have come from outside the Ballets Russes circle. A biblical ballet, *Iosif prekrasnïy* (Joseph the Beautiful), with music by Vasilenko and choreography by Goleyzovsky, had premiered in Moscow at the experimental theatre in March 1925 to critical acclaim. Although neither Diaghilev nor Kochno had seen it, there is a strong likelihood that they would have been aware of it. As a result *Joseph the Beautiful* may have had a seminal influence on *L'Enfant prodigue*. (For one thing, they may have been curious to compare it with the little acclaimed 1914 Ballets Russes' presentation of the story.) Despite some difference between the main characters—Joseph forsakes luxury for a more pious life and the wanton Prodigal becomes a sinner reclaimed—both stories share a moralistic tone, timelessness and natural adaptability to the ballet, especially with their central seduction scenes. There is no "seduction" per se in the latter story, but the words of the envious brother (a character deleted in the ballet) seem to grant a poetic (read: theatrical) license: "But when this son of yours who has squandered your property with prostitutes comes home, you kill the fatted calf for him," (Gospel of St Luke 15:30). Musically and choreographically speaking *Joseph the Beautiful* offered no model, despite the unavoidable parallels in telling the respective stories: violence against the protagonist and his emotive suffering, grotesque gestures by the villains, the use of symbolism, and so on. Some of the lifts, formations and poses in the seduction scenes, danced by Potipar's wife and the Seductress, respectively, bespeak a similar contemporaneity, however the results are, of course, completely different.[2]

In late June 1927 Diaghilev was offered, but declined to produce Vaughan Williams's proposed *Job, a Masque for Dancing*, conceived by William Blake scholar Geoffrey Keynes and based on the artist's *Illustrations of the Book of Job*. Presented with a French version of the scenario and full-sized reproductions of Blake's engravings, Diaghilev pronounced the plan "too English" and "too old-fashioned."[3] In addition to these precursors there was also the Ballets Russes production of Ravel's *L'Enfant et les sortilèges* in 1925, another moralistic work with a chastened hero. Paris had witnessed a number of theatrical works with a more retrospective and dramatic quality by this time, such as Honegger's *Judith* (1925–26) and *Antigone* (1927), his ballets *Les Noces d'Amour et de Psyché* (1928, reorchestrations of the music of J.S. Bach) and Stravinsky's *Œdipus Rex*

(1927) and *Apollon musagète* (1928). What turned out to be Diaghilev's swan-song was clearly a product of its time.

L'Enfant prodigue had the least amount of precompositional collaboration of any of Prokofiev's ballets for Diaghilev. Once he finally accepted the impresario's commission, Prokofiev composed the ballet over the next four months based on his discussions with Diaghilev and Kochno and the latter's ten-part reduction of the biblical parable (see below). The scenic design and choreography followed in turn. Prokofiev composed quickly at first, hoping to finish the rough draft before beginning his concert tour in Russia at the first of the year. He started work on the ballet during the second week of November 1928. Diaghilev arrived in Paris almost two weeks later to attend the season of Ida Rubinstein's ballet company, and before he departed for England in early December he was able to hear the work in progress on two occasions. Around mid-December Prokofiev's trip to Russia was finally scuttled, yet he pressed on with the ballet. It was finished, not without some difficulty, by 14 March (in a mid-January letter to Myaskovsky, Prokofiev said he was having difficulty finishing the ballet and had to set it aside for a while).

This was the first time that Prokofiev composed a ballet from a dramatically sound libretto, that is, one unladen with fine points. Just how much of it should be credited to Diaghilev, Kochno, or the composer's own perusal of the Bible remains unknown. Kochno had already demonstrated his dramaturgical talent by writing the libretto based on Pushkin for Stravinsky's opera *Mavra* (premiered by the company in 1922) as well as the libretti for the ballets *Zéphyr et Flore* and *Les Matelots* (1925), *La Pastorale* (1926), *La Chatte* (1927) and *Ode* (1928). Prokofiev received Kochno's libretto outline, written in the author's typically large and florid script, on 12 November. Its brevity suggests that many details had been exchanged verbally. Kochno's customary practice, as noted by *Zéphyr et Flore* composer Dukelsky, was to add details to the story for the choreographer's benefit after he heard the completed score. Kochno did send Prokofiev a more detailed libretto a week later but it arrived too late to be of use. He first heard the work in progress on 1 December in the company of Diaghilev (much to the composer's displeasure—he did not want Kochno to hear the ballet until the short score was finished). The original libretto differs at certain points from the stage instructions in the published score, as well as the version published in the catalog of Balanchine's works and especially the highly embellished, undoubtedly revised account in his book of ballet stories written many years hence.[4] Yet it is important to know what Prokofiev had in front of him as he composed. This libretto was written in Russian on two pages of Grand Hotel Paris stationery. It was not dated but the composer marked that it was received on 12 November 1928. Translated it reads:

Scheme
"Tale of the Prodigal Son"

Cast of Characters
Prodigal Son
Father
Seductress
12 Friends (comrades)
2 Female servants (or sisters)
2 Male servants

1. Departure of the Prodigal Son from home (middle part trio) and farewell with father 4 minutes
2. Meeting of Prodigal Son with 12 comrades and preparation for feast 3 minutes
3. Appearance of "Dance of Seductress" 2½ minutes
4. Dance of 2 male servants 2 minutes
5. Dance of Prodigal Son with Seductress 3 minutes
6. Getting Drunk of Prodigal Son 2 minutes
7. Comrades, Seductress and 2 male servants rob the sleeping Prodigal Son and steal away 1½ minutes
8. Awakening and "Dance of the Prodigal Son" 2 minutes
9. (After the exit of the Prodigal Son)—appearance and passing by (carousing) of the Seductress, comrades and male servants (in the cloak of the Prodigal Son)—who at the sight of the approaching Prodigal Son scatter 2 minutes
10. Return of the Prodigal Son to [his] father 4 minutes

Total 26 minutes
May be longer by 1 minute
[signed] Kochno

The discrepancy between Kochno's timings (presumably approved by Diaghilev) and the average performance time of the published score (usually about 37 minutes) is immediately striking. Since it is doubtful that Kochno collaborated with anyone but Diaghilev and Prokofiev at this stage (it appears that Balanchine was not brought onboard until early January), the timings were surely intended as guidelines to assure proper dramatic pacing rather than allotments for specific choreographic concepts (in the Petipa/Chaikovsky manner). Though Prokofiev approached the targeted time only in the Seductress's number—one he reworked at Diaghilev's request—the remainder approximate Kochno's ratio of timings between movements. The impresario's subsequent adjustments of tempi and requests for cuts are also factors in this dissimilarity. The lack of scene changes is also surprising; apparently it had been decided not to fill them with music. As performed the ballet unfolds in three scenes, the second commencing with no. 2 and the last with no. 10. Any variance between this arrangement and the layout of scenes in the published scores probably results from the composer's desire to distance himself from Kochno's work. On 14 April 1929 Prokofiev discussed the titles of the ten numbers and names of the characters with Souvtchinsky, stating in his Diary "I wanted no Kochno names/titles to remain in the future score."

Since the concept of the ballet and some of its details had been presented verbally by Diaghilev and Kochno, just a brief outline was all that was needed at the start. Presumably Prokofiev already knew the purpose of the trio in no. 1 and when to introduce the male and female servants. Nevertheless in comparison with Kochno's documented contribution to the ballet, Prokofiev's looms even larger. Decisions about the character, style and even the role of the music may have been consensual, but innumerable details must have been the composer's alone. Kochno's subsequent fleshed-out libretto may or may not have complimented these decisions (recall Prokofiev's claim that some of Kochno's ideas were "stupid"). But this was really nothing new. Since the time Prokofiev took control of the *Ala i Lolli* collaboration in 1914, he had followed the path Stravinsky established with *Petrouchka*, that is, making music, as Lincoln Kirstein phrased it, "not to serve the dance, but to control it."[5] Diaghilev's willingness to grant such license is proof of his confidence in Prokofiev's ability. On the other hand, this was the impresario's modus operandi; it was successful in that he strove to select composers he felt he could trust, or, at least, manipulate.

Although Prokofiev had begun to turn to a simpler, more accessible style with *Le Pas d'acier*, it is *L'Enfant prodigue* that provides the obvious paradigm for his later style. Only two completely new works stand between these ballets: the Overture in B-flat for Seventeen Instrumentalists (the "American" Overture) written during the summer of 1926 for the Aeolian Company of New York City, and the two-part *Choses en soi* for piano from 1928. Compared with the subsequent ballet both works demonstrate the not uncommon familial similarity in thematic content between Prokofiev's neighboring works. Beyond that the Overture for Seventeen Instrumentalists clearly reveals the composer's duplicitous tendencies at the time: its deliberately simplified harmonic idiom and long-breathed lyricism appear alongside echoes of *Le Pas d'acier* and popular Parisian styles. The Overture is cast in rondo form (ABACA) with a simple, compound meter refrain that is somewhat reminiscent of Les Six's music. Prokofiev's Russolo-like futurist experiment in orchestral sonority—using the lowest notes of the harps and celesta as "resonators" for the two pianos—links the Overture with the preceding ballet, as does the commission itself, music for the opening of a "new skyscraper," in the composer's words, with a "not very large concert hall," the Aeolian Building at Fifth Avenue and Fifty-fourth in Manhattan.[6] Prokofiev described the music of the Overture as "definitely tonal, all three themes without accidental signs, the second in Dorian mode, very little development and no coda."[7] The first episode is especially two-faced: it shares with *Le Pas d'acier* the *à la mode* use of syncopation and some harsh sounding chromaticism, but it just as clearly anticipates *L'Enfant prodigue* both texturally and melodically. Compare reh. 12 in the Overture with the seductress's theme in the ballet (see Exx. 5.1 and 5.2). The most memorable cadential phrase at the end

Ex. 5.1   Compare reh. 12 in the Overture, op. 42

Ex. 5.2   With the seductress's theme at reh. 57 in the ballet

of the Overture's refrain (for example, four before reh. 4, and so on) prefigures a similarly forceful closing phrase in that ballet (see, for example, three before reh. 6). The reduced size of the orchestra and the unusual combination of instruments do reflect contemporary trends, but the former was required by the modest size of the hall where the work was to have been performed. Prokofiev later admitted that the experimental instrumentation (flute, oboe, two clarinets, bassoon, two trumpets, trombone, two harps, two pianos, one cello, two double basses, celesta and percussion) was impractical and rescored the work for a full symphony orchestra (published as op. 42a).[8]

In *L'Enfant prodigue* Prokofiev's lyricism and stylistic downsizing became an immediately recognized phenomenon. Indeed, as with the Paris premier of his lyrical, introspective First Violin Concerto in 1923, it garnered misunderstanding along with some accusations of old-fashionedness. Despite the increasing prominence of neoclassicism as the decade unfolded, Prokofiev's stylistic redirection would disappoint many listeners. They still associated him with the raucous, neoprimitivistic style of the *Scythian Suite* and *They Are Seven*, the stridently colored, neonational *Chout*, and the factory finale of *Le Pas d'acier*. Many years would pass before his lyrical side would be as highly regarded as his aggressive, modern one. Prokofiev complained in his 1930 interview with Olin Downes, not without some hyperbole, "Why do they [the critics] continue to speak of me only as a satirist or a sarcastic composer, or as an 'enfant terrible' of discord, etc.? Perhaps this was true fifteen years ago, when that was my spirit, and somewhat my style. But I have left that period behind." Answering Mr. Downes next question, "What have you become?" Prokofiev responded, "I hope simpler, and more melodic."[9]

After hearing Prokofiev's score the second time, Diaghilev wrote to Lifar on 1 December: "Much is very good. The last scene, the Prodigal's return is beautiful. Your variation, the awakening after the orgy is, for Prokofiev, quite new. A sort of profound and majestic nocturne. Good too is the tender theme of the sisters." He also remarked that the pillage is "very good in the genuine Prokofiev manner."[10] Later in the compositional process Diaghilev would frequently boast about the ballet, for example proudly declaring to the writer and critic Sergey Volkonsky, "Such a masterpiece he has composed for me, such a masterpiece." The composer, too, sensed that this ballet would be one of his most successful works. He even made light of this in a letter to Koussevitzky's wife, Natalia: "The ballet is turning out to be simple, clear, melodic—in other words, just right for [the conservative tastes in] Brooklyn."[11] The timeless biblical parable provided the perfect vehicle for Prokofiev's "new simplicity." But for the first time in his collaboration with the Ballets Russes the composer strenuously objected to the choreographic interpretation of his music. George Balanchine's stylized modern movements conflicted with Prokofiev's realistic vision. The choreographer later complained that the composer was "passé," wanting it to be done in an outdated manner. Apparently Prokofiev wanted to embrace more of the past than just lyrical, emotive music.

Along with the deepest emotions he had yet to portray in a ballet, the story all but demanded an unprecedented amount of *ballet d'action*. But Prokofiev remembered his lesson from the overly presentational 1915 version of *Chout*. Avoiding that trap, he opted to tell the story almost exclusively through *dansante*, rather than mimetic music. By this time he had envisioned mime and dance to be musically indistinguishable: his presentational skills had been subsumed into his highly characterful dance music. For example, Prokofiev's music for the drinking and pillaging scenes is dramatically charged but nonspecific—like Chaikovsky's battle music for the Nutcracker and the Mouse King. There are some humorous sounds such as the the suggestion of orchestral laughter (one before reh. 30), and the pervasive chattering winds, and so on, which pass by without interrupting the musical flow. But there are no presentational sounds of bottles being emptied or drunks stumbling about. Prokofiev composed *L'Enfant prodigue* to be danced. It was Balanchine and Kochno through his fine points who were responsible for turning *L'Enfant* into a heavily mimed ballet.

As described in the Ballets Russes program the ballet transpired as follows:

I

I. Le Fils Prodigue quitte la maison paternelle, accompagné pas ses deux confidents.

II

II. Le Fils Prodigue rencontre ses amis et prend part à leur festin.
III. Entrée et danse de la Séductrice qui prend place à côté du Fils Prodigue.
IV. Les Confidents du Fils Prodigue divertissent les convives.
V. Le Fils Prodigue danse avec la Séductrice.
VI. La Séductrice et les Amis du Fils Prodigue le forcent à boire.
VII. Les Confidents, les Amis et la Séductrice dépouillent le Fils Prodigue endormi et s'enfuient.
VIII. Réveil et lamentation du Fils Prodigue.
IX. Promenade de la Séductrice, des Confidents et des Amis du Fils Prodigue, chargés de ses dépouilles.

III

X.   Retour du Fils Prodigue repentant dans la maison paternelle.[12]

In the opening scene only the Prodigal dances, and the last one-third is practically all *ballet d'action*. Admittedly Prokofiev's alternation of highly characterized dance passages pretty much controls the opening number, with its recurring dance of defiance for the Prodigal interwoven with reflective episodes. Based on the slightly revised choreography to a cut score recorded for Public Broadcasting Corporation's Dance in America series in 1978, Balanchine completely ignores a great deal of Prokofiev's musical cues throughout the ballet (for example, repetitions, and changes in orchestration, register, and even tempi, and so on). This divergence is especially noticeable in no. 2, "Rencoute avec des camarades." At reh. 40 Balanchine does follow the composer's repeat of a theme from no. 1 (reh. 7) by featuring wine jug activities in both spots. But there are many instances of curious discontinuity, such as the parading around the stage to a *piano* restatement of the lyrical first episode at reh. 41. Prokofiev was correct in pointing out the lack of correspondence between movement and music when he first saw it. But this freedom was a basic tenet of modern choreography, and details in the music unheeded by Balanchine still served the ballet's realization.

The composer was not alone in finding the last minutes of the staging—with the repentant Prodigal crawling home and pulling himself up into his father's arms—the most successful part. But this was probably due as much to Lifar's poignant performance as Balanchine's simple concept. Prokofiev strongly disliked the rest of his choreography, with its gymnastically inspired abstract dances, stylized and contorted movements and poses. He openly criticized Balanchine and Kochno (who may well have thought up some of the moves) during final rehearsals, apparently expecting something more realistic and ennobled in keeping with the seriousness of the story. One can imagine Prokofiev's rage when he first saw Balanchine's bald-pated male revelers parading across the stage (no. 2), in a squatting position, knees to the side, flat-footed with tucked arms flapping like some sort of gargantuan segmented insect. This use of grotesque gestures and movements stemmed from the use of gymnastics in the experimental ballet theatres in Russia. Goleyzovsky had relied upon them as well for his characterization of Joseph's brothers in *Joseph the Beautiful*.[13] The blatant sexuality of the Seductress and her erotic partnering with the Prodigal incensed him. He cursed at Diaghilev but in calmer tone wrote to Myaskovsky, "the choreography was poorly coordinated with the music and not without annoying inventions which did not go with the plot." From his point of view, the eccentric, modernistic staging was anachronistic. But with his own modernistic music for the revelers ("hammering nails") and his sultry, exotic characterization of the seductress, Prokofiev, too, had departed from a classical stance. Balanchine recognized this: "It's a biblical story, but the music was, of course, quite modern. And I did what I thought would be best for the music."[14]

Since he admitted having difficulty creating sufficient action to fill-out the music, Balanchine may not have been too keen on this assignment. His first task that spring was to choreograph the ballet *Le Bal* (music by Vittorio Rieti) for a Monte Carlo premier on 7 May. His complaint that Prokofiev would not change any of the ballet's music is self-incriminating and smacks of insubordination to Diaghilev.[15] (When was this supposed to have happened? Prokofiev did not work with him in Monte Carlo. Besides, Diaghilev was in charge of cuts.) Balanchine recalled that Prokofiev "was a bastard; so I had to invent to fill the music; the big prop [the table] is my invention to fill time. The piece was never right, but I left it."[16] Some critics did complain that the inverted trestle table being used as a boat was more appropriate for a vaudeville review than a ballet. Despite the obvious last minute haste, Balanchine's complaints and his heavy dependence on mime and a prop suggests a certain lack of empathy with the subject and the music. When David Lichine staged the ballet for De Basil's Ballets Russes in 1939, he reportedly used much more dancing, even in his equally effective homecoming scene."[17] The ballerina Danilova remembered Balanchine during the early stages of rehearsals sitting on their hotel terrance on the beach at Monte Carlo, lamenting, "I don't know what to do when the son comes home crawling on his knees—there are *six pages of music*."[18] Balanchine remained relatively tight-lipped about this ballet throughout his career, even the few times he revived it. His reminiscences are mostly embittered, suggesting painful memories. Prokofiev's demeaning refusal to share his royalties from La Société des Auteurs et Compositeurs with the choreographer—which was a customary practice—certainly must have been one of them. But in light of the legal action Balanchine's friend and collaborator Kochno tried to take against the composer it should not have been that surprising. Despite or perhaps because of Balanchine's struggles and rash solutions, his contribution brought just the right degree of breeziness to complement Rouault's somber décor and Prokofiev's highly characterful dance music. It is in fact this friction between the classical and modern, the literal and the stylized that elevates *L'Enfant prodigue* beyond a traditional, localized story into one of the masterpieces in the Ballets Russes' history.

Diaghilev's continued guidance

With *L'Enfant prodigue* come the first extant examples of rejected material since the 1915 version of *Chout*. These outtakes survive in other works: the symphony based on the music of the ballet (the Fourth), his *Divertissement*, op. 43, and the five-movement ballet Suite.[19] Prokofiev was very thrifty, unused material usually resurfaced in some other guise. For example, leftover material from *Romeo and*

Juliet reappeared as the main theme in the second movement of his Symphony no. 5. Almost all of the material in Symphony no. 4 (the original op. 47 version, not the adulterated, or "Sovietized" revision, op. 112) was either borrowed from, or intended for *L'Enfant prodigue*. Prokofiev described the "construction" of his Fourth Symphony in a letter to Myaskovsky:

> Introduction and sonata-allegro are totally new [sic] with the exception of the main part (see reh. 82 in the ballet). II is constructed on themes at reh. 210, reh. 197, and on the same theme as the introduction to the symphony. III is entirely the Seductress [movement]. IV is built on music with which the ballet begins (beginning to reh. 2) and on themes reh. 30 and reh. 44, especially on reh. 30, which develops in many combinations not found in the ballet.[20]

The idea of creating a symphony from this material came halfway through the ballet's composition.[21] Although he feared that "they will throw stones at me" for making another symphony out of a theatrical work, he was clearly proud of both the tone and the thematic material of his ballet and he did not want the unused portions to go to waste. Furthermore, the rationale that spawned the Third Symphony based on his opera *Fiery Angel* applied here as well: a symphony would undoubtedly garner greater exposure than a theatrical composition. Or so he thought. From our perspective, however, Prokofiev misjudged the ballet's durability vis-à-vis both the Symphony and the Suite (the latter of which was made "just in case" the other two misfired).

Other ballet discards or sketches formed the finale and possibly also the second movement of *Divertissement* which Prokofiev "assembled" in 1929. The first and third movements of that work are revised versions of the interpolations Romanov requested for *Trapèze*. Since *Trapèze* was essentially dead by 1928 and Romanov had yet to pay him for the interpolations, Prokofiev tried to recycle "Matelote" as no. 4 in the new ballet but Diaghilev objected.

On 26 November 1928 Diaghilev wrote to Lifar that Prokofiev "had composed a good half of his ballet. A lot of it is very good. As yet he hasn't got the female part quite right, but is quite prepared to rewrite it."[22] A second audition (on 1 December) and an argument would take place before he did, however. Prokofiev's original characterization might have been akin to the gentle and warmly expressive "love theme"[23] from the movement of *Trapèze*, another piece for Romanov he was keen to recycle (it became the first movement of *Divertissement*; the love theme portion reappears as the second episode in the work's finale, see Ex. 5.3). His second attempt was exactly what Diaghilev wanted, music that clearly evoked an exotic temptress (*scherzoso* oboe solo; see Fig. 16 and Ex. 5.4). As such, it is difficult to empathize with the composer's complaint that Balanchine's choreography sullied her character.[24] Once again the impresario's judgment well served both Prokofiev's music and the ballet.

Regarding the rest of the *Divertissement* finale, the lack of thematic resemblance with the ballet precludes anything but speculation as to the music's

Ex. 5.3 *Divertissement*, **op. 43, finale**

Ex. 5.4 **Oboe solo at the opening of "L'enjôleuse"**

original role. Whereas whole themes are not similar, it is obvious that some figures and motives are cut from the same cloth as the ballet, for example, the first violin and clarinet at four and five measures after reh. 56. If the finale retains the original key, then its C Major realm identifies the refrain as music for the Prodigal and his male servants. Much of it does have the character of a male variation. But since the second version of "Les Danseurs" (no. 4) went into the first movement of the Symphony, this refrain probably evolved from an unused sketch.

Before the second version of no. 4 was rejected Prokofiev drew up what he called a "General Aid" (*obshcheobrazovatel'noye posobiye*) on 10 February 1929, to help orient Diaghilev to the music (see Fig. 17). This was done because four days earlier Kochno could not come up with any action to accompany this sonata-allegro form movement, a most unusual framework for dance music. In turn this led to accusations that the music was not danceable. Slower, contrasting lyrical music is expected to follow the opening theme in a sonata form, but Prokofiev's music corresponding to the "secondary/fem." (that is, "secondary theme/feminine"; fourth box from left) was criticized as being out of place in a movement intended for two of the company's star danseurs: Anton Dolin and Leon Woizikovsky. Who would dance at this point? Barring an ungainly Odette-like flashback of the servants/sisters from scene one (reh. 8) the only female at hand was the seductress, and this number was intended to separate her two dances. Introducing another female would have resulted in detracting attention from her. Prokofiev's plan does make dramatic sense, however, calling upon the seductress ("fem.") in both exposition and recapitulation and perhaps in the "evil" (development) section as well to foreshadow her and the companions' complicity in plundering the Prodigal. Nevertheless, Diaghilev stuffed the "General Aid" in his pocket and a week later took a different tack, arguing that the music Prokofiev had composed was better suited to fighting than dancing and the latter was what he wanted. This angered Prokofiev—he "was extraordinarily satisfied" with this number, one that had cost him "not a little trouble and torment." Indeed, the main theme foretells the "Dance of the Knights" in *Romeo and Juliet* of 1935. After Diaghilev left that evening Prokofiev played the rejected music for Souvtchinsky and Nabokov who both found it to be both good and danceable. Nevertheless, he had calmly acquiesced to the impresario, knowing that the music would serve nicely in his Symphony.[25]

On 9 March Prokofiev finished the disputed number, having thought up a new theme two days before, "I don't know if it's good or not but in any case, it is not an everyday one." He need not have worried as Diaghilev gave his approval straight-away, commanding only a small cut. Yet after all the trouble the rewritten fourth number still retained much that was rejected in its predecessor. Now cast as a rondo with introduction and coda, the first episode continues to evoke a decidedly feminine character with its change to a slower tempo, prominent flutes, homophonic texture, reduced dynamics and sustained accompaniment. And the second episode (reh. 82) still belongs to the fight topos. Why? Because it is identical to the former version's main theme. Prokofiev simply reduced the prominence of the offending music, changing it from a main theme in a sonata allegro form to a once-occurring rondo episode. The new running 5/4 main theme or refrain (*Allegro brusco*) hardly seems the "glittering" sort of music Diaghilev requested, although it does provide a nice textural and character resemblance to the companion's music in the opening number (compare Ex. 5.5 and Ex. 5.6). In light of all its birth pains (recall that the number originally was going to be a borrowed number from *Trapèze*), it is sad to report that the "Dance of the Two Servants" was cut from Balanchine's 1977 revival and the 1978 film.

The curiousness of this example notwithstanding, Diaghilev's guidance during Prokofiev's creation of *L'Enfant prodigue* was considerable. From the start he had overseen issues of tone and style, it was to be "simpler" and not so "dry" as *Choses en soi*. He heard the work-in-progress on seven occasions between 23 November and 10 March and along the way gave many "practical directions" according to the composer, and controlled the ballet's musical character, dynamics and tempi. He continually fine-tuned the music with cuts and even asked for a new final cadence. For that he convinced Prokofiev to extend the last group of notes from a pedestrian four beats to five and one half (that is, adding the cambiata in the basses). The varying quality of the outtakes as compared to the published score once again points out the value of Diaghilev's criticism.

Ex. 5.5   Unison opening music, *L'Enfant prodigue*

Ex. 5.6   Unison *Allegro brusco* in no. 4

Nestyev and others have rightly remarked that Prokofiev did his best theatrical work when guided by respected mentors, for example, Diaghilev, Eisenstein, Meyerhold, and so on. Perhaps the best proof comes in their absence—in Prokofiev's first post-Ballets Russes ballet, *Sur le Borysthène* (Na Dnepre; On the Dnieper), written for Lifar and the Paris Opéra. Here, quite uncharacteristically, Prokofiev seemed content to repeat himself to a certain extent, and without Diaghilev around to point out the shortcomings of the production, the ballet did not enjoy success. The score's subdued coloration, unrelieved stretches in minor keys and prominent Russian "soul" or melancholia do foreshadow, for example, the quintessentially Russian tone of Danilo's and Katerina's music in *Tale of the Stone Flower*. Indeed, the ballet was undoubtedly written as much for Soviet audiences as for Parisians—it represents a politically far safer second try for success in his homeland in the wake of the brouhaha surrounding *Le Pas d'acier*'s canceled production.[26] Stravinsky, Myaskovsky and other colleagues praised the new ballet score, but most Parisians at its December 1932 premier found it pallid. The *Le Figaro* critic wrote: "The music is some of the weakest M. Prokofiev has written ... a score S. Diaghilev would not have wanted."[27] Each of Prokofiev's ballets for the Ballets Russes had reached its final form with Diaghilev's guidance. The significance of their 15-year professional relationship is exemplified by the major revision of *Chout* at its outset and the no less important revisions in the seductress's music and elsewhere in *L'Enfant prodigue* at its close.

Prokofiev's new simplicity versus contemporary trends

The term neoclassical has been so overused in regard to music over the years that it has almost become a catchall. It was first applied to Stravinsky's music in a 1923 discussion of *Symphonies d'instruments à vent* by fellow émigré Boris de Schlœzer in order to distinguish what he perceived as its emotionless "systems of sounds" from the "Tristanesque neoromanticism" of Schoenberg.[28] Stravinsky did not discourage the use of this descriptive at that time, or even as its application broadened to become essentially a password that furnished "a wary public with an easy access for coming to terms with the composer's music of the 1920s," as Scott Messing has observed.[29] As noted in the comparison of Prokofiev's first ballets with Stravinsky's above, superficial labels that sometimes fit both composers' music (clarity, simplicity, sobriety) do not prove any stylistic debt. Prokofiev's redirection of style in *Le Pas d'acier* and *L'Enfant prodigue* does not necessarily imply a conscious response to the Stravinsky-led neoclassical thrust of the 1920s, even though the latter did draw many composers into its wake.

Ever the individualist, Prokofiev vociferously parted company with his colleague's "pseudo-Bachisms," as he called them earlier in the decade, causing their relations to become strained for some time. While the Stravinsky neoclassical bandwagon powered-up, his criticisms were harsh but consistent, claiming at one point that "Stravinsky has taken Bach as his father."[30] Prokofiev disliked the "Bachness" or "stylized imitation of Bach" in the finale of the Octet (1923); he referred to the Concerto for Piano and Winds (1924) as "scratched-up Bach," and the Piano Sonata (1924) as "some kind of Bach covered with smallpox."[31] In early 1924 he recorded in his Diary the wish to be able to have the time (and a commission) to write a nonet for winds and double bass "in order to do battle with" Stravinsky and his neoclassical bellwether Octet. In his Autobiography he recalled:

> I did not approve of Stravinsky's predilection for Bachian techniques ... or rather I did not approve of adopting someone else's idiom and calling it one's own. True, I had written a 'Classical' Symphony myself [partly as a practical exercise in composing without a keyboard], but that was only a passing phase. With Stravinsky the 'Bachism' was becoming the basic line of his music.[32]

Prokofiev even went so far as to distance himself from his popular Symphony in a 1925 letter to Asafyev: "In general I don't think highly of things like *Pulcinella* or even my own "Classical" Symphony (sorry, I wasn't thinking of this when I dedicated it to you), which are written 'under the influence' of something else."

A degree of at-all-costs distancing from the opposition is at work here (recall that in 1920 Prokofiev had expressed his approval of *Pulcinella*), nevertheless there is truth behind his claims. According to the composer Nabokov, Prokofiev "used to laugh at all the complicated discussions among critics about his 'neoclassical style' of which the *Classical Symphony* was supposed to be such a striking example."[33] He continues, "The rest of Prokofiev's music is, of course, far from being neoclassical in the narrow sense of the word." I read Nabokov's "narrow sense" as the Stravinsky line, and there is more to it than form and texture. Prokofiev had used classical forms since his opus one Piano Sonata (1909) and even before. Contrapuntal texture was not his forte. If retrospectivism is neoclassicism's key criterion then why not grant Diaghilev primary status in its "invention"? The concept behind *La Boutique fantasque* and *Pulcinella* was, after all, his. Simply put, Prokofiev's "new simplicity" is *not* neoclassicism. His lyrical style provides the proof: it does not belong with the cool and objective, anti-romantic trend. By comparison, his lyricism is warm, often expansive, highly subjective and sometimes downright sentimental—closer to the characterful and colorful melodies of Rimsky-Korsakov and Lyadov than Stravinsky's comparatively dispassionate strains. Diaghilev loved the way Prokofiev's cellos sang out in *L'Enfant prodigue*, and by comparison he considered Stravinsky's latest music to be dry. Strip away the layers and there is an underlying clarity, indeed, elegance to Prokofiev's music. But this "classicism" should not be confused with the neoclassicism of Stravinsky and his followers.

Though the timing of his refocus on lyricism might seem opportunistic, Prokofiev preferred to remain, for the most part, stylistically aloof and relatively low-key in his self-promotion. It is doubtful that he was much interested in the "anti-isms" agenda that Stravinsky promoted or allowed to be promoted on his behalf (anti-romanticism, anti-Wagneriansim, anti-impressionism).[34] As "standard bearer for the new objectivity,"[35] Stravinsky even went so far as to disavow anything but an abstract basis in his earlier music, including *Petrouchka* and *L'Oiseau de feu*. In an interview in 1921 he asserted: "I have never tried, in my stage works to make music illustrate the action, or the action the music ... I have never made 'applied music' of any kind. Even in the early days, the 'Firebird,' I was concerned with a purely *musical* construction."[36] Given Stravinsky's mendacity and the stubborn self-righteousness on the part of both composers, it is not surprising that their relationship became fractious. Ever since the time of *Chout* they trod stylistically diverging paths. Not surprisingly Stravinsky considered that ballet to be Prokofiev's "most successful piece."[37] For his part Prokofiev continued to be interested in his colleague's music, admitting in an August 1926 letter to Asafyev "I am wary of taking him to task [regarding the Serenade in A, 1925], since Stravinsky has so often deceived us, and what seems ugly at first glance has become interesting with the passage of time." His concluding words on this subject, however, point out the two composers' remove: "But the paucity of melody [in the piece] is obvious."[38] Prokofiev's aesthetic was closer to composer Ferruccio Busoni's somewhat analogous concept of a *junge Klassizität*, which promoted musical evolution and rejuvenation instead of retrospectivism.[39] Nevertheless, while Stravinsky's commitment and success with neoclassicism was not directly influential, it did no doubt offer indirect encouragement for Prokofiev's stylistic redirection away from the more extroverted aspects of Parisian modernism.

Stravinsky's experiments under the banner of neoclassicism in the 1920s had included a rejection of strings for winds (and later vice versa), his newly proclaimed espousal of counterpoint and traditional forms, his rejection of overt Russian color for cooler classical strains, his rejection and subsequent reembrace of *ballet d'action*, and his eclectic stylistic appropriations ranging from Bach and Handel to Verdi and Chaikovsky (and more, if you believe Prokofiev). Conveniently there are nearly contemporary ballets which allow a comparison of Prokofiev's "new simplicity" on the one hand and Stravinsky's neoclassicism on the other. In contrasting *L'Enfant prodigue* and *Apollon musagète* it is important to separate musical influence from extramusical trends: both used timeless, or "classical" themes, a reserved, serious tone, and not totally dissimilar action in the finales. But Stravinsky's serene *ballet blanc* for string orchestra bears no significant musical similarity to Prokofiev's dramatic, colorful, sometimes humorous music.

Prokofiev saw *Apollon musagète* in Paris in June 1928 and, not surprisingly, found it terribly boring and full of "pitiful" material "stolen ... from the most disgraceful pockets: Gounod, and Delibes, and Wagner, even Minkus."[40] For his part Stravinsky had greatly disliked *Le Pas d'acier* and panned Prokofiev's recently premiered labor of love, *Fiery Angel*. Polemics aside, their music is quite different. Perhaps the most conspicuous feature of *Apollon musagète* after its austere orchestral resources and emotional reserve is its texture—transparent, yet highly contrapuntal. Prokofiev's high water mark of polyphony in this period had been his Second Symphony, a notoriously opaque work. But Prokofiev was never an adherent of strict imitative counterpoint or quasi-fugal writing, certainly not in his ballets. Nabokov pointed this out in his summary of his colleague's style: "Prokofiev's music ... lacks any consistent polyphonic development. Prokofiev seems to have a particular dislike for the style of imitative counterpoint, and used to make fun of his contemporaries for writing fugues and fugatos. He contended that this made their style necessarily derivative."[41] The rare examples of imitative and non-imitative counterpoint in his ballets are most arresting, indeed, dramatically conceived, like the fugato in the second scene in *Chout* and the end of *L'Enfant prodigue*. Reluctantly he combined three themes in the latter; "this almost never sounds as it should," he observed, but nevertheless felt that "in the given instance after all the homophonic music this union should summon tension before the prodigal son falls into his father's embrace and make more prominent the entrance of my lyrical theme."

His use of thinner orchestration and sparse instrumentation in parts of *L'Enfant prodigue* has been overstated and bears no real likeness to Stravinsky's string writing in *Apollon musagète*. Confusing the issue is the composer's acknowledgment of some debt to Stravinsky in his Autobiography in reference to the contemporary *Divertissement*, op. 43 (completed in the summer of 1929). He wrote: "The tone-color of the orchestration was subdued ... in this it bore some traces of the influence of Stravinsky with whom I was now on good terms."[42] The first number's orchestration *was* "subdued" in comparison to its former state in *Le Pas d'acier*. And "some traces" should not be interpreted too broadly; Prokofiev's next ballet, *Sur le Borysthène*, is closer to *Apollon musagète*'s monochrome style than is *L'Enfant prodigue*, although this style serves different ends. Summaries that emphasize the ballet's "austere yet lyrical" style misrepresent Prokofiev's continued used of a well-rounded theatrical style. The "emotional nuances" and "delicate timbres" mentioned by Nestyev regarding *L'Enfant prodigue* are not new.[43] Transparent and euphonious orchestration can be found in works such as the First Violin Concerto and in short sections of the ballets we have already encountered, for example the treatment of the love theme in no. 4 of *Le Pas d'acier*. The increased prominence, however, *is* new. Still, *L'Enfant prodigue*'s passages in unison or simple homophonic style remain in the minority. The first example of the latter does not appear until the end of the opening number, and as soon as the final notes of the clarinet solo and chordal accompaniment fade away, we are immediately thrust back to the familiar Prokofievian boisterous, multilayered ostinati at the outset of no. 2. A glance at these two facing pages in Boosey and Hawkes's orchestral score (pp. 30–31) is instructive: they set the stylistic extremes not only for *L'Enfant prodigue* but for all the ballets from the mid-1920s onward (see Ex. 5.7). Although the march at the beginning of no. 2 (which reappears in no. 6 and no. 7) is a pronounced case, ostinati remain vital elements of Prokofiev's style in this ballet. There are few passages without some sort of rhythmically reiterative device (the theme at reh. 62 in no. 3, and the end of no. 7 are two of the few examples). The real textural change in *L'Enfant prodigue* is the increased amount of unison passages appearing in lieu of ostinati in toccata-like movements. Prokofiev had used this texture at the beginning of *Le Pas d'acier* but now exploits it in no. 1 and no. 4. Quite unlike *Apollon musagète*, *L'Enfant prodigue* exhibits a variety of textures and orchestral colors. As in *Chout* and *Le Pas d'acier*, Prokofiev availed himself of his full stylistic palette in his quest for maximum dramatic effect.

Common themes in Prokofiev's ballets for Diaghilev

In 1927 the Russian critic Leonid Sabaneyev astutely observed that Prokofiev "belongs to the species of composers who do not go through an evolution, but find themselves once and for all, successfully and exactly, and after that evolve their own manner and inevitably repeat themselves."[44] Prokofiev's friend and fellow composer Nicholas Nabokov seconded this notion from a much later

Ex. 5.7   **End of scene 1, beginning of scene 2, *L'Enfant prodigue***
(Diaghilev: "You have so much softness, and then you hammer in
nails," Chapter 1, p. 87)

No. 2. Rencontre avec des camarades

vantage point: "[His] is a kind of music which since 1914 and 1915 has undergone very little change."[45] Prokofiev himself acknowledged that "from my twenty-third or twenty-fourth year I have had my dictionary of idioms," but added that this was not an artistically satisfying end, that renewal was needed: "if a composer has discovered a language, an idiom, of his own, and then goes on using it forever, he dies as an artist. In the main I have my language, but I don't want to be satisfied with it and go to sleep in the happy belief that having mastered the 'Prokofiev language' I need not look for anything new."[46] Malcolm Brown reconciles the critically observed "curious constancy [which] characterizes Prokofiev's creative behavior from first to last"[47] with the composer's need for personal renewal thusly:

> This paradox is resolved if the 'new' sought by Prokofiev is understood as 'new combinations' of his own, long-established private language. The basic vocabulary of that private language typifies his creative utterance in every period, in all types and forms of expression. Within this referential context, renewal is achieved by subtle but substantive modification of musical syntax, by changes in emphasis, and by refining into certainty those characteristic combinations which occur tentatively or in gross form in another period.[48]

We have seen these "new combinations" and "changes in emphasis" called into service by different dramatic and musical ends in *Chout* (its Russianness), *Le Pas d'acier* ("new simplicity") and *L'Enfant prodigue* (unflinchingly human portrayals). Prokofiev's constancy (his "dictionary of idioms"), first in terms of compositional techniques and then with respect to his characterizations, serves as a summation of his ballets for Diaghilev. Occasionally the discussion will include the later ballets and other theatrical or programmatic works as supporting evidence.

Continuity of compositional techniques

Formal and melodic organization

Despite his keen theatrical sensitivity Prokofiev did not abandon abstract considerations such as symmetry and balance in his ballet music, he clearly sought to make the music formally satisfying whenever possible. He was aided in this by the lack of specific choreographic demands. The musical numbers in *Le Pas d'acier* and *L'Enfant prodigue* (and *Sur le Borysthène*, as well) are more often than not cast in rounded forms. Even in lengthy narrative sections some sort of form ("dramatic form") is present, no matter how unusual it might be. *Chout* has the most examples of the latter due to its long-winded scenario and its highly representational nature. Its structural clarity comes more from the motivic interplay between the tableaux than from organization within. Nevertheless, there are sections within each tableaux, such as the dances, that have recognizable forms.[49] Through-composed numbers are a rarity in Prokofiev's ballets.[50]

Prokofiev was partial towards the symmetry of the rondo, rounded binary or song form (ABA) whenever the story would allow it. Considering the frequency of major dramatic turns that occur with the scenes of these ballets, examples of unrounded structures are surprisingly rare but they do exist, for example, the Entrée in *Le Pas d'acier* and nos. 5 and 6 in *L'Enfant prodigue*, the pas de deux and "L'ivresse" (Drunkenness) respectively.[51] Prokofiev favored two-episode rondos with or without introduction and coda; "The Dancers," no. 4 from *L'Enfant prodigue*, is an example with both. Typically, the refrain was newly composed whereas the episodes recalled previous numbers, for example the love theme from *Le Pas d'acier* no. 6 returns as the second episode in no. 9, "L'Usine." Borrowings can also occur at closer range, for example, the episodes in the "Danse des bouffonnes" from *Chout* reuse material from the opening of that scene as well as from the scene before.

Though they lack the sophistication of the tightly organized network of themes in the Soviet-period works, recurring themes are important unifying devices in Prokofiev's early ballets. The extent of thematic recurrence depends upon the density of the drama, while the manner of variation depends on the peculiarity of the role. Simple recollection suffices except in the case of a metamorphosing character such as the Prodigal (or Romeo or Juliet). *Le Pas d'acier* has the fewest examples of recalled themes (the *Scythian Suite* and *Trapèze* aside) due to its divertissement-like first scene. With its story about love lost and love regained, *Sur le Borysthène*, all but invites their use and Prokofiev duly complied.[52] Dramatic unity is also sought on a smaller scale, as for instance, in the last three numbers of *Le Pas d'acier*: "L'Usine," "Les Marteaux," and "Finale." Not unlike the balcony scene in *Romeo and Juliet* (but without its framing passage), these factory numbers are linked temporally as well as thematically. All this is not to imply that Prokofiev is stingy with themes, quite the contrary. But he is ultimately concerned with dramatic clarity and unity. At the very least he likes to conclude his ballets with thematic material introduced at the outset, and to be sure, his love themes are prominent features, and they recur.

A few exceptions aside, the foregoing summarizes the extent of restatements in *Le Pas d'acier*. The finale has no new material at all (nor does *Sur le Borysthène*'s): its first two themes are borrowed from the opening number, "Entrée des personages" (reh. 4 and reh. 6), and its third comes from "Les Marteaux" (no. 10, theme B at reh. 145). The middle episode of "Trains des paysans-ravitailleurs" becomes the refrain of "L'Orateur." Prokofiev's distinctively lyrical love theme from the middle of no. 6 ("Matelot à bracelets et ouvrière") recurs during the factory finale, literally in "L'Usine" and chameleon-like in "Les Marteaux (reh. 152–153). Its reappearance resolves the ballet's sole romantic issue as well as providing a touch of humanity amidst the din of the factory. Other seemingly incongruous restatements suggest cinematic flashbacks, for example the sudden reappearance of the "train-like" episode from no. 2 (reh. 26) as a secondary theme in the otherwise leisurely paced "Les Commissaires."

L'Enfant prodigue reveals similar formal characteristics. Its penultimate number, "Partage du butin" (no. 9; subtitled "Intermède"), is a rondo whose refrain repeats thematic material from "Rencontre avec des camarades" (no. 2) linked together by a brief ostinato that recalls the opening of that number. The episodes are "flashbacks" from "Pillage" (no. 7) and from "L'ivresse" (no. 6). In the finale only the "trudging" ostinato at the opening is new, the rest—all three themes—come from the opening number. The worlds of the Prodigal's family and his new friends are largely kept apart, just one musical link occurs between scenes ones and two (at reh. 40 recalling reh. 7), which may or may not have had a dramatic rationale.[53] Due to the dramatic nature of the ballet every number shares thematic material with at least one other, except for "Les danseurs" (no. 4), which is nevertheless related by style with the opening. Indeed parts of this well-crafted, two-episode rondo seem like a repository of thematic sketches and drafts found elsewhere in their final form (this may be due to its being a last minute rewrite). A sense of symmetry even emerges around "Les Danseurs" due to the repetition of the "false friends" march in nos 2, 6 and 7, and the seductress's music in nos 3 and 5, not to mention the symmetry of the opening and closing numbers (1 and 10). Indeed, after no. 4 the Prodigal's life is changed forever. "Les Danseurs" even brings to mind the melodramatic technique found in early nineteenth-century French theatrical productions whereby tension is heightened by delaying the climactic scene, in this case the pas de deux. Although there is no main, generative motive as there was in *Chout*, the manner of varying thematic repetitions and the exploitation of certain musical figures, such as the anapest in the inner numbers, are similar.

Whereas the basic character of the dramatic personae in *Chout* remained constant, the opposite is true for the Prodigal in *L'Enfant prodigue*. Accordingly, his music reflects his different states of mind. Prokofiev had foreshadowed such a metamorphosis with *Le Pas d'acier*'s love theme: when recalled during "L'Usine" it is stated literally (reh. 127) but in the next number, "Les Marteaux," it was not only combined with a representative sort of factory theme (suggestive of bellows or a piston, reh. 152, bass line), but was reshaped to incorporate some of that theme's features. In *L'Enfant prodigue* Prokofiev underscored the ballet's dramatic climax through similar thematic treatment. In the opening number he restates what seems like a "yearning" theme (Ex. 5.8) with its characteristic staccato semiquaver followed by an accented sustained note in a typical manner, using motivic manipulation, intervallic expansion, changes in register and harmony.[54] Despite the variations, however, the musical character, like the Prodigal's resolve, remains unchanged. The repeated figure of a descending semiquaver to accented minim even seems to represent a restless, forced sigh.

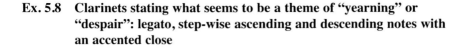

Ex. 5.8 Clarinets stating what seems to be a theme of "yearning" or "despair": legato, step-wise ascending and descending notes with an accented close

The ensuing "paternal devotion" theme (reh. 14 to 19; curiously not dissimilar from the head motive of the main *Chout* theme) is in a far greater state of flux — it is continuously varied or sequenced (much like the *Chout* theme had been), as if to depict the uneasiness of the situation (Ex. 5.9). It reappears in "Réveil et remords" (reh. 157) as the primary theme; its four statements being doggedly rooted in one key (E major), as if to emphasize the Prodigal's shame (E major was the key of "L'ivresse;" this key is often associated with wickedness in Prokofiev's ballets). The complete theme reappears again near the end of the finale (reh. 207) before yielding to an appended version (three after reh. 210) which, together with a recall of the trudge-like ostinati from earlier in the movement, carries us to the coda (and the father taking the Prodigal into his arms). Though organically varied, the "paternal devotion" theme has not only persevered, but it sounds the quiet, triumphal conclusion to the ballet. The Prodigal's "yearning" theme, on the other hand, is greatly changed for its fleeting reappearance in the finale (one after reh. 202), retaining only the opening and closing motives and having lost the prominent "forced sigh" figure.

L'Enfant prodigue was the first ballet in which Prokofiev portrayed profound depth of character, thus it more clearly linked with his later ballets of the Soviet period. The "tragedy" that befell the merchant in *Chout* was treated to musical mocking (the pompous, augmented statement of the hero's theme) in keeping with the tone of the ballet. The love interest in *Le Pas d'acier* was merely incidental to the plot. On the other hand, the more serious *L'Enfant prodigue* broached a wider emotional range: from lust and drunkenness to shame and redemption. Prokofiev's skill at characterization shone once more, allowing the audience to empathize with the humanity and the pathos through the music as well as the acting on stage.

Tonal organization

Keys and key centers do not play as consistent or important a role in organizing *Chout* as they do in the later ballets. But nevertheless they are present.[55] Even in the *Scythian Suite* Prokofiev makes a nod towards character delineation by key

**Ex. 5.9   First (top system) and last two (bottom system) of the six
statements of the father's theme between reh. 14 and reh. 19**

center. It opens with Veles's strength depicted in C major and closes with his
sunrise in B-flat major, exploiting mostly adjacent (stepwise, not circle of fifths-
wise) and occasional mediant relations in between. Ala first appears in D-Dorian.
As the mortal Lolli sets out to rescue her in the final movement, his music is
centered in C# major. Only the enemy Chuzhbog has a "contrasting" key (in a
Prokofievian sense), E major.

   Chout's main characters are not only similarly delineated by tonal centers but
their tonal centers change along with their fate. The seven buffoons are presented
in the tonal center of G until they kill their wives; thereafter they become
vengeful and are heard either in the tonal center of E or else without a distinctive
tonality. The hero's music centers around C, with an emphasis on A-Aeolian
when he appears as Molodukha. His (or "her") music re-centers a tritone away
during some of the more hectic action in the middle movements. Other key
relationships in *Chout* provide a sense of continuity without any underlying
dramatic function. The opening key of each scene is established by the final
cadence of the preceding *priskazka* or entr'acte (in succession: A, E, E, F#, D,
A). Similarly, the entr'actes begin in the key of the preceding scene. However the
scenes do not center around only one tonality. The ballet opens in A minor and
ends on a unison C, and the region of C is exploited throughout, most often in
the guise of the relative minor (hence, Diaghilev's complaint in 1920). The use
of keys for characterization and organization in the *Scythian Suite* and *Chout*
modestly prefigure a bigger role to come.

   Since *Le Pas d'acier* is little more than a divertissement, key centers and
progressions are understandably more organizational than dramatically

significant. The central tonality is A with subsidiary interest in C. Rather than a mediant relationship in the nineteenth-century sense, this is another example of Prokofiev's expanded concept of tonal centers, in this case incorporating not only A major and A minor, but C major and related modes as well. The ballet opens and closes in A. The overriding cadential progression of D/D# to E/G# to A in the three factory numbers imparts a culminating effect which is reinforced by temporal linking. Earlier, "Les Commissaries," "L'Orateur," and "Matelot à bracelets et ouvrière" feature typically Prokofievian ambiguity of tonal center. In each case the thematic line cadences clearly while the accompanying harmony remains rather unsettled between A, C or the Lydian mode on F. As this occurs in two of his so-called "white" movements, it is probably safe to assume that Prokofiev intended the ironic combination (or piquancy) of simple "white key" themes and ambiguous tonal centers.

L'Enfant prodigue is the first Prokofiev ballet score to use key signatures and coincidentally the first in which keys play an important dramatic role. However, his use of keys is not as dramatically significant as in *Romeo and Juliet* where they nearly tell the story by themselves.[56] The Prodigal is introduced in Prokofiev's favorite key center of C. Against his father's pleas in rather fluid tonality, his key is as entrenched as his defiant resolve to break free. His companions ("Les Danseurs," no. 4) emulate him in their C major refrain but reveal a darker side in their second episode in E. The false friends march in, and later rob the Prodigal in the region of D (nos 2 and 7, respectively) and share the bounty in D-flat (amidst recollections in the original keys, no. 9). The Prodigal's interaction with them is demonstrated through recurring thematic material in C during their march and during the drinking number (no. 6) in E. Similarly, though the seductress has her own key of B (no. 3), her pas de deux with the Prodigal (no. 5) unfolds in his key until near the end when her "triumph" is signaled by a statement of her theme in her key. The subtlety of Prokofiev's key usage becomes apparent in his treatment of the chastened Prodigal. Both as isolated pitch and as a key, E serves as a nightmarish reminder of his drunkenness and debauchery amidst the harmonic haze of "Réveil et remords" (no. 8). Even as the repentant Prodigal trudges homeward in the finale, he cannot quite shake off E: the ostinato stubbornly turns from C to E every four bars. Only at the climactic resolution— dominant to tonic in C—is the Prodigal truly freed, or forgiven of his sins. The touch of D (first bassoon, second violins) clouding the otherwise pure C sonority at the very end provides an example of Prokofiev's chiaroscuro-like highlighting technique rather than any sort of reminder of the false friends.

Consistency of characterization

Prokofiev has the uncanny ability to immediately and unmistakably suggest a mood, define a character, or capture an emotion. The opening few measures of any of his ballets are sufficient to set the stage for the work to follow: from the fantasy of the *priskazka* in *Chout*, to the oppression felt by Cinderella, from the brilliance of the Queen's realm in *Stone Flower* to the industrial atmosphere of *Le Pas d'acier*. Another highly distinguishing practice of his is consistency of characterization. From the buffoons in *Chout* to the earnest Danilo and the evil Severyan in *Tale of the Stone Flower*, Prokofiev's character portrayals are some of his greatest achievements. Almost all the basic character types are introduced in the ballets for Diaghilev. The depth of his characterizations correspond to the dramatic situation (for example, the ouvrière in *Le Pas d'acier* versus Juliet). Most distinctive and profound are his highly personal love themes ranging from ethereal to opaque. Some struggle to overcome lugubrious starts, many build through upwards octave displacement, and most end stratospherically, occasionally with a delicate lattice of arpeggios and high pedals. Almost every ballet has at least one energetic toccata-like number (for example, "Danse des filles des bouffons" in *Chout*, "Train des paysans-ravitailleurs" in *Le Pas d'acier*, "Pillage" in *L'Enfant prodigue*, "Morning Dance," "Duel," and "Dance of the Five Couples" in *Romeo and Juliet*, and so forth). Equally distinctive are his percussive, ostinati-driven character marches (for example, the "Entrée" of the seven buffoons in *Chout*, and the march of the false friends in *L'Enfant prodigue*). Though biting sarcasm and malicious humor are found only in *Chout*, humorous and grotesque passages occur in every ballet (for example, the Nurse in *Romeo and Juliet*, Skinny and Fatty in *Cinderella*, and the repulsively vile Severyan in *Stone Flower*). Taken together these stylistic traits help make Prokofiev's ballet scores a distinctively personal body of works. The following survey will demonstrate that these qualities were established in his ballets for Diaghilev, that is, long before *Romeo and Juliet*, the work generally taken as the benchmark of his work in the genre, was written.

Three areas of characterization show amazing stylistic stability despite the obvious differences in each ballet's tone: 1. love themes and (sometimes exotic) feminine seductiveness; 2. power, evil and fighting; and 3. the grotesque or humorous. Not surprisingly, these incorporate four of the five categories that Prokofiev once claimed made up his style: 1. the "innovative line" (in regard to his "harmonic language ... melody, orchestration and drama"); 2. the "toccata, or 'motor' line"; 3. the "lyrical" line; and 4. the "various degrees of the scherzo—jesting, laughter, mockery" ("grotesque" is really a more apt term, despite the composer's objection to its overuse).[57] Each of the areas discussed below reveals indebtedness to western theatrical tradition, the latter two—power, evil, fighting (henceforth referred to as "power/fighting") and the grotesque—more specifically to the Russian tradition of realistic characterization.

Love themes and seductiveness

Although they have varying degrees of dramatic importance, the love themes (or, heroine's themes) in Prokofiev's ballets always stand out in great relief. The composer obviously relished the opportunity for emotive lyrical display, especially early on when many were unaware of this aspect of his talent. In the ballets for Diaghilev the softly stated, simple diatonic (or modally pure) lyricism of the love themes often affords high contrast with its more harmonically and rhythmically aggressive surroundings. Later, amidst a more euphonic context, these impassioned numbers still stand out because of their thicker orchestration and exploitation of extreme registers (for example, "Love Dance," no. 21 in *Romeo and Juliet*). The complicated love affair in that ballet also necessitated a greater variety of this type of music, some of it has tragic undertones whereas other examples suggest transcendence. The love/feminine themes in the ballets for Diaghilev lack such emotional shading, yet they reveal similarities in instrumentation, melodic style and harmony.

Most common is the use of a solo flute's pure timbre to introduce the heroine (Ala, Molodukha, the ouvrière, Natasha in *Sur le Borysthène*, and so forth). If the heroine (or an important female character) is "exotic" rather than "pure," Prokofiev will most likely introduce her with a double reed, for example, the seductress (oboe), the maiden in "Orientalia" from *Cinderella* (cor anglais), and the gypsy in *Stone Flower* (cor anglais, no. 32 at reh. 279). The unusual female characters are given less traditional instrumentation. The wives of the seven buffoons, certainly more earthy (or exotic) than pure, are introduced in a tutti *pesante* setting, and later dance to solo clarinet, oboe, flute and harp. Despite the lyrical nature of these themes, Prokofiev often adds characteristic rhythmic accompaniments, thereby avoiding any sense of nineteenth-century languorous *volupté*. These motoric devices range from simple arpeggiations or steady demarcations of the beat, half-beat or after beat, to even more impelling figures such as: ⁷ ♪ ♪ which is used in the ouvrière's, seductress's and the gypsy's themes (and less conspicuously in Ala's). Countersubjects sometimes provide this same rhythmic drive, as in "Scène" (no. 2) of *Sur le Borysthène*.

Harmonization also separates "pure" from "exotic" types but not so rigorously. Prokofiev usually characterizes the former with "white" keys—C major (for example, the ouvrière), A-Aeolian (for example, Molodukha), D-Dorian (Ala)—or at least without chromaticism in the melody. The exotic creatures, perhaps appropriately, are harmonically enigmatic or unstable. The deception behind the seductress's flirtatious character is underscored by the play between tonal centers a half-step apart (B minor and B-flat major).

Certain melodic characterizations are common to these themes. Curiously, the themes often begin with pitch reiteration. Although distinguished by different performing instructions (*dolce* versus *scherzoso*, and legato versus staccato), the opening phrase of the seven wives' dance in *Chout* seems like a prototype to the one for the seductress. In *Cinderella* reiterated notes also open the magical signature tune of the Beggar woman-turned fairy as well as the scene setting music just before Cinderella enters the ball. Akin to these examples are Ala's and Molodukha's themes with their repetition of sustained notes and appending figures. The ornamentation in Ala's theme is a rather traditional feature of musical exoticism as is the ornamentation in the gypsy dance in *Stone Flower* (yet another example with repeated notes at the outset). Like Molodukha's music, the ouvrière's theme opens with a repeated figure that evokes a berceuse-like lilt. One can only speculate what all this repetition is supposed to signify, if anything. Certainly the resultant ethereal, gliding quality is appropriate for ballerinas either "pure" or "exotic." Perhaps the accessibility gained through accumulated repetition suggests an inviting character, be it sultry, vulnerable or maternal.

Power/fighting

Prokofiev's apposite, trenchant portrayals in this category are made with broadly accented strokes. Where understanding is enhanced by great contrasts, dramatic subtleties are superfluous. The characters in this category either undergo no transformation (like Chuzhbog, they persist or are vanquished), or they acquire this trait at some point in the drama (the Prodigal at the outset, or the seven buffoons beating the cook). Power also may be displayed inanimately as in the themes in the last two factory numbers in *Le Pas d'acier*.

As before, this group is distinguished by traditional instrumentation and melodic character: a loud brass sonority and themes with dotted or steadily reiterated rhythms being the primary traits. However, the type of brass instrument that bears the theme is not as consistent, nor is the association as memorable as the flute vs. double reed dichotomy noted above. And while bold, primary colors remains a dominant feature, the strings and winds are often called upon to share in thematic presentation. With forces of good battling forces of evil, as in the *Scythian Suite*, the trumpets clearly represent the former (Veles, Lolli) and the horns, the latter (Chuzhbog). Other conflicts are not so neatly delineated, however. Beginning with *L'Enfant prodigue*, Prokofiev also used unison strings to depict masculine vigor (the 5/4 main theme in "Les Danseurs"), fighting (no. 4 in *Cinderella*) and supremacy or power ("Danse du fiancé" in *Sur le Borysthène*, and "Dance of the Knights" in *Romeo and Juliet*). Boldly stated unison writing has traditionally been used to depict forcefulness or resolve: Musorgsky used it, for example, at the outset of "Gnomus" and "'Samuel' Goldenburg and 'Schmuÿle'" in *Pictures at an Exhibition*. Prokofiev chose the sonority of unison woodwind and *marcato* strings to open *L'Enfant prodigue* and to set the tone for the Prodigal's defiant departure. This surprised Diaghilev when he first saw the full score—he thought there would only be winds. Prokofiev replied that it was more "energetic" with the strings.

Two characteristics emerge to define the melodic content of these power/fighting themes: accentuated, détaché reiteration of notes or figures and the use of dotted rhythms. Reiterative "hammering" quite naturally occurs at the climax of the factory scene in *Le Pas d'acier* and as the seven buffoons beat the matchmakers in *Chout*. But it is also used less specifically to signify strength or power, to emphasize closure (reh. 190 to the end of "Partage du butin" in *L'Enfant prodigue*), or as a component of more lyrical themes ("Fight," no. 9 in *Sur le Borysthène*). This hammering occurs at the level of the crotchet or quaver, in steady pulses or through repeated dactyls or anapests. The close of *Le Pas d'acier* features all three. Such characterization is, once again, traditional. Remaining with the Musorgsky paradigm, the wicked Baba-Yaga's "Hut on Hen's Legs" similarly utilizes all three rhythmic types. The extreme case occurs at the conclusion to *Le Pas d'acier* (and in variation vi in Symphony no. 2) where Prokofiev made such an elemental display of pounding rhythm that it overpowered the harmony and practically obliterated any sense of melody.[58] The evocation of power in these examples also derives from the reiteration of harmonically defining chord tones in a clearly tonal context. Indeed, the clear diatonicism and undisguised cadences are features of these power/fighting themes. Dotted rhythms occur frequently—perhaps the most memorable example being the galloping theme in *Romeo and Juliet*'s "Dance of the Knights" and its antecedent, the second episode in "Les Danseurs" in *L'Enfant prodigue*. The latter may be the quintessential example of this category as it features not only dotted rhythms, a unison statement of the theme and accentuated repeated notes and figures, but also has a characteristic emphatic cadence that leaves the impression of absolute authority (see Ex. 5.10).

The grotesque or humorous

The theatrical works that best demonstrate Prokofiev's humorous and grotesque vein are *Chout*, its near contemporary, *L'Amour des trois oranges*, and *Cinderella*. Characterizations in these works are often unsubtle—musical equivalents of circus clown antics such as pratfalls, pies-in-the-face, and so forth. By the mid-1920s, the composer's musical humor had become far less biting and malevolent, yet it remained direct, effective and an important element of his style. Probably the most extreme example is the noisy entrée music for the seven buffoons with its limping ostinato (very similar to the Fata Morgana music in *Oranges*) and its highly disjunct theme that suggests a bizarre physical character. The range of humor expressed in the ballet characterizations for Diaghilev runs from this sort of trenchant, grotesque music to the odd sort of music for the vermin in *Ala i Lolli* and the sailor-turned-worker in *Le Pas d'acier* (no. 8). In addition, his scherzando movements without specific representation, such as "Les petits camelots," use some of the same musical techniques; Prokofiev obviously relished the humor of unusual instrumental sounds. Despite the serious tone of *L'Enfant prodigue*, he did not refrain from adding some overt humorous touches, in fact, "Pillage" is almost entirely in this character.

Once again instrumentation is a distinguishing factor. In company with other Russian composers Prokofiev exploits the humorous potential of the bassoon and contrabassoon.[59] In his ballets he most often used the bassoons to provide

Ex. 5.10   Second episode, no. 4, *L'Enfant prodigue*

accompaniment, often a walking bass line of staccato quavers reiterating chordal intervals, usually thirds, in the lower range.[60] In certain contexts this alone may be humorous. For melodies with a humorous character Prokofiev usually turned to the clarinets (including bass, but not, surprisingly, the little E-flat), often exploiting the lower extremes of their range. The collective thought process of the seven buffoons in *Chout* is represented by the steady staccato beat of three bassoons and a wandering, legato phrase marked *penseroso* for one clarinet in A and one bass clarinet. The grotesque humor in *L'Enfant*'s "Pillage"—a real tour de force for bass clarinet and two B-flat clarinets—is due in large measure to the rapid traversal of notes across a very wide range (D to d³), the phantasmagorical manipulation of rather slender melodic material, as well as the unusual instrumentation and exploitation of extreme tessitura. The movement ends with a solo piccolo stating the primary triadic ostinato from d⁴ to a⁴, five octaves above the pedal bass. This is also a magical moment on stage thanks to Balanchine's choreography, as the last of the pillaging, grotesque false friends quickly waddles off stage. The clarinet writing in "Pillage" is briefly foreshadowed in the desert scene of *Oranges* as Princess Ninetta is transformed into a rat by the nasty Sméraldine (bassoons and 3 clarinets, reh. 451). The theme of the vermin in *Ala i Lolli* is also stated by a trio of clarinets (reh. 53). In the nearly contemporaneous opera *The Gambler*, Prokofiev again used the clarinets and bassoons to reinforce a similar comically-blustering, yet ineffectual character, the retired General (a basso).

Prokofiev was also fond of capitalizing on the rather unflattering sonorities of instruments, especially the winds, having them make passing comical noises suggestive of "chattering," "squeaks," "grunts," or "gurgles." It is not surprising that he was so enamored of the drinking song "Kornilo" in Stravinsky's *Pribautki*. First, it was highly presentational—the oboe and clarinet accurately mimic the "gurgle of an emptying bottle"—and second, it sounded quite comical as well. Although the dynamic and textural disjunctions and galloping 6/8 meter contribute greatly, the scherzando quality of the vendor's movement in *Le Pas d'acier* is largely due to an eclectic compilation of such sounds. Outstanding among the bizarre motives are a recurring "gurgle" for two bassoons (three after reh 51, and so on) and a passage reminiscent of a someone banging out arbitrary chords up and down a piano keyboard (beginning reh. 66, and so on).[61] The exaggerated climactic statement of this silliness also contributes to the humorous effect. But the whole movement is rife with orchestrational tricks: wide *portamenti*, *al tallone* bowing and *col legno* triple and quadruple stops, the close juxtaposition of muted and unmuted trumpets, and Prokofiev's only use of the castanets in a Diaghilev ballet. Clarinets make important motivic statements but can hardly be said to stand out in a movement so pointillistically scored as this. Nevertheless, at least one passage for three clarinets (including bass) shows a strong affinity with that in "Pillage" and elsewhere (three before reh. 68).

A similar example of this scherzando style occurs in the fourth movement in the *Scythian Suite* (reh. 53 to 56). The choice of clarinets to state the theme, the extreme disjunctions of range and dynamics, and instances of bizarre instrumental effects conspire to make these vermin more comical than fearsome. The softly stated "chattering" by the flutes in octaves and the odd three and one-half octave leaps beginning at reh. 54 with their delightful, piccolo-accentuated climaxes create a distinctive caricature, perhaps intended as comic relief (this is certainly not *Le Sacre du printemps*!). A similar example where capricious-sounding details help to temporarily deflect the overriding character of the work occurs during the false friends march in *L'Enfant prodigue*. The descending cadential motive appended to the march sounds quite like mocking laughter. Features like this perhaps helped inspire Balanchine's "grotesque" choreography.[62]

This is by no means an exhaustive survey. Further consistencies may be found in other types of characterizations in Prokofiev's ballets, from deeply dramatic "seriousness" or "oppression" to presentations of the inanimate or evocations of nature. Despite this constancy, the composer did not resort to the "cookie-cutter" approach often found in the ballet music written by nineteenth-century specialist composers. Like them, however, Prokofiev borrowed from and relied upon the audience's knowledge of the corpus of operatic clichés that date back to Rossini and *mélodrame*. But he went beyond the stereotypical, adding personalizing touches that intensified his characterizations. Whether it is a poignant subtlety during the Prodigal's return (for example, the sub-contra doubling of the final thematic statement as the Prodigal crawls towards his father) or the deliberate circus-like gaudiness as the seven buffoons come on stage (for example, the riot of glissandi and busy percussion), his characterizations are unfailingly incisive and, despite the occasional unexpected wry turn, they are also dramatically apt. Couched in his distinctive harmonic language, orchestration and melodic style, they are also highly individualistic. And thanks to his tutorial with Diaghilev, they were always expressed through remarkably *dansante* music. It is both the consistency and variegation of the "Prokofiev Language" that gives the composer's ballets for Diaghilev their profound sense of drama and dance.

Prokofiev's ballets for Diaghilev: coda

Diaghilev's influence on Prokofiev's ballet career was tremendous: with each Ballets Russes commission he provided direction and guidance. In 1914 Diaghilev persuaded the young, opera-minded composer to write for the ballet (*Ala i Lolli*). The next year he convinced him to adopt a recognizably Russian style (*Chout*). In 1920 he directed the revision of *Chout*, providing a much belated choreographic tutorial. In 1925, at a low point in the composer's career in the West, Diaghilev encouraged his turn towards a new simplicity and offered him a great opportunity for career renewal with a topical ballet on Soviet life (*Le Pas d'acier*). Even as late as 1928–29 the impresario compelled Prokofiev to achieve new heights of expressivity in characterization (*L'Enfant prodigue*). Surely this was not all done with only the company's bottom line in mind—there must have been a special rapport between them. Yet it was slow to develop. For a long time there remained a formal distance between them, no doubt due to Prokofiev's respect for his esteemed elder as well as his customary ingratiation towards those in authority whom he trusted. For all they went through together the two addressed each other in conversations and correspondence using the formal Russian *vï* (you) until October 1927. The previous summer amidst the backstage excitement celebrating *Le Pas d'acier*'s highly successful premier run, Prokofiev had let slip the familiar form *tï* (you) while dedicating the score to the impresario. Embarrassed, he quickly apologized. Nevertheless, in the wake of their estrangement in 1924, they had become much closer and Diaghilev eventually suggested that they *tïkat'* (*tutoyer*). Though theirs would never be the camaraderie of equals that Diaghilev and Stravinsky shared in the best of times, they had arrived just the same at a new plateau of mutual dependence and respect.

Prokofiev held the impresario in highest esteem, seeking his approval and readily accepting his calls for revisions. Other composers who worked for Diaghilev during the 1920s remarked about his uncanny intuitive discernment about music and his ability to stimulate his artists to achieve new heights. Prokofiev seconded the former in his writings and the latter through his ballets for Diaghilev. A comparison of the composer's originals with their replacements from both ends of this collaboration proves the value of Diaghilev's musical and theatrical gift. Prokofiev rarely disputed his judgment and rarer still did so personally (quite unlike his frank confrontations with Stravinsky). The composer meekly accepted the rejection of *Ala i Lolli*, but in a subsequent letter teased the impresario good-naturedly about his lack of understanding. Given Diaghilev's lack of enthusiasm for the project, his captivation with modernism and the company's precarious circumstances, *Ala i Lolli* had no chance whatsoever with the Ballets Russes in 1915. Turned into a concert suite, however, the rejected ballet came back to haunt him. But Diaghilev was wise enough to see Prokofiev's potential as a great ballet composer and offered him another chance, and then another. This faith provides further proof of the impresario's amazing musical discernment.

One piece of sage advice that Diaghilev offered Prokofiev early on after hearing *Ala i Lolli* was to warn him that being enamored of too many kinds of music was folly. In his autobiography the composer recalled objecting, "But surely that will lead to narrowness." Diaghilev's reply was something that took about nine years to sink in, "The cannon shoots far because it doesn't scatter its fire." Prokofiev's quest for fame in the West resulted in some outstanding music to be sure, but it also brought on a degree of tentativeness as well. The estimable critic of *La Revue musicale*, Boris de Schlœzer, sensed this: after the premier of the composer's Second Symphony he wrote, "Each time one hears a new work of Prokofiev, the same question always arises: where does it lead to? And one is tempted to answer, nowhere." Sensing that Prokofiev did not know what he really wanted, de Schlœzer admonished, much as Diaghilev had done, "It is necessary to choose, to be limited and be determined."[63] In June 1925 Prokofiev finally did focalize; his new aesthetic, the one which would remain for the rest of his career, was revealed in *Le Pas d'acier*. With that ballet's success came the freedom to consider a new path for his career. For better or worse, Diaghilev's advice had pointed him homeward. Prokofiev's Russian tour in early 1927 was highly gratifying: he discovered an unconditionally receptive venue for the kind of music he wished to write. The vexing problem of how to cope and appease in post-revolutionary Russia was then hardly a consideration. When at long last he settled his family in Moscow at their Chkalov Street apartment in June 1936, Prokofiev respectfully hung a portrait of the top-hatted impresario on the wall above his desk (see Fig. 18).[64] Over the course of 15 years Diaghilev had exerted a positive influence on both his music and his career. And now under the gray skies of Stalin's Moscow the impresario's dancing eyes and satisfied smile must have given rise to some bouts of warming nostalgia.

Though Prokofiev followed Stravinsky to the Ballets Russes, he worked there on his own stylistic terms. The proof lies in the music. His ballets for Diaghilev are so fundamentally different in concept and style from those of his older colleague that it is difficult to understand why commentators still claim Prokofiev was swayed by Stravinsky. Prokofiev certainly knew his older colleague's music and could play it from memory at the piano, but in spite of their common heritage, the two remained stylistically independent. The confusion lies in the fact that both composers were inspired by similar elements: Russian fairly tales, *khorovods*, neoprimitivism, Diaghilev-approved (that is, exportable) Russianness, and so forth. *Chout* is not *Sacre*'s "clumsy clone," nor is it "modeled after *Petrouchka*."[65] To make such claims is to deny the individuality of one of the century's most individual composers. How can one equate Prokofiev's fundamentally lyrical style with Stravinsky's, which, after *L'Oiseau de feu*, exploited the manipulation of melodic cells to harmonic, rhythmic and melodic ends? One almost suspects a degree of envy for Prokofiev's knack for writing such memorable tunes. Expressive, characterful and accessible melodies meant everything to Prokofiev. Harmonic piquancy came next. Although his rhythms became more engaging they were still only meant for propulsion. That is the ballet style of Prokofiev. Even in the face of Diaghilev's conversion and Stravinsky's tutelage Prokofiev upheld his personal ethos of originality and stylistic independence.

Prokofiev's ballets for Diaghilev are essential to understanding the composer's oeuvre. They offer perhaps the best vantage point to observe his constancy of musical style. These ballets certainly stand apart from their Soviet successors in their greater proportion of dissonance, rhythmic intensity, density of lines and restive juxtaposition of thematic material. Yet it is significant that this is a question of degree. Every ballet from *Chout* to *Tale of the Stone Flower* was created using the same stylistic palette—only the emphasis differs. *Le Pas d'acier* marks the beginning of his turn from a predominantly modern outlook to one that featured simpler harmonies and emotive lyricism. His self-proclaimed new simplicity became more noticeable in *L'Enfant prodigue*, but it is important to remember that this style is evident in even earlier works, just as strident harmonies and restless ostinati can be found both here and in his subsequent works.

The ballets for Diaghilev fully demonstrate Prokofiev's innate sense of theatricality. That his skills were honed as a result of collaborations with the likes of Massine, Larionov, Yakulov, Kochno, and especially Diaghilev is obvious. But the first ballet of Prokofiev's to be produced, *Chout*, is a mature and polished piece of dance theatre, in its own way as dramatically satisfying and *dansante* as *Romeo and Juliet*. The composer's lyricism, clear rhythm and phrasing obviously contributed greatly to the music's danceable quality. It is paradoxical that so natural a composer for the dance—one whose music expresses the movements almost by itself—had to be converted to the genre. It is also paradoxical that Prokofiev's greatest fame in western theatres in the 1920s came not from his beloved operas but from his ballets for Diaghilev.[66]

Following Stravinsky's lead with *Petrouchka* and *Le Sacre du printemps*, Prokofiev's ballet scores controlled, to a great extent, the choreographic response; this even after he sublimed his presentational style into the realm of eminently danceable music. Though given a narrative, suggested timings and sometimes a visual concept, Prokofiev was left with enormous latitude. The composer determined the narrative's defining movements through the music, quite unlike Chaikovsky for whom the balletmaster dictated the tempo, meter, style, duration and musical character. Larionov, Massine and Balanchine were given essentially completed scores. Only Diaghilev could ask for changes in the music. Perhaps modern ballet choreography, with its movement against the dictates of the music, evolved in self-defense.

Finally one must acknowledge the artistry of the music itself. Although the appraisal of ballet music ought to be made in light of the collaboration, the music often deserves further examination on its own merits. This is especially true regarding the ballet music Prokofiev composed for Diaghilev, not because it was a poor partner, quite the contrary, by degrees it outclassed the ballets it served. Only *L'Enfant prodigue* survives as a ballet entity. The earlier ballets disappeared from the repertory for reasons other than their music.

As Prokofiev's musical achievement was variable, so too his ballets for Diaghilev. Nevertheless, each displays sound craftsmanship along with plenty of arresting turns of phrase and beguiling charm. The importance of *Le Pas d'acier* is unmistakable, with its multivalent combination of topical allusions and new simplicity, its humor and its romance. Nabokov called it "Prokofiev's greatest success in Paris." Yet there is no denying that this score is not the musical achievement that *Chout* or *L'Enfant prodigue* are. Prokofiev labored over these scores far longer than he did with *Le Pas d'acier*. And Diaghilev was more involved (perhaps interested, as well) in making them the best that they could be. The composer recalled that the impresario rated *L'Enfant prodigue* "above all my other works."[67]

As a ballet score *L'Enfant prodigue* surpasses *Chout*. The musical integrity of *Chout* suffers, as do many ballets, from precompositional strictures. The story was laden with fine points and with the added entr'actes the music had an unfortunate repetitiveness, a fault that was duly noted by the critics. The Suite extracted from the ballet might seem to be a good alternative except for its regrettable omissions, such as the seven buffoons' entry/exit music, their "council music," and many felicitous narrative links which are not included. Nevertheless, *Chout* is Prokofiev's most accomplished score for Diaghilev. It represents not only his second and third chance to please the impresario, but the showpiece for his Paris and London theatrical debuts as well. It is obvious that the composer was driven to excel in *Chout*.

Each of Prokofiev's ballets for Diaghilev fulfilled its purpose splendidly. Their well-considered colors, distinct characterizations and appealing tunefulness makes them enjoyable even without theatrical trappings. There should be no need to cast the Diaghilev ballets against the Soviet ones; certainly no Prokofiev enthusiast would wish to be without either. But in light of their neglect at the expense of *Romeo and Juliet* and *Cinderella*, we might call attention to Prokofiev's ballets for Diaghilev so that a wider audience can savor their youthful optimism and exuberance and their reflection of an important period in the composer's life. Above all, the ballet *Chout* is most deserving of a revival, Larionov's madcap décor, costumes, choreography and all. Prokofiev remained justifiably proud of his music for this ballet, later admonishing his biographer Nestyev that "it should be recommended to the reader."[68] This music clearly captures the flavor of Russian fantasy as successfully as the canonized examples by Rimsky-Korsakov, Musorgsky, Lyadov and Stravinsky. *Chout* does what only the best ballet scores can do: satisfy musically and fire the imagination of dancers and listeners alike. It made an auspicious beginning for Prokofiev's ballet career.

Notes

1. "Prokofieff Speaks," *New York Times*, 2 February 1930. In an article for Moscow's *Izvestiya* in November 1934, Prokofiev again called for a "new simplicity," this time to suit the needs of Soviet Russia. Quoted in Harlow Robinson, *Sergei Prokofiev: A Biography* (New York, 1987), p. 294.
2. See Elizabeth Souritz, *Soviet Choreographers in the 1920s*, trans. by Lynn Visson, ed. with additional trans. by Sally Burne (Durham, NC, 1990), pp. 185-96, for a detailed account of *Joseph the Beautiful*.
3. Michael Kennedy, *The Works of Ralph Vaughan Williams* (London, 1964; second edn, 1980), pp. 200–202. Vaughan Williams, a balletophobe, was apparently relieved by the rejection. He wrote Keynes' sister-in-law, "it really wdnt. [sic] have suited the sham serious really decadent and frivolous attitude of the R.B. [Russian Ballet] toward everything—can you imagine *Job* sandwiched between *Les Biches* and *Cimarosiana*—and that dreadful pseudo-cultured audience saying to each other 'My dear, have you seen God at the Ballets Russes?'" The first staged performance of *Job* was given in London in July 1931, with Anton Dolin as Satan and John MacNair as Job).
4. See George Balanchine's *Choreography By George Balanchine, a Catalog of Works* (New York, 1984), p. 92, and *Balanchine's Complete Stories of the Great Ballets* (Garden City, NY, 1977), pp. 451–6.
5. Lincoln Kirstein, *Four Centuries of Ballet: Fifty Masterworks* (New York, NY, 1970; reprint edn., 1984), p. 194.
6. In actuality, this "skyscraper," erected in 1926, was a modest-sized, 14-story building, and its "medium sized concert hall" was just a 150-seat recital room on the second floor. Its stage was large enough to hold a nine-foot concert grand, but not much more. The building had its "golden key" ceremony on 23 February 1927, but without a performance of Prokofiev's Overture. By then the piece had been premiered in Moscow by the conductorless Persimfans (on 7 February 1927) during the composer's ten-week visit to Russia. This new Aeolian Building should not be confused with the company's previous headquarters on 42nd Street, whose 1100-seat Aeolian Hall saw the premier of Gershwin's *Rhapsody in Blue* with Paul Whiteman's Orchestra in 1924. The Aeolian Company manufactured pianos and sold Aeolian Duo-Art piano rolls; Prokofiev was one of their recording artists.
7. Autobiography, in *S. S. Prokof'yev, materialï, dokumentï, vospominaniya* (Moscow, 1961), p. 281. By writing "without accidentals" Prokofiev means that his three main themes have no chromaticism. The first episode (reh. 12) belies this, however, although it begins in the Dorian mode. The overture opens and closes in B-flat major. The refrain (A) is in three parts, the middle of which is in the key of A major, but with no accidentals in its key signature. Section C (reh. 30) is also in A major, this time with the proper key signature.

8. In his diary he admitted that orchestrating the "American" Overture for this unusual combination of instruments was a lot more trouble than he had thought it would be. He finished the piece on 24 August.

9. "Prokofiev Speaks," *New York Times*, 2 February 1930.

10. Letter to Lifar dated 1 December 1928. Serge Lifar, *Serge Diaghilev, his life his work his legend, an intimate biography* (New York, 1940), p. 341.

11. Letter dated 26 December 1928 from Paris from Harlow Robinson, *Selected Letters of Sergei Prokofiev* (Boston, 1998), p. 199. Serge Koussevitzky had became the conductor of the Boston Symphony Orchestra in 1924.

12. A more detailed synopsis "adapted from the program" by Alexander Schouvaloff in his *The Art of the Ballets Russes* (New Haven, CT, and London, 1997), p. 300, is as follows:

> Scene 1: Home. Two confidants of the prodigal son arrange a store of wine jugs as if embarking on a journey. The prodigal son comes out of the tent followed by his two [female] servants [sisters in Prokofiev's score]. They try to engage his attention but he is in high spirits and dances energetically, acting out the adventures he and his confidantes will have when he leaves home. His dance stops when he finds himself face to face with his stern father. The father beckons to him, but then the prodigal son backs away. Finally he ignores his father and the servants, summons up his two confidants and points to the open road. With a flourish they leave. The servants watch in dismay but the father raises his hand in unacknowledged farewell.

> Scene 2: In a far country. A scene of great revelry in a tent by a group of grotesquely bald men is interrupted by the entrance of the prodigal son and his confidants. The group is suspicious at first but when the prodigal son offers them his wine they all begin to dance exuberantly again. They are joined by the seductress who voluptuously captivates the prodigal son until he is completely in her power. She then makes him drink and so completely intoxicates him that he collapses in a stupor. He is then robbed by his confidants and the other revelers, with the seductress snatching the medallion from round his neck. Slowly the prodigal son awakens. He realizes what has happened and acknowledges the betrayal of his confidants and his own self-betrayal. He drags himself on his knees back towards his home. The others return and divide their loot.

> Scene 3: Home. The prodigal son, exhausted, returns crawling and suddenly sees that he has reached his home. The servants see him, and, overjoyed, help him. The father comes out of the tent and remains motionless while the prodigal son struggles towards him. Finally the father shows his forgiveness and holds him in his arms like a child.

13. See Souritz, *Soviet Choreographers*, p. 194.

14. Solomon Volkov, *Balanchine's Tchaikovsky: Interviews with George Balanchine*, trans. Antonina W. Bouis (New York, 1985), p. 210.

15. From Balanchine's interview with Emile Ardolino, producer of the 1978 video taped production of *The Prodigal Son* for Dance in America (included in the program booklet accompanying Nonesuch Dance Collection video tape no. 40179-3, 1995).

16. Ibid.

17. Katherine Sorly Walker, *De Basil's Ballets Russes* (London and Melbourne, 1982), p. 90.

18. Danilova, p. 89.

19. Prokofiev constructed the Suite in 1929 and led its premier in Paris on 7 March 1931. He told Dukelsky in a June 1932 letter that the Suite "was made from the material that did not go into the Fourth Symphony. So it's no wonder that it does not include

the best numbers, for example, the A-minor rondo or the concluding andante. They make up the middle two movements of the Symphony ... the Fourth, which is infinitely more significant than the Suite, which [Bruno] Walter performed ... I didn't foresee that Walter would become so fixated on the Suite." Letter quoted from Robinson, *Selected Letters*, p. 149.

This five-movement Suite is not Prokofiev's best; the opening and closing movements sound forced. Unlike his previous ballets Suites this one's music does not proceed in chronological order. The middle three movements are the most successful because they are based on whole numbers from the ballet, Drunkenness, Pillage, and Awakening/Remorse with a section from the finale, respectively. The latter movement includes a felicitous new touch added to its conclusion, which perhaps compensates for the workaday transition linking bar 209 in the finale back to bar 165 for the close. In the first movement the grafting of material from the opening of the pas de deux onto the first number, The Departure and the resulting stops and starts are not altogether successful. The last movement is largely derived from no.2 (Meeting of Friends) but opens and closes with material from or intended for no. 4 (The Dancers): the beginning is reh. 74–76 of the latter and the end must surely be an outtake from the old no. 4. If this assumption is correct, Diaghilev's dissatisfaction is understandable. The ending sounds insipid.

20. Letter dated 30 May 1929. M.G. Kozlova and N.R. Yatsenko, eds, *Prokof'yev i N. Ya. Myaskovskiy perepiska* (Moscow, 1977), p. 313. The introduction to the Symphony's first movement was newly written, but the rest of the movement was not (see below).

21. In early October 1929 Koussevitzky and Prokofiev agreed to delay the premier of this Symphony, saving it for the fiftieth anniversary season of the Boston Symphony. The composer set it aside, finishing it on 23 June 1930. It was premiered in Boston on 14 November 1930.

22. Lifar, *Diaghilev*, p. 338.

23. This appellation comes by way of Prokofiev, who, in a letter to Romanov dated 17 October 1925 referred to this music as such: "then in the middle of the Overture there must be a love scene, of real tenderness."

24. See Bernard Taper *Balanchine: A Biography* (New York, 1984), p. 111.

25. The "Matelote" replacement for no. 4 appears beginning at reh. 6 (*allegro eroico*) in the Symphony, op. 47 (the slow introduction was apparently newly composed). The disputed "fem." secondary theme follows at reh. 16 (*più tranquillo*; 2:41 into Järvi's Chandos recording). Despite Prokofiev's affection for the original, I believe Diaghilev landed the better movement, if for no other reason than the feebleness of "fem."

26. See Ch. 4 footnote 50 and my "*On the Dnieper*: Reappraisal of an Unfairly Rejected Opus,'" in *Three Oranges Journal*, 2 (November 2001), p. 24–9.

27. Robert Brussel, *Le Figaro*, 20 December 1932. This is yet another example of western audiences' resistance to Prokofiev's redirection towards lyricism.

28. Boris de Schlœzer, "La Musique," *La Revue contemporaine*, 1 February 1923, p. 248. Taruskin notes the irony of de Schlœzer's example, "a *tombeau* for Debussy that faithfully mimics an Orthodox funeral service," that is actually "Stravinsky's valedictory to his Russian period." This review appeared some months before the premier of Stravinsky's incontestably neoclassical *Octour*. Richard Taruskin, "Back to Whom?" Neoclassicism As Ideology," *Nineteenth-Century Music*, **16**, no. 3 (Spring 1993), p. 290.

29. Scott Messing, *Neoclassicism in Music: From the Genesis of the Concept through the Schoenberg/Stravinsky Polemic*. (Ann Arbor, MI, 1988; reprint edn, Rochester, NY, 1996), p. 153.

30. When questioned by an interviewer from the Russian Warsaw newspaper, *Za svobodu!* in January 1925, "does he really come from Bach? And is he not along a lateral line from his predecessor Vivaldi?" Prokofiev answered, "In essence it is not that important: it is important that it is from the epoch which Bach crowned." Diary entry, 23 January 1925.

31. For his part Stravinsky angrily (jealously?) attacked Prokofiev's popular Third Piano Concerto: "This is unbearable! This is some sort of pseudo-classical Russian style! It is some kind of phoney Bach [Bachestov]." This tirade, witnessed by Dukelsky, occurred after a performance of the Concerto at Princess Polignac's in June 1925.

32. Sergey Sergeyevich Prokofiev, "Autobiography", trans. and ed. by Oleg Prokofiev; assoc. ed. Christopher Plamer, in *Sergei Prokofiev Secret Diary, 1927 and Other Writings* (Boston, MA, 1992), p. 273.

33. Nicholas Nabokov, *Old Friends and New Music* (Boston, MA, 1951), p. 162.

34. Messing cites the conductor Ansermet as being an important promoter of Stravinsky's aesthetics as well as his music in the 1920s (p. 99ff).

35. Ibid., p. 102. Since the summer of 1915 when he censured impressionism during an interview for Carl Van Vechten's book *Music After the War*, Stravinsky regularly promoted himself as champion of "simplicity" (that is, anti-romanticism and anti-impressionism).

36. *Observer*, 3 July 1921, quoted in Messing, p. 104.

37. Diary entry, 3 June 1926.

38. Letter of 9 August 1926 from Robinson, *Selected Letters*, p. 108.

39. Messing, pp. 65–7. During his Soviet career Prokofiev did turn towards retrospectivism (for example, *Cinderella*) but partly out of political expedience.

40. Letter to Myaskovsky, dated 9 July 1928; as translated in Robinson, *Selected Letters*, pp. 274–5.

41. Nabokov, *Old Friends*, pp. 169–70.

42. Prokofiev, "Autobiography," p. 288.

43. Nestyev, *Prokoviev*, p. 230.

44. Leonid Sabaneyeff, *Modern Russian Composers* (London, 1927), p. 93.

45. Nabokov, *Old Friends*, p. 167.

46. Quoted by Alexander Werth in "The Real Prokofiev," *The Nation*, 176 (4 April 1953), p. 286. Prokofiev's "dictionary of idioms" (his compositional palette) may be sampled quite conveniently by listening to his set of 20 piano pieces, *Visions fugitives*, op. 22 (1915–17).

47. Brown, p. 6.

48. Ibid., p. 8.

49. For example, the "Danse du rire" is a double period, and the deployment of the entrée and "Danse du rire" forms a symmetry around the intervening *ballet d'action*.

50. The finale of the *Scythian Suite* is a dubious example in that the suite does not represent the entirety or the organization of the original ballet scene.

51. Another example is the finale of *Sur le Borysthène*.

52. In a nutshell the scenario Prokofiev composed to is as follows: Natasha realizes she has lost her former love Serge to Olga when he arrives home from a lengthy absence, in the middle of the ballet Olga is forced to abandon Serge for a prearranged marriage, and at the end, after helping the reunite the lovers, Natasha, with a broken heart, watches them depart. The opening of the Prologue returns as the B section of the Epilogue, and its middle section reappears in the middle of the Betrothal (no. 5). Natasha's flute motive is heard in each of her numbers (nos. 2, 8, 10); the first half of no. 10 is basically a rearrangement of no. 2; the theme from Olga's and Serge's pas de deux (no. 3) returns in no. 8 (Olga's melancholy solo); and the A theme of the

Betrothal becomes the A section of the Epilogue. Unity is also promoted by the recurrence of cadential passages (for example, bars 8–9 in no. 7 returns in the Betrothal).

53. Balanchine took advantage of this by having the servants relocate the jugs of wine in both spots.

Prokofiev's ballet music did not always have a visual conception or a dramatic justification behind it. When the choreographer Lavrovsky asked the composer what the twelve arresting, equally spaced tutti chords at the end of Romeo's and Tybalt's duel in *Romeo and Juliet* were supposed to signify, he replied, "Nothing," in an "obviously nettled" tone according to the choreographer. "But what am I supposed to do on stage at that point?" Lavrovsky persisted. "Whatever you like," was his laconic reply. Leonid Lavrovsky, "Repository of Creative Talent," in *S. Prokofiev: Autobiography, Articles, Reminiscences*, ed. S. Shlifshteyn (Moscow, n.d.), p. 270.

54. In the 1978 film Balanchine cuts the first statement of this theme and has the Prodigal emerge from his tent during the second, in a manner which in no way reflects the character of Prokofiev's theme. In this production the Prodigal is all defiance and exuberance in no. 1.

55. Tonal centers in Prokofiev's enriched harmonic language are best considered on a macro level, encompassing all related keys that can gravitate to the primary one. Thus music centering around his favorite "C" incorporates not only the usual A minor and C minor, but keys a half step away and their relatives and parallels.

56. Romeo is introduced in the key of F in no. 2, Juliet in C in no. 10. They fall in love in "Madrigal," no. 16, in G. They declare their love in the balcony scene in B-flat, and consummate it at the opening of Act III by ascending a whole step to their "eternal love key," of C major. Because of their forced separation, Juliet obtains a potion and acquiesces to marry Paris (E minor). She sleeps in the crypt in C major. Romeo believes her dead and kills himself in distant F minor (but the parallel minor of his original key). Juliet awakens and seeing Romeo dead, kills herself in F# minor, a tritone away from her key. But almost immediately they are reunited for eternity in pure C major.

57. Translated from Prokofiev "Autobiography," in *S. S. Prokof'yev, materialï, dokumentï, vospominaniya* (Moscow, 1961), pp. 148–9. Prokofiev considered the last mentioned to be inflections of the other lines rather that a separate entity, obviously an attempt to counteract its prominence in critical notices. Prokofiev also referred to a "classical line," for which he mentions his use of traditional forms (sonatas, concertos) and his imitation of eighteenth-century formal dances. The latter appear in only two of the nine ballets, both politically safe retrospective works from his Soviet period.

58. This was Stravinsky's primary complaint about Prokofiev's score.

59. I do not mean to imply that Russians have a monopoly on comic bassoon characterizations; Ravel's *Daphnis et Chloë*, to cite just one example from Ballets Russes fare, exploited the bassoons' sonority in order to establish the grotesque character of Dorcon's dance (reh. 32).

60. Earlier Prokofiev had relied on the the instrument's inherent jocularity in his piano piece op. 12, no. 9, entitled "Humorous Scherzo (for four bassoons)."

61. Despite the impression, this is a passage of willfully conceived polymodality. A rising and falling tritone motive accompanies a series of unrelated triads (beginning C, B, D, E and so forth). At the bubbly climax two after reh. 71 C is colored by the D-flats and B's on either side.

62. It is so labeled by the choreographer in his *Balanchine's Complete Stories*, p. 453.

63. Boris de Schlœzer, "2e Symphonie de Serge Prokofieff" *La Revue musicale* 4 (7 January 1925), p. 61.

64. Natalia Savkina, "Back in the USSR," *Three Oranges*, 1 (January 2001), p. 12.

65. These accusations have been made by Taruskin and Austin, respectively.

66. A letter from the composer to Berlin choreographer Max Terpis dated 17 June 1925 is telling: "Do they want to perform the opera [*Oranges*] and the ballet [*Chout*]? Or if they perform the ballet they will not perform the opera? The performance of the opera is of great importance for me and the performance of the ballet is a question of minor importance. Therefore if the performance of the ballet excludes the performance of the opera I will not perform the ballet."

67. Prokofiev made this claim to Nestyev in defense of his period abroad and his association with Diaghilev and Koussevitzky. Nestyev, "New Discoveries,", in *Sergei Prokofiev: Materials, Articles, Interviews* (Moscow, 1975), p. 90.

68. Ibid., p. 91.

Select bibliography

Afanas'yev, A.N. (1957), *Narodnïye russkiye skazki*, vol. 3, reprint edn, Moscow: Gosudarstvennoye izdatel'stvo khudozhestvennoy literaturï.

Aladzhalov, S. (1971), *Georgiy Yakulov*, Erevan: Armyanskoye teatral'noye obshchestvo, Institut iskusstv Akademii nauk Arm. SSR.

Ansermet, E. (1996), *Ernest Ansermet: Correspondences avec des Compositeurs Européens (1916–1966)*, ed. C. Tappolet, Geneva: Georg Éditeur.

Antheil, G. (1946), *Bad Boy of Music*, Garden City, NY: Doubleday, Doran.

Archer, K. and Hodson, M. (1995), "Skating Rink: cubism on wheels," *Dance Now*, **4** (4), Winter, 14–18.

Baer, N. Van Norman (ed.) (1988), *The Art of Enchantment: Diaghilev's Ballets Russes 1909–1929*, San Francisco: Fine Arts Museum of San Francisco.

—— (ed.) (1995), *Paris Modern: The Swedish Ballet 1920–1925*, San Francisco: Fine Arts Museum of San Francisco.

—— (ed.) (1991), *Theatre in Revolution: Russian Avant-Garde Stage Design 1913–1925*, New York: Thames and Hudson.

Banes, S. (1978), "Introduction to the Ballet Suédois," *Ballet Review*, **7**, 28–59.

Beaumont, C.W. (1975), *Bookseller at the Ballet: Memoirs 1891 to 1929* [incorporating *The Diaghilev Ballet in London*], London: C.W. Beaumont.

Berlin, E. (1980), *Ragtime: A Musical and Cultural History*, Berkeley and Los Angeles, CA: University of California Press.

Bibliothèque Nationale. (1979), *Diaghilev. Les Ballets Russes* [exhibition guide], Foreword by G. Le Rider, Paris: Bibliothèque Nationale.

Blok, V. (ed.) (1978), *Sergei Prokofiev: Materials, Articles, Interviews* [English translation of *Materialï, stat'i, interv'yu*], Moscow: Progress Publishers.

Boganova, T.V. (1961), *Natsional'no-russkiye traditsii v muzïke S.S. Prokof'yeva*, Moscow: Sovetskiy kompozitor.

Bowlt, J.E. (1977), "Constructivism and Russian stage design," *Performing Arts Journal*, **1** (3), Winter, 62–84.

—— (1982), *Russian Stage Design: Scenic Innovation 1900–1930*, Jackson, MS: Mississippi Museum of Art.

—— (1984), "When life was a cabaret," *ART News*, December, 123–7.

Brown, M.H. (1967), "The symphonies of Sergei Prokofiev," PhD dissertation, Florida State University.

—— (1985), "Prokofiev's Correspondence with Stravinsky and Shostakovich," in *Slavonic and Western Music: Essays for Gerald Abraham*, Eds. M.H.

Brown and R.J. Wiley, Russian Music Studies, no. 12, Ann Arbor, MI: UMI Research Press, pp. 271–92.

——— (1986), "Stravinsky and Prokofiev: Sizing Up the Competition," in *Confronting Stravinsky: Man, Musician and Modernist*, ed. J. Pasler, Berkeley and Los Angeles, CA: University of California Press, pp. 39–50.

Buckle, R. (1979), *Diaghilev*, New York: Atheneum.

——— (1988), *George Balanchine, Balletmaster*, New York: Random House.

Calvocoressi, M.D. (1933), *Musicians' Gallery: Music and Ballet in Paris and London*, London: Faber and Faber.

"Catalog of the Ballet Material and Manuscripts from the Serge Lifar Collection," prepared by Sotheby's of London for a public auction held on 9 May 1984.

Craft, R. (1982–85), *Stravinsky: Selected Correspondence*, 3 vols, New York: Knopf.

Drummond, J. (1997), *Speaking of Diaghilev*, London: Faber and Faber.

Duke, V. (1945), *Passport to Paris*, Boston, MA: Little, Brown.

Egorova, E. (1999), "The Diaghilev family in Perm," trans. I. Huntoon, in *The Ballets Russes and Its World*, eds. L. Garafola and N. van Norman Baer, New Haven, CT, and London: Yale University Press, pp. 13–21.

Fokine, M. (1961), *Fokine: Memoirs of a Ballet Master*, trans. V. Fokine, ed. A. Chujoy, Boston, MA, and Toronto: Little, Brown.

Fülöp-Miller, R. and Gregor, J. (1930), *Russian Theatre: Its Character and History with especial Reference to the Revolutionary Period*, trans. P. England, New York: Benjamin Blom.

Garafola, L. (1989), *Diaghilev's Ballets Russes*, New York: Oxford University Press.

García-Márquez, V. (1995), *The Ballets Russes: Colonel de Basil's Ballets Russes de Monte Carlo 1932–1952*, New York: Knopf.

George, W. (1966), *Larionov*, Paris: La Bibliothèque des Paris Arts.

Glebov, I. (Boris Asafyev) (1927), *Sergei Prokof'yev*, Leningrad: Triton.

Goossens, E. (1951), *Overture and Beginners. A Musical Autobiography*, London: Methuen.

Grigoriev, S.L. (1960), *The Diaghilev Ballet 1909–1929*, trans. V. Bowen, London: Constable, 1953; reprint edn, Harmondsworth: Penguin Books.

Häger, B. (ed.) (1990), *Ballets Suédois*, trans. R. Sherman, New York: H 3arry N. Abrams.

Halbreich, H. (1992), *Honegger: Un musicien dans la cité des hommes*, Paris: Fayard.

Haskell, A. (1934), *Balletomania: The Story of an Obsession*, New York: Simon and Schuster.

Haskell, A. and Nouvel, W. (1978), *Diaghileff: His Artistic and Private Life*, New York: Simon and Schuster, 1935; reprint edn, New York: Da Capo Press.

Jablonski, E. (1987), *Gershwin*, New York: Doubleday.

Kameneff, V. (1936), *Russian Ballet through Russian Eyes*, London: Russian Books and Library.

Kennedy, M. (1980), *The Works of Ralph Vaughan Williams*, London: Oxford University Press, 1964; second edn.

Kholopov, Y.N. (1967), "Diatonicheskiye ladï i tertsovïye khromaticheskiye sistemï v muzïke Prokof'yeva," in *Ot Lyulli do nashikh dney*, ed. V.D. Konen, Moscow: Muzïka, pp. 256–79.

—— (1967), *Sovremennïe chertï garmonii Prokof'yeva*, Moscow: Izdatel'stvo muzïka.

Kirby, M. (1971), *Futurist Performance*, New York: E.P. Dutton.

Kochno, B. (1970), *Diaghilev and the Ballets Russes*, trans. A. Foulke, New York: Harper and Row.

Lifar, S. (1940), *Serge Diaghilev: His Life, Work and Legend; an Intimate Biography*, New York: Putnam's Sons.

Lourié, A. (1931), *Sergei Koussevitzky and His Epoch*, New York: Knopf.

Macdonald, N. (1975), *Diaghilev Observed by Critics in England and the United States 1911–1929*, New York: Dance Horizons.

Massine, L. (1968), *My Life in Ballet*, eds P. Hartnoll and R. Rubens, London: Macmillan.

Messing, S. (1996), *Neoclassicism in Music: From the Genesis of the Concept Through the Schoenberg/Stravinsky Polemic*, Ann Arbor, MI: UMI Research Press, 1988; reprint edn, Rochester, NY: University of Rochester Press.

Milhaud, D. (1952), *Notes without Music*, trans. D. Evans, ed. R.H. Myers, London: Dennis Dobson.

Minturn, N. (1997), *The Music of Sergei Prokofiev*, Composers of the Twentieth Century series, New Haven, CT, and London: Yale University Press.

Nabokov, N. (1942), "Sergei Prokofiev," *Atlantic Monthly*, July, 62–70.

—— (1951), *Old Friends and New Music*, Boston, MA: Little, Brown.

Nestyev, I. (1971), *Prokofiev*, trans. F. Jonas. Stanford, CA: Stanford University Press, 1960; reprint edn.

—— (1973), *Zhizn' Sergeya Prokof'yeva*, Moscow: Sovetskiy kompozitor.

—— (1999), "Diaghilev's musical education," trans. R. Johnson, in *The Ballets Russes and Its World*, ed. L. Garafola and N. Van Norman Baer, New Haven, CT, and London: Yale University Press, pp. 23–42.

Nest'yev, I.V. and Edel'man, G.Y., eds (1965), *Sergey Prokof'yev: Stat'i i materialï*, revised second edn (originally *Sergey Prokof'yev 1953–63: Stat'i i materialï*, 1962), Moscow: Izdatel'stvo Muzïka.

Oberzaucher-Schüller, G. (1992), "'Schrieben Sie die Musik so, daß sie russische ist …' Der Balletkomponist Sergej Prokofjew in der ästhetischen Pflicht seiner Auftraggeber," in *Bericht über das Internationale Symposium 'Sergej Prokofjew—Aspekte seines Werkes und der Biographie,'* ed. K. Niemöller, Regensburg: Gustav Bosse Verlag, pp. 207–50.

Orenstein, A. (1975), *Ravel: Man and Musician*, New York: Columbia University Press.

Parton, A. (1993), *Mikhail Larionov and the Russian Avant-Garde*, Princeton, NJ: Princeton University Press.

Payton, R.J. (1974), "The futurist musicians: Francesco Balilla Pratella and Luigi Russolo," PhD dissertation, University of Chicago.

—— (1976),"The music of futurism: concerts and polemics," *Musical Quarterly*, **62** (1), January, 25–45.

Perloff, N. (1993), *Art and the Everyday: Popular Entertainment and the Circle of Erik Satie*, Oxford: Clarendon Press.

Pisani, M.V. (1997), "A Kapustnik in the American Opera House: modernism and Prokofiev's *Love for Three Oranges*," *Musical Quarterly*, Winter, 487–515.

Pollack, H. (1995), *Skyscraper Lullaby: The Life and Music of John Alden Carpenter*, Washington, DC, and London: Smithsonian Institution Press.

Poulenc, F. (1978), *My Friends and Myself*, trans. J. Harding, ed. S. Audel, London: Dennis Dobson.

Prokofiev, S.S. (1979), *Prokofiev by Prokofiev: A Composer's Memoir*, trans. G. Daniels, ed. D.H. Appel, Garden City, NJ: Doubleday.

—— (1984), "Prokofiev's Correspondence with Stravinsky and Shostakovich," trans.N. Rodrigues and M.H. Brown, in *Slavic and Western Music: Essays for Gerald Abraham*, ed. M.H. Brown, Russian Music Studies, no. 12, Ann Arbor, MI: UMII Research Press, pp. 271–92.

—— (1998), *Selected Letters of Sergei Prokofiev*, ed. and trans. H. Robinson, Boston, MA: Northeastern University Press.

—— (1992), *Sergei Prokofiev Soviet Diary 1927 and Other Writings*, trans. and ed. O. Prokofiev, associate ed. C. Palmer, Boston, MA: Northeastern University Press.

—— (2002), *Dnevnik 1907–33* [Diary 1907–33], 2 vols, ed. and foreword Svyatoslav Prokofiev, Paris: sprkfv.

Prokof'yev, S.S. and Myaskovsky, N.Y. (1976), *S.S. Prokof'yev i N. Ya. Myaskovsky Perepiska*, eds. M.G. Kozlova and N.R. Yatsenko, Moscow: Sovetskiy kompozitor.

Propert, W.A. (1931), *The Russian Ballet in Western Europe 1921–1929*, London: John Lane and the Bodley Head.

—— (1972), *The Russian Ballet in Western Europe 1909–1920*, New York: John Lane, 1921; reprint edn, Benjamin Blom.

Ries, F.W.D. (1986), *The Dance Theatre of Jean Cocteau*, Theatre and Dramatic Studies, no. 33, Ann Arbor, MI: UMI Research Press.

Rimsky-Korsakov, N.A. (1951), *Sto russkikh narodnïkh pesen*, St Petersburg, 1877; reprint edn, Moscow and Leningrad: Gosudarstvennoye muzïkal'noye izdatel'stvo.

Robinson, H. (1987), *Sergei Prokofiev: A Biography*, New York: Viking Penguin.

Sabaneyeff, L. [Sabaneyev] (1927), "Two more Russian critiques," trans. S.W. Pring, *Music and Letters*, 8, October, 425–31.

—— (1928), "Russia's strong man," *Modern Music*, 6, January–February, 3–9.

Savkina, N. (1984), *Prokofiev, His Life and Times*, trans. C. Young, Neptune City, NJ: Paganiniana Publications [translation of *Sergey Sergeyevich Prokof'yev*, Moscow: Muzïka, 1982].

—— (2001), "Back in the USSR," *Three Oranges*, 1, January, 12–13.

Sayers, L.-A. (1996), "Sergei Diaghilev's 'Soviet' ballet: *Les Pas d'acier* and its relationship to Russian constructivism," *Experiment/Eksperiment*, 2, 100–125.

Scholl, T. (1994), *From Petipa to Balanchine*, London: Routledge.

Shlifshteyn, S.I. (ed.) (n.d.) *S. Prokofiev: Autobiography, Articles, Reminiscences*, trans. R. Prokofieva, Moscow: Foreign Languages Publishing House.

—— (ed.) (1961), *S. S. Prokof'yev: Materialï, dokumentï, vospominaniya*, second edn, Moscow: Gosudarstvennoye muzïkal'noye izdatel'stvo.

—— (ed.) (1965), *Sergey Prokof'yev: Al'bom*, Moscow: Muzïka.

Smith, M.E. (1988), "Music for the ballet-pantomime at the Paris Opéra, 1825–1850," PhD dissertation, Yale University.

Sokolova, L. (1989), *Dancing for Diaghilev*, ed. R. Buckle, London: John Murray, 1960; reprint edn., San Francisco, CA: Mercury House.

Souritz, E. [Surits, E.]. (1980), "Soviet ballet of the 1920s and the influence of constructivism," *Soviet Union/Sovétique Union*, 7, 112–37.

—— (1990), *Soviet Choreographers in the 1920s*, trans. L. Visson, ed. with additional translations by S. Banes, Durham, NC: Duke University Press.

—— (1990), "The Young Balanchine in Russia," *Ballet Review*, 18, Summer, 66–71.

—— (1991), "Constructivism and Dance," in *Theatre in Revolution: Russian Avant-Garde Stage Design 1913–1925*, ed. N. van Norman Baer, New York: Thames and Hudson, pp. 129–43.

Stravinsky, I. (1953), "The Diaghilev I Knew," trans. M. de Acosta, *Atlantic Monthly*, November, 33–6.

—— (1962), *An Autobiography*, New York: Simon and Schuster, 1936; reprint edn., New York: Norton.

Stravinsky, I. and Craft, R. (1980), *Conversations with Igor Stravinsky*, Garden City, NY: Doubleday, 1959; reprint edn., Berkeley and Los Angeles, CA: University of California Press.

—— (1981), *Expositions and Developments*, Garden City, NY: Doubleday, 1962; reprint edn., Berkeley and Los Angeles, CA: University of California Press.

—— (1981), *Memories and Commentaries*, Garden City, NY: Doubleday, 1960; reprint edn., Berkeley and Los Angeles, CA: University of California Press.

Stravinsky, V. and Craft, R. (1978), *Stravinsky in Pictures and Documents*, New York: Simon and Schuster.

Styan, J.L. (1982), *Max Reinhardt*, Cambridge: Cambridge University Press.

Taper, B. (1984), *Balanchine: A Biography*, New York: Times Books.

Tarakanov, M. (1991), "Prokofjew: Legende und Wahrheit," trans. M. Weiss, in program book for the symposium "Sergej Prokofjew—Aspekte seines Werkes und der Biographie" held in Cologne, 16–25.

—— (ed.) (1991), *Sergey Prokof'yev 1891–1991, dnevnik, pis'ma, besedï, vospominaniya*, Moscow: Sovetskiy kompozitor.

Taruskin, R. (1980), "Russian folk melodies in *The Rite of Spring*," *Journal of the American Musicological Society*, **33**, 501–43.

—— (1982), "From *Firebird to The Rite*: folk elements in Stravinsky's scores," *Ballet Review*, **10**, Summer, 72–87.

—— (1983), "How the acorn took root: a tale of Russia," *Nineteenth-Century Music*, **6**, Spring, 189–212.

—— (1985), "Chernomor to Kashchei: harmonic sorcery; or Stravinsky's 'Angle,'" *Journal of the American Musicological Society*, **38**, 72–142.

—— (1987), "Chez Pétrouchka: harmony and tonality chez Stravinsky," *Nineteenth-Century Music*, **10**, Spring, 265–86.

—— (1988), "The Anti-Literary Man: Diaghilev and Music," in *The Art of Enchantment: Diaghilev's Ballets Russes 1909–1929*, ed. N. van Norman Baer, San Francisco: Fine Arts Museum of San Francisco, pp. 112–21.

—— (1988), "Tone, Style, and Form in Prokofiev's Soviet Operas: Some Preliminary Observations," in *Studies in the History of Music*, vol. 2, Music and Drama, New York: Broude Brothers, pp. 215–39.

—— (1991), "Prokofiev, hail ... and farewell?" *New York Times*, 21 April, "Arts and Leisure," section 2, pp. 25 and 32.

—— (1992–93), "Back to whom? Neoclassicism as ideology," *Nineteenth-Century Music*, **16**, no. 3, 286–302.

—— (1996), *Stravinsky and the Russian Traditions. A Biography of Works through Mavra*, 2 vols, Berkeley and Los Angeles, CA: University of California Press.

—— (1997), *Defining Russia Musically. Historical and Hermeneutical Essays*, Princeton, NJ: Princeton University Press.

Van den Toorn, P.C. (1986), "Octatonic Pitch Structure in Stravinsky," in *Confronting Stravinsky: Man, Musician, Modernist*, ed. J. Pasler, Berkeley and Los Angeles, CA: University of California Press, pp. 130–56.

Varunts, V.P. (ed.) (1991), *Prokof'yev o Prokof'yeve: stat'i i interv'yu*, Moscow: Sovetskiy kompozitor.

—— (1991), "Prokof'yev o Stravinskom," in *Prokof'yev o Prokof'yeve: stat'i i interv'yu*, Moscow: Sovetskiy kompozitor, pp. 236–53.

Ville de Strasbourg, Deuxième Exposition Européenne [15 May to 15 September, 1969] (1969), *Les Ballets Russes de Serge de Diaghilev 1909–1929*, preface by S. Lifar, introduction by V. Beyer, Strasbourg: SOPIC.

Volkov, S. (1985), *Balanchine's Tchaikovsky: Interviews with George Balanchine*, trans. A.W. Bouis, New York, NY: Simon and Schuster.

Walker, K.S. (1982), *De Basil's Ballets Russes*, London: Hutchinson.

Walsh, S. (1993), *The Music of Stravinsky*, reprint edn, Oxford, New York, Toronto: Oxford University Press.

—— (1999), *Stravinsky: A Creative Spring: Russia and France 1882–1934*, New York: Knopf.

Wearing, J.P. (ed.) (1984), *The London Stage 1910–19: A Calendar of Plays and Players*. 2 vols, Metuchen, NJ, and London: Scarecrow Press.

—— (ed.) (1984), *The London Stage 1920–29: A Calendar of Plays and Players*, 2 vols, Metuchen, NJ, and London: Scarecrow Press.

Yenisherlova, V.P. (ed.) (1984), *Sergey Gorodetskiy, Zhizn' neukrotimaya. Stat'i, ocherki, vospominaniya*, Moscow: Sovremennik.

Zil'bershtein, I.S. and Samkov, V.A. (eds) (1982), *Sergey Dyagilev i russkoye iskusstvo*, 2 vols, Moscow: Izobrazitel'noye iskusstvo.

Index

DATE DUE

PRINTED IN U.S.A.